Soft Coal, Hard Choices

Soft Coal, Hard Choices

The Economic Welfare of Bituminous Coal Miners, 1890–1930

PRICE V. FISHBACK

New York Oxford
OXFORD UNIVERSITY PRESS
1992

Oxford University Press

Oxford New York Toronto
Delhi Bombay Calcutta Madras Karachi
Kuala Lumpur Singapore Hong Kong Tokyo
Nairobi Dar es Salaam Cape Town
Melbourne Auckland

and associated companies in
Berlin Ibadan

Published by Oxford University Press, Inc.,
200 Madison Avenue, New York, New York 10016

Library of Congress Cataloging-in-Publication Data
Fishback, Price Van Meter
Soft coal, hard choices : the economic welfare of bituminous coal
miners, 1890–1930 / Price V. Fishback.
p. cm. Includes bibliographical references and index.
ISBN 0-19-506725-8
1. Coal miners—United States—History. 2. Bituminous coal
industry—United States—History. I. Title.
HD8039.M6152U64 1992
331.7'622334'0973—dc20 91-22925

1 3 5 7 9 8 6 4 2

Printed in the United States of America
on acid-free paper

PREFACE

My first studies of the bituminous industry dealt with the treatment of blacks and immigrants, applying economic analysis and modern statistical techniques to test for discrimination. While reading about the coal industry, the descriptions puzzled me. There were constant references to monopolistic company stores and towns, yet the workers were described as constantly moving from town to town. Rather than focus on local monopolies, it seemed to me that the relevant market to study was the regional labor market. The coal labor market is particularly fascinating because the employment package included not only wages and working conditions but also the conditions in the town. Insights derived from the study of economics led me to ask a series of questions about the coal labor market in the early 1900s. Why did companies own their own housing? Did miners really owe their souls to the company store and pay exorbitant prices? How did housing in company towns compare to housing in towns of similar size? Did wages rise to compensate miners for higher store prices, higher accident rates, higher rents, or other negative features? Why pay some workers piece rates and other workers by the day? How did coal miners' hourly and annual earnings compare to those in manufacturing? How much did unionization raise wages? Did labor unions and government regulations improve mine safety? What was the miner's net gain from striking? Why did operators and miners resort to violence? This book seeks to provide answers to those questions. Several of the findings were originally reported in journal articles. Those findings are summarized here along with the results of additional inquiries.

Looking back over ten years of writing a dissertation, journal articles, and a book manuscript about bituminous coal miners, I realize that an enormous number of people have helped me along the way. My deepest scholarly debts are owed to professors and friends from graduate school. Robert Higgs has helped guide my studies from the time I started writing a dissertation. He has served as mentor, friend, editor, and critic. Throughout I have valued his advice, and more importantly his friendship. Douglass North first attracted my interest to economic history. After luring me into the field, he has always encouraged my efforts and opened the door to many opportunities. Morris Morris opened my eyes to the enormous complexities of studying economic history, while Daniel Benjamin encouraged me to dig deeply into the subject. John Wallis, Sumner LaCroix, and Mark Plummer shared the travails of completing a dissertation and have been valuable friends and critics ever since. Lee Alston, Mark Schmitz, Randy Rucker, and Torben Andersen read substantial parts of all my studies and offered valuable comments. Mary Wellnitz shared the worst and the best of my life during the early phases of this study.

Gary Libecap, Stanley Engerman, Lance Davis, David Galenson, Claudia Goldin, Daniel Slesnick, and Robert Margo have all given valuable comments on several chapters of the manuscript. Along the way I have received useful comments and insights from numerous others: Jeremy Atack, Scott Atkinson, Thomas Borcherding, John Brown, Louis Cain, Leonard Carlson, Phil Cartwright, Pae Kun Choi, Harry Cleaver, Christopher Cornwell, Cletus Coughlin, Douglas Dacy, Richard Dusansky, Christian Dustmann, Thomas Eaton, Richard Epstein, Robert Fogel, Gerald Friedman, John Garen, Vince Geraci, Mason Gerety, Doc Ghose, Shubha Ghosh, Caren Ginsburg, Victor Goldberg, Myron Gutman, David Haddock, Michael Haines, Nori Hashimoto, Carol Heim, R. Carter Hill, Betsy Hoffman, Mark Isaac, Ronald Johnson, Shawn Kantor, James Kau, Donald Keenan, Seung Wook Kim, Tom Kniesner, Ken Kroner, Subal Kumbhakar, Dwight Lee, James McCann, Fred McChesney, Donald McCloskey, David Mitch, Joel Mokyr, Michael Munger, Larry Neal, Hugh Nourse, Ron Oaxaca, Tony O'Brien, James Rebitzer, Joseph Reid, W. Craig Riddell, Joseph Ritter, Sheri Rochford, Paul Rothstein, Paul Rubin, Andrew Rutten, Barbara Sands, Raymond Sauer, Frank Scott, Ken Sokoloff, Dale Stahl, Leslie Stratton, Richard Sutch, Cynthia Taft-Morris, Peter Temin, Joseph Terza, Fred Thum, Richard Timberlake, Steve Tomlinson, Joseph Trotter, Gordon Tullock, Manuelita Ureta, Georgia Villaflor, Susan Walcott, Ronald Warren, Thomas Weiss, Warren Whatley, David Wheelock, Rudy White, Oliver Williamson, Paul Wilson, Gavin Wright, and several anonymous referees.

Various parts of the book were enhanced greatly by the discussions in sessions at the Economic History Association meetings, the Cliometrics meetings, the Southern Economic Association meetings, the NBER Summer Institute, the Greater Washington, D.C. Economic History Seminar, and the Social Science History Association meetings. Similar benefits came from presentations of the research at the political science and history departments at the University of Texas at Austin and the economics departments at the following: University of Arizona, University of California at Berkeley, Carnegie Mellon University, University of Chicago, Claremont College Graduate School, Clemson University, University of Georgia, Emory University, Harvard University, University of Illinois, Indiana University at Bloomington, University of Kentucky, University of Michigan, University of New Mexico, Northwestern University, Stanford University, University of Texas at Austin, Washington University, and University of Washington.

In preparing the articles and this manuscript I have received valuable editorial advice from Kathy Wright, Lynn Bryant, and David Robinson. Paul Betz encouraged me to write a book based on the original journal articles. Herb Addison and Mary Sutherland guided me through the process of turning a manuscript into a book.

Financial support came from several sources. The Earhart Foundation and the Bradley Foundation each provided support to allow me to travel and devote summers to completing the manuscript. I also received funds from a University of Georgia Faculty Research Grant, an Arthur Cole Foundation Research in Economic History Grant, and a National Endowment for the Humanities Travel-to-Collections Grant. The Economics Department at the University of Georgia was generous with summer salaries, graduate assistants, and other resources. Dean Albert Niemi of

Georgia's College of Business was especially encouraging and fostered a research environment that was beneficial. Throughout I have benefitted from the help of the staffs in the Economics Departments at the University of Georgia, the University of Texas at Austin, and the University of Arizona. Carolyn Hale, Marian Bolan, Cindy Russell, Lorraine Beach, Nadine Flaherty, Linda Goodfader, Liz Trotter, Judy Griffin, Kimberly Fettig, Mary Flannery, Jean Keyes, Rose Marie Rouse, and Nancy York all have helped me get my ideas onto the printed page.

While gathering evidence, I greatly appreciated the help of the staffs at the West Virginia Regional and History Collection in the University of West Virginia Library, the Hagley Museum and Library, the Beckley Exhibition Mine, the Department of Labor Library, the Suitland Branch of the National Archives, the Birmingham Public Library, the Western Kentucky University Library, Alice Lloyd College Oral History Project, and the University of Washington Library. John Rumm and Richmond Williams were particularly helpful. Matthew Wellnitz, Ted van der Aart, Mark Botsch, Josh Gotkin, and Mary Evans helped transfer data from the printed page onto computer readable files.

Fran Fishback and William Fishback helped shape my life. I cannot thank them enough for the wonderful things they have done for me. I dedicate the book to the person who has brought great joy to my life, Pamela Slaten.

Tucson
July, 1991

P.V.F.

CONTENTS

Soft Coal, Hard Choices

1

The Miners' Choices: Voice or Exit

Coal miners had two means of bettering their conditions: voice and exit. They could band together in unions and raise their collective voices, using strikes to focus attention on their grievances. Or each miner could act alone, moving to other mines or other industries to improve his position. Most studies of laborers in the coal industry and in other industries at the turn of the century focus on collective action. The studies offer detailed descriptions of the workers' attempts to organize into unions, the internal politics of the unions, and the struggles between miners and coal employers in strikes. Discussions of wages and working conditions are generally brief, emphasize the workers' discontent, and offer limited quantitative evidence. Economic institutions like the company store and company town are portrayed as the employer's means of limiting the mobility of workers and preventing them from joining unions. In sum, unions are considered necessary for the miners to prevent exploitation and to improve working conditions.

The impact of exit often is ignored or described as inconsequential. Yet it was a powerful force in improving the economic welfare of the miners. There were thousands of mines hiring coal workers. Since many miners had originally migrated to reach the coal fields and then lived in rental housing, they were willing and able to move on to the next mine or switch to other industries. Thus coal operators who tried to pay wages below the prevailing wage for labor often lost workers or could hire only the least productive miners.

Maybe the role of exit receives less attention because the miners themselves were not comfortable in relying upon exit. Switching mines or industries was not costless and could be disruptive to family life. The workings of the invisible hand in labor markets are not always obvious. Individual miners thus felt like they had no control of the wage-setting process, that they were buffeted by forces beyond their control. While coal mining boomed, the miners fared relatively well, as real hourly wages rose almost 2.7 times between 1890 and 1923. But coal demand fluctuated even during the boom era, and miners experienced temporary wage cuts in some downturns. Miners felt that they could prevent wage cuts through collective action. After 1923, unionized workers were able to maintain wages for a while in the face of stagnating coal demand. Eventually collective action could not stem the tide, and by 1929 more than one fourth of the miners had migrated to new industries to avoid the decline in wages. The decline in wages did not necessarily mean that the employers were all powerful captains of industry. Given the intense competition in the coal product market, the employers were also buffeted by forces beyond their control. When the coal market declined, employers seemed like villains when seeking wage cuts, but more often they were the bearer of bad tidings.

One problem with studying the impact of exit is that its effects on working conditions are subtle. There are no major events like bargaining sessions and strikes that clearly mark when wage rates change. The effects of exit are evolutionary, not revolutionary. Exit limits the employers' ability to exploit workers through the migration of workers to different areas, and often all that is needed is the threat of migration of thousands of workers. To show the impact of exit requires information on the actions of thousands of workers. But we can infer its impact from the relationship of wages in coal mining to wages in other sectors, to coal prices, to improvements in worker productivity, and to other factors influencing the demand and supply of labor.

In fact, as shown in Chapter 6 on earnings, probably the most powerful cause of the rise in coal earnings during the early 1900s was the improvement in earnings in the miners' next best alternative, in manufacturing. This does not mean that collective action was not important. The earnings chapter also shows that changes in the strength of the United Mine Workers of America (UMWA) had important effects on coal miners' earnings both in the long run and in the short run. One goal of this book is to show how both exit and voice played important roles in determining the coal miner's welfare.

When assessing the conditions in coal mining in the early 1900s, the standards of comparison are extremely important. To a modern reader, a straightforward description of wages, working conditions, and living conditions in a coal company town is horrifying. In 1910, many coal workers were paid 28 cents an hour or 40 cents a ton to mine coal. Three out of every thousand miners died in coal accidents each year. Most coal houses had no running water, no inside bathrooms, and six to eight people might be crammed into a four-room house. Little wonder that the modern reader would be horrified; when the minimum wage today is $4.25 an hour and miners receive $13.30 an hour, coal accident rates are one-fourth as high; nearly everybody in our society has the modern conveniences of running water and flush toilets; and the typical family has less than one person per room in the house. However, the modern reader should be careful. After adjusting for inflation, the coal workers of 1910 earned roughly $3.70 per hour in 1989 dollars. Further, U.S. coal miners in 1910 had a standard of living that exceeds the average standard of living of countries where 65 to 80 percent of the world's population lives today. Comparisons with modern conditions show how much the standard of living of American workers has improved during this century, largely due to technological changes and other improvements unavailable to miners in the early 1900s.

An alternative standard of comparison is to show how coal miners fared relative to other industrial workers at the time. Relative to today's standards, coal mining was a miserable occupation, but jobs in manufacturing and agriculture were equally if not more miserable. By putting coal miners into the context of their times, we can better assess the workers' choices between coal mining, agriculture, and other industries. In 1910 or 1920, an unskilled or semiskilled worker found coal mining to be a reasonable alternative. Hourly wages were higher than in most industries, but this in part was compensation for fewer opportunities to work and acceptance of more dangerous conditions. Throughout the book, conditions in coal mining are compared with conditions in other industries.

A number of excellent books on bituminous coal miners in the early 1900s have appeared in recent years. To name a few, David Corbin's study of southern West Virginia miners offers many insights into coal miners' culture and reasons why they failed to unionize for many years and then chose to unionize. Ronald Lewis illuminates the experience of black miners, particularly their relations with miners' unions. Keith Dix shows the inner workings of a coal mine and the forces affecting the introduction of various technologies. Progressive Era efforts by government to improve mine safety are well documented by William Graebner. Howard Gitelman weaves the story of how Rockefeller and MacKenzie King responded to the political and public pressures following the Ludlow Massacre by introducing the company union into Colorado mining. Dubovsky and Van Tyne show the inner workings of the United Mine Workers of America in their fascinating biography of John L. Lewis. Dorothy Schwieder presents a detailed study of community life in Iowa coal towns, while Alan Kent Powell documents the struggle of Utah's miners to unionize.[1]

So why read this book?

This study is written from an alternative perspective, based on *cliometric* analysis. Cliometrics involves the use of economic theory and statistics to examine history. Ideally, the goal is to expose the models hidden in many descriptions of events, and then test their internal consistency and various hypotheses that are generated. The goal here is to try to combine the old and new economic history, using both qualitative and quantitative evidence to examine the bituminous coal labor market.

The basic models applied and tested come from the modern literature on labor economics and institutional change. Debates over the impact of voice and exit on labor markets are a primary topic in modern labor economics and many of its tools are directly applicable to the study of coal markets in the early 1900s. At the same time, the recognition that transaction costs and monitoring costs are important factors has led to a virtual revolution in the way economists study institutions. The study of transactions costs helps explain a wide variety of ways in which coal operators organized their businesses, from the choice of wage payments (piece rates or time rates) to the development of company towns and company stores.

In some ways the quantitative evidence and use of economic theory offers a view that contradicts previous versions of what happened. Labor historians have done excellent work describing the roles played by key individuals, the development and internal politics of unions, the progress of negotiations, and the basic attitudes of workers. In describing how workers developed solidarity with the labor movement, they have given us a better understanding of workers' aspirations, their grievances, their culture, and their relations with fellow workers and employers. In the process historians generally did not address the issues of wages and working conditions with the economist's eye. Few have challenged age-old descriptions that were often based on scattered evidence and/or the demands of workers. Such an evidence base for describing working conditions can be misleading. Comparing actual wages to workers' demands almost by definition implies that workers will be seen as exploited. After all, in nearly all bargaining situations, both sides start with demands that exceed what they are willing to accept. The use of scattered evidence also leads to problems, because extreme situations may be overemphasized relative to their actual occurrence. The extremes give us information about the worst that could happen but do not tell us necessarily how the majority of miners lived. This book challenges some traditional interpretations while reconfirming others by testing statements made by observers with an expanded data base on wages, working conditions, and company towns.

In many ways the use of quantitative evidence and economic theory complements the studies done by earlier labor historians. Certainly, someone interested in the coal industry should go beyond this book and read the fine studies cited earlier. Economists and cliometricians often ask an entirely different set of questions. How much of the rise in coal earnings can be explained by changes in coal demand and workers' opportunities in other industries, as compared with unionization? How did miners' earnings compare with those of similarly skilled workers in other industries? Why pay piece rates for some jobs and hourly rates for others? Did wages rise to compensate workers for limits on working time or more dangerous jobs? Does safety legislation actually lower accident rates? Do accident rates rise and fall over the course of the business cycle? Were blacks, immigrants, and native whites treated similarly after we adjust for differences in their skills? How did workers' compensation laws change incentives in the workplace and what impact did they have on accidents? What were the net benefits to the miners of going on strike? In the process of answering these questions we obtain a better understanding of the labor market in the early 1900s.

A full-scale study of the bituminous coal labor market requires a description of the analytical framework, conditions in the labor market, the nature of coal mining, and then detailed descriptions of wage rates, earnings, safety, company stores, company towns, strikes, and violence.[2]

Chapter 2 lays out the analytical framework, which shows how competition (exit) and collective action (voice) affected the economic welfare of coal miners. The framework starts with a basic economic model in which employers compete with hundreds of other mines when hiring labor. The model of labor market competition is expanded to consider the impact of positive information and transportation costs. In competing for labor, employers could alter not only wages but a number of other features of the employment package, like safety or the quality of life in the company town. One of the major implications of the competition framework is that the value of employment packages will be roughly similar for miners with similar skills. Therefore, when one part of the employment package worsens, say store prices are raised, wages or other parts of the package will improve to compensate. Unionization alters the nature of bargaining between miners and employers. Neoclassical labor economists argue that labor unions, by limiting labor supply to employers, raise wages for their members at the expense of nonunion workers and employers. Some of the gains of union membership may be dissipated for new members as they pay dues or spend long apprenticeships trying to join the union. On the other hand, unions in some settings can provide benefits to both employers and workers by helping workers negotiate workplace public goods, by cutting turnover, and by raising morale.

To see how well the analytical framework fits the coal industry, Chapter 3 describes the coal labor market in the early 1900s. The coal labor market boomed through World War I and then began to stagnate, although even during the boom coal mining experienced downturns. Miners most commonly exercised voice through the United Mine Workers, who developed a stronghold in the Central Competitive Field by 1902, received a major boost during World War I, but then declined in strength in the 1920s. Throughout the period miners also practiced exit. In seeking new opportunities miners obtained information from word-of-mouth networks, supplemented by labor agents and advertisements. Most observers described miners as highly mobile, particularly in nonunion districts. During downturns miners were less mobile within the industry, but still could switch industries.

Chapter 4 describes the nature of jobs in coal mining, including the skills required, wages paid, and differences in accident risk. Workers were placed in broad categories based on the type of wage rate they were paid: Tonnage men were paid piece rates and daymen were paid time rates.

Chapter 5 explores the economic reasoning behind the different forms of wage payments, focusing on differences in the costs of measuring output, supervising workers, and ensuring quality. Employers tried to ensure quality with screens and docking systems. The payment of piece rates was also complicated by differences in mining conditions, and the chapter shows how both union and nonunion areas adjusted piece rates to compensate. The nature of wage payments, weighing the coal, and quality control were often sources of dispute between miners and coal operators. Miners at times complained that payment methods were designed to cheat them. There were limits to cheating, however, because the miners' hourly earnings had at least to match miners' alternative earnings in other industries.

Chapter 6 offers comparisons of coal miners' hourly and annual earnings with the earnings in other industries. Coal miners generally earned substantially more per hour than manufacturing workers, but their annual earnings were similar or slightly lower. On the plus side, coal miners had more workplace independence and worked roughly seventy days less than manufacturing workers for similar annual earnings. However, the higher hourly earnings compensated miners for limits on the number of days the mines were open, for greater accident risk, and for living in more isolated areas. During the hand-loading era, real wages in coal mining rose substantially. Labor histories give the impression that advances in wages came about only through collective action. Examination of time series on coal wages shows that between 1890 and 1929 most of the rise in coal wages is attributable to a rise in the opportunity cost wage in manufacturing. Collective bargaining through the UMWA made some contributions to the overall rise and affected the short-run timing of wage increases much more, boosting wages for workers earlier than if wages had only kept pace with manufacturing wages. In comparisons of wage rates across states within the coal industry, miners earned more in states where they struck or joined the union. But again other factors were as important. Earnings rose in response to higher coal prices, greater productivity, and fewer work opportunities.

Coal mining was one of the more dangerous occupations in the early 1900s.

Chapter 7 discusses several aspects of workplace safety. There was a distinct division of labor with respect to mine safety. The tonnage worker was primarily responsible for the safety in his own workplace, while mine management was responsible for factors like ventilation and dusting of the mine, which could not be easily controlled by individual workers. Workers were mobile enough that they reduced their labor supply to states where the mines were more dangerous. The UMWA helped miners receive higher wages holding the accident rate constant but had little impact on lowering accident rates. In the early 1900s state governments increased regulation of mine safety, while the U.S. Bureau of Mines was formed to develop and spread information about better mine safety. Most of the legislation was disappointing. A statistical study of accident rates confirms William Graebner's suspicions that most state laws had very little impact on accident rates. The environment of legal liability also changed dramatically, shifting from the common law standards of negligence liability to workers' compensation. The switch led to a substantial increase in the number of workers compensated for injuries and an increase in the amount each received. The change in incentives led to the unexpected result that accident rates actually rose after workers' compensation was introduced.

Many consider the company store as a device used by coal employers to exploit the miners. Because employers owned the store, some have argued that they exercised monopoly power, paying people in scrip that could be used only at the store, charging exorbitant prices, and keeping miners in debt to the store. Chapter 8 on company stores examines these claims theoretically and with evidence from the period. Since store prices were part of the employment package offered to miners, attempts to charge high store prices were limited by the competition for labor with hundreds of other mines. Evidence on company store prices shows that in many regions they were similar to prices at nearby independent stores. Generally, miners were not in debt to the store after payday. They received scrip as an advance on payday and typically received around half their earnings in cash on payday.

The company's ownership of the houses at the mine, the short tenure of leases, and the requirement that the miner remain employed to stay in the house have been controversial. Chapter 9 on company towns examines company ownership of housing. In part, the companies used their ownership to break strikes. Yet both the miners and the company actually gained from company ownership of housing given the fluctuating nature of coal demand and the contracting problems that arise because the mine was the only source of employment in isolated coal towns. In addition to housing, company towns also provided services, like sanitation and supplements to schooling, that are typically provided by local governments. The standard image of the coal company town is of a squalid place, where few would want to live. Part of the chapter shows the results of statistical comparisons of the quality of life and sanitation in company towns and independent towns. On average, sanitation in coal towns was similar to sanitation in smaller communities and rural areas, although lagging behind the quality of sanitation offered in major cities. Sanitation across coal towns varied substantially in part because towns faced different costs of providing better services. Since company towns were owned by the employer, there is a tendency to believe that the employers sacrificed sanitation for higher profits. However, employers had to pay higher wages to miners in towns with lesser sanitation. There was no guarantee of better sanitation in independent towns because towns with local governments faced free rider problems in getting the votes for new sanitation facilities. An empirical study shows that after adjusting for population, company towns and towns with independent governments typically offered similar levels of sanitation.

The coal industry employed large numbers of blacks and immigrants. Chapter 10 examines the extent of discrimination against blacks and immigrants. Although the national policy of the UMWA called for equal treatment of workers of all colors and creeds, black workers for a long time faced barriers erected by local unions to their migration into northern coal fields. In West Virginia the substantial competition for labor eroded most forms of workplace discrimination. The major exception was that blacks were denied management positions unless they supervised an all-black work crew. The extensive competition for black labor among coal employers reached beyond the workplace and even eroded discrimination by local governments in West Virginia. Coal employers were an important force in equalizing expenditures on education in West Virginia's segregated schools.

Bituminous coal mining was notorious for prolonged strikes and for the violence that marred some strikes. Chapter 11 compares the strike activity in bituminous coal mining and other industries and assesses the pecuniary costs and benefits of strikes. Miners gave up earnings during the strike to achieve improvements in wages and working conditions. Unless the strike was over union recognition, the loss in earnings while on strike exceeded the gains from obtaining a higher wage rate. In union recognition strikes, the gains from unionization had to last several years before the expected gain from the strike exceeded the lost earnings in the course of the strike.

Although most strikes were settled peacefully, the coal industry became infamous for a series of violent episodes, some that developed into full-scale warfare. Rather than trying to fix blame on one side or the other, Chapter 11 suggests that both miners and employers armed themselves in self-defense. Both sides faced problems in controlling their more headstrong members. Often the ill-considered actions of a few people forced large groups of miners and operators to become involved with major conflagrations.

Looking back, we should appreciate how much the standards of living and working conditions of workers have improved over the course of the century. Workers in the early 1900s did not have the option of working with better machinery in the cleaner, safer confines of the modern workplace. They faced a series of hard choices about whether to work in agriculture, manufacturing, or mining. Coal mining offered the opportunity to earn money quickly during booms, but it was a dirty, dangerous job often located in isolated little towns. Those who were bothered less by the danger and the dirt generally stayed in mining. Others came to the industry in the good times but moved on when times turned bad. When men tried to alter their positions through collective action their sacrifices often exceeded the rewards. Over the long run, however, conditions improved as employers and workers found better ways to mine coal and a complex interaction of technological changes, improvements in organization, educational improvements, advances in consumer products, and other factors raised the standard of living of all workers in the United States.

NOTES

1. David Corbin, *Life, Work, and Rebellion: The Southern West Virginia Miners, 1880–1922* (Chicago: University of Illinois Press, 1981); Keith Dix, *Work Relations in the Coal Industry: The Hand-Loading Era, 1880–1930*, (West Virginia University Bulletin, Series 78, No. 7-2, January 1978); Ronald Lewis, *Black Coal Miners in America: Race, Class, and Community Conflict 1780–1980* (Lexington: The University Press of Kentucky, 1987); William Graebner, *Coal-Mining Safety in the Progressive Era* (Lexington: The University Press of Kentucky, 1976); Howard M. Gitelman, *Legacy of the Ludlow Massacre: A Chapter in American Industrial Relations* (Philadelphia: University of Pennsylvania Press, 1988); Melvyn Dubofsky and Warren Van Tyne, *John L. Lewis: A Biography* (New York: Quadrangle/The New York Times Book Company, 1977); Dorothy Schwieder, *Black Diamonds: Life and Work in Iowa's Coal Mining Communities, 1895–1925* (Ames: Iowa State University Press, 1983); and Alan Kent Powell, *The Next Time We Strike: Labor in Utah's Coal Fields, 1900–1933* (Logan: Utah State University Press, 1985).

2. Portions of the analysis have appeared in print in the following publications: Price Fishback, "Workplace Safety During the Progressive Era: Bituminous Coal Mining, 1912–1913," *Explorations in Economic History* 23 (July 1986): 269–98; Price Fishback, "Liability Rules and Accident Prevention in the Workplace: Empirical Evidence from the Early Twentieth Century," *Journal of Legal Studies* 16 (June 1987): 305–28; Price Fishback, "Did Coal Miners 'Owe Their Souls to the Company Store'? Theory and Evidence from the Early 1900s," *Journal of Economic History* 46 (December 1986): 1011–29; Price Fishback and Dieter Lauszus, "The Quality of Services in Company Towns: Sanitation in Coal Towns During the 1920s," *Journal of Economic History* 49 (March 1989): 125–44; Price Fishback, "Employment Conditions of Blacks in the Coal Mining Industry, 1900–1930," unpublished Ph.D dissertation, University of Washington, 1983, summarized in *Journal of Economic History* 44 (June 1984): 605–08; Price Fishback, "Segregation in Job Hierarchies: West Virginia Coal Mining, 1906–1932," *Journal of Economic History* 44 (September 1984): 755–74; Price Fishback, "Discrimination on Nonwage Margins: Safety in the West Virginia Coal Industry, 1906–1925," *Economic Inquiry* 23 (October 1985): 651–69; and Price Fishback, "The Economics of Company Housing: Historical Perspectives from the Coal Fields," *Journal of Law, Economics, and Organization* 8 (Spring 1992): forthcoming.

2

The Analytical Framework

Many coal mines were isolated. Coal seams often were located in Appalachian hollows or in rural settings where few had ever settled. Mining coal became the impetus for settlement with coal companies often building and owning the town around the mine. The isolation of the mines and the company's ownership of housing and stores led many to focus on powerful companies and helpless miners. In economic terms, they describe the employer as both monopsonist, single buyer, in the labor market, and monopolist, single seller, in the sale of housing and store goods. The economics of coal mining at the time were far more competitive. There were thousands of coal companies throughout the United States and they sold coal in a highly competitive market. Their power in the labor market was also limited becaused they hired in a regional labor market. Mines and mining towns competed against other mines and other industries for workers.

Few doubt that, given the opportunity, coal operators would have "exploited" miners by paying lower wages. Similarly, miners would have "exploited" the operators by extracting higher wages if possible. The operators faced two constraints in their efforts to maximize their profits at the expense of the miners: Adam Smith's Invisible Hand of competition and collective action by miners. Under competition when one employer sought to pay workers below-market wages, other employers hired them away by offering higher wages. Miners used collective action to raise wages by controlling the labor supply available to employers and changing the nature of negotiations. The implications for the miners' welfare of competition and collective action are examined here using the analytical framework developed in standard labor economics textbooks.[1]

The Implications of Competition

When competing for labor, the coal operator offered an entire employment package to the miner. The employment package, as in most employment situations, included earnings and working conditions. Miners' earnings were determined by the wage rate, opportunities to work more hours, probability of layoffs, and the opportunities for training and advancement. The specifics of working conditions included safety, the comfort of workplaces (temperature, wetness, and spaciousness), and the miners' independence in making workplace decisions. In many work settings the employers' package was limited to attributes in the workplace. In coal mining, however, many employers owned the town, with more direct control over housing and rents, store prices and the quality of goods, public health, and education for children. The attributes of the town therefore became part of the coal-mining employment package.

To examine how the attributes of employment packages interact under competition, start by assuming a perfectly fluid labor market with large numbers of buyers and sellers. Further assume that miners have perfect information about the components of the package: they face no costs of migration, no costs of negotiating with employers, and all miners are homogeneous, that is, they have the same tastes and similar productivity. Under this setting, competition among employers equilibrates the value of employment packages to the miners across all mines. To see why, consider a situation where an employer reduces the value of the package by charging higher store prices. If he fails to offset the decline in value elsewhere in the package, miners would migrate to other mines where the value is greater. To continue to attract and keep workers, the employer has to improve another part of the package, say by raising wages or improving safety. In actuality, a higher wage was probably the most common form of compensation, since it was the easiest attribute to alter. After adjustments, the packages might have different combinations of attributes, but the overall value of employment packages is the same across mines.

During the early 1900s, the composition of employment packages might have differed because the costs of providing various components differed across mines.[2] Employers faced higher costs of making the mine safe in areas where gas deposits were naturally more common or impurities in the soil made roof falls more likely. More isolated mines faced higher costs of transporting store goods, while mines located in valleys could enhance public health more easily than mines on mountainsides. Although higher costs placed some mines at a disadvantage, theoretically to attract labor they had to enhance the value of other parts of the package to equal the value of employment packages elsewhere.

Different employment packages reflected differences in the miners' tastes. Younger, single miners were more attracted to mines paying higher wages but offering low-quality housing because they cared more about earnings than housing. Immigrants commonly saved to support families back home or to bring family members over. They were more likely to choose mines with higher wages and higher store prices because they expected to spend relatively small amounts at the store. Similarly, miners with families might choose lower-wage mines with lower store prices and better quality education. Seeing these differences, employers emphasized certain parts of the package to attract the types of miners who matched their current labor demands. For example, a marginal mine in business because of a jump in coal prices chose packages more attractive to younger miners to reduce spending on durable factors like housing. An operator with a larger mine in business for the long run chose packages more attractive to families because he expected long-run returns to better housing.

The value of an employment package, which is directly tied to the miner's marginal product and coal prices in competitive markets, was likely to rise and fall with fluctuations in the coal industry.[3] Therefore, we should expect that the value of the employment package rose and fell with increases and declines in coal prices. Competition for miners among employers fluctuated with the coal cycle. Upturns were typically associated with tight labor markets, with employers' demands for labor growing faster than labor supply; downturns with looser labor markets. "Exploitation" of miners was therefore likely to be more common during downturns. Even during downturns, "reputation effects" constrained the actions of employers. Harsh exploitation during a downturn gave the employer a bad reputation, which hindered his ability to attract labor during the next upturn. The reputation effect probably had more impact on mines in the industry for the long run, since they were more likely to be operating in both good times and bad.

Potentially, the typical coal operator in an isolated company town had a monopoly on store goods or housing. However, when he hired in a competitive labor market, characterized by zero costs of migration, information, and transactions, the coal operator was unable to exploit effectively his store or housing monopoly. If he tried to raise store prices or rents to monopoly levels, he had to raise wages or improve other parts of the employment package in order to continue to attract workers.

Generally, there were large numbers of mines, so there was a substantial amount of competition among mines from labor. However, the assumptions of zero transactions costs were not met in the coal regions. Migration costs were positive. Migrants paid railroad fares, spent time moving, and faced both the direct costs of moving possessions and the psychological costs of leaving friends and family. The costs of moving varied across miners, higher for families than for single miners, and higher for those with more possessions. Accurate information clearly was not free. Labor agents and handbills at times played fast and loose with the truth. As with migration costs, information costs varied with the miners. Illiterate miners and immigrants who spoke no English faced greater problems with obtaining accurate information. Although the costs were present, they should not be overemphasized. Chapter 3 shows that migration costs were low enough that miners moved freely from mine to mine.

The presence of migration and information costs gave coal operators some room to earn short-term profits by exploiting a local monopoly. Companies could charge higher store prices or rents without raising wages to the extent that miners faced costs of moving. Under costly migration, local competition became a more important constraint on the operator's ability to charge high store prices or rents. Therefore, store prices and rents were likely to be lower in towns near independent towns or near local stores. Higher prices were more likely in more isolated towns, although migration costs were low enough that the higher prices probably would have been at least partially compensated for by higher wages or improvements in other parts of the employment package.

Information costs varied across different parts of the employment package. They were often lower for earnings than for working conditions, safety, and the quality of the company town. Earnings information was widely publicized by the mines and was accurately described by a dollar amount. Acquiring accurate information about the other factors required an inspection of the mine or town or talks with miners employed there; each process was more costly than reading a handbill about earnings. Even when the prospective miner inspected the mine or town, accurate descriptions of safety and the town were more costly because there was no single index like a dollar amount that accurately portrayed the situation. Higher information costs on nonearnings aspects gave the employer more room to charge higher store prices and to skimp on safety, given the wage, than to pay lower wages, given store prices and safety. When the coal operator raised store prices or reduced safety, the miner was less likely to move than when earnings were lowered because it was more costly to compare store prices and safety than it was to compare earnings across mines.

That companies at times exploited these differences in information costs is probably the reason that miners suspected the integrity of coal operators. There was an element of "bait and switch" when companies offered high wages without describing other facets of the employment package in detail. At times miners arrived and discovered that other aspects of the package failed to meet their expectations. The situation worsened when the employer claimed high earnings and failed to deliver on them. Disappointed miners either left the mining town or stayed and remained disgruntled. There were limits to "bait and switch" tactics because over a period of time the mine developed a reputation for dishonesty. Miners within the region avoided the mine, and the mine would continue to have to rely on migrants from elsewhere. Reliance on in-migrants might also be hindered when the mine's reputation extended outside the region. Companies followed those practices more often if they were only short-run operations. Companies that expected to remain in business much longer were likely to follow more honest practices.

The Impact of Collective Action and Unions

The results of competition in the previous section stem from miners exercising their right to "exit." If conditions were not satisfactory, miners could vote with their feet and migrate to the next town. However, miners developed varying degrees of attachment to coal mining communities. Exit was most likely to be practiced by more mobile miners: the young, those without families, workers with general and not mine-specific skills, and in-migrants whether from Europe or other regions. Others found it more costly to move. Either they and their families had established roots in the area, like Appalachian natives, or they had developed skills that could not be easily transferred to other mines or other industries without a significant loss of earnings. Such individuals were more likely to "voice" their dissatisfaction with conditions at any one mine.[4] Voice often took the form of strikes or the development of unions. Economists describe the impact of collective action in two major ways, talking of the monopoly face of unions and Freeman and Medoff's positive face of unions.[5]

In the monopoly model of unions, miners band together to raise their earnings or the quality of other facets of the employment package. In a competitive labor market, they do so by controlling the amount of labor available to employers through strikes and other forms of collective action. The union often trades jobs for higher wages.[6] As a successful union raises the value of employment packages, it moves the employer back upward along his labor demand curve, reducing the number of workers that he hires. The consequent reduction in employment in the unionized area leads the extra workers to spill over and seek employment in nonunion sectors, increasing the supply of labor and reducing the value of employment packages in the nonunion sectors. The final result is that employment packages in the union sector are more valuable than those in nonunion areas of the coal industry.

The spillover effect on nonunion wages assumes that workers who are unemployed in union areas are absorbed into the labor market in the nonunion areas. Employers in nonunion areas, however, may perceive a threat of unionization in their own firms and respond by raising the value of employment packages.[7] The threat effect causes unemployment because nonunion firms will not absorb the unemployed from the union sector and may actually reduce employment in the nonunion sector. Generally, economists have found that the presence of unions leads to a wage differential between the union and nonunion sectors. The difference on average has been between 10 and 20 percent, although the difference varies across time and industries.[8] Although relatively few studies have tried to separate spillover and threat effects on nonunion wages, limited modern evidence suggests that the spillover effect outweighs the threat effects in modern cities.[9]

Other facets of modern employment packages also appear to be more valuable in union than in nonunion settings. Freeman and Medoff show that fringe benefits (pensions, life and accident insurance, and vacations) are generally more common in union settings.[10] However, the gain in wages and fringes is partially offset in modern times. Blue-collar workers in union firms tend to have more hazardous jobs, more structured work settings, and less employee independence in labor-leisure decisions.[11]

Differences in earnings and fringes may overstate the gain from unionization. Some of the gains may be dissipated because resources are required to develop the union. In today's setting, workers interested in the union and union officials devote resources to campaigning for union elections. The resource costs to workers were much higher prior to the initiation of the National Labor Relations Board in the 1930s. In the face of legal barriers and employer opposition, workers campaigned for recognition of unions through strikes and walkouts. In each strike workers gave up earnings (although in coal mining there was some latitude to make up for lost time) and went through varying degrees of hardship. Longer strikes often meant living in tent colonies and facing deprivation for both miners and their families. More violent strikes led to injuries and deaths. Employers lost earnings from reduced or delayed coal production and dissipated resources spent on mine guards and fortifications.

Once the union is in place, the original members (and possibly the leadership) can capture rents from new members. The union-nonunion difference in employment packages creates incentives for nonunion workers to compete to get into union jobs. Some may accept unemployment and give up earnings for a while to obtain entry into the union. No one gains from this prospect, because the value of the lost time goes to no one in society. Union members may capture rents from the competition for union jobs by charging initiation fees, union dues, or requiring apprenticeships at low earnings. The gains may not be purely monetary, as union members allocate union slots among friends and relatives. Unfortunately, these forms of dissipation are relatively hard to measure; thus, few have examined them empirically.

Even after the union has formed, the dissipation of gains may continue for its members. Unionized firms typically are less profitable than nonunion firms.[12] As a result, nonunion firms generally expand relative to union firms, threatening the strength of the union. To protect its position, the union would try to organize nonunion areas, again leading to the dissipation of resources associated with organization.

The monopoly description of unions generally portrays them in a negative light. Union workers gain at the expense of nonunion workers. Unionism leads to the misallocation of workers between sectors and thus lower overall productivity in the economy. Union-negotiated contract provisions retard productivity by requiring minimum work crews, establishing inefficient work rules, and misaligning work incentives through pay schedules that are unrelated to productivity.

Recently, Freeman and Medoff and their students at Harvard have portrayed unions in a more positive light, emphasizing that unions offer a collective voice for workers.[13] They argue that collective rather than individual bargaining with an employer is necessary for effective voice in the workplace for two reasons. First, there are "public goods" in the workplace that benefit all workers simultaneously; one worker's gains from the goods are not affected by other workers' gains. Some aspects of safety, grievance procedures, pension plans, layoff plans, lighting, and the comfort of workplaces have public good qualities. Thus individual employees might act as "free riders" when they negotiate with employers, focusing on their own wages and welfare, hoping that others will use their time to negotiate for the public goods. The free rider hopes to get the benefits of the public goods without having to spend resources in negotiating for them. If the union negotiates as a single agent, it is more likely to represent the total demands of all workers with regard to these public goods. Second, they argue that workers are less willing to reveal their true feelings about conditions for fear of being fired. Therefore, firms fail to have adequate information about the workers' demands and suggestions for productivity improvements. In a sense, the union lowers the information costs to firms of collecting information about their workers' preferences and lowers the costs of negotiation in cases where the workers have similar demands. In such cases unionism can raise productivity by improving worker morale, reducing voluntary quits and the waste of resources devoted to developing firm-specific skills, and allowing workers more input into the production process.

Summary of Implications

Employers' efforts to "exploit" workers were constrained in two ways: by competition from other employers and by collective action by workers. In nonunion areas, competition among employers causes the value of employment packages to be similar for similarly productive workers. Reductions in the value of one part of the package are at least partially compensated for by improvements in other parts of the package. Such compensations restrict a coal operator's ability to exploit local monopolies on store goods or housing. The compensating differences are diminished and local competition becomes more important as a constraint on coal operators' behavior to the extent that there are positive information and migration costs for miners.

Collective action by miners enhances the value of employment packages for union members relative to those of nonunion members. Spillover effects from the union districts cause nonunion employment packages to be less valuable, although this will be tempered to the extent that nonunion employers respond to the threat of unionization by increasing the value of their employment packages. To the extent that the threat effect is present, unemployment increases. Union gains may be dissipated by the costs of establishing the union, and gains to new members are dissipated to the extent that they use up resources in competing to join the union. The development of the union has varying impacts on productivity in the coal industry. The monopoly face implies that unions retard productivity, while collective-voice arguments imply that unions may actually enhance productivity.

NOTES

1. For example, see Ronald Ehrenberg and Robert Smith, *Modern Labor Economics: Theory and Public Policy*, 3rd ed. (Glenview, Ill.: Scott, Foresman and Company, 1988); Belton Fleisher and Thomas Kniesner, *Labor Economics: Theory, Evidence, and Policy*, 3rd ed. (Englewood Cliffs, New Jersey: Prentice-Hall Inc., 1984).

2. For a seminal article on compensating differences, see Sherwin Rosen, "Hedonic Prices and Implicit Markets: Product Differentiation in Pure Competition," *Journal of Political Economy* 82 (January 1974): 34–35.

3. The marginal product is the additional output a miner produces from an additional amount of effort. The value of the marginal product is the marginal product multiplied by the price of coal.

4. See Albert O. Hirschman, *Exit, Voice, and Loyalty* (Cambridge, Mass.: Harvard University Press, 1971).

5. Richard Freeman and James Medoff, *What Do Unions Do?* (New York: Basic Books Inc., 1984).

6. It is possible that when the union first forms, it successfully maintains employment at existing levels while raising wages. In the long run this is not a stable solution for a firm in a competitive product market. With no changes in demand for labor, the employer would go out of business. Alternatively, if the demand for labor rose, the employer might stay in business at the higher wage but the amount of employment will be less than would be the case without the union.

7. The spillover and threat terminology is found in Ehrenberg and Smith, *Modern Labor Economics*, pp. 473–79.

8. Ehrenberg and Smith, *Modern Labor Economics*, p. 480; Barry Hirsch and John Addison, *The Economic Analysis of Unions: New Approaches and Evidence* (Boston: Allen and Unwin, 1986), pp. 116–55.

9. Kahn found that wages of nonunion workers are lower in cities with higher percent-

ages of union members. Lawrence Kahn, "The Effect of Unions on the Earnings of Nonunion Workers," *Industrial and Labor Relations Review* 31 (January 1978): 205–16; Ehrenberg and Smith, *Modern Labor Economics*, p. 481.

10. Freeman and Medoff, *What Do Unions Do?*, pp. 61–77.

11. Greg Duncan and Frank Stafford, "Do Union Members Receive Compensating Wage Differentials?" *American Economic Review* 70 (June 1980): 355–71; Ehrenberg and Smith, p. 483.

12. Freeman and Medoff, *What Do Unions Do?*, pp. 181–90; Ehrenberg and Smith, *Modern Labor Economics*, p. 489; Richard Ruback and Martin Zimmerman, "Unionization and Profitability: Evidence from the Capital Market," *Journal of Political Economy* 92 (December 1984): 1134–57.

13. Freeman and Medoff, *What Do Unions Do?*, pp. 8–9.

3

The Coal Labor Market, 1890–1930

Coal miners exercised voice and exit within a labor market constrained by swings in the coal product market. The coal industry expanded rapidly with some cyclical fluctuations until the early 1920s, when coal demand stagnated and began to decline. Although the concentration of ownership increased slightly, existing mines were not operating at full capacity, and "cutthroat" competition dominated the product market. Miners exercised collective action primarily through the United Mine Workers of America (UMWA), which controlled the labor force in northern, midwestern, and many western mines, claiming a membership in 1920 of about two-thirds of American coal miners. In nonunion areas miners had ample opportunities for exit, as nonunion districts generally expanded more rapidly than union districts. Although operators' associations fought unionization in the nonunion regions, the period of expansion led to substantial competition among employers hiring labor. Miners in the nonunion regions moved often. Some were brought to the coal fields by operators and labor agents; many more came in response to reports of relatives and friends who had already migrated. Inside the fields an even stronger word-of-mouth network alerted miners to new opportunities.

Long-term Trends in the Coal Product Market

From the Civil War into the early 1920s, miners' opportunities expanded as the bituminous coal industry grew rapidly. Between 1870 and 1890 bituminous coal production expanded from 17 to 111 million tons. Despite the depression in the mid-1890s, coal tonnage nearly doubled from 1890 to 1900, more than doubling again to 478 million tons in 1913 (see Table 3-1). As demand for coal expanded, new firms entered the industry and new coal fields developed. Although coal production was originally concentrated in Pennsylvania, Illinois, and Ohio as late as 1890, the expansion touched off a boom in the southern Appalachian areas in West Virginia, eastern Kentucky, and Alabama, and spread to smaller fields in the West and Southwest. The expansion of existing fields and opening of new fields more than matched the rising demand for coal; the average coal price at the mine therefore

TABLE 3-1. Coal Production, Employment, Days Worked, Prices, and Wages

Year	Output (millions)	Employment	Days	Price	WPI (1926 = 100)	Hourly Earnings (1967$)
1890	111.3	192204	226	0.99	56.2	0.67
1891	117.9	205803	223	0.99	55.8	0.63
1892	126.9	212893	219	0.99	52.2	0.66
1893	128.4	230365	204	0.96	53.4	0.70
1894	118.8	244603	171	0.91	47.9	0.66
1895	135.1	239962	194	0.86	48.8	0.63
1896	137.6	244171	192	0.83	46.5	0.59
1897	147.6	247817	196	0.81	46.6	0.55
1898	166.6	255717	211	0.80	48.5	0.68
1899	193.3	271027	234	0.87	52.2	0.74
1900	212.3	304975	234	1.04	56.1	0.85
1901	225.8	340235	225	1.05	55.3	0.95
1902	260.2	370056	230	1.12	58.9	0.93
1903	282.7	415777	225	1.24	59.6	0.98
1904	278.7	437832	202	1.10	59.7	0.99
1905	315.1	460629	211	1.06	60.1	1.00
1906	342.9	478425	213	1.11	61.8	1.06
1907	394.8	513258	234	1.14	65.2	1.03
1908	332.6	516264	193	1.12	62.9	1.04
1909	379.7	543152	209	1.07	67.6	1.03
1910	417.1	555533	217	1.12	70.4	1.02
1911	405.9	549775	211	1.11	64.9	1.05
1912	450.1	548632	223	1.15	69.1	1.07
1913	478.4	571882	232	1.18	69.8	1.04
1914	422.7	583506	195	1.17	68.1	1.05
1915	442.6	557456	203	1.13	69.5	1.09
1916	502.5	561102	230	1.32	85.5	1.14
1917	551.8	603143	243	2.26	117.5	1.25
1918	579.4	615305	249	2.58	131.3	1.32
1919	465.9	621998	195	2.49	138.6	1.35
1920	568.7	639547	220	3.75	154.4	1.56
1921	415.9	663754	149	2.89	97.6	1.71
1922	422.3	687958	142	3.02	96.7	1.80
1923	564.6	704793	179	2.68	100.6	1.80
1924	483.7	619604	171	2.20	98.1	1.58
1925	520.0	588493	195	2.04	103.5	1.38
1926	573.4	593647	215	2.06	100.0	1.36
1927	517.8	593918	191	1.99	95.4	1.33
1928	500.7	522150	203	1.86	96.7	1.31
1929	535.0	502993	219	1.78	95.3	1.28
1930	467.5	493202	187	1.70	86.4	1.29
1931	382.1	450213	160	1.54	73.0	1.34
1932	309.7	406380	146	1.31	64.8	1.24
1933	333.6	418703	167	1.34	65.9	1.21
1934	359.4	458011	178	1.75	74.9	1.57
1935	372.4	462403	179	1.77	80.0	1.71
1936	439.1	477204	199	1.76	80.8	1.78
1937	445.5	491864	193	1.94	86.3	1.91
1938	348.5	441333	162	1.95	78.6	2.06

(continued)

TABLE 3-1. (*Continued*)

Year	*Output (millions)*	*Employment*	*Days*	*Price*	*WPI (1926 = 100)*	*Hourly Earnings (1967\$)*
1939	394.9	421788	178	1.84	77.1	2.00
1940	460.8	439075	202	1.91	78.6	1.99

Sources: Output in millions, employment, average days the mines were open, and average coal price at the mine come from various issues of the U.S. Geological Survey (and later U.S. Bureau of Mines), *Mineral Resources of the United States: Nonmetals* (Washington, DC: U.S. Government Printing Office, various years), and is summarized after 1900 in Morton S. Baratz, *The Union and the Coal Industry* (New Haven, CT: Yale University Press, 1955), pp. 40–43. Real hourly earnings (1967\$) come from dividing the CPI into Greenslade's estimates of hourly earnings. Rush V. Greenslade, "The Economic Effects of Collective Bargaining in Bituminous Coal Mining," Ph.D. dissertation: University of Chicago, 1952, pp. 39–41. For more details on the construction of the wage rate, see Appendix A and Chapter 6. The Consumer Price Index (series E-135) and the Wholesale Price Index (series E-40) are from U.S. Bureau of the Census, *Historical Statistics of the United States: Colonial Times to 1957* (Washington, DC: U.S. Government Printing Office, 1961), pp. 200, 211.

rose more slowly than the wholesale price index from 1900 to 1913 (see Table 3-1). The expansion in tonnage required more and more labor, causing employment to nearly triple between 1890 and 1913 to 571,882 miners, roughly 1.5 percent of the labor force in the United States. The demand for labor apparently outstripped labor supply, as bituminous miners' annual earnings grew at a slightly faster pace than those for manufacturing workers. After a sharp drop in the mid 1890s, the miner's hourly wage in real terms rose (see Table 3-1), as the work week declined in length.[1]

The demands of World War I reversed a short decline following 1913. Production and nominal coal prices rose sharply to levels of 579 million tons and \$2.58 in 1918. The nominal coal price rose faster than the wholesale price index and might have risen still higher without government ceilings on fuel prices. After the war, the coal market began to stagnate. Coal tonnage fluctuated around 510 million tons during the 1920s, as end users increased their fuel efficiency and substituted other fuels for coal.[2] The average coal price soared temporarily to \$3.75 a ton in 1920, as a coal shortage, caused by a major coal strike in 1919 and inadequate provision of railroad cars to the mines, was exacerbated further by winter storms and a railroad switchmen's strike.[3] Afterward the coal price declined more slowly than the wholesale price index, in part because a major coal strike in 1922 created another temporary shortage. The high coal prices drew more commercial mines into the industry, peaking in 1923 at 9331 mines. At the same time, miners' real hourly earnings peaked, and mining employment expanded to 704,793 miners. A slump followed, as employment declined to 502,993 and the number of mines fell to 6057 in 1929.[4] The situation worsened with the Great Depression.

Both coal operators and miners shared in the decline. The coal industry's net income reported to the Bureau of Internal Revenue fell from \$200 million dollars in 1918 and \$250 million during the 1920 shortage to negative levels in the late 1920s. After 1924, less than 40 percent of the firms in the coal industry reported positive net incomes.[5] Although miners received high hourly earnings in the early 1920s, average days worked fell to record lows. During the coal boom miners generally worked between 200 to 220 days per year with peaks above 240 in 1917 and 1918 (see Table 3-1). In 1921 and 1922 the average mine was open less than 150 days. In 1924 the miners worked fewer days than they worked at any time between 1895 and 1920. Annual earnings for miners rose more slowly than for all workers from 1913 to 1926.[6] The national average hourly earnings were held artificially high by the United Mine Workers in the Central Competitive Field (western Pennsylvania, Illinois, Indiana, and Ohio) and the Southwest, while nonunion mines in the South had begun cutting wages. Southern mines had expanded relative to the union regions prior to World War I and continued to capture a larger share of the stagnating coal market. In response, operators in the unionized fields began repudiating their contracts. In the midst of the labor strife that followed, wages followed prices downward.[7]

Even during the coal expansion through World War I, the fortunes of the industry fluctuated markedly. Heating demand dropped during mild winters. During economic downturns, industrial demand for coal declined with the demand for industrial products. The troughs in coal production in Table 3-1 closely coincided with downturns in American business activity.[8] Demand fluctuations did not affect mines equally. Mines with natural advantages and captive mines, owned by coal buyers like utilities and steel companies, often continued to produce during downturns. During upturns, some mines starved in the midst of plenty when railroads could not supply enough coal cars to satisfy the large number of mines.[9] The success of individual mines was also determined by railroad rates set by the Interstate Commerce Commission, a source of dispute among coal operators from different regions.[10]

The rapid expansion of the industry led to major changes in mining techniques and the specialization of labor. The pick miner of the 1890s performed numerous tasks with hand tools. He used a pick to make cuts at the base of the wall; drilled holes for charges with a hand auger; and then measured and prepared the explosive himself. After blasting the coal down, he shovelled it into a car, and then pushed the car to a passageway where it was hauled out of the mine by a driver and mule. The only task that was not altered greatly over the following forty years was loading the coal into the cars, causing scholars to refer to the period as the hand-loading era.[11]

The major technological development of the era was the cutting machine, which made the cut at the base of wall. Developed in the 1870s, the machine in various forms cut 25 percent of the tonnage produced in the United States in 1900. Diffusion continued as mines used cutting machines to produce 81 percent of U.S. coal by 1930.[12] The diffusion varied across mining districts in response to the relative prices of capital and labor, physical conditions, and the improvements of machines.[13] In West Virginia cutting machines produced only 15 percent of output in 1900, increasing to 87 percent in 1930. In Colorado as late as 1930, only 57 percent of the coal was mined with cutting machines.[14] Transportation inside the mines improved with the introduction of electric motors and electric lights in the main passageways. Prepackaged charges reduced the dangers of explosives, while electric drills replaced the hand auger.

Over the course of the hand-loading era, each mine worker's task became increasingly specialized in larger mines. A machine cutter and his helper made the cut, shot firers drilled the holes and blasted the coal, loaders loaded the coal into cars, and motormen and brakemen hauled them out of the mines. In many mines, though, the coal loader still set the charges and drilled the blast holes before loading the coal. By 1930 the stage had been set for the next major coal technologies. The machine loader had been introduced in the early 1920s. Some areas had begun strip mining, using bulldozers to tear the earth's surface off the coal seam.

Exercising Voice Through the Union

The most prominent institution through which miners acted collectively was the United Mine Workers of America. Over the long term, membership in the UMWA rose and fell with the coal industry. Although various miners' unions had organized earlier, the UMWA developed in 1890 and has been the dominant coal miners' union ever since. Starting with a membership of 17,000 to 20,000 (of a total work force of 255,244 bituminous and anthracite miners in the United States), the union added another 50,000 members within one year. The depression of the mid 1890s led to a drop in membership to 10,000. After winning a three-month strike in 1897, union membership again expanded. The union's position solidified when in Joint Conferences of 1898 and 1902, the coal operators in the Central Competitive Field of Ohio, western Pennsylvania, Indiana, and Illinois agreed to collective bargaining.[15] By 1902 union membership accounted for approximately 50 percent of the miners in the United States.[16] The percentage held relatively steady until World War I, when pressure from the United States Fuel Administration forced many nonunion mines to operate under collective bargaining agreements. In West Virginia, for example, both the New River and Winding Gulf fields operated under an agreement with the UMWA from June 1917 until 1919, although it is unclear whether they had officially recognized the UMWA.[17] UMWA membership rose to around 60 percent during the war and peaked at around 484,468 members in December of 1922, representing approximately 75 percent of bituminous miners.[18]

The core of union strength was the Central Competitive Field. As shown in Table 3-2, the UMWA was also strong in much of the West and Southwest. The union was weakest in southern mines. From 1900 to the early 1920s, paid-up membership accounted for at best one-third of the employees in the mines of Kentucky, Virginia, and Tennessee; an even smaller proportion of the coal workers in West Virginia and Maryland; and a negligible proportion after 1905 in Alabama. Mine operators in nonunion areas opposed the UMWA every step of the way. As part of employment, they required miners to sign nonunion pledges, disparaged by the union as "yellow-dog contracts." Company police were instructed to keep union organizers out of the towns. In several strikes, violence was used as a deterrent and was often returned in kind by the miners. Another strategy was to improve conditions at the mines. In several fields in southern West Virginia miners did not join because they were not convinced the union offered a better alternative.[19]

As the demand for coal declined in the mid-1920s, the union lost its foothold in a series of bitter struggles. Nonunion fields, paying lower wages than the $7.50 per day scale in the Central Competitive Field, kept expanding market share relative to union districts. Faced with this increasing competition, operators in field after field

TABLE 3-2. Paid-up Membership in the United Mine Workers of America as a Percentage of the Average Number of Employees

State	*1899*	*1902*	*1905*	*1908*	*1912*	*1915*	*1918*	*1921*	*1923*
Alabama	23	65	16	4	*a*	*a*	26	5	2
Arkansas, Oklahoma, and Texas	22	15	84	87	80	80	89	61	33
Colorado and New Mexico		14	3	10	7	3	15	29	3
Illinois	76	91	89	100	94	95	100	92	88
Indiana	74	85	59	99	83	88	89	73	74
Iowa	50	93	73	71	96	84	100	100	88
Kansas	78	50	76	73	89	67	88	19	86
Kentucky, Tennessee, and Virginia	26	31	19	21	11	10	23	23	21
Maryland and West Virginia	3	7	12	3	3	5	30	29	22
Michigan	67	100	62	82	78	83	67	83	80
Missouri		52	87	89	68	58	75	85	61
Montana					90	100	100	93	89
Ohio	55	75	80	80	85	76	85	78	77
Pennsylvania	12	23	41	38	39	40	38	29	41
Washington			10	59	85	68	100	49	10
Wyoming and Utah			26	97	67	57	63	66	54

Source: United States Coal Commission, "Bituminous Mine Workers and Their Homes," *Report,* 68th Congress, 2d Session (Washington, DC: U.S. Government Printing Office, 1925), p. 1052. The percentages in the table are based on the paid-up membership of the United Mine Workers of America as reported for fiscal years ending November 30 and the average number of employees in each areas as reported by the U.S. Geological Survey. The number of employees in the various areas was not available for the years 1922 and 1923. Therefore the percentages for those years were computed on the number employed in 1921.

[a]Less than 1 percent.

either refused to negotiate new agreements or repudiated existing agreements. The New River field in West Virginia failed to come to an agreement in 1921. Colorado went nonunion in 1922. In Kansas and western Kentucky operators broke agreements in 1924, while northern West Virginia broke ranks in 1925. Operators in western and central Pennsylvania, Ohio, Oklahoma, Arkansas, Maryland, and Iowa all discontinued bargaining after 1925.[20] In 1927 the UMWA struck the Central Competitive District for five months in an unsuccessful attempt to stave off a decline in wages. Throughout the period union membership declined, falling to 380,556 in 1923, the last year in which the UMWA published membership figures. By 1929 only 84,395 members were paying dues.[21]

Collective action was not limited to the members of the United Mine Workers. Paid-up membership in the UMWA probably underestimates the number of miners willing to join an UMWA strike. Miners often let their dues lapse when they found other uses for the money. Miners in nonunion districts and at individual mines at times went on strike. Some short-lived, regional unions formed. In Alabama strikes during the early 1890s, the workers claimed membership in the United Mine Workers of Alabama; similar initials but a different union.[22] As the UMWA's power declined during the 1920s, several splinter unions developed, including the Pennsylvania and Ohio Miners Union and West Virginia Miners Union after the strike settlement of 1922, the National Miners Union in the late 1920s, and the Progressive Miners Union in Illinois in the early 1930s.[23]

Competition Among Employers for Labor

While the product market remained highly competitive throughout the period, the structure of the labor market varied across coal districts. In areas where the United Mine Workers of America were strong, the labor market became almost a bilateral monopoly, as operators' associations and the union participated in collective bargaining.[24] In nonunion regions the labor market expanded and was relatively competitive, despite combinations of operators that tried to prevent unionization.

With product market competition ubiquitous, competition among coal operators for labor was bound to follow. During the nineteenth century small owner-operators with offices tucked in their hats typified the industry. As the demand for coal expanded and new technologies became available, greater capital requirements favored larger firms and absentee ownership. U.S. Steel, the Consolidation Coal Company, and other large firms expanded operations and acquired a number of mines, yet they could not dominate the industry. In 1920 the eighty firms that produced over one million tons per year sold only 34.2 percent of the total tonnage in the United States. Another 1000 firms, each producing more than 100,000 tons of coal, sold 45 percent of the coal in the market.[25] The market also contained a strong competitive fringe. When demand expanded, new mines entered the industry, closed mines reopened, and existing mines increased production. Miners themselves often worked outcroppings of coal and hauled their diggings in wagons to the railroad. Contemporary observers bemoaned the presence of this "overcapacity," which led to substantial price competition.[26] Large-scale collusion on a national level with this many operations was highly unlikely. The National Coal Association was the only national organization of coal operators. Its membership included only the owners of 60 percent of commercial coal tonnage in the United States. Further, the members excluded labor relations from the national association's programs by mutual consent.[27]

Firms more often joined local operators' associations. In union districts the primary purpose of many local associations was to negotiate with the union. Some operators' associations paralleled the subdivisions of the United Mine Workers. Isador Lubin suggested that the UMWA therefore had the advantage in negotiations because it was more closely knit than the larger number of operators' associations with which it negotiated.[28] In the nonunion fields of southern West Virginia, for example, the operators freely admitted that they joined forces to prevent union organizing. They pooled monies to press for legislation restricting unions, to form publicity bureaus that attacked unions, and to hire guards to keep union organizers out of their coal fields.[29] These efforts and improvements in working conditions generally curtailed unionization, except during World War I.

The operators' associations' resistence to the UMWA in southern West Virginia did not imply that there was no competition for labor in those areas. The labor force was relatively mobile, and during booms, competition for labor was fierce. The number of firms in southern West Virginia alone was large and they were spread among several associations. In 1913 thirty firms employed over 300 workers in the seven major coal counties in southern West Virginia, an additional one hundred employed over a hundred workers, and at least eighty more employed more than fifty workers.[30] At least six operators' associations were founded in the field.[31] Although some associations set up wage scales, these scales had to be competitive with the wages paid in other associations, union districts, nonunion districts, as well as in other industries. Miners in southern West Virginia easily crossed state borders into eastern Kentucky where there were at least another 150 companies hiring more than ten workers per year and into Virginia where there were another twenty to forty companies.[32] The associations may have tried to keep wages down while stopping unionization, but the average wage for miners rose significantly after their formation. Wages for brakemen in the union and nonunion districts ranged from 15 to 25 cents per hour in 1913. By 1923 the average wage in the area had risen to between 75 and 91 cents, a narrower range in percentage terms.[33] Firms or associations that did not follow this trend experienced an outmigration of labor.

The operators' associations could not prevent internal competition. The typical member faced incentives to follow the association's rules as long as he found them beneficial and break them otherwise. Since each association had little market power in the product market, there were few effective means of enforcing the association's rules.[34] In some instances operators quit or switched associations when they disagreed with policy changes. W.P. Tams, a charter member, quit the Winding Gulf Association in 1917 when it showed sign of weakening its stance against unions. Justus Collins quit the Winding Gulf Association for the Pocahontas Association. He later rejoined and then quit again in 1928.[35] Walter Thurmond, an operator in Logan County, noted that "some members broke loose from time to time" from the Logan County Association, although it continued to speak for the bulk of the tonnage in the field.[36]

Although associations at times set wage scales, some operators felt free to pay wages that differed. In one instance in 1917, when southern West Virginia operators increased wages in response to increases in the coal price allowed by the Fuel Administration, the operators in the New River district raised their wages beyond the level desired by many in the Winding Gulf region. One firm offered a Winding Gulf Colliery worker a wage 25 percent higher than what he would have received from the Winding Gulf increase. In another instance in 1927, Winding Gulf broke away from the group to pay lower wages.[37] In 1920 at least one operator began hiring workers who had been discharged from other mines for affiliating with the UMWA. The operator stated that he would not recognize the UMWA as long as the others did not, but he saw no reason not to hire both union and nonunion workers.[38] Corbin suggests that "the coal companies, always in need of good miners, often procured workers from other companies by offering them bonuses and individual contracts."[39] The competition extended beyond wages. Model mining towns offered better housing, more activities and a better quality of education; others adjusted work rules. Miners responded to these incentives.[40]

Recently, William Boal tested for the presence of labor monopsony power in the nonunion counties of West Virginia over the period from 1897 to 1932. If coal firms had a labor monopsony, we would expect to find a gap between the wage paid coal miners and their marginal revenue product. Boal set up empirical models based on two common theoretical solutions to bargaining situations. He then performed quantitative analysis with a panel of county-level data over the entire period from the annual reports of the West Virginia Department of Mines. Since the county-level data prevented the study from capturing competition within the county, the analysis was biased toward finding monopsony power on the part of coal employers. Despite the bias, the analysis showed that coal employers enjoyed only a small amount of monopsony power in the short run, and the power diminished greatly in the long run. The results are consistent with the qualitative evidence that positive information and migration costs imposed some limits on labor market competition in the short run, but the limits were overcome when miners had more time to adjust in the long run.[41]

The competition for workers was not limited to firms in the coal industry. Opportunities outside the coal industry improved, as real wages for skilled and unskilled laborers rose through much of the early twentieth century.[42] For coal mining to continue to expand into the early 1920s, employers had to pay wages in mining for both skilled and unskilled wage earners that kept pace with this trend. Unskilled laborers could relatively easily match their mining wages, holding risk of injury constant, in other industries. The U.S. Immigration Commission, for example, found that wages in Pennsylvania mining rose to meet the competition of other industries that used unskilled labor.[43] About half of coal mining operatives were considered semiskilled workers by students of the occupational structure, because their skills could be learned within one to two years. The other half were considered laborers because their work was heavy, coarse work that required no special training, judgment, or manual dexterity.[44] In the short run, semiskilled and more skilled miners relied more on coal opportunities. With skills specific to mining but not other industries, they were unlikely to match the coal wages initially in other endeavors. In the longer run, however, skilled miners' wages had to rise to remain competitive with those of other equally skilled workers. Opportunities for betterment within the industry depended on the period in the coal cycle. During booms, opportunities opened up as both skilled and unskilled labor were in demand. During the boom of the early 1900s, the United States Immigration Commission repeatedly found that more experienced native miners and immigrant miners from England, Germany, and Scotland, who had been in the fields a long time moved up into the more skilled positions rapidly if they had not moved on to other regions.[45] However, during busts, the miners' alternatives were few within the industry. As coal mining contracted after 1923, almost 200,000, or 30 percent, of the miners left the industry by 1929. Another 100,000 left the industry in the first three years of the Great Depression.[46]

The Miners' Mobility

The large number of employers inside and outside the coal industry was no guarantee of labor market competition if miners were immobile. Workers could not avail themselves of opportunities elsewhere if they were stuck in one place, trapped by high costs of migration and lack of information on opportunities elsewhere. While migration was not costless and information about mining towns was not perfect, miners, particularly in nonunion districts, were mobile and consistently exited.

One sign that miners were able to move is high turnover rates. The U.S. Coal Commission collected information on turnover in 1921 from company payrolls throughout the United States. The Commission calculated the turnover rate as total separations divided by the average number of workers on the payroll during the year.[47] They also offered an alternative measure, the stable labor force, which is the percentage of workers who stayed on the payroll throughout the year. Both measures, shown in Table 3-3, offer a similar picture of movement. The turnover rate in coal mining for the United States as a whole was approximately 100 percent, which was slightly lower than the 115 percent ratio found for 160 firms in other industries in 1913–1914, but substantially lower than the 146 percent rate for firms employing under 1000 workers, which are more comparable with the size of coal mines. The rate for other industries during World War I was 180 percent for all firms and 221 percent for smaller firms.[48] However, all evidence suggests that coal mining turnover rates were also substantially higher during World War I. These comparisons are striking because most industries were located in urban areas where workers could change jobs without moving. In coal mining changing employers often meant migrating to a new town.

Further, the U.S. average for coal mining disguises enormous differences between districts. Table 3-3 shows that low turnover in union districts brought the national coal average down. In the states where the United Mine Workers were strongest—Ohio, Indiana, Illinois, and the union section of Pennsylvania—the turnover rates were less than 80 percent; approximately 60 percent of the work force stayed on the payroll throughout the year. In contrast, in the nonunion Appalachian fields, where miners relied more upon exit, turnover rates rivaled the levels for smaller firms during World War I at 211 percent; approximately 31 percent of the work force stayed on the payroll throughout the year.

The evidence on turnover by occupation is inconsistent with views that high turnover rates reflected an unskilled population that was constantly drifting from mine to mine while the skilled workers all stayed put. Coal mining was similar to other industries in that skilled workers displayed lower turnover, but the gap in turnover rates was not large. The national average turnover rate for machine miners, the highest paid occupation, was 76 percent compared with 110 percent for loaders, the group most likely to be characterized as a floating population.[49] The turnover rates were high enough for all groups to cast aside images of the immobile mine worker.

There are caveats about using turnover rates as a picture of the miners' mobility. Separations may have negative connotations and 1921 was a severe recession year. The Coal Commission suggested that nonunion mines discharged miners more easily, and miners moved in nonunion districts to avoid wage cuts, while union wage rates stayed constant.[50] However, high turnover rates are also a sign of low costs of moving from mine to mine, as miners moved to take advantage of small differences in wage rates and work opportunities across mines. During the 1921 recession, the movement was generated by wage cutting and slack work, while in

TABLE 3-3. Labor Turnover and Stable Work Force Rates in Union and Nonunion Areas, 1921

Area	*Turnover Rate*	*Stable Force*
Nonunion West Virginia, Virginia and Kentucky[a]	211.3	31.0
Mixed West Virginia[b]	148.0	46.0
Union West Virginia[c]	133.0	44.5
Nonunion West[d]	131.5	43.0
Mixed Tennessee	122.0	51.0
Nonunion Pennsylvania[e]	118.3	50.0
Union Montana and Wyoming	105.0	52.0
Nonunion Alabama and Georgia	80.0	60.0
Union Pennsylvania[f]	78.5	56.0
Nonunion Maryland[g]	77.0	57.0
Union Ohio, Indiana, and Illinois[h]	64.1	63.2
Union Midwest and Southwest[i]	60.8	65.8
Union Washington	51.0	66.0

Source: U.S. Coal Commission, "Labor Turnover in the Bituminous Coal Industry," *Report*, Part 3, 68th Cong., 2nd sess. (Washington, DC: U.S. Government Printing Office, 1925), pp. 1264–65.

Notes: The turnover rate is the total number of separations lasting longer than one month as a percentage of the average number of employees on the payroll. The stable force rate is the number of workers who were on the payroll throughout the year as a percentage of the average number of employees on the payroll.

[a]Southern Appalachian, Northeastern Kentucky, Virginia, Logan, Kenova-Thacker, Pocahontas, and Tug River districts.

[b]Winding Gulf and New River districts.

[c]Panhandle, Fairmont, Kanawha, and Coal River districts.

[d]Utah, New Mexico, and Colorado districts.

[e]Somerset, Westmoreland, and Connellsville districts.

[f]Central Pennsylvania, Northwestern Pennsylvania, and Pittsburgh districts.

[g]Cumberland and Piedmont districts.

[h]Northern Ohio, Southern Ohio, Indiana, and the following districts in Ilinois: Danville, Northern Illinois, Fulton, Peoria, Central, Belleville, and Southern.

[i]Iowa, Michigan, Oklahoma, Arkansas, Texas, Kansas, and Missouri.

earlier booms wage increases and more work generated the movement. Although lower turnover in union districts may imply greater job satisfaction, it may also reflect higher opportunity costs of moving. For example, in unionized Illinois in 1909, the presence of a number of unemployed workers willing to wait for high-wage spots in each union mine made it very costly for a union member to quit to move to a new mine.[51] When combined with evidence from boom years, the turnover rates in 1921 suggest that where miners did not exercise voice through the union, they responded with exits.

Other sources confirm the high degree of mobility in the Appalachian nonunion fields at other times. Corbin's examination of the Stevens Coal Company Acme Mine payroll in Kanawha County, West Virginia shows that only twelve of fifty-eight men working at the mine in November 1904 were still there sixteen months later, despite an increase in the number of men on the payroll.[52] During the major surges of labor demand relative to local supply in the early 1900s, the Immigration Commission commented on the constant shifting of immigrants within fields, across the country, and back to Europe.[53] The movement was not limited to immigrants nor to unmarried miners. A U.S. Children's Bureau study of Raleigh County, West Virginia in 1920 found that almost 60 percent of the families interviewed had lived in the same community for three years or less. The percentage was similar for native whites, blacks, and immigrants.[54] The moves were caused by a combination of push and pull factors. Sometimes mines closed or hit slack periods, at other times new mines and better opportunities beckoned.

Corbin argues that, with the exception of more experienced miners, the movement in southern West Virginia was limited to just that area.[55] But he underestimates the opportunities for movement across coal districts and in and out of coal mining. During the early 1900s, the United States Immigration Commission found a strong tendency of native white miners to leave West Virginia and Virginia coal fields for other coal mining sections, in part because they were dissatisfied by the results of early strikes.[56] Other groups moved with similar facility. In the 1890s and early 1900s, many immigrants in midwestern fields and the majority of immigrants in southwestern fields came from other coal mining sections of the United States.[57] Numerous workers came to West Virginia, Virginia, and Alabama from Pennsylvania fields and other regions in search of new opportunities.[58] In Pennsylvania many left the mines for employment in other industries in Pittsburgh.[59] In general, the U.S. Immigration Commission found that the immigrants moved "readily from one community to another of the coal industry, and with equal facility from coal mining to another industry, according to the fluctuating demands for labor."[60] The immigrants also moved easily back and forth between the United States and Europe. Often during strikes, immigrants left for home and returned when operations resumed.[61]

Black miners shared similar experiences, except they often faced barriers to migration into union mines in Illinois, Ohio, Pennsylvania, and northern West Virginia.[62] The West Virginia Bureau of Negro Welfare and Statistics noted that during downturns numerous blacks returned to farms that they or their relatives owned.[63] Numerous southern blacks used the West Virginia fields as springboards to jobs in other areas, stopping for a few years to earn high wages before migrating farther north.[64]

Many miners were mobile because they originally had to migrate to reach the coal fields, whether located in the Appalachian regions of Kentucky, West Virginia, Virginia, and Pennsylvania, or in the midwest or west. Throughout the hand-loading era, migrants dominated work forces in many fields. The most obvious group was the foreign-born, who accounted for over half the mining population in Pennsylvania in 1907, approximately 30 percent in West Virginia between 1902 and World War I, and 37 percent of bituminous coal miners in the United States in 1920.[65] Small local populations in most areas where coal was found and constant expansion of mines and employment meant that most American-born miners also migrated from some other area. As late as 1932, after thirty to forty years of coal production, only 14 percent of the 600 black miners James Laing interviewed were natives of the state.[66] Although some of the black out-of-state miners had migrated as children, numerous children of miners left the fields for other occupations.[67] In Pennsylvania, the Immigration Commission found that children of native-born miners refused to enter the industry.[68] In general, migrants faced lower costs of moving than natives of a district when considering further migration. Previous migrants generally did not have the natives' attachment to the locale. Further, they already had accumulated valuable experience that lowered both economic and psychological costs of moving.

Conditions in the mining industry probably caused more mobile workers to enter and remain in the industry. By moving from mine to mine, the more mobile workers potentially earned higher incomes. If one mine was laying off workers, chances were that another mine was hiring. When nonunion operators talked to the U.S. Coal Commission, they stated that men moved quickly when work slackened, "and there [was] the faintest rumor of work elsewhere."[69] The Kentucky Department of Mines noted in 1915 the tendency of mine workers to shift from place to place during the larger part of the year.[70] During strikes, men at times left strike districts for other areas, returning at the end of the turmoil. During downturns, the U.S. Immigration Commission found that miners constantly moved in search of work.[71] During economy-wide downturns, the miners' opportunities were restricted in the same way that other workers' opportunities were. The benefits of mobility were then reduced not just for mine workers but also for other workers.

Clearly the most mobile group of workers were single miners, who generally had few possessions. In 1909 approximately 28 percent of native white miners, 37 percent of black miners, and 33 percent of foreign-born miners were single; another 19 percent of foreign-born miners had left their wives in Europe.[72] Even many married men with families remained relatively mobile, because they generally rented housing. They did not incur the costs of selling property, nor did they suffer capital losses from selling property after the mine closed.

The direct costs of moving fell during the hand-loading era. Transportation between mines was originally provided by railroads and improved throughout the period. Railroads connected all of the mines, but their primary use was for coal freight in the early stages of the industry. Most passenger cars were found on lines between major towns. As mining expanded, the number of mines and mining towns increased, shortening the distance between mines. The number of trains to more isolated areas also increased, although many operated sporadically. Travel costs were lowered even further by the introduction of paved roads and automobiles during the late 1910s and early 1920s.[73] A surprising number of miners owned automobiles in the 1920s and 1930s.[74]

The Miners' Information

Obtaining accurate information about opportunities was another potential obstacle to miners' mobility. Workers and mine employers closed this "information gap" in a variety of ways.[75] Some workers entered the coalfields through other jobs or because they lived nearby. Many discovered opportunities through word-of-mouth networks of relatives and friends. Others were recruited by labor agents in cities or by coal company agents who traveled within the coal region, outside the region, or in Europe.

Some miners entered the coalfields in other activities and stayed on as miners. Many of the first miners in the Appalachian fields in both West Virginia and eastern Kentucky worked on the railroad construction crews that laid the track to the mines.[76] Others came greater distances to the fields on the basis of rumors of high wages. About 4 percent of the black miners interviewed by James Laing about migrating to West Virginia were attracted by general knowledge of a boom in the coalfields.[77]

Word-of-mouth networks offered the most important source of information about jobs at the mines. A migrant who discovered conditions to his liking initiated a stream of additional migration. He was a valuable source of information for friends and relatives because they already knew him and could gauge the accuracy of the information he provided. If he were a trusted friend, his descriptions were more accurate and more detailed than those available from labor agents and in advertisements. For the non-English speaking individual, the network was even more important. Moving to an area where others spoke his language alleviated problems of adjusting to a new culture and information difficulties until he was able to learn English. The Immigration Commission constantly emphasized the importance of this network throughout its report.[78]

At least 20 percent of the black migrants to West Virginia interviewed by James Laing mentioned some form of the relative/friend network.

> The decision of relatives to go to the mining fields is a factor that brings many more Negroes than just those making the decision . . . It is not unusual to find a man, his wife, and their sons and their families all living in the same mining town. Not infrequently some of their old neighbors in the south will be found there also. This tendency may be compared to the situation sometimes found in the cities when a lawyer would sometimes have about the same clientele in Chicago as he did in Mississippi or Georgia. Others visited relatives in West Virginia and decided to stay themselves.
>
> Hardly less potent as a pull toward West Virginia were friends of Negroes already in the mining fields. Friends returning from the mines for a visit to their old homes and neighbors were living evidence of the prosperity to be found there. In a sense their return was more or less a triumphal entry—and they made the most of it. Over-loaded with clothes and money, they left little doubt in the minds of their old neighbors that better things must be in store for the Negro who went north.[79]

The potential word-of-mouth flows among miners within the industry were even greater. As miners moved from town to town, the number of informants increased. Shorter distances allowed the network to work more effectively. The UMWA's efforts to organize workers generally enhanced the word-of-mouth networks. According to Fred Mooney, secretary-treasurer of the United Mine Workers in District 17 in northern West Virginia in the early 1920s, "the knowledge of one's neighbors and their whereabouts over hundreds of square miles was prevalent in all communities where the organization had spread in the years from 1917 to 1925."[80]

The coal companies, seeking an effective work force, tried to tap the word-of-mouth flows. When they found a good worker from distant places, they might reasonably have inferred that his friends and relatives were good workers. The inference was subject to error, but hiring the friend was more likely to turn out well than hiring an unknown. In periods when companies sought labor, they at times offered payments or trips home to workers if they would recruit friends or relatives. In many cases the company arranged transportation for the new workers. One black miner in the Paint Creek district in West Virginia told senate investigators that he had made six to eight trips home to North Carolina at company expense.[81] Another black miner stated that on trips home he often spent all his money. When ready to return, he wrote his boss and received transport expenses for him and a few others.[82] Generally, workers repaid the transport expenses out of future pay. In the Southwest, companies paid transport expenses from Europe for miners' friends and relatives when two or more would stand good for the amount.[83]

When mines first opened or during peak periods of production, word-of-mouth networks at times failed to satisfy increases in the companies' demand for labor. Companies then sent their own agents to recruit in rural areas or other coalfields. Alternatively, they hired existing agents in areas where they sought workers. Many Kentucky, West Virginia, and Virginia mines were initially filled with blacks and whites transported from rural parts of Virginia and the Carolinas. Immigrants were funnelled into coalfields all over the country by New York agents who met them when they came off the boats, and by agents who organized transportation from existing fields.[84] George Williams, an agent from New York, brought workers from various eastern cities to Kanawha county during the strike of 1912 and 1913. He was employed by the Winding Gulf Operators' Association during World War I.[85] Bowlegged Jones operated in Alabama during and after World War I. He usually set up a table in the woods near the Alabama mines and coordinated transport for miners who wanted to migrate to West Virginia. When asked how long he planned to stay in business, he stated that he would "keep on sending 'em until his legs got straight."[86] The labor agents generally worked for a fee, one to two dollars per man or five dollars per family with the company paying transport expenses in 1910.[87] Williams worked for a salary with the employer paying transport expenses. Use of labor agents to bring in labor was a costly proposition, but the effect on labor migration was potentially enormous. If workers found conditions were favorable, positive feedback through the new connections in the word-of-mouth network stimulated larger influxes of new labor.

At times in nearly every field, companies brought miners in on transport during strikes. Spero and Harris believe that black strikebreaking broke down barriers to black employment in several mines in northern West Virginia and Pennsylvania in the mid-1920s.[88] However, the importance of strikebreaking to long-term migration should not be overemphasized. Strikebreakers often entered very tense environments, which sometimes exploded into violence. When the strike ended, returning strikers often ostracized strikebreakers. Dissatisfied nonstrikers often left, stifling additional migration from the word-of-mouth network.

In the absence of the word-of-mouth network, the companies found other means of informing potential workers from a great distance. The successful labor agent probably was a persuasive salesman. The accuracy of the information depended on the agent's desire to continue operating in an area or working for his employer. In larger cities, the company or the agent passed out handbills or advertised in the paper for potential laborers. Dishonest claims may have been effective in the short run, but workers who were fooled discredited the agent when they returned home. Further, newcomers whose expectations were not met, especially the immigrants, commonly moved on before the coal companies could collect transportation costs from their wages.[89] The Stonega Coke and Coal Company records show that between 16 and 37 percent of the men who came to the Stonega mines in Virginia on transportation left without working. Many left for other mines.[90] Employers who wanted a more permanent labor force had little need for an agent who could not effectively supply them with one. Employers who wanted only a temporary increase in their work force might have used dishonest agents. Unfortunately, when workers were fooled by dishonest agents, the worker most often bore the costs of returning home or finding work elsewhere.

Although we have no recordings of the agent's verbal descriptions, there are examples of advertisements. The complexity and type of information varied. An Alabama coal operator during the early 1890s sought black workers with the following ad.

> . . . job at Blue Creek is a desirable one. This is a rare chance for all first class colored miners to have a permanent home. They can have their own churches, schools, and societies, and conduct their social affairs in a manner to suit themselves, and there need be no conflict between the races. This can be a colored man's colony.
>
> Colored miners come along; let us see whether you can have an Eden of your own or not. I will see that you will have a fair show. You can then prove that there is intelligence enough among colored people to manage their social and domestic affairs by themselves in such a way as to command respect of the people at large. It is not likely you will have another chance to demonstrate to the world that you are capable of governing your social affairs without the aid of interference of the white race H. F. DeBardeleben[91]

There is no mention of mining conditions, but the ad seems to be written to attract first-class miners and actually appears to be written for them. Laing found that more articulate black miners were more likely to focus on civic and social reasons for migration than others whom he interviewed.[92] The advertisement was apparently placed during a major strike and drew a number of black workers to the Blue Creek mine. DeBardeleben's sons later ran company towns known for the provision of paternal services to blacks, which have been described as part of an all-out, no-holds-barred effort to prevent unions.[93]

In the 1920s, the Spruce River Coal Company in Boone county, West Virginia ran the following ad, which similarly focused on town conditions and not mining.

Miners Wanted

Best	Good	Hospitals
Conditions	Schools	and
in the	Church	Amusements
STATE	YMCA	

Apply at Office of the SPRUCE RIVER COAL CO.[94]

Other advertisements were more pragmatic. The following handbill, meant specifically for experienced black miners in the Birmingham district in the 1890s, provided a great deal of information about work at the mine.

> *Colored Coal Miners Wanted* for Weir City District, Kansas. Coal 3 feet 10 inches high. Since issue of first circular, price paid for mining had been advanced to one dollar per ton in winter and ninety cents in summer, for lump coal screened over seven-eights inch screen. Payday twice a month in cash. Transportation will not exceed 10 dollars, which will be advanced. Special train leaves Birmingham Tuesday night, June 13. Leave your name at Kansas City railway office, 1714 Morris Avenue.[95]

Note the amount of information provided in the circular. The number of paydays, the size of coal seams, the size of the coal screen, and the costs of transport were deemed important enough to be included with the piece-rate wage. All of these factors affected the miner's net earnings and were especially important to an experienced miner. The major piece of information not provided was that these miners were strikebreakers. The company actually paid for that omission. A large percentage of the 175 men attracted to Kansas by this offer returned to Birmingham at company expense when they discovered a strike in progress.[96]

Another ad from the early teens was targeted at New York workers with much less mining experience.

> Miners and Laborers for coal mine. Blacksmiths, track layers, drum runners, motor runners, motor helpers, trappers, greasers, slate men, tipple boys, mule drivers, tipple bosses, and men. Good steady job all the year around; family men of all nationalities preferred. Transportation furnished; long contract; also strong men used to pick work can make $6 per day. Strike on. Homes all furnished. All the coal you want. $1 per month. Here is your chance to make money and a good home. Apply early. Joseph Knowles, Room 302–303 Wallace Block. Call from 8 A.M. to 9 P.M.[97]

The ad emphasizes the continuity of work and the potential for earning high wages. Descriptions of furnished homes and cheap fuel offer added information about living conditions. The contract the men signed before embarking contained a more detailed list of wages and described the terms of repaying transport costs. Both the ad and the contract stated that there was a strike. The mine owner was apparently interested in keeping the new workers. He was honest about the strike, and in the contract he offered workers free transport if they worked more than ninety days.[98]

Summary

While the coal labor market was not the pristine market of neoclassical economic theory, it still seemed to operate in ways predicted by the theory. Miners' opportunities were determined in part by the conditions in the coal product market and in part by the general conditions for all workers. Coal employment rose and opportunities improved when the industry boomed, and declined when the industry declined. The miners took advantage of their opportunities in two ways. They exercised their collective voice through the UMWA in northern, midwestern, and western regions until the mid-1920s. Where the UMWA did not maintain a strong foothold, miners were quick to practice exit. Adjustments were not instantaneous, but miners faced low costs of migration and information. Many observers described substantial mobility of miners, particularly in nonunion regions, and the description is borne out by rudimentary statistics from the period. Aside from the barriers to movement into union districts, miners moved relatively freely within coal mining as well as in and out of coal mining. When miners did poorly, it could not be blamed on them being stuck in one place without the ability to move. External conditions in the coal market or in the overall economy were more likely to be the cause of their plight.

NOTES

1. From 1890 to 1913 the average annual manufacturing wage in current dollars rose 32 percent, while average annual earnings in coal mining rose 51 percent. The difference in growth rates is smaller for the period 1890–1910 when coal earnings rose 22.6 percent compared to 18 percent in all industries. See Table 6-1. The workweek data are from series 595 in U.S. Bureau of the Census, *Historical Statistics of the United States: Colonial Times to 1957* (Washington, DC: U.S. Government Printing Office, 1961), p. 91.

2. Glen Lawhon Parker, *The Coal Industry: A Study in Social Control* (Washington, DC: American Council on Public Affairs, 1940), p. 40; National Industrial Conference Board, *The Competitive Position of Coal in the United States* (New York: National Industrial Conference Board, 1931).

3. Parker, *The Coal Industry*, pp. 35–36.

4. Morton S. Baratz, *The Union and the Coal Industry* (New Haven, CT: Yale University Press, 1955), pp. 40–41.

5. Waldo Fisher and Charles James, *Minimum Price Fixing in the Bituminous Coal Industry* (Princeton, NJ: Princeton University Press, 1955) p. 18; Parker, *The Coal Industry*, p. 63.

6. Nominal annual earnings for miners rose 111 percent from 1913 to 1926, compared with an 138 percent rise for manufacturing workers. See Table 6-1.

7. Parker, *The Coal Industry*, pp. 40, 70–72.

8. The downturn in 1904 coincides with the Rich Man's Panic; the fall in 1908 with short-term problems in 1907; 1919 is the postwar depression; 1921 and 1922 were a second postwar depression that combined with strikes. Other smaller downturns occurred in recessions of 1911 and 1914. In 1927 and 1928 business activity slowed relative to the years surrounding. See Figure 1-4 in Albert W. Niemi, *U.S. Economic History*, 2nd ed. (Chicago, IL: Rand McNally, 1980), p. 11.

9. Waldo Fisher and Anne Bezanson, *Wage Rates and Working Time in the Bituminous Coal Industry, 1912–1922* (Philadelphia: University of Pennsylvania Press, 1932), p. 17. U.S. Geological Survey, *Mineral Resources of the United States, Part II Nonmetals* (Washington, DC: U.S. Government Printing Office, various years), 1915, p. 347; 1916, pp. 930, 987; 1917, p. 906; 1918, p. 697; 1921, pp. 459, 489–91; 1926, p. 466.

10. Fisher and James, *Minimum Price Fixing*, pp. 8–9; Baratz, *The Union and Coal*, p. 33.

11. Much of the description here is derived from the following sources: Keith Dix, *Work Relations in the Coal Industry: The Hand-Loading Era, 1880–1930* (West Virginia University Bulletin, Series 78, No. 7–2, January 1978), pp. 8-38; Carter Goodrich, *The Miner's Freedom* (Boston, MA: Marshall Jones Co., 1925; reprinted, New York: Arno Press, 1977); Hugh Archbald, *The Four-Hour Day in Coal*, New York: H.W. Wilson Co., 1922); I. Lubin, *Miner's Wages and the Cost of Coal* (New York: McGraw-Hill, 1924); United States Coal Commission, *Report*, 5 parts. Senate Document 195, 68th Cong., 2nd Sess. (Washington, DC: U.S. Government Printing Office, 1925), p. 1054.

12. Dix, *Work Relations*, p. 20.

13. Christian Dustmann, "The Diffusion of the Cutting Machine Technology in the U.S. Bituminous Coal Industry, 1901–1930," M.A. Thesis, University of Georgia, 1986.

14. Dix, *Work Relations*, p. 20; U.S. Bureau of Mines, *Mineral Resources of the United States, Part II Nonmetals, 1930* (Washington, DC: U.S. Government Printing Office, various years).

15. Baratz, *Union and Coal*, pp. 51–52.

16. H.G. Lewis, *Unionism and Relative Wages in the United States* (Chicago, IL: University of Chicago Press Midway Reprint, 1973, pp.73–75.

17. Letter to Justus Collins from George Wolfe, August 27, 1917, in Justus Collins Papers, West Virginia Regional and History Collection, West Virginia University Library, Morgantown, West Virginia. Collins owned several mines in the Winding Gulf field and helped found the Winding Gulf Coal Operator's Association. Wolfe was his manager at the Winding Gulf Colliery Company and served as an officer in the Winding Gulf Operators' Association.

18. Parker, *The Coal Industry*, p. 76; Lewis, *Unionism and Wages*, p. 73–75.

19. David Corbin, *Life, Work, and Rebellion in the Coal Fields: The Southern West Virginia Miners 1880–1922* (Chicago: University of Illinois Press, 1981), pp. 43–52.

20. Parker, *The Coal Industry*, pp. 70–71.

21. Ibid., p. 76; Baratz, *Union and Coal*, p. 61.

22. Ronald Lewis, *Black Coal Miners in America: Race, Class and Community Conflict 1780–1980* (Lexington: The University Press of Kentucky, 1987), pp. 42–43; Robert D. Ward and William W. Rogers, *Labor Revolt in Alabama: The Great Strike of 1894* (University: University of Alabama Press, 1965).

23. Parker, *The Coal Industry*, p. 78.

24. Bilateral monopoly refers to a situation where there is only one buyer and one seller.

25. These figures do not take into account interlocking directorates and therefore underestimate the concentration in the industry. U.S. Coal Commission, *Report*, p. 1888.

26. Fisher and Bezanson, *Wage Rates*, pp. 12, 13.

27. Lubin, *Miner's Wages*, p. 39.

28. Ibid., pp. 39–42.

29. Corbin, *Life, Work, and Rebellion*, pp. 112–14.

30. Operations with more than one mine were counted as one operation. Interlocking directorates were not taken into account. The seven counties are McDowell, Fayette, Kanawha, Raleigh, Mercer, Logan, and Mingo. Data are from West Virginia Department of Mines, *Annual Report* for the Year Ending June 30, 1913, pp. 110–24.

31. Associations dotted the map in West Virginia. The Kanawha County Coal Operator's Associations contracted with the UMWA. The Guyan Valley Coal Operators' Association formed in Logan County and later took the name of the county. McDowell County contained three operators' groups, the Tug River, Pocahontas, and Winding Gulf Operators' Associations. The Williamson Coal Operators' Association was founded in Mingo County.

32. Kentucky Department of Mines, *Annual Report for the Year 1915*, p. 15; and U.S.

Bureau of Mines, *Bulletin* No. 115, "Coal-Mine Fatalities in the United States, 1870–1914," by Albert Fay (Washington, DC: U.S. Government Printing Office, 1916), pp. 210–11, 329. For the Virginia mines I assumed each company owned between 1.5 and three mines.

33. Brakemen's wages serve as an index of general changes in wages. Changes over time in other wage rates were similar. U.S. Coal Commission, *Report, Part V: Atlas of Statistical Tables*, pp. 208–09, 218–19.

34. Some of the associations had defense funds to which operators contributed, but these were not necessarily means of keeping operators in the association. In some cases the funds were spent on guards and antiunion publicity, testimony before Senate and Fact Finders' committees, and legislative lobbying. When the Associations were broke, they tapped the operators for further funds. Corbin, *Life, Work, and Rebellion*, p. 113; letter to Justus Collins from S.R. Anderson, August 13, 1923, Justus Collins Papers. Rather than holding members in the association the spending of funds and subsequent requests for money have caused the operator to reassess his membership with each contribution.

35. There may have been some interlocking of associations as George Wolfe, the manager and treasurer of Justus Collins' Winding Gulf Colliery, was an officer of the Winding Gulf Operators' Association and of the Tug River Operators' Association in 1920. This might have led to some confusion about the wages the Winding Gulf Colliery would pay since the wage scales for the two associations were different. Letters to Justus Collins from George Wolfe, May 5, 1917, May 16, 1917; Bulletin "I" of the Winding Gulf Operators' Association, July 16, 1920; Bulletin No. 124 of the Tug River Coal Operators' Association, George Wolfe, secretary, October 2, 1920; letter to L. Epperly from P. M. Snyder, president of the Winding Gulf Operators' Association, May 7, 1928; all from the Justus Collins Papers.

36. Walter Thurmond, *The Logan Coal Fields of West Virginia: A Brief History* (Morgantown: West Virginia University Library, 1964), p. 42.

37. Letter to Justus Collins from George Wolfe, November 12, 1917; letter to L. Epperly from P. M. Snyder, May 7, 1928, Justus Collins Papers.

38. Letter to Justus Collins from George Wolfe, July 16, 1920, Justus Collins Papers.

39. Corbin, *Life, Work, and Rebellion*, p. 42.

40. It is clear that miners valued nonwage aspects of the package. Several authors cite several instances where miners moved to camps for nonwage reasons. See ibid., p. 42; James T. Laing, "The Negro Miner in West Virginia," Ph.D. dissertation, Ohio State University, 1933, pp. 146–51. Operators who ran model towns felt that they could attract, select out, and keep more productive workers by enhancing the housing, schools, and other facets of the town. For an example in Alabama, see Marlene Hunt Rikard, "An Experiment in Welfare Capitalism: The Health Care Services of the Tennessee, Coal, Iron, and Railroad Company," Ph.D. dissertation, University of Alabama, 1983.

41. William M. Boal, "Testing for Employer Monopsony in Turn-of-the-Century Coal Mining," Ohio State University Department of Economics Working Paper #90-05, unpublished manuscript, August 1990. Marginal revenue product rather than the value of marginal product is used in situations where the firm has market power. Marginal revenue product is the miner's marginal product multiplied by the firm's marginal revenue.

42. Average annual earnings of employees in 1914 dollars (after adjusting for unemployment) rose from $445 in 1900 to $546 in 1910 to $648 in 1919, fell to 566 in 1921, and rose again to $793 in 1929. See United States Bureau of the Census, *Historical Statistics of the United States, Colonial Times to 1970* (Washington, DC: U.S. Government Printing Office, 1975), series D-725, p. 164. Average Annual Earnings for wage earners in manufacturing (D-781) deflated by Douglass's Cost-of-Living index (E-185) rose from $410.37 in 1890–99 dollars in 1900 to $435.94 in 1910 to $474.8 in 1920 to $543.1 in 1926. Average Annual Earnings for Farm Labor (D-789) deflated by Douglass's Cost-of-Living index rose from

$233.02 in 1900 to $262.50 in 1910 to $283.22 in 1920, but fell to $246.1 in 1926. Average Annual Earnings in Bituminous Coal (D-788) deflated by the Douglass Cost-of-Living index rose from $413.21 in 1900 to $435.94 in 1910 to $484.61 in 1920 to $517.43 in 1926.

43. U.S. Immigration Commission, *Report on Immigrants in Industries, Part I: Bituminous Coal Mining*, 2 vols. Senate Document no. 633, 61st Cong., 2nd sess. (Washington, DC: U.S. Government Printing Office, 1911), vol. I, p. 424.

44. Alba Edwards, "Social-Economic Groups of the United States," *Journal of the American Statistical Association* 15 (June 1917): 643–51; Alba Edwards, *Comparative Occupation Statistics for the United States, 1870–1940*, (Washington, DC: U.S. Government Printing Office, 1943).

45. U.S. Immigration Commission, *Immigrants in Coal*, vol II, p. 222.

46. Baratz, *Union and Coal*, pp. 40–41.

47. A miner was considered to have separated from the firm if he was absent from the payroll for longer than one month.

48. U.S. Coal Commission, "Labor Turnover in the Bituminous Coal Industry," *Report*, pp. 1263–64.

49. Ibid., pp. 1267–69.

50. Ibid., p. 1266. Miners might also be forced to go when the mine shuts down, although that is not a problem for these turnover rates, which focused on mines working the full year.

51. "[O]lder miners allege even in normal periods, there are areas in Illinois where there are two miners for every place that offers steady work to one miner." U.S. Immigration Commission, *Immigrants in Coal*, vol. I, p. 669.

52. Corbin, *Life, Work, and Rebellion*, p. 40. The Stevens Coal Company owned three mines. Some of the men might have moved to one of the other mines; therefore, the figures may overestimate the amount of turnover. Stevens Coal Company Records, West Virginia Regional and History Collection, University of West Virginia Library, Morgantown, West Virginia.

53. U.S. Immigration Commission, *Immigrants in Coal*, vol. I, p. 164; vol. II, pp. 27, 148–49, 151–52, 155, 158, 218. The Commission most prominently mentioned high mobility in West Virginia, Alabama, Virginia, and Kansas.

54. U.S. Department of Labor, Children's Bureau, "The Welfare of Children in Bituminous Coal Mining Communities," *Bureau Publication* No. 117, by Nettie P. McGill (Washington, DC: U.S. Government Printing Office, 1923), p. 5. Also cited in Corbin, *Life, Work, and Rebellion*, p. 40.

55. Corbin, *Life, Work, and Rebellion*, p. 42.

56. U.S. Immigration Commission, *Immigrants in Coal*, vol. II, p. 222; vol. II, pp. 151–52, 148–49.

57. Ibid., vol. I, p. 606, vol. II, pp. 27, 61.

58. Ibid., vol. II, pp. 147, 149, 152, 153, 156–58, 164–66, 216.

59. Ibid., vol. I, pp. 260–61.

60. Ibid., vol. I, p. 164. This tendency was especially noticeable during industrial depressions, when there was an exodus of immigrant mine workers from the affected districts and an influx into communities and localities where work was still available.

61. Ibid., vol. I, p. 164.

62. Lewis, *Black Coal Miners*, pp. 79–118.

63. West Virginia Bureau of Negro Welfare and Statistics, *Report*, 1923–24, p. 39.

64. James T. Laing, "The Negro Miner in West Virginia," Ph.D. dissertation, Ohio State University, 1933.

65. U.S. Immigration Commission, *Immigrants in Coal*, vol I, p. 227; West Virginia

Department of Mines, *Report*, various years; United States Bureau of the Census, *Thirteenth Census of the United States, Population, 1920*, Vol. IV, Table VII (Washington, DC: U.S. Government Printing Office, 1923).

66. Laing, "The Negro Miner," p. 108.

67. Ibid., pp. 108–25.

68. U.S. Immigration Commission, *Immigrants in Coal*, vol. I, p. 425. The Commission commented: "Only the less ambitious, less intelligent, and less thrifty of the second generation enter the mines. The others seek different work."

69. U.S. Coal Commission, "Labor turnover," p. 1266.

70. Kentucky Department of Mines, *Annual Report*, 1915, p. 15.

71. U.S. Immigration Commission, *Immigrants in Coal*, vol. I, p. 164.

72. Ibid., vol. I, p. 144.

73. For example, in West Virginia the number of commercial lines rose from 35 in 1870 to 325 in 1900 to a peak of 1702 in 1923. Laing, "Negro Miner," pp. 39–52; West Virginia Department of Mines, *Annual Report*, for the years 1901 (p. 2) and 1923 (p. 265).

74. Laing's study of black miners showed that approximately 20 percent of black miners owned automobiles in 1932. He speculated that the percentage had declined from the beginning of the Depression. Laing, "Negro Miner," pp. 292–300.

75. Murayama uses this phrase in describing Japanese attempts to overcome this same problem. Yuzo Murayama, "The Economic History of Japanese Immigration to the Pacific Northwest: 1890–1920," Ph.D. dissertation, University of Washington, 1982.

76. Harry Caudill, *Night Comes to the Cumberlands: A Biography of a Depressed Area* (Boston, MA: Little, Brown, and Company, 1963), p. 102. This was also the case for several groups of Italians in the West Virginia fields, U.S. Immigration Commission, *Immigrants in Coal*, vol. II, pp. 151, 157.

77. Laing, "The Negro Miner," p. 152.

78. U.S. Immigration Commission, *Immigrants in Coal*, vol. I, pp. 257, vol. II, pp. 17, 27, 61, 152, 156–58, 164–65.

79. Laing, "The Negro Miner," pp. 151–52.

80. Fred Mooney, *Struggle in the Coal Fields: The Autobiography of Fred Mooney*, edited by J. W. Hess (Morgantown: West Virginia University Library, 1967), p. 142.

81. Tom Gray estimated that he brought 200 to 300 men from North Carolina to the mines. Inaccuracies in this testimony suggest that he overestimated his importance to the migratory flow. However, his description of the company's aid appears to be accurate. U.S. Senate Committee on Education and Labor, *Hearings on Conditions in the Paint Creek District, West Virginia*, 63rd Cong., 1st sess. (Washington, DC: U.S. Government Printing Office, 1913), p. 1137.

82. Laing, "The Negro Miner," pp. 127–28.

83. U.S. Immigration Commission, *Immigrants in Coal*, vol. II, p. 61.

84. U.S. Immigration Commission, *Immigrants in Coal*, vol. II, pp. 16, 26, 149, 151–65, 220–21.

85. Committee on Education and Labor, *Conditions in the Paint Creek District*, pp. 1202, 1266; letters to Justus Collins from George Wolfe, October 19, 1917, October 10, 1917, Justus Collins Papers; U.S. Immigration Commission, *Immigrants in Coal*, vol. II, p. 61.

86. Oral history interview with William (Major) Veasley, conducted by Keith Dix with U.G. Carter, October 28, 1976, Charleston, West Virginia Oral History Project, West Virginia Regional and History Collection, West Virginia University, Morgantown, West Virginia.

87. U.S. Immigration Commission, *Immigrants in Coal*, vol. II, p. 220–21.

88. Sterling Spero and Abram Harris, *The Black Worker* (New York: New York University Press, 1931), pp. 210–26.

89. Letter to John J. Tierney from L. E. Johnson, March 21, 1900 from Pocahontas Company Letterbook, cited in Jerry Bruce Thomas, "Coal County: The Rise of the Southern, Smokeless Coal Industry and Its Effect on Area Development," Ph.D. dissertation, University of North Carolina, 1971, p. 193.

90. Annual Operating Report, 1923, Box 212, Stonega Coke and Coal Company Collection, Series II, within the Westmoreland Coal Collection at the Hagley Museum and Library, Wilmington, Delaware.

91. Birmingham *Daily News*, April 20, 1894, cited in Justin Fuller, "History of Tennessee Coal, Iron, and Railroad Company, 1852–1907," Ph.D. dissertation, University of North Carolina, 1966.

92. Laing noted that there were some cases of less articulate blacks who gave social reasons for migrating as well. Laing, "The Negro Miner," pp. 146–48.

93. Lewis, *Black Coal Miners*, pp. 41, 70–74.

94. Found in Mining Community Schedule A from Spruce River Coal Company, Boxes 24–32, Entry 62, U.S. Coal Commission Records, Record Group 68 at the National Archives in Suitland, Maryland.

95. Spero and Harris, *The Black Worker*, p. 211.

96. Ibid.

97. Committee on Education and Labor, *Conditions in the Paint Creek District*, p. 1826.

98. Ibid., pp. 1330–40.

4

Working in a Coal Mine

During the hand-loading era, the mining jobs often were divided into four broad categories.[1] Tonnage men, who were paid by the ton of coal, were the most numerous group, including pick miners, coal loaders, machine cutters and their helpers. Inside daymen, who were paid by the hour or by the day, transported the coal and provided other services for the miners and the operators. Among the daymen were drivers, trackmen, timbermen, and motormen. Outside daymen made the final preparations of the coal for market and cleaned and repaired coal cars, or performed skilled work as blacksmiths, carpenters, and engineers. Managers assigned the miners to their places and daymen to their daily tasks but provided little direct supervision. Although the broad categories remained the same over time, increasing specialization and technological change created many new jobs and moved some jobs across categories.

Much of the skill in mining involved knowing how to avoid injury while performing the job. Driving a motor and loading coal, relatively simple tasks when done outside or in a factory, increased in complexity when executed in dark, narrow passageways with tons of rock overhead. Skilled mine workers worked under conditions that inexperienced workers could not handle and recognized danger signals that nonminers could not perceive. Mine workers gained their skills through experience and on-the-job training as helpers of experienced miners. Late in the hand-loading era some mines and the state mining department began providing safety training. Even then, the skills were learned most effectively on the job.

Tonnage Men

The pick miner of the late 1800s was a jack of all trades underground. He used his pick to undercut the coal seam, drilled holes for the blast, made his own explosives, and blasted the coal. He then loaded the coal into a car and positioned it where a mule driver carted it out of the mine. The pick miner owned his own hand auger, pick, and shovel, and purchased the powder for blasting. Because he was paid by the piece and the coal operator had little capital equipment in the workplace, the pick miner received little supervision beyond the initial assignment of his workplace and cursory visits by the foreman. The pick miner determined his own comfort and safety, laying track to make it easier to push the coal car, bailing water from his place to stay dry, and timbering the roof to insure his own safety. In addition, he determined his own hours and how much to produce. When the miner felt that he had loaded enough coal for the day, he left the mine. At times, however, he left early because of factors he could not control: the failure of drivers to deliver empty coal cars, flooding in his place, or a charge that did not explode. In most mines the miner had a form of property rights to his room. Even after surprisingly long absences, he could expect to return to work in the same room.

In many ways the pick miner was a rough artisan. The diversity of his task made his job complex, and he was expected to extract large chunks of coal from the seam. Delivering large chunks of coal to the surface was especially important in that era, because coal dust and small chunks of coal had little market value. The miner determined the size of the chunks by the depth and width of his undercut; the depth, angle, and number of explosive holes that he drilled; and the size of the charge he prepared. Adjusting these decisions in response to different seam thickness and qualities of coal while remaining safe was an art that might require several years of experience to master. In the 1880s in Pennsylvania and England, miners with more than four years' experience were described as "skilled" miners.[2] As the miner obtained more experience, his productivity generally increased. Since he was paid by the amount of coal produced, his hourly earnings also typically rose to reflect his increased productivity.

The pick miner obtained experience through personalized on-the-job training by experienced miners.[3] The miner's helper often performed many of the same tasks as the pick miner and learned the craft of coal mining in the process. Many early miners learned the trade from their fathers, who rewarded their efforts with a share of the pay. In his autobiography, John Brophy describes his father's role in his own introduction to pick mining:

> He would explain to me patiently how things were done and why, but it took some time and added strength before I could apply the knowledge as a fully competent miner. I shoveled coal from the far ends of the workplace over nearer the track, and helped as best I could with loading the cars. I brought him his tools and supplies, filled his lamp with oil, and did such other jobs as came my way. I had to be busy doing something to keep warm. . . .
>
> My father had arranged for us to start in a new place, so he and I had our full two turns with the cars, just as though we were two men. To keep up with our turn he had to work much harder, because I could not do my full share. He had to do all the pick work, undercutting and such, for both of us, and much more than half of all the other work, though I tried my best, to the limit of my strength. He went to work early, and often went in on days when the mine was idle, to loosen coal for us to get out when we had a working day. . . .
>
> After a few months, or a year, as I gained strength, weight, and experience, I began to try undercutting. I could get the cut started in a few inches, working standing up or squatting; then my father had to take over the harder part of the job, which he had to do lying on his side. It was a long time before I could manage that work.[4]

Those without fathers in the mines learned from other relatives or friends.

The introduction of the cutting machine divided the pick miner's job into several occupations and lessened the similarity between the tonnage worker and the independent artisan. The cutting machine made the cut at the base of the wall, either with a pneumatic pick that drove repeatedly into the wall or with a large blade that worked much like a chain saw. *Survey* magazine described the latter as like a sea turtle with a swordfish's snout, spinning chains in and out of itself like a spider.[5] The machine runner and his helper moved the machine from room to room and undercut the wall. They anchored the machine in place with two large jacks and made sure that the cutting bits did not become clogged with coal or slate. The machine cutter's primary skill was the operation of the machine, which he learned as a machine helper. His tasks often did not require the detailed knowledge of coal required by the pick miner. In a number of mines, the foreman marked the width of the cut, while the length of the blade determined its depth.

Aside from operating the machine, the machine cutter was expected to be a more dependable and responsible worker than pick miners and the loaders, even when he was paid by the ton. He operated valuable equipment, which he was expected to keep in proper working order. Since the work of several loaders depended on his cuts, mine operators frowned on absenteeism and expected the machine cutter to work full shifts without direct supervision. Often the machine cutter and his helper worked at night, so they could move more freely throughout the mines and make their designated cuts.[6]

After the undercut the loader typically performed the rest of the pick miner's original tasks. He set the charges and blasted or shot the coal, loaded the cars, and was directly responsible for the safety and comfort of his place. In some mines the loader's task was restricted to loading the coal. By the early 1920s in many West Virginia mines, daymen began taking over the tasks of laying track, pushing cars, and handling slate.[7] In some mines shot firers blasted the coal and timbermen propped the roof. Like the pick miners, the loaders were assigned to rooms where they worked alone or in pairs for piece rates, retaining the freedom to choose their own hours and production pace.

New loaders often received their training in the helper system. In Illinois state law made it illegal for an inexperienced miner or loader to work alone.[8] In West Virginia training under the helper system was often perfunctory, and many loaders learned safety skills on their own. The following exchange between Keith Dix and Charles Elekes, a Hungarian-born coal loader who arrived in West Virginia in 1911, describes one example of the training of a loader whose tasks were limited to drilling and loading.

DIX: Who taught you to drill and tamp the powder?

ELEKES: The good Lord. They showed me one time and that was all. Every once in a while somebody from my boarding house would sneak over to see how I was doing.

DIX: You were put in a place by yourself?

ELEKES: Yes. The first day all three of us (with his cousin and brother) was in one place. The second day my cousin and I worked on a place, so the third day everybody was separated. We all had a place.

DIX: In other words, in three days, you were expected to learn the basics and take off on your own?

ELEKES: I'll tell you, in six months' time, I load as much coal as any man.[9]

Daymen

At the beginning of the hand-loading era the occupational structure was relatively simple. The job structure at mines in the Pennsylvania county in Table 4-1 was typical in the 1890s. Roughly 80 percent of the workers were miners or miners' helpers. The major distinguishable company position underground was the mule driver. Increases in coal demand brought more specialization and technological change and created more job categories. In addition to the cutting machine, mines increasingly were electrified. Electric motors replaced mules in hauling cars through the mines, some mines were lighted electrically, and in some cases electric charges ignited explosives. Table 4-2 shows the occupational structure in the same Pennsylvania county in 1930. The percentage of pick miners fell to 9.2 percent of the work force, as the percentage of daymen rose from under 20 percent to 32 percent. The number of specific job titles for company men also rose substantially. The following describes the nature of the jobs.

> Before the pick miner or the machine runner and loader go down into the mine in the morning, a fire boss has tested all the working places for weak roofs, rock falls and dangerous accumulations of deadly gases. The miner goes down the shaft in a

TABLE 4-1. Percentage of Workers in Each Job in Bituminous Coal Mines, Allegheny County, Pennsylvania, 1890[a]

Job Title	*Percentage of Workforce (%)*
Inside the Mines	
Foremen	0.8
Miners	75.5
Miners' laborers (helpers)	5.9
Drivers and helpers	4.8
Door boys	0.3
All other company men	2.8
Outside the Mines	
Foremen	0.3
Superintendents	1.3
Blacksmiths and carpenters	1.4
Engineers and firemen	1.0
All other company men	5.9

Source: Based on table compiled by Keith Dix from *Reports of Inspectors of Coal Mines,* Pennsylvania Department of Internal Affairs, 1890, Part V (Harrisburg, 1891). Keith Dix, *Work Relations in the Coal Industry: The Hand-Loading Era, 1880–1930* (West Virginia University Bulletin, Series 78, No. 7-2, January 1978), p. 14.

[a]Total number in work force = 10,464.

TABLE 4-2. Percentage of Workers in Each Job in Bituminous Coal Mines, Allegheny County, Pennsylvania, 1930[a]

Job Title	*Percentage of Workforce*
Inside the Mines	
Mine foremen	0.7%
Assistant mine foremen	0.9
Fire bosses	0.8
Shot firers	1.3
Pick miners	9.2
Machine miners (loaders)	53.4
Machine runners and helpers	5.1
Motormen	2.5
Motormen's assistant	2.2
Drivers	2.0
Car handlers	0.5
Trackmen	3.0
Bratticemen	0.4
Timbermen and rockmen	1.2
Pumpmen and pipemen	1.1
Electricians	0.8
Doorboys	0.03
All other employees	4.8
Outside the Mines	
Superintendents	0.5
Foremen	0.2
Blacksmiths	0.5
Carpenters	0.5
Engineers and firemen	0.6
Tipplemen	3.1
Machinists	0.3
Trackmen	0.2
Office employees	0.7
All other employees	3.3

Source: Based on table compiled by Dix, *Work Relations*, p. 37.

[a]Total number in work force = 15,189.

cage the operation of which is controlled by an engineer. His tools are sharpened at a blacksmith shop in charge of a blacksmith and his helper. Where mules are used, a stable boss and stable boys care for the animals in underground quarters. There are also machine shops, frequently underground as well as on the surface, in the charge of machinists and helpers who make repairs to mine equipment. Electricians or wiremen string the wires which carry the current that gives a ghostly illumination to the underground workings and feeds energy to the electric locomotives of the underground haulage system. A motorman runs the locomotive and a trip rider looks after the train. Track layers are busy putting down new track and repairing old. Where the grade is steep, a spragger brakes the speed of the mine cars by thrusting a piece of wood—a sprag—between the spokes of the car wheels.

. . . The power plant above ground means the employment of an engineer and fireman. In the tipple are the men in charge of preparing the coal, with a weighboss

> to supervise the weighing of the contents of the mine cars because the miners are paid by the ton. On the ground are cleaners looking for the occasional piece of rock or slate that escaped the eyes of the underground and tipple men, car trimmers, slate dumpers, who look after the mine cars loaded with refuse, car repairmen and yardmen. Inside the mine at the bottom of the shaft are cagers pushing loaded cars into the cage in which the cars will be hoisted to the tipple, and removing the empties that come down. In some mines pumpmen and pipemen are employed to prevent flooding; there are other mines where it is necessary to sprinkle the roadways to keep down dust and so minimize the chances of dust explosions. Brattice men put up partitions in cross entries to control air currents and force them into the working places. The great fans that keep the mine supplied with fresh air are in charge of a special crew. When the entry that is to be partitioned off by the brattice men must be used for the passage of workers and cars, the brattice contains a door that is opened and shut by a trapper boy.[10]

In many electrified mines, mules were not entirely replaced by underground motor locomotives. Drivers using mules gathered coal cars from the miners in their rooms and brought them to the main switches, where the coal cars were collected by motors. The increase in the division of labor created jobs for timbermen, slatemen, and shaftmen. Timbermen placed timbers in passageways and sometimes in the miners' places. Slatemen removed slate from the seams and loaded it into cars to be removed from the mines. Shot firers set the charges for blasting down the coal in many mines where electricity was used for ignition of the charge.

Most of the company jobs were similar with respect to the skill levels they required. All daymen learned relatively simple, mechanical or manual tasks. Since the work of loaders and miners depended on the company men completing their tasks, mine management expected the company men to be in regular attendance and work full shifts when the mine was open. Additional responsibility was given to those workers who used machinery or other important capital equipment. The company men often worked a number of days when the mine was not sending coal out to the tipple to ensure that mine conditions did not deteriorate while the mine was not producing coal.[11] As with the other mining jobs, the safety training made the jobs more complex than if they had been above ground. For example, Charles Fowler noted that the "well-trained mule driver must learn to stand on a tail chain with one hand on the mule's rump and the other on the front end of the car to keep the car from bumping the mule. It require[d] a well-trained acrobat to ride at full speed on a tail chain, in a 4-foot vein of coal."[12]

Daymen were trained on the job under the helper system. Motormen taught their brakemen or motor helpers, timbermen taught timber helpers, and so on. Children of workmen often gained valuable safety experience as trappers before promotion to company tasks or tonnage tasks when they reached maturity.

Management

Mine management included the superintendent and his helpers, the mine foreman, section bosses, and company bosses. Mine owners were represented by the superintendent. He and his assistants oversaw the purchase of supplies and the maintenance of the mining equipment, established the general work rules and employment policy of the mines, and supervised the provision of housing, education, and stores in the company town.

The actual production decisions were left to the mine foreman. He made the hiring decisions and in nonunion mines could promote or fire workers at will.[13] In addition the foreman assigned rooms to the tonnage workers and controlled the daily work activity of the company men. In union mines, the foreman retained many of these powers, but a worker who felt he had been unfairly treated could appeal the foreman's decisions through a pit committee. The collective bargaining agreements specifically constrained the pit committee's role to the settlement of disputes. Members of the pit committee were not allowed to go through the mine inspecting conditions; they became involved only after it had been "referred by the employee affected and only after he ha[d] made an attempt to settle his grievance with the mine manager."[14]

State mining laws made the foreman more than an agent of the mine owner by making him legally responsible for ensuring several aspects of the safety of the mine. By 1915 most of the coal mining states required that the foreman visit each workplace at least once a day, although Illinois required a visit only once every two weeks.[15] In many states the foreman also was charged with supplying adequate timbers to the miners for propping the roofs, with ensuring proper breakthroughs for ventilation, maintaining the haulage system in safe condition, and instructing new miners in mine safety techniques.[16]

During the early phase of the pick mining era, the foreman's primary job had been to supervise the haulage system and make workplace assignments. Since most workers acted as independent contractors paid by the piece, the foreman made only cursory visits to workplaces, as he travelled long distances throughout the mines each day. Table 4-1 shows that there was roughly one foreman for every one hundred workers. The rise of specialization and the state-required increase in the safety role of the foreman brought new layers of management. Table 4-2 shows that by 1930 the typical mine foreman had at least one assistant mine foreman who was in charge of a group of rooms or even an entire entry way. As the number of company men increased, motor bosses, driver bosses, machine bosses, and timber bosses were given authority over the men assigned to the various company tasks. The mines also added fire bosses who did not supervise men but aided the foreman in insuring the safety of all the inside workers.

Throughout the hand-loading era advancement to all but the superintendent's position came by gaining work experience. According to the U.S. Bureau of Mines in 1918, the coal mining foremen required the following qualifications:

> Physical strength; good health; more than average ability; ability to handle men. He should have large practical experience and a general knowledge of coal-mining conditions as to methods, safety requirements, etc. He should have had experience as pusher, repairman and coalminer, or engineer, and be capable of reading mine maps and laying out work at coal mines. He should have a certificate of competency.
>
> Schooling: Common or high school.[17]

By the mid-1920s all states required foremen and fire bosses to leap the additional hurdle of competency examinations. In West Virginia, which began requiring foremen to pass exams after 1910, the foreman was also required to have at least five years of experience in the working, ventilation, and drainage of coal mines. Although several of the state universities sponsored mine extension training programs, formal education was not necessary to pass the exams.[18] Among those who passed the exam without formal training was John Pattison, the black safety director of the West Virginia Department of Mines in the late 1920s. He could not take an extension course because none existed for blacks prior to 1937.[19]

On-the-job training became less important for achieving the superintendent position as the mine operations became more complex. During the early period many owners operated their own mines. Many superintendents gained their positions by working their way up through the ranks from pick miner to foreman to superintendent. Some even started their own mines. Eventually, ownership was separated from management, and the mines became more specialized. Collegiate or specialized training became more important than on-the-job training. College-trained civil and mining engineers with good administrative capabilities were generally desired by most absentee owners, although nepotism was sometimes practiced by owners with trained relatives.[20]

Rewards in the Occupational Hierarchy

Since the primary reason that workers entered the mines was to earn wages, the relative earnings of the jobs in the mine give a rough indication of the desirability of each job.[21] To give a complete picture of the earnings capability of each job, indexes of earnings per hour, per start (day), and per half-month are reported for West Virginia in 1922 and 1924 in Tables 4-3 through 4-5. Comparisons of earnings per half-month alone can be deceiving because some workers earned more by working many more hours. Hourly earnings come the closest to showing how much mine workers earned for a particular unit of effort, but they do not show the impact of restricted work opportunities.

The United States Bureau of Labor Statistics gathered earnings information for West Virginia from the payrolls of 47 mines in 1922 and 142 mines in 1924.[22] The Bureau of Labor Statistics calculated the average earnings per half-month for each job simply by dividing the total earnings per half-month in that job by the number of workers in the job. Calculating earnings per hour was more complex. For company men, who were paid by the hour, the wage reported was the hourly wage paid for time actually worked, excluding time for lunch and travel time inside the mine. Since few mines normally recorded the hours of tonnage men, the Bureau of Labor Statistics requested special records for tonnage men on both total time spent in the mine and, after deducting travel time, the time spent at the face (in their workplace) including lunch. Since travel time was excluded from the hours of daymen, the hourly wage of tonnage men in the tables is based on the time at the face including time for lunch. To the extent that tonnage men took lunch breaks at the face, the hourly wage index understates the relative desirability of the tonnage jobs.[23] In Tables 4-3 through 4-5 the motormen's average earnings are given a value of one

TABLE 4-3. Hourly Wages in the West Virginia Job Hierarchy, 1922, 1924 (Motorman's Wage = 100)

Occupation	*Wage Index*
Inside	
Machine runner	179.3
Hand or pick miner	132.0
Loader	124.6
Cager	104.6
Driver	102.4
Motorman	100.0[a]
Trackman	99.4
Bratticeman and timberman	97.2
Brakeman	95.7
Pumpman	91.8
Laborer	83.6
Trapper	61.6
Outside	
Blacksmith	109.5
Carpenter	99.4
Engineer	86.5
Fireman	78.3
Laborer	75.3

Source: Compiled from U.S. Department of Labor, U.S. Bureau of Labor Statistics, "Hours and Earnings in Bituminous and Anthracite Coal Mining, 1922 and 1924," *Bulletin* Number 416 (Washington, DC: U.S. Government Printing Office, 1926), pp. 44–52. The index is an unweighted average of the indexes in 1922 and 1924. Hourly earnings for tonnage men are net of deductions for powder, dynamite, other explosives, tool sharpening and blacksmithing. The hourly earnings for daymen are based on time actually worked, excluding lunch and travel time. The hourly earnings for tonnage men are based on time at the face including lunch but excluding travel time. The indexes based on total time in the mine (including travel time) for tonnage men are 167.1 for machine cutters, 121.8 for pick miners, and 115.2 for hand loaders.

[a]The motormen's wage was $0.781 in 1922, and $0.623 in 1924.

hundred in 1922 and 1924. The wage index of each occupation in each year is then calculated relative to that figure. The overall index for each job is a simple average of the index in 1922 and 1924.

The rankings show that tonnage workers received hourly earnings that exceeded the earnings of motormen and other daymen by more than 24 percent.[24] Machine cutters were paid the highest hourly wages, commensurate with the greater responsibility required of the occupation. They also earned the most over a half-month period. Although pick miners and loaders earned significantly higher hourly earnings than daymen, they earned less per half-month than most daymen. The pick miners and loaders worked fewer hours per start than the full-shift workers, but they still earned more on average per start (see Table 4-4). They also tended to work

TABLE 4-4. Earnings per Start in the West Virginia Job Hierarchy, 1922, 1924 (Motorman's Earnings = 100)

Occupation	*1922*	*1924*	*Average*
Inside			
Machine runner	168.0	171.0	169.5
Hand or pick miner	105.0	111.3	108.2
Cager	102.4	110.6	106.5
Loader	95.6	105.8	100.7
Motorman	100.0	100.0	100.0
Trackman	96.4	97.2	96.8
Pumpman	93.8	97.6	95.7
Driver	98.0	95.5	96.8
Bratticeman and timberman	94.4	95.9	95.2
Brakeman	89.3	90.7	90.0
Laborer	76.7	94.4	85.6
Trapper	58.0	57.8	57.9
Outsiee			
Blacksmith	108.3	110.0	109.2
Engineer	101.4	105.2	103.3
Carpenter	96.8	99.4	98.1
Fireman	84.7	103.3	93.9
Laborer	72.8	75.2	74.0

Source: Compiled from U.S. Department of Labor, U.S. Bureau of Labor Statistics, "Hours and Earnings in Anthracite and Bituminous Coal Mining," *Bulletin Numbers* 316, pp. 35–50; Number 416, pp. 44–52. The motorman's earnings per day were $6.62 in 1922 and $5.38 in 1924.

TABLE 4-5. Earnings per Half-Month in the West Virginia Job Hierarchy, 1922, 1924 (Motorman's Earnings = 100)

Occupation	*1922*	*1924*	*Average*
Inside			
Machine runner	159.3	154.4	156.9
Pumpman	114.3	111.0	112.7
Motorman	100.0	100.0	100.0
Cager	101.3	93.8	97.6
Trackman	97.9	94.5	96.2
Bratticeman and timberman	94.5	92.4	91.2
Hand or pick miner	87.3	95.1	91.2
Loader	84.1	87.1	85.6
Driver	91.0	84.8	87.9
Brakeman	84.6	81.9	83.3
Laborer	74.1	74.1	74.1
Trapper	57.6	53.4	70.5
Outside			
Engineer	—	134.9	134.9
Blacksmith	117.7	119.8	118.8
Fireman	127.2	103.3	115.3
Carpenter	107.9	106.1	107.0
Laborer	71.4	75.1	73.3

Source: Compiled from U.S. Department of Labor, U.S. Bureau of Labor Statistics, "Hours and Earnings in Anthracite and Bituminous Coal Mining," *Bulletins* Number 316, pp. 35–50; Number 416, pp. 44–52. The motorman's earnings per half-month were $64.68 in 1922 and $53.83 in 1924.

fewer days, which lowered their fortnightly earnings almost 10 percent below those of the motormen (see Table 4-5). Pick miners and loaders earned less per start and per half-month in part because they chose leisure, quitting work early or not coming to work at times when work was available. However, the tonnage workers' absences from work were at times involuntary when coal cars were not available or the place was worked out. The U.S. Coal Commission studied absences and found no way to separate the voluntary absences from involuntary ones.[25] Further, most tonnage men, particularly motormen, bratticemen and timbermen, and trackmen, often worked when the mine was not producing. The higher earnings per start for tonnage men thus acted in part as compensation for reduced opportunities to work. As Chapter 6 shows, a similar situation existed when comparing the earnings of coal miners to earnings in manufacturing jobs.

The payment of piece rates to tonnage men caused greater dispersion around mean hourly earnings than for company men. Figure 4-1 shows the frequency distributions of hourly earnings for motormen and loaders in 1924 in West Virginia.[26] Nearly 80 percent of the motormen received hourly wages between 50 and 70 cents, less than 2 percent earned less than 50 cents per hour, while almost no one earned more than $1 per hour. In contrast, because the loaders' earnings were determined directly by how much coal they loaded, the loaders' frequency distribution was far more dispersed. Roughly 8 percent of the loaders earned less than 50 cents per hour, while 24.7 percent earned more than $1 per hour.[27]

One important cause of the differences in the percentage of workers at the low end of the scale for motormen and loaders was differences in the range of mining experience of the workers. Loading coal was often an entry position in the mines. Thus many men with low hourly earnings had just started in the mines. In contrast, few of the motormen would have earned less than 50 cents an hour, even had they worked as loaders, because nearly all motormen had some mining experience. The foreman often screened workers to ensure that they were reliable and would care for machines before he allowed them to become motormen. The differences at the high end of the earnings distribution were probably caused by self-selection among the motormen. Men who were unable to earn high hourly earnings as loaders were likely to seek jobs as motormen to ensure stable earnings.

Not all of the dispersion in loader's earnings was due to differences in experience. Some of the dispersion might reflect random fluctuations in the amount of uncompensated "deadwork" the miner had to perform when he ran into flooding in his room, or slate in the coal seam, or a more dangerous roof. The dispersion reflects in part differences in how regularly the miners or the mine was working. As loaders worked more hours and more regularly, they earned higher hourly wages, because they spent less time cleaning and timbering the workplace to compensate for deterioration of the workplace while not working.[28] To the extent that these factors caused the dispersion in loaders' earnings, the higher hourly wage for loaders may have acted also as a premium to offset greater fluctuations in the earnings of loaders relative to motormen.

The disparity in the dispersion of loaders' and motormen's earnings was not nearly so large for half-monthly earnings. Figure 4-2 shows the frequency distributions of half-monthly earnings for motormen and loaders in West Virginia in 1924.

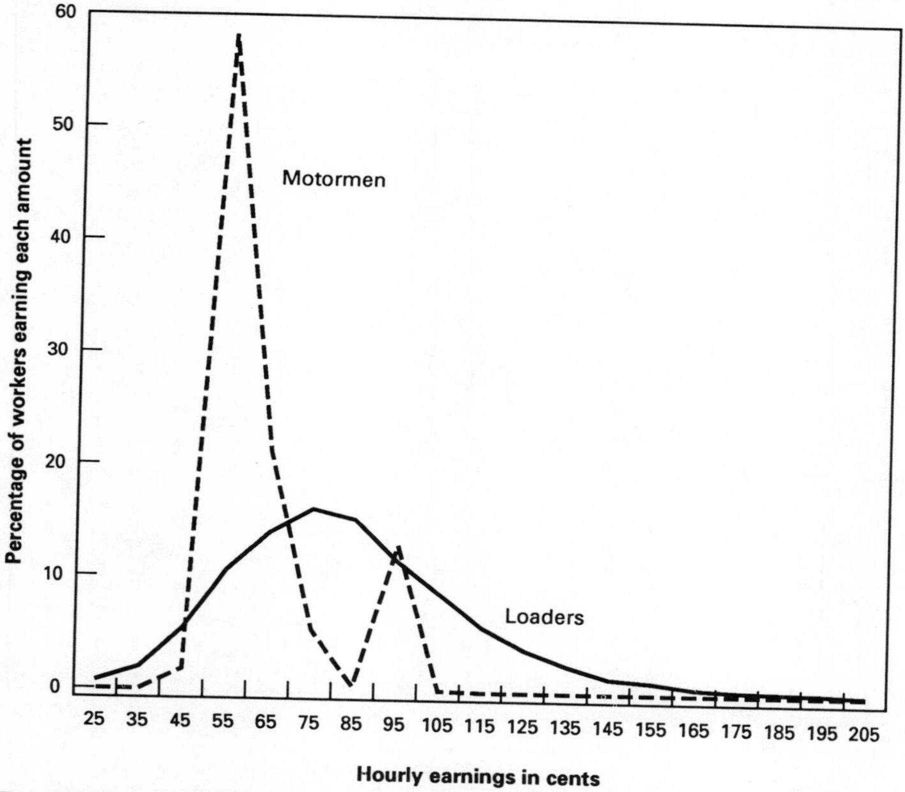

FIGURE 4-1. Distribution of Hourly Earnings for Motormen and Loaders, West Virginia, 1924. *Source:* U.S. Bureau of Labor Statistics, "Hours and Earnings in Bituminous and Anthracite Coal Mining, 1922 and 1924," *Bulletin* No. 416 (Washington, DC: U.S. Government Printing Office, 1926), pp. 54–48.

While the standard deviation of hourly earnings for loaders (28.8 cents) more than doubled the standard deviation for motormen (13.7 cents), the standard deviation of the loader's half-monthly earnings ($24.4) was only 22 percent greater than the standard deviation of the motormen's half-monthly earnings ($20.0).

Among daymen, the hourly earnings rankings indicate that motormen, cagers, drivers, timbermen, and trackmen earned similar wages. Brakemen and pumpmen earned significantly less than the initial group, followed by unskilled inside laborers and the trapper position, which was given mostly to boys. One surprising finding is that mule drivers earned slightly more per hour than motormen in West Virginia. Contemporaries considered the motorman to be the most skilled of the company positions. In areas where machine runners were paid by the day, the motormen's and machine runners' wages were often equivalent.[29] Other evidence suggests that this ranking may be incorrect. Motormen earned more than drivers in the unionized Central Competitive Field and in alternative wage rankings in West Virginia reported by the Coal Commission show that drivers were paid less than motormen.[30]

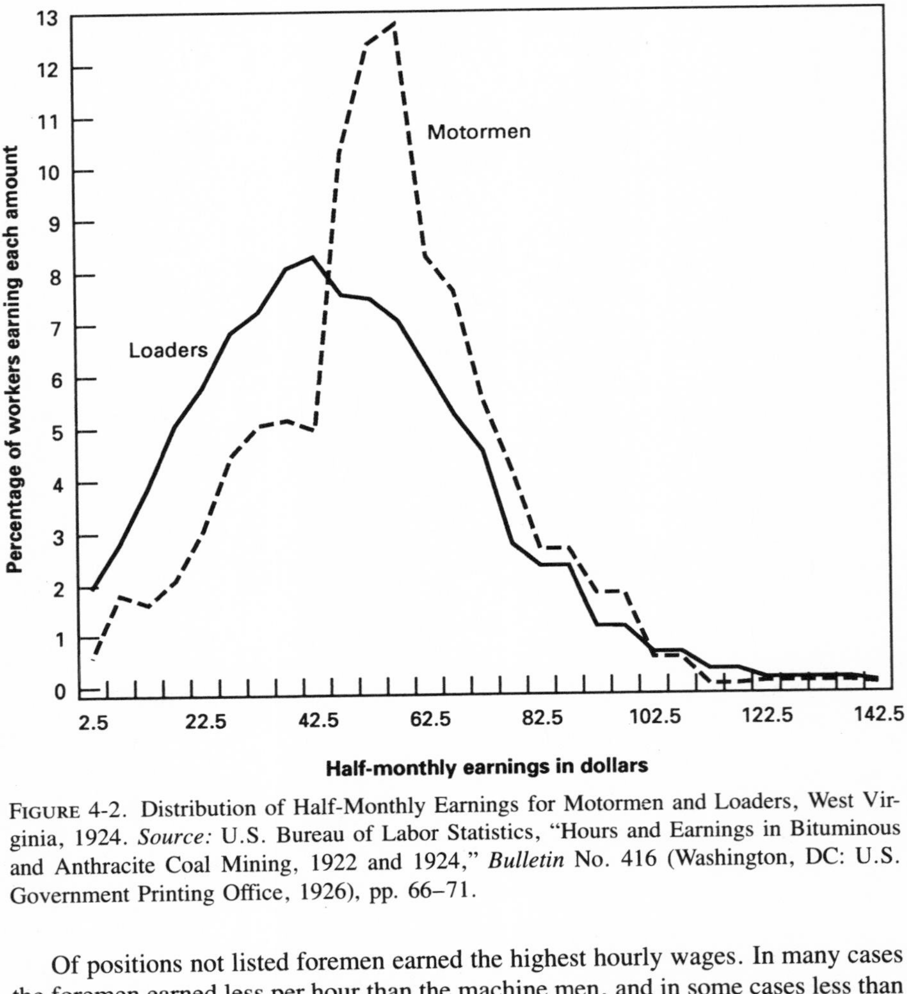

FIGURE 4-2. Distribution of Half-Monthly Earnings for Motormen and Loaders, West Virginia, 1924. *Source:* U.S. Bureau of Labor Statistics, "Hours and Earnings in Bituminous and Anthracite Coal Mining, 1922 and 1924," *Bulletin* No. 416 (Washington, DC: U.S. Government Printing Office, 1926), pp. 66–71.

Of positions not listed foremen earned the highest hourly wages. In many cases the foremen earned less per hour than the machine men, and in some cases less than the best loaders and pick miners. The foreman's job was attractive because he was on salary the year round and thus was paid during short-term shutdowns of the mine. Slatemen were usually paid about the same as brakemen and pumpmen, while helpers for day jobs were usually paid more than laborers but less than the workers in the specific jobs.

Part of the difference in wages among the various mining occupations arose from differences in the risk of accidents. Accident risk premiums are most obvious when comparing inside and outside jobs. In West Virginia from 1920 to 1924, the risk of fatal accidents for inside workers was roughly 2.3 times the level of risk faced by outside workers.[31] In consequence, outside workers were paid less than inside workers of equal, or often lesser, nonsafety skills. The leading outside workers were blacksmiths, followed by carpenters. Both were skilled artisans, trained away from the mine and paid on the basis of the wage for noncoal mine artisans, yet they received hourly wages that were well below those for such "semi-skilled" inside workers as machine miners, pick miners, and loaders. General laborers working outside the mines received about 14 percent less per hour than the same group inside the mines. Similarly, engineers and firemen, who had similar nonsafety skills to those of trackmen and timbermen, earned about 9 percent less because they worked outside.

Inside the mine the higher hourly earnings of tonnage workers may have resulted in part because they faced greater risk of fatal accidents than most daymen. Table 4-6 shows rough estimates of fatal accidents per million man-hours for inside jobs in Pennsylvania in 1921 and 1922. The most dangerous of the daymen's jobs, not surprisingly, involved driving electric motors that pulled coal cars through relatively dark passageways. The increase in speed when using motors raised the risk of pulling cars dramatically, as the motormen's risk of a fatal accident was more than double the risk of drivers who pulled cars with mules. The tonnage jobs of loader, pick miner, and machine cutter were clearly more dangerous than the remaining day jobs. A key difference between tonnage jobs and most day jobs stemmed from the dangers of roof falls at or near the face where coal was being mined. Roof falls caused more than half of the accidents in the mines and most of those occurred in the miner's room. All three tonnage occupations involved performing several tasks at the point where coal was extracted and often required the men to make numerous decisions about propping the roof. These same decisions were made by the most dangerous of the remaining day occupations, the timbermen and rockmen. The timberman was responsible for insuring that the roof was properly propped, while rockmen were often close to the face when they were removing slate. The tonnage jobs were more dangerous than the timberman's jobs because in addition to their work propping the roofs, many loaders and pick miners also handled explosives and at times pushed mine cars. Meanwhile, the machine cutters also faced the risks associated with handling heavy electrical equipment, including driving it from room to room.

The hourly rankings do not offer a complete view of the relative desirability of the coal mining jobs because of differences in work opportunities and the risk of accidents. There are two additional factors to consider when examining the relative desirability of tonnage and daymen's jobs: differences in the control over decision making and in work intensity. The two factors tend to offset each other. Tonnage workers had greater control over when and how long they worked. They could choose to be absent, quit early, and determine their own production pace without fear of management interference. Since control over the labor-leisure decision is a desirable attribute in any job, hourly wage comparisons understate the relative desirability of tonnage jobs. On the other hand, high hourly wages for tonnage men might have overstated the desirability of their jobs to the extent that most tonnage men worked more intensively per hour than daymen to obtain an equivalent hourly wage. Because the piece rate worker's earnings were directly related to how much he produced in the short run, he tended to work more intensively than the dayman when faced with the same amount of supervision.[32] The work-intensity bias may not

TABLE 4-6. Risks of Fatal Accidents for Inside Jobs in Pennsylvania, 1921–1922

Occupation	*Fatal Accidents per Million Manhours*
Tonnage Men	
Pick miners	1.92
Machine runners	1.88
Hand loaders	1.60
Daymen	
Motormen and motormen's helpers	2.11
Timbermen and rockmen	1.30
Trackmen and bratticemen	0.89
Drivers	0.81
Pumpmen and pipemen	0.44
Door boys	0.00

Sources: Fatalities per man hour were calculated as: (*FAT21* + *FAT22*)/[(*EMP21* × *DAYS21* + *EMP22* × *DAYS22*) × *%TIPPLE* × *HOURS*]. The number of men killed (*FAT21* and *FAT22*) and employed (*EMP21* and *EMP22*) and days the mines were open (*DAYS21* and *DAY22*) in 1921 and 1922 in each occupation are from Pennsylvania Department of Mines, *Report, Part II, Bituminous,* pp. 10–13, 35–39. Since the typical pick miner often started only 88.4 percent of the days that the mine started, and motormen worked 161 percent of the days the mines were officially open, the days the mines were open are adjusted for the percentage of days the men in the occupation actually worked (*%TIPPLE*). *%TIPPLE* is the ratio of man starts to mine starts for the tonnage jobs and for daymen is the ratio of eight-hour days worked relative to days the mine was open, from Waldo Fisher and Anne Bezanson, *Wage Rates and Working Time in the Bituminous Coal Industry* (Philadelphia: University of Pennsylvania Press, 1932), pp. 131–38. For the daymen, the number of hours per day (*HOURS*) is eight. For tonnage men, HOURS is the average number of hours spent in the mine per start in Pennsylvania, from U.S. Bureau of Labor Statistics, "Hours and Earnings in Anthracite and Bituminous Coal Mining," *Bulletin* Number 316 (Washington, DC: U.S. Government Printing Office, 1922), pp. 18–37.

Notes: The risk measure for tonnage men is not exactly comparable to that for daymen, due to problems in comparing starts by tonnage workers and days worked by daymen. Generally, there were few problems in using days the mines were open to calculate total hours worked by daymen. The problems arise in obtaining hours for tonnage men, for whom starts and hours per start were reported. The standard means of reporting days the mines were open was to treat half-days as half-days, such that if a mine was listed as open for 200 days, that mine might have had 205 starts if it worked ten half-days. Thus the number of starts made by tonnage men is understated when I multiplied *%TIPPLE* by days the mine was open. This problem causes the risk measure to overstate the risks of tonnage men relative to daymen. In contrast, the risks of tonnage men relative to daymen may by understated due to problems in comparing the number of hours worked per day. For tonnage men, I have the total time in the mine per start reported by the Bureau of Labor Statistics. For daymen it is eight hours, because Fisher and Bezanson's measure of tipple time was reported in eight-hour days. Unfortunately, Fisher and Bezanson do not state whether these eight-hour days include travel time and time for lunch for the daymen or not. The hours per day in the mine for daymen therefore might be understated, overstating their risks of fatal accidents.

have been large, however. As shown in the next chapter, daymen were supervised more closely, although often in an indirect manner. Although daymen were paid by the hour, closer supervision insured that they would not shirk extensively.[33]

NOTES

The quote from John Brophy, *A Miner's Life: An Autobiography* © 1964 (Madison: The University of Wisconsin Press) is used by permission of the publisher.

1. For excellent discussions of the task of the miner and other workers in the mines, see Keith Dix, *Work Relations in the Coal Industry: The Hand-Loading Era, 1880–1930* (West Virginia University Bulletin, Series 78, No. 7-2, January 1978); Carter Goodrich, *The Miner's Freedom* (Boston: Marshall Jones Company, 1925); Edward Hunt, F.G. Tryon, and Joseph Willits, eds., *What the Coal Commission Found* (Baltimore, MD: Williams and Wilkins Co., 1925); and Hugh Archbald, *The Four-Hour Day in Coal* (New York: The H. W. Wilson Company, 1922).

2. Frederick Ryan, *The Rehabilitation of Oklahoma Coal Mining Communities* (Norman: University of Oklahoma Press, 1935), p. 37.

3. On-the-job training in Alabama sometimes was not highly personalized. A large number of black pick miners learned their trade through experience gained in convict mines. U.S. Immigration Commission, *Report on Immigrants in Industries, Part I: Bituminous Coal Mining*, Vol. II, 61st Cong., 2nd Sess. (Washington, DC: U.S. Government Printing Office, 1911), pp. 218–19.

4. John Brophy, *A Miner's Life* (Madison: University of Wisconsin Press, 1964), pp. 48–49.

5. Cited in Goodrich, *The Miner's Freedom*, p. 46.

6. Goodrich, *The Miner's Freedom*, pp. 43–46.

7. U.S. Coal Commission, "Wage Rates in the Bituminous Coal Industry," *Report*, 68th Cong., 2nd Sess. (Washington, DC: U.S. Government Printing Office, 1925) p. 1055.

8. Dix, *Work Relations*, p. 115.

9. Ibid., pp. 35–36.

10. Hunt, et al., *What the Coal Commission Found*, pp. 59–60.

11. On average inside daymen worked about 120.8 percent of tipple time, outside daymen worked 141.6 percent of tipple time, and tonnage men made about 90.3 percent of the mine starts. Waldo Fisher and Anne Bezanson, *Wage Rates and Working Time in the Bituminous Coal Industry* (Philadelphia: University of Pennsylvania Press, 1932), pp. 131–38.

12. Charles B. Fowler, *Collective Bargaining in the Bituminous Coal Industry* (New York: Prentice-Hall, Inc., 1927), p. 24.

13. Goodrich (*The Miner's Freedom*, pp. 72–73) claims that firings over everyday work were rare in union fields in the 1920s. Nor was it "clear that they were any more numerous in the past—an operator of fifteen years ago declared that in his experience 'suspensions (were) simply and solely for loading dirty coal;' and it is not even clear that they are much more frequent in the non-union fields, except where the weapon of a wholesale discharge is used as a campaign measure to get rid of union men and 'agitators' or to force the men to sign the 'yellow-dog' anti-union contracts. Both union and non-union bosses know how to 'freeze men out' or ease them off' by giving them poor working places, but in ordinary operation outright discharge is comparatively rare in either part of the industry."

14. Louis Bloch, *Labor Agreements in Coal Mines: A Case Study of Agreements Between Miners' and Operator's Organizations in the Bituminous Coal Mines of Illinois* (New York: Russell Sage Foundation, 1931), pp. 178–82.

15. Price V. Fishback, "Workplace Safety During the Progressive Era: Fatal Accidents in Bituminous Coal Mining, 1912–1923," *Explorations in Economic History* 23 (1986): 285.

16. Dix, *Work Relations*, p. 46.

17. United States Bureau of Mines, prepared for the Department of Labor, *Descriptions of Occupations: Mines and Mining* (Washington, DC: U.S. Government Printing Office, 1918), p. 20.

18. Dix, *Work Relations*, p. 45.

19. Interview with U.G. Carter conducted by Keith Dix, West Virginia Oral History Project. West Virginia Sound Archives, West Virginia Regional and History Collection, West Virginia University Library. Morgantown, West Virginia.

20. Dix, *Work Relations*, p. 42

21. Sociologists also include other factors such as prestige, skill, and responsibility as attributes that make jobs desirable. The wage often reflects these factors, since it tends to rise with the skills and responsibility of the job. In many cases, prestige is linked to higher incomes.

22. U.S. Bureau of Labor Statistics, "Hours and Earnings in Anthracite and Bituminous Coal Mining," *Bulletin No. 316* (Washington, DC: U.S. Government Printing Office, 1922); idem, "Hours and Earnings in Anthracite and Bituminous Coal Mining, 1922 and 1924," *Bulletin No. 416* (Washington, DC: U.S. Government Printing Office, 1926).

23. Hourly earnings were determined by dividing the total earnings in the half-month by the number of hours worked in that half-month. For comparisons of tonnage men with other industries in Chapter 6, I used the hourly wage based on total time in the mine, for which the index is listed in the notes of Table 4-3. Total time in the mine per day was generally about 6.5 to 7.5 percent greater than the time spent at the face.

24. The earnings measure for tonnage men is net earnings after deductions for powder, dynamite and other explosives, tool sharpening, and blacksmithing. See U.S. Bureau of Labor Statistics, *Bulletin No. 416,* "Hours and Earnings in 1922 and 1924," p. 9. The earnings measure for tonnage men does not subtract the pick miners' and loaders' expenditures on picks, shovels, and hand drills. In 1922 in the New River district of West Virginia, the Coal Commission found that the price of pick heads was $0.64, of pick handles was $0.40, and of shovels was $1.76. Assuming that miners and loaders replaced their equipment four times a year, the average cost per half-month would be $0.47, which was roughly 1 percent of the miner's half-monthly earnings. See U.S. Coal Commission, "Bituminous Mine Workers and Their Homes," *Report*, p. 1529.

25. U. S. Coal Commission, "Irregularity of Employment, Attendance, and Absenteeism," *Report*, p. 1128.

26. The loader's hourly earnings are based on time at the face. The U.S. Bureau of Labor Statistics reported the number of workers earning each amount for 10 cent intervals for hourly wages and $5 intervals for half-monthly earnings. Above $2 an hour and $80 a half-month the wage intervals increased. Above those levels, I divided the number of workers evenly among the 10 cent and $5 intervals.

27. When the loader's hourly wage is based on total time in the mine, roughly 13 percent of the loaders earned less than 50 cents per hour, while nearly 17 percent earned more than $1 per hour.

28. U. S. Coal Commission, "Earnings of Bituminous Coal Mine Workers," *Report*, pp. 1168–72.

29. Goodrich, *The Miner's Freedom*, p. 53.

30. U.S. Coal Commission, Part 5: Atlas of Statistical Tables, *Report*, pp. 218–30.

31. The fatal accident risk for inside workers was 3.145 fatalities per million man-hours, for outside workers was 1.36 fatalities per million man-hours. The formula used to calculate

the risks appears in the notes to Table 4-6. The number of deaths, number of workers, days the mines were open, and average work-hours are from U. S. Bureau of Mines, "Coal-Mine Fatalities in the United States, for the year in question," *Bulletin Nos. 355* for 1930, pp. 82–83; *283* for 1926, pp. 58–62; *241* for 1923, pp. 31–36, 52–55. The percent figure for tipple time worked was 141.6 for outside daymen and 100.0 for inside workers (120 percent for inside daymen multiplied by 35 percent of the work force and 90 percent for tonnage men multiplied by 65 percent of the work force) from Fisher and Bezanson, *Wage Rates*, pp. 131–40.

32. The discussion of work intensity presumes, using the logic of the next chapter, that hourly wages are paid for day jobs because it is harder to measure the productivity of day workers. Mine owners have a harder time discovering changes in productivity and adjusting the wage accordingly in the short run for day men. With the piece rate, the tonnage men's earnings are automatically adjusted if his productivity rises or falls.

33. Neither group was directly supervised by a monitor for more than short periods of time during the day, because both groups were spread among numerous places throughout the mine. However, foremen kept closer tabs on daymen through "knocking" and the task assignments, as described in Chapter 5. See Dix, *Work Relations*, pp. 47–49 and Goodrich, *The Miner's Freedom*, pp. 50–55.

5

Methods of Wage Paym

Employers paid piece rates for some occupations and time rates for others. In addition, coal employers used various fines and means of measuring coal to ensure that the coal delivered to the surface was of marketable quality. The payment methods at times were major sources of controversy. Many of the miners' complaints about low wages dealt specifically with the level of piece rates. Miners at times accused employers of "labor larceny," abuses of methods for weighing coal and the fine schedules established for loading low-quality coal.[1] Were the various payment schemes designed so that the coal operators could nibble away at the miners' hard-earned gains? Or did the forms of payment serve other purposes?

Peculiar payment methods often are seen as prima facie evidence that employers were exploiting miners or cheating them by not paying for all the coal they mined.[2] Such inferences may be mistaken. Faced with problems of measuring work effort and supervising workers, employers designed many of the payment devices to give miners incentives to produce more coal without sacrificing quality. Low piece rates by themselves are not evidence of low earnings, because piece rates tended to be lower at mines where it took less effort for miners to produce a given amount of coal. The best way to examine how miners fared with respect to wages is to compare their hourly and annual earnings with those of workers in other industries, which is the subject of Chapter 6.

Piece Rates, Time Rates, and Transactions Costs

Employers paid two types of wages: piece rates and time rates. Most coal workers were paid piece rates for removing the coal from the seam and loading it into coal cars. These tonnage men included the pick miners, loaders, and cutting machine operators and helpers described in Chapter 4. In a sense these men were not laborers, but independent firms or contractors. The company leased them a room at zero rent, and they "sold" the coal they produced there to the mine operator for a stipulated price. The relationship became more explicit in cases, more common in anthracite mining, where the operator hired a contractor and paid him a fixed amount per ton. The contractor then hired his own work force and made his own work decisions.[3] The remaining workers, the daymen who provided transport services, safety precautions, and other auxiliary services both inside and outside the mine, were generally paid by the day or by the hour.

Two types of transactions costs help explain why the mine operators paid piece rates to tonnage men and time rates to daymen: the costs of measuring the worker's output and the costs of directly monitoring his work activity.[4] The mine worker contracts with his employer, explicitly or implicitly, to provide a certain quantity and quality of labor effort for the wage he is paid. While the employer prefers that workers offer more intense effort for a given amount of pay, workers prefer less effort for a given amount. Therefore employer-worker relationships are often marred by problems with shirking, where workers seek to receive the stipulated wage while offering labor effort below the level agreed upon. Employers also can shirk by not meeting their full obligations. The focus here is on shirking by workers, since we are discussing why mine operators chose different payment forms for different occupations.

In a world with zero transactions costs, there are no problems with shirking. The employer measures the worker's output precisely and pays him directly for his production. Supervisors are not needed to monitor the worker's effort because the worker's own actions determine his output. If he works longer and harder, he receives more pay. When he slackens his pace, he receives lower earnings. When the cost of measuring the worker's output is positive, however, the employer cannot measure each worker's product precisely. The employer must therefore weigh the costs and benefits of less accurate measures. The less accurate his measure, the greater the problems he faces with shirking. Problems with shirking are solved partially by hiring supervisors to monitor the worker's efforts. Thus in the less pristine world with positive transactions costs, the employer chooses payment schemes with an eye on the costs of measuring the worker's output, the costs of direct supervision of the worker, and the losses from shirking resulting from inaccurate measurement and incomplete supervision. The employer chooses a piece rate more often when the worker's final product is more easily measured or when the costs of directly supervising the worker are higher.[5]

Economists who study transactions costs propose two simple rules for ranking the costs of measuring output of different occupations.[6] The costs of measuring output are higher, when the final output of the worker is more complex, and/or when a worker works more interdependently with other workers.

The final output of the worker may be complex for several reasons. The sheer number of final outputs produced by the worker may be large and the mix of outputs produced at any one time may vary. Each final output by itself may be easy to measure, but the process of negotiating piece rates and measuring and recording all of the separate outputs may be more costly than just paying a time rate and hiring a monitor. For this reason, the National Industrial Conference Board suggested that it was hard to apply piece rates to repair work, assembling, trucking, stockroom work, pattern making or common labor, which is constantly shifted from one job to another.[7]

Certain outputs by their nature are more complex. Consider the output of lifeguards. They provide the service of protecting swimmers from drowning, and in the modern era, the pool owner from liability suits. One measure of their output might be the number of drownings at the pool, but drownings happen so seldom that they are not a very accurate measure of safety at pools where drownings do not occur. The number of saves is another potential measure, yet good lifeguards rarely are required to make saves. The safety of the pool might actually decrease if lifeguards were paid by the save because they have incentives to increase the save count by allowing people to endanger themselves. The most effective payment method might be a time rate with a penalty for drownings. The lifeguards' protection of the swimmers is reasonably correlated with their time spent watching the pool, and the penalty ensures that they remain alert.

Interdependence creates measurement problems because each worker's contribution to the final output is hard to measure. Team production is used when members working together complete the task more efficiently than if they each worked separately. The measurement problems arise because it is hard to determine how the increased productivity of the team should be apportioned among workers. The problem is compounded when team members shirk by placing more of the work burden on other members. Hiring a monitor to enforce work effort and using a less accurate measure is a possible solution to this problem. Another possibility is to pay the team as a group for the final output and allow them to divide the earnings among themselves.[8]

Wage systems in the coal industry broadly conformed to the reasoning above. Pick miners and loaders were paid piece rates because the amount of coal they produced was a reasonably accurate measure of their efforts. The pick miner performed several tasks; he made the cut at the base of the seam, blasted the coal, loaded it, cleaned his workplace, laid track to the seam, and ensured his own safety. Many loaders performed the same tasks except making the cut. Yet all these tasks were aimed at one goal, producing a mine car full of coal to be delivered to the surface. By paying the miner by the coal ton, the employer reduced the problem of miners shirking by performing easier tasks that did not remove coal from the seam. The employer faced low costs in using coal tonnage to measure the miner's output because he already measured the coal for market. Thus, the added cost of attributing the amount weighed to the miner was relatively low. Coal output was a reasonable estimate of the miner's productivity within mines where there was little variation in seam size, flooding of rooms, or other mine conditions affecting the ease of mining. Where substantial variation existed, the measurement problem was solved by adjusting piece rates or negotiating other forms of payment.

Payment of piece rates offered an added advantage by reducing the amount of supervision required of individual miners and loaders inside the mine.[9] The costs of supervision in a typical mine were relatively high because each miner or pair of miners was assigned to a room. In the mine the distance between rooms was likely to be at least 150 feet, along dark passageways. "In passing from one room to the next, a man would have to duck his head as he goes through the cross-cut, perhaps crawl on his hands and knees when the coal is low." Five miles was "a short day's tramp" for a coal mine foreman, who might make cursory visits to sixty men in a day.[10] Often the rooms were considerable distances apart. Further, low ceilings in the mines prevented foremen from supervising several workers at once, as they might in a factory. To closely monitor the miners' work effort required a relatively high ratio of supervisors to miners or a transportation technology that did not exist at the mine.[11] Paying piece rates saved on supervision costs, because the miner's output directly determined his earnings.[12]

John R. Commons and large manufacturers in the 1920s noted that payment of piece rates did not always elicit maximum effort from factory workers. At times workers "held back" because they feared the employer would cut piece rates if they displayed a higher level of productivity. Several large corporations tried to eliminate this fear by guaranteeing piece rates. A number had policies of not changing piece rates even if a few workers earned high earnings, or of changing piece rates only when new techniques were introduced. Problems with piece rate cutting were most common when the piece rates were originally set, because setting piece rates was an imprecise art. A number of companies experimented with developmental rates and then moved to the permanent rates after a testing period.[13] The contemporary literature on the coal industry generally did not mention piece rate cutting due to higher productivity and the consequent holding back by workers. Cuts in piece rates were associated with declines in the market for coal and not with increased productivity. Coal miners had less incentive to hold back than factory workers because mines were open an average of four days a week compared with six days in factories. Miners thus had more incentive to work intensively during periods when work was available.[14] Further, the coal industry in the 1900s did not face the factory's problems of introducing piece rates because coal mines had a long history of using piece rates. Coal operators had a greater body of knowledge to tap when setting them and were less likely to err by setting new piece rates too high relative to the rest of the market.

The introduction of the cutting machine generally did not affect the payment of piece rates for the tonnage jobs. Instead of paying a single piece rate to the pick miner for undercutting and blasting and loading the coal, the mines paid separate piece rates to the cutting machine operator and his helper for undercutting the coal and the loader for blasting and loading it. Paying a piece rate to the machine cutters made sense because the amount of coal produced by each cut was a reasonable measure of the work involved in making the cut.[15] Even when the machine cutter made cuts of varying length in different rooms, the amount of coal produced was likely to be highly correlated with the length of the cut. If he worked quickly, he could make more cuts and total coal production from all his rooms would rise. Further, where and how the machine cutter made the cut in the wall might also determine the amount of coal produced, giving the cutter incentive to make more productive cuts.

Payment by tonnage was not a perfect measure of the cutting machine operator's output due to team production in the room. The output of the cut was also determined by the loader's skill in blasting and how quickly he worked. Problems of mismeasuring the machine cutter's contributions were resolved at least partially when his assignments were rotated through the mine, reducing the effect any one loader had on the output from his cuts. The revolving assignments also solved problems with mismeasuring the loader's output, since his output was affected less by the productivity of one machine cutter. Not all mines felt that they could effectively solve the measurement problems arising from team production. The U. S. Bureau of Labor Statistics reported in 1919 that roughly 50 percent of the machine miners in Virginia and nearly all of the machine miners in Oklahoma were paid time rates.[16] The anthracite coal industry solved the team production problem differently. The men who ran the cutting machines worked on contract for a specific tonnage rate and then hired their own helpers to blast and load the coal.[17]

Introduction of loading machines and loading conveyors in the late 1920s led to the elimination of piece rates. With the loading conveyors several men shovelled coal onto the conveyor belt as it moved past. Mine managers told Carter Goodrich that they stopped paying piece rates because they had no good way of marking who had shoveled a particular amount of coal onto the belt.[18] Heavier investment in machinery by the company may also have been an important contributor to the elimination of piece rates. Pick miners and loaders generally owned their own tools, picks, shovels, and handdrills. In contrast, the mine owners made the large-scale investment in loading machines, giving them incentives to supervise the use of the equipment more carefully. Given that they were already supervising the use of machinery, the marginal cost of supervising the workers was lower, thus reducing the shirking problems from paying time rates.[19]

The payment of time rates to daymen is also broadly consistent with transaction-cost reasoning. Employers faced problems in measuring their output because of the complex nature of their final outputs and the team production aspects of their jobs. Consider the motorman's task. He delivered coal-filled mine cars from the rooms to the surface and then distributed the empty cars among the rooms. At first glance, his output seems easy to measure; pay him on the basis of the number of mine cars he delivers. But his mine car output was dependent on the number of loaders and pick miners in the mine on any particular day. On the Monday following payday, fewer miners and loaders came to work. The motorman might drive the same distances in the mine as when there were twice as many miners and yet he would be paid less. He might be paid by the miles driven, but that was also determined by the number of miners reporting for work and where they were located. Further, such payments gave him incentive to drive extra miles unnecessarily. The motorman's output was hard to measure because it clearly depended on the productivity of other workers; therefore, time rates made more sense as the form of payment.

Consider the timberman. His efforts ensured the safety of the roof, an output as hard to measure as the lifeguard's. How do you determine his final output, by the number of timbers he places? In his rush to prop more timbers, he might not support the roof in more dangerous areas, and placing too many timbers could cause accidents for drivers and miners travelling through the mines. Safety in the mine was complex enough that any single measure would not effectively capture the productivity of the timberman.

Since daymen were paid a time rate, limiting shirking required that the foreman spend more resources directly supervising the daymen's activities. The problems of directly supervising daymen and tonnage men were similar because daymen also were spread throughout the mines. Mine management overcame this problem in several ways. The foreman kept time books on when daymen entered and left the mines. Because most of the daymen's activities were interdependent with the work of other men, the foreman often supervised through a system of "knocking." The foreman could tell if the motorman had relaxed when it took him a long time to bring coal cars to the surface. Had the motorman been delayed by an accident caused by poorly laid track, he would "knock" the tracklayer. Loaders who had not received their share of cars knocked the motorman, or they might knock the track-layer if new switches were not laid.[20] If men complained of ventilation problems, the foremen knew that the bratticemen had not erected the proper doors for sealing off passageways. Some jobs—bratticeman, pumpman, trackman, and slatemen—were mine maintenance jobs, which could be divided into tasks. The foreman assigned them to the specific tasks with rough estimates of the time required. He then examined the final results at roughly the time they were expected to finish. When the Gary, West Virginia, mine of the United States Coal and Coke Company began trying to practice more scientific management of the mines in the 1920s, they adopted this method for closer supervision of loaders. They increased the number of assistants to the foremen, and these assistants moved about the mine discussing with each loader how long it would take to blast and load the coal. Later in the day they checked the loader's progress.[21] As mines became more specialized, the foreman established bosses for work crews. A motor boss supervised the motormen, and a track boss led groups of trackmen.[22]

Piece Rates and Quality Control

Measuring the tonnage man's output included determining both the quality and the quantity of coal he produced. Loaders and pick miners typically were paid by the ton in union districts and by the car in nonunion districts.[23] The operator could count cars or weigh each coal car, but miners had incentives to increase their tonnage by loading the car with slate or with coal dust, which had less commercial value than chunk coal.[24] The companies solved these problems in several ways.

To rid the car of coal dust and smaller chunks of coal, operators at the turn of the century ran the car's contents over screens before weighing. Miners and operators constantly negotiated over the screenings. The UMWA contracts with operators' associations provided for specific dimensions of the screen, describing the size of the holes and the density of the bars.[25] An alternative to screening was to pay miners a "run-of-mine" piece rate for all coal the miner loaded into the car. The UMWA consistently pushed for the payment of run of mine rates on the grounds that miners were not being paid for the fine coal falling through the screens. They argued, correctly after 1900, that fine coal had nearly the same commercial value as chunk coal when sold to industrial users. The operators countered, also correctly, that they implicitly paid the miners for the fine coal, because the piece rates paid for screened coal were substantially higher than those paid for run-of-mine coal.[26] In West Virginia counties in 1907, the average wage differential between a screened ton and a run-of-mine ton ranged from 10 to 34 cents per ton.[27] Further, use of screens gave the miners incentives to continue to undercut and blast the coal in order to produce larger chunks of coal, which were more valuable because they could be sold to more types of coal consumers. In Illinois after 1897 run-of-mine payments were made for all coal, but the United Mine Workers did not achieve universal payment of run-of-mine rates in the Central Competitive Field until 1916.[28] The trend toward run-of-mine payments also developed in primarily nonunion West Virginia during the early 1900s. By 1914 only four counties, none among the leading producers, bothered to report payments for screened coal.[29]

Several factors contributed to the operators' willingness to shift toward run-of-mine piece rates. First, improvements in coal consumption technologies placed a lower premium on the production of chunk coal. Second, the spread of cutting machines meant that chunk coal was more likely to be produced even when miners were being paid run-of-mine rates. The major problem with run-of-mine rates had been the tendency for miners to shoot off the solid, or blast the coal without an undercut, which caused more of the coal to fall in smaller sizes. The trend toward run-of-mine payments also eliminated a source of irritation over measuring the miners' wages. In negotiations the miners charged that unscrupulous operators were slow to replace damaged screens through which larger chunks of coal fell. They also accused the operators of placing breakers on the screen that broke the chunks into smaller sizes that fell through the screens.

The other serious quality issue was the loading of "dirty" coal, coal filled with slate dust or chunks of slate. To prevent this practice, most operators adopted a punitive docking system. In nonunion districts a miner could lose credit for as much as a whole coal car if several chunks of slate were found in the car.[30] The companies went further. At least one operator claimed that in his fifteen years of experience loading dirty coal was the sole cause of suspensions of miners in day-to-day operations.[31] In union districts, loading dirty coal was also subject to fines beyond just deducting the weight of the impurities from the miner's tonnage. The United Mine Workers' contract in District 12 in Illinois provided for a three-step procedure for miners who loaded dirty coal. For the first offense in any given month the miner was fined 50 cents; for the second offense in the same month the operator could fine him $2 or suspend him for two working days; and for the third offense in the month or malicious or aggravated cases for the first or any subsequent offense, the operator could indefinitely suspend or discharge the miner.[32]

Miners complained that they were cheated by the punitive docking system in nonunion areas.[33] Yet the punishments for loading dirty coal were clearly designed as strong deterrents. If the miner lost only the weight of the impurities when he loaded dirty coal, he still might have continued to load the impurities. He could shovel coal into the car with abandon and allow the dock boss or the coal cleaners to sort out what was valuable and what was not. Given that such inspection was costly, the miner gained when the dock boss missed some of the impurities. In essence, the loader shifted the full cost of ensuring clean coal onto other workers in the mining process. It was more efficient to remove the impurities before the coal left the mine, if only because valuable coal car space was not wasted on transporting impurities to the surface. In the face of punitive punishments, the miner faced substantial incentives to remove the impurities from his coal. The coal companies were particularly sensitive to coal quality because a reputation for marketing low-quality coal severely damaged their ability to sell in a highly competitive product market.

Even after the issues of quality were settled, there remained an element of distrust over weighing the coal. The following joke from the *United Mine Workers Journal* typified such distrust:

> Two brothers were coal operators, operating a non-union mine in Eastern Kentucky. The elder brother of the firm was converted during a series of revival meetings that had stirred the town. For weeks afterward, the brother who had acquired religion endeavored to persuade the other to join the church. One day during a strenuous effort to bring his brother to his way of believing, he asked: "Why can't you, Richard, join the church as I did?" "It's all right for you to be religious," replied Richard, "but if I join the church too, who's going to weigh the coal?"[34]

The UMWA generally demanded a checkweighman who acted as the watchdog for the scales and sometimes collected union dues. In nonunion districts checkweighmen were relatively uncommon. West Virginia mining law required the operator to have a weighman on the tipple and allowed the miners to hire their own checkweighman if the majority desired one. Hinrichs found in some cases that miners in the nonunion fields refused to pay the extra cost of having their own checkweighman. They may have felt that the company's weighman was generally honest so that the cost of hiring their own man to check him was unwarranted. Although there were abuses of the weighing process, we don't know whether they were more than isolated instances. In some cases, however, Hinrichs found that the miners feared to vote for a checkweighman because employers might have perceived a favorable vote as advancing unionization and fired the men thought to be the leaders.[35]

Despite union claims, the operators' opposition to checkweighman does not imply that they continually cheated the miners through dishonest weighing. Coal operators generally opposed checkweighmen on several grounds. First, they argued that the checkweighman imposed unnecessary costs on the miners. Second, weighing was a matter of constant dispute. One operator claimed that "no real loader ever admits that he is satisfied with the weight you give him," and the checkweighman had incentives to aggravate the situation. Hinrichs believed that there was some truth to these claims because the checkweighman's job was a negative one. If he discovered no problems, the men wondered why they were paying him for a pleasant and prestigious job with little purpose. At times therefore he might protest unnecessarily.[36] The third and probably most compelling reason for the operators' opposition was that many checkweighmen became leaders in union organizing. A checkweighman already had the imprimatur of a leader because the men had selected him, and many sought to make the position a general ombudsman for the miners. The operators saw the development of a union as infringing upon their right to decide the best policies for running the mine. Since many operators operated on tight profit margins, the operators felt that changes to accommodate the union, whether through higher wages or changes in the operation of the mine, threatened their survival.

In mines where payment was by the car, the size of the car and its fullness were matters of dispute. In some mines the car was expected to be full enough to have a hump which could hit a board set above the weight scales. Some miners felt that they lost a large amount of the coal they had produced when the hump hit the board.[37] Mine owners might have used such arcane practices to reduce wages unfairly. Information about unrepaired screens and the fullness of the coal car was probably harder for miners to obtain than direct wage-rate information. Yet if the mine continued such practices, eventually it developed a reputation for cheating. Many practices were common knowledge among the miners and were often practiced all over the fields. "Shortweighting" was not necessarily cheating if all the men knew about it when they came to the mine. They just incorporated the weighing practices in their calculations of their potential earnings. The amount of coal required for a full car was itself responsive to changes in demand and supply, as one miner in Mingo County, West Virginia noted:

> Where they needed men and miners, then in those cases those cars were level full, but where they have plenty of men at the operations they compelled them to heap the cars up, what is known as the O-2 hump, and the drivers are instructed to set their elbows on the edge of the miner's cars like this and sight over their fingers, and if they could not see any coal over their fingers, they would let it stand until the men loaded them up until they could see the coal over their fingers.[38]

Miners who complained apparently expected that if such practices were stopped they would end up earning higher wages. In essence, they said they were cheated by not being paid for every part of the coal they loaded. However, the practices of screening the coal, requiring full cars, and docking for dirty coal seems to have served the economic purpose of reducing shirking on quality. Had the companies been denied the use of these techniques, they were likely to have lowered piece rates, so that overall earnings were roughly the same as before. If by eliminating these practices, the costs of ensuring quality rose, the miners' hourly earnings might have fallen as the employer forced miners to share the burden of the extra costs of quality control. The key factor that employers were forced to consider in hiring miners was that they pay earnings high enough to attract an adequate work force. The guidance for that payment came from what the workers could earn in their next best alternative.

Piece Rates and Variation in Mine Conditions

The payment schemes for tonnage men were complicated by the variety of conditions found in the miner's workplace. Conditions varied from mine to mine and within the same mine, affecting both the miner's earnings and his physical comfort. The miner could produce more per day as the height of the coal seam increased toward 8 feet.[39] Larger seams allowed him to blast down more coal per cut. The seam size also determined the height of the room; taller seams allowed the miner more freedom of movement and more relief for his aching joints. Mining very low seams often required digging out as much slate as coal, as did mining seams split by clay veins or slate formations, like "horsebacks." Places near ground water flooded at times, requiring the miner to bail before he could dig coal. Differences in the geological structure of the mine caused the hazards of roof falls and methane gas to be greater in some places than in others.[40] Miners in more dangerous places either spent more time timbering and checking for gas, or risked being carried from the mine in a pine box.

Holding worker productivity constant in a competitive labor market with mobile workers, piece rate wages adjust to differences in working conditions.[41] Adjustments were made in piece rates in situations where the conditions differed in a consistent manner. Variations in conditions between mines were probably greater and more consistent than those within the mine; therefore, piece rates probably differed more across mines than within mines. Where they were adjusted, piece rates were higher in mines and workplaces with worse conditions: smaller seams, more water-filled places, less firm roofs, or fewer days of work.

The best place to test whether competition among mines in the labor market caused piece rates to compensate for differences in natural mine conditions is in primarily nonunion areas. In studying black miners in West Virginia, an area dominated by nonunion mines, I performed a rough test on the proposition that piece rates were higher in areas where natural conditions made it harder to mine coal. First, an overall measure of the ease of mining coal in various counties in West Virginia was developed. For pick mining in each county, the measure was tons of pick-mined coal per pick miner per day, calculated as total tonnage of pick-mined coal in the county divided by the number of pick miners and by the average days worked. For hand loaders, the measure was coal tons produced using cutting machines per hand loader per day. Output per man day captures differences in the ease of mining coal to the extent that the average productivity of the miners did not differ across counties.

Weighted least squares regressions were then run with the average run-of-mine pick mining rate per 2240 lb. ton in the county as the dependent variable and the measure of pick mining productivity and other variables discussed in Appendix G as explanatory variables. Similar regressions were run with the average run-of-mine machine mining rate per 2240 lb. ton in the county as the dependent variable and the measure of machine mining productivity as one of several explanatory variables. Both sets of regressions were run for each of the following years: 1907, 1910, 1914, 1915, 1918, and 1923.

The elasticities of the piece rates with respect to the output per man hour are reported in Table 5-1. They show that in general piece rates were higher in areas where it was harder to mine coal. The elasticities are negative for all six years in the pick-mining regressions and negative in five of the six years in the hand-loading regressions. We can reject the hypothesis that the coefficients are zero with a two-tailed t-test at the 90 percent level in three years in the pick-mining regressions and three years in the hand-loading regressions. The largest response of pick rates to changes in output per man hour was in 1915, when the elasticity implied that a 10 percent reduction in the productivity measure led to nearly a 5 percent increase in the pick-mining rate. The elasticities for hand loading were on average of smaller magnitude, with the largest showing a 3 percent increase in the loaders' piece rate when the productivity measure rose by 10 percent. Since the elasticities were all less

TABLE 5-1. Elasticities of Piece Rates with Respect to Output per Man Day, West Virginia Counties in the Early 1900s

Year	*Pick Mining*	*Hand Loading*
1907	−0.253[a]	−0.305[a]
1910	−0.387[a]	−0.130[a]
1914	−0.041	−0.183[a]
1915	−0.498[a]	−0.082
1918	−0.031	0.029
1923	−0.014	−0.088[a]

Source: Based on regression coefficients in Table G-1 in Appendix G.

[a]Coefficient on which elasticity is based is statistically significant.

than one in absolute value, the piece rates did not adjust fully to equate earnings for similar workers across all mines.

This test of how piece rates adjusted to differences in the ease of mining coal is only a rough test for several reasons. First, the measures are all aggregated at the county level and therefore miss the variations in piece rates and ease of mining coal within the counties. This aggregation bias may cause the elasticities to show smaller compensating differentials than actually were present. Second, output per man-day is an imperfect measure of the ease of mining coal to the extent that it reflects differences in the productivity of the miners themselves. The use of county averages may be a plus in this sense, since the average productivity of miners probably varied less from county to county than it did from mine to mine. The output per man-hour measure offers one advantage because it economizes on information by summarizing in one measure all of the factors that might affect the ease of mining coal—seam sizes, problems with water and slate, roof compositions, and so on.[42]

The evidence above suggests that the primarily nonunion labor market in West Virginia put pressure on piece rates to rise in areas where coal was harder to mine. The UMWA tried to exert similar pressures on piece rates in the Central Competitive Field and other areas where collective bargaining determined wage rates. The UMWA sought "competitive equality" of wage rates, so that miners earned the same amount for the same effort throughout the union districts. Isador Lubin analyzed the determination of piece rates in the Interstate Agreements between the UMWA and various operators' associations in Illinois, Ohio, Indiana, and western Pennsylvania in terms of countervailing theories of competitive equality. He cited a number of examples where miners were paid higher piece rates in areas where the seams were smaller.

Lubin also found countervailing pressure by operators in the opposite direction. The operators defined competitive equality to mean making wage adjustments so that all mines could continue operating. Thus, they pressed for lower piece rates at mines facing higher coal freight charges, lower seams and/or other disadvantageous natural conditions. Lubin suggests that the Interstate Joint Agreements and agreements at the district and subdistrict levels were often contradictory because they tried to follow both the operators' and the miners' view of competitive equality.[43] Piece rates were adjusted partially to favor operators faced with higher transport and production costs, but piece rates also were set for smaller seams such that miners and operators shared the burden of their disadvantage. The UMWA succeeded more in imposing its view of competitive equality on the hourly wage rates paid to daymen. The day rates for similar jobs were almost uniform across the Central Competitive Field.[44]

As the cutting machine diffused, another issue that arose in setting piece rates was establishing the "machine differential," the rate paid pick miners minus the sum of the rates paid to loaders, machine cutters, and their helpers. The cutting machine allowed men to make the cut at the base of the seam faster, less arduously, and with less skill, increasing the coal workers' daily output.[45] As a result, the machine differential was positive, that is, the pick-mining rate exceeded the sum of the machine rates.

The differential varied from area to area. In West Virginia in 1905 the machine differential ranged from $.02 per ton (4.5 percent of the pick rate) in Harrison county to $.28 per ton of screened coal (28 percent of the pick rate) in Marshall county. In 1929 the average machine differential in West Virginia was $.14 (18 percent of the pick rate) with a low of $.02 (2.7 percent of the pick rate) in Grant County and a high of $.25 (29 percent) in Tucker County.[46] In the Central Competitive Field the UMWA negotiated a variety of machine differentials. The original differential negotiated in 1898 in Illinois was based on the prior nonunion differential. By the 1920s in Ohio, the districts established several machine differentials based on different seam sizes.

The size of the machine differential helped determine the diffusion of the cutting machine. The UMWA claimed that they did not oppose the introduction of new technologies. They argued, however, that the machine rates should be set to pay the owner of the machine the cost of installation, upkeep, and depreciation, as well as a "fair" profit, so that no advantage accrued to the machine mine over pick mines. The operators insisted on sharing in the lower costs from using machines. Although small machine differentials might have slowed the diffusion of machines, any obstacles the machine differentials created were generally overcome. In most major mining states the cutting machine aided in mining at least 70 percent of the coal by 1930.[47]

Within a mine the nature of wage adjustments depended on how conditions varied. When conditions varied greatly and with consistency, the piece rate was likely to be renegotiated. For example, miners received different rates for working in their rooms than for driving entries and crosscuts.[48] Generally, piece rates were higher for miners who "robbed pillars" because such work was substantially more dangerous.[49] In one mine where miners were paid by the car and there were two seam sizes, the mine operation used different-sized cars, although the miners there complained that the company at times delivered the larger cars to the smaller seams.[50] The U.S. Coal Commission found in 1923 that in mines where slate, clay, bone, or sulphur were consistently a problem, miners were paid yardage for removing impurities in addition to their regular tonnage or car rates.[51]

Where variations in conditions were large and consistent, the transactions costs of paying different piece rates were low because the consistency of the difference allowed its effect on output to be measured effectively. When differences in natural conditions within the mine were small and fluctuated randomly, we would expect that companies were less likely to pay different piece rates. In those cases the costs of negotiating different piece rates were probably higher than the losses to the miner and the coal operator from not having completely accurate piece rates.

In a number of mines the variations in conditions were sporadic and inconsistent, although large. Renegotiating the piece rate for each of these changes was costly because the variability of conditions made it harder to measure their impact on output. Each new change affected coal output in ways not easily comparable with previous changes, causing coal output to be a less accurate measure of the miner's output. In mines with greater division of labor, one means of handling a problem like flooding of the room was to move the miner to a different room and bring in pumpmen to handle the problem. A number of mines paid the miner an hourly rate for periods of "deadwork," such as bailing water or loading slate out of the room.

Often the value of time spent on the task was determined by the miner performing the task and telling the foreman how much deadwork he had done. At times the foreman's estimate and the miner's estimate differed dramatically. In one case cited by the Coal Commission a loader requested pay for eleven hours of work for removing twenty-seven cubic feet of slate. The manager in turn felt it should only have taken a half hour.[52] Some disagreements led to displays of temper. A miner claimed that the pool of water in his room was four to five feet deep, despite the manager's assurances that it measured only a foot. After the point was argued back and forth, the miner decided to prove his point and threw the foreman into the pool of water. The miner kept his job because his estimate was correct. In general, Goodrich found that during the 1920s bargaining over deadwork went on in a manner of considerable equality between the miner and the foreman.[53]

In the unionized Central Competitive Field payment for deadwork was generally not negotiated in interstate conferences.[54] Instead, negotiations over whether to pay for deadwork were held at the district or subdistrict level. The nature of the payments varied widely from district to district.[55] The UMWA claimed that nonunion mines rarely paid for deadwork. The absence of deadwork payments is not necessarily damning in and of itself. If miners performed a substantial amount of deadwork in producing coal at a particular mine, they might have been compensated with higher piece rates. In fact, the negative relationship between piece rates and output per man day in Table 5-1 suggest some compensation for deadwork. The absence of deadwork payments may have harmed miners more where the amount of deadwork varied within mines. Even then, the harm was not likely to be great if the amount of deadwork was relatively small and varied randomly for all miners. Over the course of the year, the deadwork was likely to even out, just like an umpire's bad calls in baseball games. The absence of deadwork payments became a more serious issue when the variations were large and nonrandom. Even if piece rates contained a premium to offset the risk of running into large amounts of deadwork, miners stuck with more deadwork were placed at a disadvantage.

Firms may not have paid for deadwork because they used workplace assignments to reward more productive miners. Rather than lower the wage rate to less productive workers, the foreman may have put them into less productive workplaces. As a miner became more productive, the foreman may have rewarded him with safer workplaces, places with taller seams, less water, or less slate, more coal cars, and more opportunities to work.[56] By using such hierarchical assignments to reward the most productive miners, the mine could reduce turnover among that important group.

The UMWA generally opposed such practices on the grounds that all miners should be treated equally. They also argued that mine assignments were used at times to punish workers for union-related activities, for not purchasing at the store, or because the foreman wished to punish his enemies. UMWA contracts therefore included clauses requiring that mine cars be distributed equally to all miners (the square turn) and establishing detailed rules about workplace assignments. The square turn and other rules were not confined to UMWA contracts. In many cases Goodrich suggests that the square turn and other rules in the union contracts codified the customs and rules already established in the mines.[57] Such rules helped the mine owner eliminate problems that might arise when it was costly to supervise the foreman's activities. If the foreman followed his own agenda, he might use car distribution or workplace assignments to reward friends or punish enemies. Even with the square turn and other rules, it was not uncommon to find miners cultivating friendships with the foreman or the driver who distributed empty coal cars.

Summary

The wage payment methods in the coal industry can be explained as a response to the transactions costs involved in monitoring laborers. Employers paid piece rates to workers for whom the amount of coal offered a reasonable measure of their productivity, and time rates to workers whose productivity was harder to measure. For piece rate workers the coal operators screened the coal and used punitive fines to ensure that miners sent larger chunks of coal without impurities to the surface. The ease of mining coal varied within mines and across mines. In nonunion labor markets and in unionized areas, piece rates rose to at least partially compensate miners at mines where it was harder to mine coal. Within mines, payment for variations in conditions probably depended on the degree of variations and how random they were. Piece rates appear to have been adjusted for consistent and large differences in working conditions. For large and inconsistent differences, mines seem to have allowed the miner and the foreman to negotiate the amount of payment.

Some might argue that the mine operators chose a relatively complex payment system because it was easier for them to practice labor larceny by not fixing screens or mismeasuring weights, and so on. Although some employers may have sought to cheat miners, the range of cheating was narrowed considerably by the fact that miners could compare their hourly and annual earnings across mines and with earnings in other industries. Low earnings offered a reasonable signal to miners to avoid that mine. Further, the "cheating" mine paid a price in the labor market in the long run, as miners required a premium to work there to guard against such cheating.

Some might argue further that the miners' mobility was limited enough that the operators could get away with such cheating in the long run. Evidence on mobility casts doubt on this view. Even if miners were immobile, the cheating interpretation of the choice of wage payment schemes faces an added problem. If mine operators had the monopsony power to get away with cheating in the long run, why bother to design a costly and complicated payment scheme purely to cheat the miners. Operators with such power could have "exploited" the miners in the open, no matter what type of wage payment scheme they chose. The choice of wage payments therefore seems to be primarily a response to other factors like the transactions costs of measuring output and monitoring labor.

NOTES

1. Arthur E. Suffern, *Conciliation and Arbitration in the Coal Industry of America* (Boston: Houghton Mifflin Company, 1915), p. 26; Keith Dix, *Work Relations in the Coal Industry: The Hand-Loading Era, 1880–1930* (West Virginia University Bulletin, Series 78, No. 7-2, January 1978), p. 56.

2. For an example of this view, see Alexander MacKenzie Thompson, *Technology, Labor and Industrial Structure of the United States Coal Industry: An Historical Perspective* (New York: Garland Publishing, Inc., 1979), pp. 131–35.

3. Following the diffusion of the cutting machine, the anthracite and bituminous industries organized themselves differently. The U.S. Bureau of Labor Statistics (BLS) reports in 1919 and 1922 that men who ran cutting machines in the anthracite industry were contract miners, who then hired their own helpers to shoot down the coal and load it. The "contract miner" was the basic occupation in the anthracite industry in the 1920s. In 1924 in the bituminous industry only 170 out of roughly 90,000 tonnage workers sampled by the BLS were listed as contract workers. U.S. Department of Labor, Bureau of Labor Statistics, "Hours and Earnings in Anthracite and Bituminous Coal Mining," *Bulletin No. 279* (Washington, DC: U.S. Government Printing Office, 1921), pp. 112–13; idem, "Hours and Earnings in Anthracite and Bituminous Coal Mining," *Bulletin No. 316* (Washington, DC: U.S. Government Printing Office, 1922), pp. 2, 60–63; idem, "Hours and Earnings in Anthracite and Bituminous Coal Mining, 1922 and 1924" *Bulletin No. 416* (Washington, DC: U.S. Government Printing Office, 1922), pp. 43–44.

The definitions of contract miners in earlier government publications were somewhat different. The mining censuses of 1889 and 1902 imply that mine operators generally hired contractors for extensive improvements or development work, such as tunnels, and shaft sinking. The practice was apparently more common in anthracite than in bituminous coal mining, and in both types of mining the payments for the contractor's services (not including wages paid to their men) were 1 percent or less of the total paid for wage earners (including men hired by contractors) by 1902. The instructions to special agents of the census in 1902 state that "Extensive improvements or development work, such as tunneling, shaft-sinking, boring test holes, etc. are frequently let out by contract and are not done by regular employees of the mine or quarry." However, the instructions specific to coal mines suggest that relatively few schedules would include such entries. In 1902 bituminous coal mines in the United States spent $1.2 million on such contract work to 5040 contractors, compared with $181.5 million on aggregate wages. Thus, 0.6 percent of the funds spent on wages and contract work went to contractors. The bituminous figure was higher in 1889 at 1.16 percent, when bituminous coal miners paid $0.82 million for contract work and $69.8 million for wages. Anthracite mining used contractors more extensively but saw a large drop in the extent of payments to contractors by 1902. In anthracite mining in 1889 roughly 5.6 percent of the $41.7 million spent on wages and contractors went to contractors; the percentage declined to 1.0 percent in 1902. See U.S. Bureau of the Census, *Mineral Industries of the United States, 1889* (Washington, DC: U.S. Government Printing Office, 1890), pp. 349–51; U.S. Bureau of the Census, *Special Reports, Mines and Quarries, 1902* (Washington, DC: U.S. Government Printing Office, 1905), pp. 706–17, 1109, 1116.

4. For a discussion of transactions costs and the payment of piece rates and time rates see Stephen Cheung, "The Contractual Nature of the Firm," *Journal of Law and Economics* 26 (April 1983): 1–21. For further discussions of transactions costs, see Douglass C. North, *Structure and Change in Economic History* (New York: W.W. Norton Company, 1981), pp. 40–41. Also see John McManus, "The Costs of Alternative Economic Organization," *Canadian Journal of Economics* 8 (August 1975): 334–50.

5. Early institutionalists led by John R. Commons recognized the importance of output measurement costs in determining the types of wage payments:

> If the worker is paid by the day or week it is usually because his product cannot be accurately measured. If he is paid by the piece the employer knows exactly what he is buying and how much he is paying for it. Piece-work furnishes accurate knowledge of labor costs and estimates of future costs. . . . Furthermore, piece-work stimulates the worker to greater exertion and attention. The rough, traditional estimate is 25 per cent greater output when paid by the piece than when paid by the day.

John R. Commons, *Industrial Goodwill* (New York: McGraw-Hill Book Company, 1919), p.7. For more recent discussions of piece rates in the economics literature, see John Pencavel, "Work Effort, on-the-Job Screening, and Alternative Methods of Remuneration," *Research in Labor Economics* vol. 1 (Greenwich, CT: JAI Press, 1977), pp. 225–58; B. R. Skelton and Bruce Yandle, "Piece Rate Pay," *Journal of Labor Research* 3 (Spring 1982): 201–09; Eric Seiler, "Piece Rate vs. Time Rate: The Effect of Incentives on Earnings," *The Review of Economics and Statistics* 46 (August 1984): 363–75.

6. Cheung, "Contractual Nature," pp. 7–8.

7. National Industrial Conference Board, *Systems of Wage Payment* (New York; National Industrial Conference Board, 1930), p. 34

8. The team may actually prefer that the owner monitor their efforts and pay them himself. Cheung describes a situation in Hong Kong where a group of boat pullers actually hired another worker to monitor their efforts and punish those who did not pull their share. Cheung, "Contractual Nature," p. 8. For the production of shoes, the U.S. Rubber Company paid certain groups gang rates where several employees were engaged in a single operation. E. S. Cowdrick, "Methods of Wage Payment: Report of a Fact-Finding Study in the Companies Associated with the Special Conference Committee," unpublished manuscript, 1927 from Record Group 23, Accession 1699, Box 241 at the Hagley Museum and Library, Wilmington, Delaware.

9. Dix, *Work Relations*, pp. 48–49 and Goodrich, *The Miner's Freedom*, pp. 30–32, both describe the advantage of reduced supervision.

10. Hugh Archbald, *The Four-Hour Day in Coal* (New York: The H. W. Wilson Company, 1922), pp. 39, 49.

11. The standard mining technique in the United States was the room and pillar method, which led to the placement of miners in rooms throughout the mines. Mines in the United States probably could have reduced supervision costs by following the long-wall method commonly used in Europe, in which a larger group of workers worked together in one place. Keith Dix (*Work Relations*, p. 7) claims that the long-wall method was not adopted in the United States because of "adverse physical conditions, such as thin and irregular coal seams

and poor roof conditions. Labor force and capital investment considerations also restricted the use of the system in this country." The irregularity of production in most American mines—caused in part by unsteady railroad car supplies, seasonal demand, and strikes—made long-wall mining less feasible because irregularity in the removal of the coal often caused the roof to shear at the face, resulting in the loss of some coal and mine equipment and considerable additional cost to reestablish the working face. Even short stoppages of operations could cause serious damage to the working area through caving of the roof.

12. Another gain to the operator from piece rate payments was that the worker paid for his own on-the-job training without explicit changes in wage rates. As his skill increased, he could produce more with the same effort as before and therefore receive higher earnings. The operators lost relatively little from allowing the worker to train in their mine, even if he left after he was skilled. The miner had paid for his training with lower earnings while he trained. The primary cost to the operator when the miner trained was the opportunity cost of having a workplace tied up by an inexperienced worker. This cost was lower during booms when the binding constraint on the mine was the labor supply.

13. Cowdrick, "Methods of Wage Payment"; National Industrial Conference Board, *Systems of Wage Payment*, p. 17; Commons, *Industrial Goodwill*, pp. 7–11.

14. The U.S. Bureau of Labor Statistics found that workers sped up when working on short time. U.S. Department of Labor, Bureau of Labor Statistics, "Hours and Earnings in Anthracite and Bituminous Coal Mining," *Bulletin No. 279* (Washington, DC: U.S. Government Printing Office, 1921), p. 10.

15. Contemporary sources suggest that the majority of cutting machine operators were paid by the piece. The U.S. Coal Commission Reports describe them as tonnage men and generally only report piece rates for them. United States Coal Commission, "Wage Rates in the Bituminous Coal Industry," *Report*, 1925, pp. 1065–75.

16. U.S. Bureau of Labor Statistics, "Hours and Earnings," *Bulletin No. 279*, p. 10. In West Virginia some cutting machine operators were paid by the day. The West Virginia Department of Mines' *Reports* from 1913 and 1929 on county averages paid to machine runners and helpers contain both piece rates and time rates. In 1913, 19 counties, including all of the leading coal-producing counties reported averages for both piece rates and time rates, while 11 smaller counties reported only averages of piece rates, and 1 county reported only averages for time rates. In 1929, 22 counties reported averages for both piece rates and time rates, 9 counties reported only piece rates, and one county reported only time rates. The problem with the West Virginia evidence is that we have no sense of how many cutting machine operators were paid piece rates and time rates in each of the counties. Without more specific evidence on the mines that paid piece rates and times rates, we can only speculate as to the reason for the difference. One reason why some mines may have paid time rates to cutting machine operators was that management in those mines supervised machine use more carefully, because of extensive investment in the machinery. Yet that explanation does not explain why some mines did not supervise machine use more closely.

17. U.S. Bureau of Labor Statistics, "Hours and Earnings," *Bulletin No. 316*, pp. 60–63.

18. Carter Goodrich, *The Miner's Freedom* (Boston: Marshall Jones Company, 1925), p. 173.

19. A similar situation developed in southern agriculture. Where landowners owned the mule or later the tractor, they were more likely to use wage labor. The marginal cost of supervising workers was lower when the landowner was already supervising the use of capital equipment. Lee Alston and Robert Higgs, "Contractual Mix in Southern Agriculture Since the Civil War: Facts, Hypotheses, and Tests," *The Journal of Economic History* 42 (June 1982): 327–54.

20. Goodrich, *The Miner's Freedom*, p. 50.

21. Ibid., pp. 125–130.

22. Keith Dix, *Work Relations*, pp. 46–51.

23. A.F. Hinrichs, *The United Mine Workers of America and the Nonunion Coal Fields* (New York: Longmans Green and Company, 1923), p. 19.

24. Prior to 1900, the coal consumption technology was such that coal chunks were far more valuable than fine coal. Around the turn of the century, industrial users began using fine coal as well as chunk coal. However, it still remained advantageous for the mine to produce coal in chunks because it could be sold for both industrial and home usage, while fine coal was limited to industrial production.

25. For example, see the scale agreement of 1898 reprinted in Louis Bloch, *Labor Agreements in Coal Mines: A Case Study of Agreements Between Miners' and Operator's Organizations in the Bituminous Coal Mines of Illinois* (New York: Russell Sage Foundation, 1931), pp. 343–44.

26. Suffern, *Conciliation*, pp. 26, 154–59.

27. West Virginia Department of Mines, *Annual Report* for the year ending June 30th 1907, p. 140. Substantial differentials were also present in the run-of-mine and screened rates negotiated by the United Mine Workers. See also Isador Lubin, *Miners' Wages and the Cost of Coal* (New York: McGraw-Hill Book Co., 1924) pp. 85–87.

28. Charles B. Fowler, *Collective Bargaining in the Bituminous Coal Industry* (New York: Prentice-Hall, Inc., 1927), pp. 77–79. Under the 1916 agreement, only the Indiana Block Coal district was allowed to retain screens.

29. See the West Virginia Department of Mines, *Report* for the year ending June 30, 1914, p. 324.

30. This was described to me by miners at the Beckley Exhibition Mine in Beckley, West Virginia. See also Suffern, *Conciliation*, p. 26.

31. Goodrich, *The Miner's Freedom*, pp. 72–73.

32. Bloch, *Labor Agreements*, pp. 374–75. The union contracts also provided a procedural safeguard. The docking boss was required to keep the impurities for seventy-two hours and could not know whose tag was on the car when inspecting the car for impurities.

33. Suffern, *Arbitration*, p. 26.

34. *United Mine Workers Journal*, August 1, 1927, p. 4.

35. Hinrichs, *The UMWA and Nonunion Fields*, pp. 15, 30–35.

36. Ibid., p. 33.

37. Discussions with miners at Beckley Exhibition Mine.

38. Quoted in Hinrichs, *The UMWA and Nonunion Fields*, p. 19.

39. The Coal Commission offers evidence that the miner's productivity rose as the seam increased to eight feet before it fell. U.S. Coal Commission, "Wage Rates in the Bituminous Coal Industry," *Report*, pp. 1056, 1076–79. The costs of mining coal for the operator apparently fell as the seam increased in height to six feet. As seams increased in height beyond six feet, the cost of mining rose because of greater labor and supplies required to timber the roof. Lubin, *The Miners' Wage*, p. 94.

40. U.S. Coal Commission, "Wage Rates," p. 1055.

41. Remember that the adjustments also could be made in other facets of the employment package, such as the quality of housing and education, and store prices.

42. For more details on the regressions and the evidence, see Appendix G.

43. In the Central Competitive Field, the Interstate Joint Agreement established the pick rates, machine differentials, and percentage changes in daymen's wages for four basing points, the Danville district in Illinois, Hocking Valley in Ohio, the Indiana Bituminous district, and the Pittsburgh district in western Pennsylvania. Each state contained several

districts, and the districts used the Interstate Agreement as a basis for their own rates. They then negotiated over local conditions that might affect the situation. Outlying union districts also paid attention to the Interstate Joint Agreement. Washington, Iowa, and the Southwest Interstate Conference generally established higher rates than in the Central Competitive Field. In union districts in western Kentucky and northern West Virginia, the rates were generally lower due to direct competition from nonunion mines in the same product markets.

44. Lubin, *The Miners' Wage*, pp. 71–75, 76, 86, 92–99, 193, 196. When the Industrial Commission described the Joint Interstate Agreements in the early 1900s, they argued that the operator's notions of competitive equality were dominant. "No attempt is made to make wages uniform or the earning capacity of the men equal between different districts, or within districts themselves, the principal object being so to regulate the scale of mining as to make cost of production practically the same in one district that it is in another regardless of whether or not the earnings of miners are equal." Quoted in Suffern, *Conciliation*, p. 145.

45. Dix (*Work Relations*, p. 28) made some rough calculations in West Virginia that showed the tons per day produced by pick miners and by machine miners were quite similar. However, his comparisons do not hold constant the natural conditions faced by the two types of mining. After controlling for safety, unionism, and other factors, Pae-Kun Choi found that labor productivity and total factor productivity generally increased with increases in the percentage of coal produced by cutting machines. Pae-Kun Choi, "Effects of Unionism and Work-Related Safety on Productivity in the U.S. Bituminous Coal Mining Industry, 1898–1945," Ph.D. dissertation, University of Georgia, 1989, pp. 186–200.

46. West Virginia Department of Mines, *Report*, 1905, pp. 86–88; 1929, p. 124.

47. Lubin, *The Miner's Wage*, pp. 101–14; Dix, *Work Relations*, p. 20. For an econometric analysis of the impact of unions and other factors on the diffusion of coal cutters, see Christian Dustmann, "The Diffusion of the Coal Cutting Machine in the United States Bituminous Coal Industry," unpublished Masters thesis, University of Georgia, 1986.

48. Entries were generally driven for haulage purposes and the miner's rooms were then driven off of them. As the miners advanced their rooms further from the entryway, crosscuts were driven between the rooms to enhance ventilation.

49. Pillars were the unmined walls of coal left between rooms to support the mine roof. When a section of the mine was finished, selected miners extracted or "robbed" the coal from the pillars. As pillars were robbed, the roof support diminished, making the work dangerous. Lubin, *The Miners' Wage*, p. 20

50. Hinrichs, *The UMW and the Nonunion Fields*, p. 20.

51. U.S. Coal Commission, "Wage Rates," p. 1055.

52. U.S. Coal Commission, *Report*, pp. 1312–13.

53. Goodrich, *The Miner's Freedom*, pp. 38–41.

54. The anthracite industry handled deadwork differently. Contract miners and laborers who ran into obstructions that caused their earnings to fall below a minimum rate were paid time rates and their status was changed to that of consideration miners. When past the obstructions and earning above the minimum, they were returned to their status as contract miners. The anthracite industry also paid slightly lower time rates to company miners who removed obstructions and prospected for new places. U.S. Bureau of Labor Statistics, "Hours and Earnings," *Bulletin No. 316*, pp. 60–63.

55. Lubin, *The Miners' Wage*, p. 121.

56. See Dix, *Work Relations*, p. 48. Dix argues that the use of workplace assignments for job discipline depended on the views of the foreman and the extent to which mine workers resisted the foreman's assignments.

57. Goodrich, *Miner's Freedom*, pp. 59, 66–67.

6

Dig Sixteen Tons and What Did You Get? Earnings

Bituminous coal miners in the early 1900s are commonly perceived as receiving low pay for dangerous work in isolated regions. The perception is only partially right. Estimates from various sources show that hourly earnings in coal mining were substantially higher than in manufacturing until the late 1920s. However, the mines typically were open seventy fewer days a year than manufacturing concerns, leaving annual earnings in coal about the same or slightly lower than in manufacturing. High hourly earnings in coal mining helped compensate miners for accepting greater risk of injury, a limit on work opportunities, and living in an isolated area. On the other hand, a worker had to face the rigors of work seventy more days in manufacturing just to earn the same or slightly higher income he could earn in coal mining. Further, a worker had far more independence in making workplace decisions in coal mining than in manufacturing.

Since the United Mine Workers of America (UMWA) was among the most successful unions in the early 1900s, the story of the coal industry has often been told in terms of union struggles. The UMWA has been given credit for much of the improvement in coal wages during the boom in coal mining through World War I. Many see the UMWA's demise as the cause of the decline in wages during the 1920s. The timing of the rise and fall of the U.S. average coal earnings and the UMWA seems so right that few question this description. Yet there were other secular trends that may be as important if not more so. Labor demand in the coal industry rose and fell with changes in coal prices, and coal companies were forced to match the secular rise in manufacturing wages if they wanted to continue to attract workers. Regression analysis of the U.S. average hourly earnings in coal mining helps sort out the relative importance of the union and these other factors.

The relationship between unions and wages also is examined within the coal industry, where hourly and annual earnings varied substantially across districts and states. Few have gone beyond cursory comparisons that suggest unionization as the primary cause of coal wage differences. Clearly other factors are important. Analysis of a pooled sample of state averages from twenty-three coal states for the years

1912 to 1923 shows the impact of union membership, strikes, coal prices, and productivity differences. Further, we can delve more deeply into aspects of wage determination not captured by time-series analysis of national averages. The pooled sample allows study of whether hourly wages within the coal industry compensated for differences in opportunities to work, in accident rates, and in the coverage of workers' compensation laws.

Why Become a Miner? High Hourly Earnings

A major attraction of coal mining was high hourly earnings. Table 6-1 shows that hourly earnings in coal mining exceeded the manufacturing average for males in nearly every year and more than doubled the earnings of hired farm labor throughout. The estimates are constructed by combining U.S. Census data with evidence from state reports and the U.S. Geological Survey; see Appendix A for more details. In the early 1890s, coal hourly earnings were roughly 11 to 13 percent higher than manufacturing earnings before plunging to 11 percent less in 1897. As the United Mine Workers established their base in the Central Competitive Field, coal hourly earnings jumped to 28 percent above male manufacturing earnings by 1900. The tremendous coal boom in the early 1900s kept coal earnings between 35 and 44 percent higher than manufacturing earnings until 1913. From 1913 through World War I coal hourly earnings stayed around 30 percent higher than manufacturing earnings. Surprisingly, during the period of labor strife and the severe economic

TABLE 6-1. Average Annual Earnings per Full-Time Equivalent Worker in Current Dollars

	Hourly Earnings			*Annual Earnings*				
				Coal Mining			*Ratios*	
Year	*Coal Mining*	*Male Manuf.*	*Ratio Coal/Manuf.*	*Greenslade*	*Census*	*Male Manuf.*	*Green./Manuf.*	*Census/Manuf.*
1890	18.0	15.8	1.14	406		483	0.84	
1891	16.9	15.8	1.07	377		486	0.78	
1892	17.9	16.0	1.12	393		491	0.80	
1893	18.8	16.6	1.13	383		462	0.83	
1894	17.1	15.3	1.12	292		425	0.69	
1895	15.8	15.2	1.04	307		458	0.67	
1896	14.7	15.8	0.93	282		447	0.63	
1897	13.8	15.4	0.90	270		449	0.60	
1898	17.0	15.1	1.13	316		453	0.70	
1899	18.5	16.1	1.15	379		469	0.81	
1900	21.3	16.6	1.28	438		479	0.92	
1901	23.7	17.4	1.36	465		502	0.93	
1902	24.2	18.2	1.33	490		520	0.94	
1903	26.5	18.7	1.42	519		535	0.97	
1904	26.7	18.6	1.44	464		525	0.88	
1905	27.0	18.9	1.43	490		543	0.90	
1906	28.5	20.2	1.41	522		579	0.94	

(*continued*)

TABLE 6-1. *(Continued)*

	Hourly Earnings			*Annual Earnings*				
				Coal Mining			*Ratios*	
Year	*Coal Mining*	*Male Manuf.*	*Ratio Coal/Manuf.*	*Greenslade*	*Census*	*Male Manuf.*	*Green./ Manuf.*	*Census/ Manuf.*
1907	27.8	21.0	1.32	560		574	0.98	
1908	28.1	20.2	1.38	466		523	0.89	
1909	27.7	20.5	1.35	498	554	570	0.87	0.97
1910	28.6	21.8	1.31	533	594	598	0.89	0.99
1911	29.3	22.2	1.32	531	593	591	0.90	1.00
1912	30.9	22.8	1.36	593	663	605	0.98	1.10
1913	30.7	24.3	1.26	612	685	636	0.96	1.08
1914	31.6	24.2	1.31	530	595	638	0.83	0.93
1915	33.1	24.9	1.33	577	649	625	0.92	1.04
1916	37.3	28.8	1.29	739	832	716	1.03	1.16
1917	47.9	34.8	1.38	966	1,090	851	1.13	1.28
1918	59.6	45.9	1.30	1,205	1,362	1,078	1.12	1.26
1919	69.7	52.5	1.33	1,097	1,251	1,274	0.86	0.98
1920	93.6	50.8	1.54	1,659	1,884	1,494	1.11	1.26
1921	91.8	53.7	1.71	1,102	1,247	1,298	0.85	0.96
1922	90.3	49.6	1.82	1,034	1,165	1,264	0.82	0.92
1923	92.0	54.9	1.68	1,325	1,487	1,379	0.96	1.08
1924	80.7	56.8	1.42	1,116	1,248	1,364	0.82	0.92
1925	72.3	56.4	1.28	1,141	1,271	1,408	0.81	0.90
1926	72.3	56.9	1.27	1,252	1,390	1,440	0.87	0.97
1927	69.2	57.4	1.21	1,070	1,183			
1928	67.2	57.4	1.17	1,100	1,211			
1929	65.5	58.7	1.12	1,142	1,253			

Sources: Coal mining hourly earnings and Greenslade estimates of annual earnings from Rush V. Greenslade, "The Economic Effects of Collective Bargaining in Bituminous Coal Mining," Ph.D. dissertation, University of Chicago, 1952, pp. 39–41. Male manufacturing hourly earnings are 1.10 times the manufacturing hourly earnings for all wage earners, which come from Albert Rees, *Real Wages in Manufacturing, 1890–1914* Princeton: Princeton University Press, 1961), p. 33, and Albert Rees, *New Measures of Wage-Earner Compensation in Manufacturing, 1914–1957*, National Bureau of Economic Research Occasional Paper 75 (New York, 1960), p. 3. The Census coal mining annual earnings are based on benchmark years in which total wages are divided by total wage earners (average for the year, including inactive periods) from U.S. Bureau of the Census, *Sixteenth Census of the United States: 1940, Mineral Industries, 1939*, vol. I (Washington, DC: U.S. Government Printing Office, 1944), p. 230. The ratio of the Census estimate to the Greenslade estimate was 1.112 in 1909, 1.14 in 1919, and 1.097 in 1929. The remaining estimates were interpolated using Greenslade's series and straight-line interpolations of the Census-Greenslade estimate. Male manufacturing annual earnings are annual manufacturing earnings for all workers multiplied by 1.10, which is an estimate of the ratio of male manufacturing earnings to manufacturing earnings for all workers. Manufacturing earnings for all workers from Paul Douglas, *Real Wages in the United States, 1890–1926* (Boston: Houghton Mifflin Company, 1930), p. 246. The figure for 1910 was corrected by subtracting $14 following the correction made by Albert Rees, *Real Wages in Manufacturing, 1890–1914* (Princeton: Princeton University Press, 1961), p. 32.

downturn of the early 1920s, coal mining hourly earnings rose relative to manufacturing hourly earnings. Although 1921 and 1922 brought significant drops in coal annual earnings, hourly earnings rose to levels 71 and 82 percent greater than manufacturing earnings. As coal demand stagnated and the strength of the United Mine Workers waned, coal hourly earnings dropped relative to manufacturing hourly earnings, bottoming out at 3 percent less in 1933.

TABLE 6-2. Hourly Wages in Bituminous Coal Mining and for Males in Manufacturing from the National Industrial Conference Board (Current Cents)

Industry	*1929*	*1928*	*1927*	*1926*	*1925*	*1924*	*1923*	*1922*	*1921*	*1920*	*1919*	*1914*
Bituminous Coal Mining												
All Workers	61.9			71.9		74.8		81.1			69.9	35.8
Tonnage men	62.6			74.9		77.7		84.5			78.9	
Daymen	60.5			66.4		69.6		75.3			53.0	
Hand loaders	59.2			71.5		74.8		83.6			77.4	
Inside laborers	54.4			62.0		65.7		69.7			58.6	
Outside laborers	49.3			54.6		57.5		64.9			50.2	
Manufacturing Payrolls												
All males	62.5	61.4	61.0	60.1	59.2	59.2	57.0	52.0	55.4	64.2		26.2
Unskilled males	48.6	47.4	47.1	46.1	45.5	45.8	44.3	40.2	43.7	52.9		20.3
Farm Labor Without Board[a]												
Hired Labor	30.3	30.4	30.8	31.0	30.8	30.5	30.6	26.8	27.1	44.5	38.8	18.0

Source: M. Ada Beney, *Wages, Hours, and Employment in the United States 1914–1936*, National Industrial Conference Board Studies Number 229 (New York: National Industrial Conference Board, 1936). Manufacturing payrolls includes the following industries: agricultural implements, automobiles, boots and shoes, chemicals, cotton (only for northern states), electrical manufacturing, foundries and machine shops, furniture, hosiery and knit goods, iron and steel, leather tannings and finishing, lumber and millwork, meat packing, paint and varnish, paper and pulp, paper products, book and job printing, news and magazine printing, rubber, silk, wool. For mining earnings: U.S. Bureau of Labor Statistics, "Hours and Earnings in Bituminous Coal Mining, 1929," *Bulletin* No. 516 (Washington, DC: U.S. Government Printing Office, 1930), pp. 2–4, 27–28. The figures for 1919 are from U.S. Bureau of Labor Statistics, "Hours and Earnings in Anthracite and Bituminous Coal Mining, 1929," *Bulletin* No. 279 (Washington, DC: U.S. Government Printing Office, 1921), pp. 9, 64, 75–83. Figures for 1914 are from U.S. Bureau of Labor Statistics, "War and Postwar Wages, Prices, and Hours, 1914–23 and 1939–44," *Bulletin* No. 852 (Washington, U.S. Government Printing Office, 1945), p. 3.

[a]Assumes farm laborers worked eight hours per day.

An alternative set of comparisons in Table 6-2 confirms that hourly earnings for all workers in coal mining generally exceeded earnings for males in manufacturing. The earnings in Table 6-2 come from direct surveys of payrolls at several hundred companies by the Bureau of Labor Statistics (coal mining) and the National Industrial Conference Board (manufacturing).[1] The gap between coal and manufacturing earnings in Table 6-2 is smaller than in Table 6-1 in part because the Conference Board's survey was skewed toward larger firms in the Northeast. However, both tables show the pattern of a sharp rise to 1922 and then a decline through the rest of the 1920s. Until the late 1920s, coal hourly earnings were higher than earnings in such industry classifications as automobiles, iron and steel, and foundries and machine shops. In fact, coal earnings exceeded the earnings of all the Conference Board industries except printing until the late 1920s.

Comparisons so far may be misleading, because the skills required in various industries differed. We can control for skill differences across industries by examining the earnings of the unskilled workers listed in Table 6-2. Unskilled workers generally had more mobility between industry than other workers because they were less likely to have skills specific to only one industry. Inside laborers and outside laborers in coal mining definitely were unskilled. There is some question about how to classify loaders. Alba Edwards, a leading researcher on occupational status, seemed to consider coal loaders to be unskilled.[2] Most loaders received minimal training, much of which was teaching the man how to stay alive while loading coal. Many saw the replacement of pick miners with cutting machines and coal loaders as a major form of deskilling of the coal miner's task.[3] However, the large differences in earnings between loaders and inside laborers in Table 6-2 suggests that loaders were more than unskilled workers. Even if coal loaders were semiskilled workers, the comparisons of their earnings and those of unskilled manufacturing workers are instructive. A coal loader who switched to manufacturing was likely to start as an unskilled worker.

The gap between the coal and manufacturing earnings of unskilled workers is wider than the gap for all workers. In 1922 outside coal laborers, the lowest paid group of unskilled coal workers, earned 61 percent more than unskilled manufacturing workers. Yet outside laborers were only a small fraction of the unskilled workers at coal mines. Working inside increased the laborer's earnings at least 10 percent, so that he earned 73 percent more per hour than the typical unskilled manufacturing worker in 1922; the advantage fell to 11 percent in 1929. The inside-outside difference is probably a premium for accident risk, since working inside was significantly more dangerous than outside the mines. Working as a coal loader raised the unskilled coal worker's earnings another order of magnitude as coal loaders earned 207 percent of the male manufacturing unskilled wage in 1922, although the difference fell to 122 percent by 1929. Clearly for unskilled workers and for loaders, the tremendous cut in hourly pay was a major obstacle they faced in moving into manufacturing.

Annual Earnings

With such high hourly earnings, why were coal miners commonly depicted as poorly paid? The impression may stem from comparisons of annual earnings. Comparisons of the earnings of full-time equivalent workers in Table 6-1 show that on average coal miners earned similar or somewhat lower earnings than manufacturing workers. Greenslade's lower-bound estimates of coal annual earnings were on average about 92 percent of male manufacturing earnings between 1900 and 1926, while the higher estimates based on Census employment data averaged about 104 percent of manufacturing earnings for the years 1909 to 1926. Appendix I describes the construction and biases of the Greenslade and Census estimates in more detail.

The averages may be deceiving. The workers' earnings experience in coal mining depended heavily on the period in which they worked because coal miners experienced tremendous fluctuations in their relative fortunes. Some fluctuations were caused by external forces. Economy-wide downturns caused greater declines in annual earnings in mining than in manufacturing. During the depression of the 1890s Greenslade's lower-bound estimates of coal earnings fell below 70 percent of manufacturing earnings. In the Great Depression, miners' annual earnings fell to lows of 50 to 60 percent of male manufacturing earnings.[4] Miners experienced milder relative drops during the recessions of 1904, 1907–08, 1914, and 1921. The increase in coal demand during World War I caused the miners' relative fortunes to peak, as their annual incomes rose between 13 and 28 percent above incomes for male manufacturing workers. Some fluctuations were caused by internal strife in the coal industry, as miners struck for higher wages or better working conditions in the face of the owners' intransigence. Major strikes in 1897, 1919, and 1922 caused large drops in coal annual earnings. Smaller strikes also contributed to reduced working time and reductions in annual earnings.[5]

The Worker's Choice

To the farm laborer in the South, coal mining offered an opportunity to earn substantially greater income than he could earn as hired labor on the farm. For example, in 1926 a farm laborer who became an outside laborer at a coal mine raised his hourly earnings from 31 cents to 54.6 cents per hour (see Table 6-2), while his annual earnings might rise by 60 percent. Even after adjustments for differences in prices between farms and the mines, the farm laborer gained roughly 28 percent in hourly wages and 17 percent in annual earnings by becoming an outside laborer in the mines.[6] It is hardly surprising that a large portion of coal workers had left work as rural laborers in the South and in Europe. In fact, some workers migrated back and forth between farms and mines. Some used coal earnings to buy land and then migrated back and forth, working the farm in summer and in the mine during the winter.[7]

The choice between mining and the typical manufacturing job was not as clear-cut. As shown in the mining-manufacturing ratios of earnings in Figure 6-1, high hourly earnings in coal were offset by more limited working time. In average years while most manufacturing concerns worked 270 to 300 days a year,[8] the typical coal mine was open only 200 to 220 days a year due to overcapacity, seasonal fluctuations, and problems in obtaining railroad cars. Thus, on average the worker's annual earnings in coal mining were 92 percent to 104 percent of annual earnings in manufacturing. The same general pattern of higher hourly earnings, more limited working time, and the same or lower annual earnings in coal mining compared with manufacturing also was present within the major coal states; see Tables A-1 and A-2 in Appendix A. Assume the worst, that coal miners earned on average 8 percent less each year than manufacturing workers. Would workers freely choose coal mining over manufacturing?

High hourly wages served to compensate coal workers for constraints on their working time caused by layoffs when the mines were closed. Consider a year like 1915, when Greenslade's lower-bound estimate of coal annual earnings was at the average of 92 percent of manufacturing earnings. In manufacturing average annual male earnings were \$625; workers worked 279 nine-hour days for 24.9 cents per hour. In coal mining the mines were closed many more days so that coal workers averaged only 203 8.6-hour days for the year. Say coal employers had tried to pay the manufacturing hourly wage of 24.9 cents an hour. They would have faced enormous problems in trying to attract workers because coal workers would have earned only \$434 for the year, while being laid off intermittently the rest of the year.

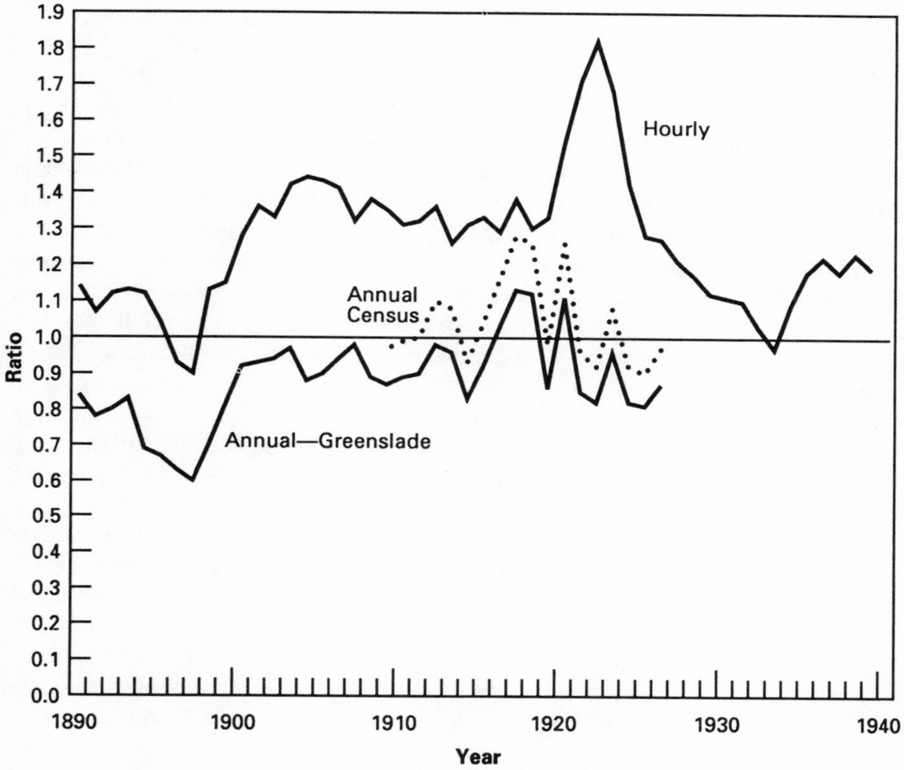

FIGURE 6-1. Ratios of Coal Mining to Male Manufaturing Earnings. *Sources:* See Table 6-1.

To attract enough workers to meet coal demand, employers had to raise hourly earnings to 33.1 cents per hour, which gave coal miners annual earnings of $577.

Coal employers did not find it necessary to raise hourly earnings enough to set coal annual earnings equal to manufacturing annual earnings because workers were willing to give up some income for a significant reduction in the time they endured at work. This willingness to make an "income-leisure tradeoff" is a standard subject in labor economics textbooks. In 1915 the worker who chose coal mining over manufacturing gave up $48 or 8 percent in annual income, but in return his rigorous workload was reduced by seventy-six days as well as almost an half hour each day.

The choice between industries above is a long-run choice, where the reduced working time in coal mining was a result of constraints beyond the control of the worker. Once the worker committed to mining, his income-leisure choices were limited because he could work no more days than the mine was open. Within that limit miners and loaders were given a great deal of latitude in deciding when to quit for the day and when to come to work. A description of the miners' independence in 1906 stated that the miner "begins and quits when he pleases, and the operator does not say a word," because if he did and the miner didn't like it, the miner would pack up and move on.[9] A number of miners and loaders chose to work less than the full number of days the mines were open. However, sometimes the choice was forced upon them when they faced slack time when coal cars were not delivered to their rooms, the room filled with water, the machine cutter had not made the undercut, or they were injured.

By choosing mining over manufacturing the worker accepted a limited work year for higher hourly earnings. Yet interviews with miners often found them grousing that there was never enough work. A number moved from mine to mine in hopes of increasing the number of days they worked. One reason was that miners could have earned substantially more if only the coal mines operated more days while still paying the high coal hourly wage. However, a longer work year in coal mining was no guarantee of a large increase in annual earnings. If the coal operators had been able to cut down on layoffs and keep the mines open longer, they would have been able to pay lower wages and still attract coal workers. Coal employers sought to pay the lowest hourly earnings that still allowed them to hire a full work force. If mines had been open the same number of days as manufacturing firms, coal employers would have paid an hourly wage much closer to the manufacturing wage of 24.9 cents per hour.

Coal employers probably could not have gotten away with paying the manufacturing hourly wage because high coal hourly earnings also compensated miners for accepting more accident risk and for living in isolated communities. Table 6-3 shows that in 1926 bituminous coal mining paid higher hourly earnings than any other industry to unskilled workers, the workers who were most likely to be able to switch industries with little loss in earning power. In part the high earnings compensated coal workers for working at least nine fewer hours per week than in any other industry. The measures of accident risk listed by industry in Table 6-3 show that coal mining was more dangerous than any manufacturing industry. State workers' compensation funds forced industries with higher fatal and nonfatal accident rates to pay higher premiums. In West Virginia bituminous coal mines paid $2.10 in workers' compensation premiums for every $100 in wage payments, 60 cents more than the next highest industry in the table and more than double the premiums paid in most industries. The coal industry's relative record for fatal accidents was far worse. U.S. bituminous mines experienced two fatal accidents per million man hours worked. The next highest industry was lumber and mill work at less than one-fourth that level.[10]

High hourly earnings in coal mining might also reflect compensation to workers for living in isolated company towns. Coal miners lived in company towns to a greater extent than workers in other industries listed in Table 6-3. By the 1920s the negative features of company towns were associated less with high prices at company stores than with living in an isolated town where there were few opportunities for wives to work, and the company was the focus of town life with the power to evict at short notice. In 1922 the average cost of living for a coal miner in the United States was at most 1.7 percent higher than for a manufacturing worker. Roughly 65 percent of the miners in the United States lived in districts similar to those in Illinois, Ohio, and Pennsylvania, where U.S. Coal Commission surveys (summarized in Table 8-1 in Chapter 8) showed food prices to be lower than in nearby manufacturing districts. The national average cost of living was up to 1.7 percent

TABLE 6-3. Hourly Earnings, Weekly Hours, and Workplace Accident Risk in 1926 (Ranked by Hourly Wage for Unskilled Males)

		Accident Measures		
Industry	*Hourly Earnings Unskilled Males*	*Workers' Compensation Premium*	*Fatalities per Million Manhours*	*Weekly Hours Unskilled Males*
Bituminous Coal Mining	62.0	2.10	2.00	36.2
Rubber	54.2	0.40		49.8
Automobiles	52.3		0.089	50.8
Chemicals	52.1	1.30	0.177	53.2
Hosiery and Knit Goods	49.9	0.15		48.4
Iron and Steel	49.3	0.80	0.200	55.1
Foundries and Machine Shops	49.0	0.75	0.206	50.0
Leather Tanning and Finishing	48.8	0.40	0.102	46.9
Agricultural Implements	48.6		0.062	50.2
Paper Products	47.7	0.40		50.5
Printing: News and Magazines	47.6	0.20		45.5
Electrical Manufacturing	47.4		0.050	47.8
Silk Textiles	46.7	0.40		52.2
Paint and Varnish	46.5	1.30		47.6
Meat Packing	46.4	0.90	0.105	49.4
Paper and Pulp	44.8	0.65	0.189	51.7
Furniture	44.5	0.80	0.028	48.8
Wool Textiles	43.8	0.40	0.334	47.2
Boots and Shoes	40.4		0.035	45.9
Lumber and Millwork	38.2	1.50	0.463	48.4
Book and Job Printing	37.9	0.20		48.4
Cotton Textiles[a]	37.8	0.40	0.003	51.1

Sources: Hours and Earnings for all but coal industry from M. Ada Beney, *Wages, Hours, and Employment in the United States 1914–1936*, National Industrial Conference Board Studies Number 229 (New York: National Industrial Conference Board, 1936). For mining earnings and hours: U.S. Bureau of Labor Statistics, "Hours and Earnings in Bituminous Coal Mining, 1929," *Bulletin* No. 516 (Washington, DC: U.S. Government Printing Office, 1930), pp. 2–4, 27–28. The listings for unskilled coal miners are for inside laborers. The Workers' Compensation Premium is the premium paid by companies per $100 on their payroll from the West Virginia State Compensation Commissioner, *Annual Report* for 1926 to 1930, pp. 31–33. The fatal accidents per million man hours are aggregated (using number of employees as weights) from state accident statistics reported in U.S. Bureau of Labor Statistics, "Statistics of Industrial Accidents in the United States to the End of 1927," *Bulletin* No. 490, pp. 19–28, 127. The fatal accident rate for bituminous coal is fatalities in 1926 divided by the product of total employment, days worked, and average hours per day from U.S. Bureau of Mines, "Coal Mine Fatalities for the year 1927," *Bulletin* No. 283.

[a]Cotton includes no payrolls from southern states.

higher because 35 percent of the mining work force was employed in southern or nonunion areas where there were generally higher food prices. Prices were 11.8 percent higher in southern West Virginia and 4.9 percent higher in the Kanawha district than in Charleston, West Virginia, although prices in the Alabama coal districts were the same as in Birmingham. In fact, the national average difference in the cost of living was probably smaller than 1.7 percent because miners generally paid lower rents and lower fuel costs than manufacturing workers.[11]

Workers clearly responded to the changes in relative wages in mining and manufacturing. Greenslade notes that when coal hourly wages rose relative to manufacturing wages, coal employment expanded. This was particularly true during the early 1920s. Coal hourly earnings reached levels 80 percent above those in manufacturing at the time. Despite a drop in days worked below 150 in 1920 and 1921, and thus low annual earnings, coal employment expanded. When coal hourly earnings fell from that peak, the exodus from coal mining was huge. Coal employment fell by over 28 percent from over 700,000 in 1923 to 500,000 in 1929.[12]

Trends in Real Earnings

Although annual earnings fluctuated greatly, coal miners experienced a long-term rise in their annual and hourly earnings over the course of the hand-loading era. Figure 6-2 shows Greenslade's estimates of hourly and annual earnings deflated by the consumer price index for all goods in 1967 dollars.[13] Real hourly earnings in coal rose 91.5 percent from 1890 to 1929, while real annual earnings rose 48 percent. Neither trend was steady. Real hourly earnings rose 169 percent from 1890 to 1923.[14] Annual earnings peaked about three years earlier, as recessions and labor strife in the early 1920s reduced days worked, and artificial shortages drove coal prices and hourly earnings higher. Both annual and hourly earnings declined after 1923, reaching a trough in 1933. Annual earnings finally reached their World War I level again during the late 1930s.

Labor historians and many contemporaries attributed the rise and fall in coal hourly earnings to the rise and fall of the United Mine Workers. Although union strength played an important role, other factors are of equal and possibly greater importance. The derived demand for labor in coal mining was stimulated by increases in coal prices. As manufacturing wages rose over time, the miners' opportunity cost rose, forcing coal employers to pay higher wages to attract miners. Further, fluctuations in days the mines were open affected wages by forcing coal employers to raise hourly earnings when days fell and allowing them to lower hourly earnings when days rose. To determine the relative importance of each factor, the following wage equation is estimated: the change in real hourly earnings in coal mining (*COALEARN*) as a function of the change in the coal price (*PRICE*), the change in the percentage of coal workers in the United Mine Workers (*UNION*), the change in real hourly earnings in manufacturing (*MANUEARN*) and the number of days the mines were open (*DAYS*) for the years 1890 to 1929.[15] All but the days variable are included in change form to eliminate statistical problems that result from time series analysis of variables with unit roots.[16] The equation is estimated with ordinary least squares. A Durbin-Watson test suggests that serial correlation was not present in the error terms. The absolute value of t-statistics are in parentheses below the coefficients.

$$\underset{(1.71)}{.184} + \underset{(3.73)}{0.080}\,PRICE + \underset{(3.84)}{0.83}\,UNION - \underset{(1.68)}{0.0009}\,DAYS + \underset{(1.84)}{0.69}\,MANUEARN. \quad (6\text{-}1)$$

$$COALEARN =$$

$R^2 = 0.50$, Durbin-Watson statistic $= 1.79$.

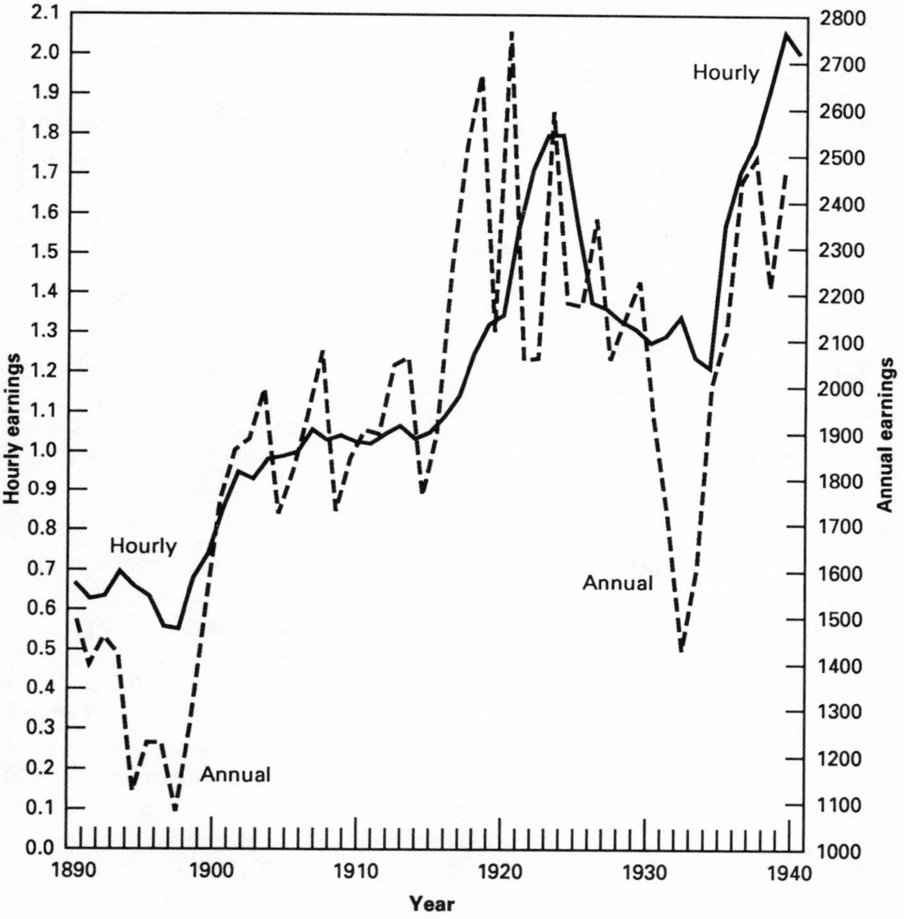

FIGURE 6-2. Annual and Hourly Earnings in Coal Mining (1967$). *Sources:* See Table 6-1 and Table A-3 in Appendix A.

All the coefficients are consistent with expectations. Increases in coal hourly earnings were associated with increases in coal prices, increases in union strength, and increases in the opportunity cost wage in manufacturing; all coefficients are statistically significant at the 90 percent level. Consistent with the discussion on the miners' choice between mining and manufacturing, the days coefficient suggests that coal earnings rose more when the mines were closed more days.

Decompositions in Table 6-4, based on the coefficients above, show that changes in union membership were not the only important determinant of the long-term rise in coal hourly earnings. The primary cause of the near doubling in coal hourly earnings over the entire period from 1890 to 1929 was an increase in the opportunity cost wage in manufacturing, which accounted for roughly 66 percent of the rise. Increased membership in the United Mine Workers, starting at 5 percent of the work force in 1890 and ending at 31 percent in 1929, contributed only 36

TABLE 6-4. Decompositions of Changes in Coal Hourly Earnings (Decomposition's Percentage Share of the Change in Coal Hourly Earnings Is Reported in Parentheses)[a]

Variable	*1890–1902*	*1902–1913*	*1913–1923*	*1923–1929*	*1890–1929*
Change in Coal Hourly Earnings	0.93–0.67 0.26	1.03–0.93 0.10	1.80–1.03 0.77	1.28–1.80 −0.52	1.28–0.67 0.61
Coal Price (1967 $)	0.05 (19.2%)	−0.03 (−30.0%)	0.10 (13.0%)	−0.14 (27.0%)	−0.02 (−3.8%)
Union	0.37 (142.3%)	0.0 (0.0%)	0.15 (19.5%)	−0.31 (60.6%)	0.22 (36.0%)
Manufacturing Wage (1967$)	0.076 (29.2%)	0.08 (80.0%)	0.18 (23.4%)	0.05 (−9.6%)	0.40 (65.6%)

[a]Decompositions were calculated by multiplying the coefficient from the regression equation 6-1 in the text by the change in the variable over the period listed. For example, the union entry in the table for 1890 to 1902 is (0.50–0.05) × 0.83 = 0.37, where the union has 50 percent of the miners in 1902, 5 percent in 1890, and the union coefficient was 0.83.

percent to the rise in coal earnings. Meanwhile changes in real coal prices had small effects on the long-term rise in hourly earnings.

Analysis of the long-term trend understates the impact of the UMWA on earnings in important subperiods of the hand-loading era. Changes in union strength had much stronger effects in the first and last subperiods in Table 6-4 than had the other explanatory variables. From 1890 to 1902, membership in the UMWA rose from 5 percent of the bituminous work force to roughly 50 percent, as the union established its major stronghold in the Central Competitive Field after a successful strike in 1897 and 1898. This gain in strength more than explains the rise in real hourly wages, and the union contribution to the rise in coal earnings is more than twice as large as the combined effects of the increases in manufacturing wages and the coal price. A sharp drop in union strength from 68 percent to 31 percent of the work force also contributed the most to the 52 cent drop in coal hourly earnings from 1923 to 1929, accounting for 61 percent of the decline. Meanwhile, a sharp drop in coal prices contributed another 36 percent to the decline. Coal earnings fell despite an increase in the miners' opportunity cost earnings in manufacturing.

Changes in union strength were not the primary contributor to the rise in coal earnings in the remaining subperiods. From 1902 to 1913, while the UMWA's relative strength remain unchanged, an increase in manufacturing earnings explains 80 percent of the rise in coal earnings. As coal hourly earnings soared from 1913 to 1923, the rise in manufacturing earnings contributed about 23 percent, while the rise in union strength from 50 to 68 percent of the work force contributed about 20 percent, and an increase in coal prices contributed 13 percent. If changes in coal prices were caused by changes in unionization, our measure of the impact of unions may be understated. Yet, even under the extreme assumption that all changes in coal prices were caused by changes in unionization, the relative importance of unionization and manufacturing earnings in explaining coal earnings in the various time periods is not changed much.

TABLE 6-5. Average Hourly Earnings for Hand Loaders Based on Time in the Mine[a]

State	*1929*	*1926*	*1924*	*1922*	*1919*
United States	59.2	71.5	74.8	83.6	77.4
Alabama	35.3	43.6	45.4	46.4	73.7
Colorado	68.8	72.6	79.9	83.7	77.4
Illinois	79.1	97.6	100.3	112.7	88.9
Indiana	86.5	104.0	103.4	109.4	87.5
Kentucky	54.7	57.9	64.6	70.4	68.6
Ohio	54.5	75.2	79.1	89.3	76.1
Pennsylvania	54.2	65.1	68.2	67.2	75.3
Tennessee	43.6	40.6	47.8		72.5
Virginia	51.3	55.6	56.9		62.7
West Virginia	59.1	71.0	76.4	84.1	77.8

Source: U.S. Bureau of Labor Statistics, "Hours and Earnings in Bituminous Coal Mining, 1929," *Bulletin* No. 516 (Washington, DC: U.S. Government Printing Office, 1930), pp. 2–4, 27–28. The 1919 figures are from U.S. Bureau of Labor Statistics, "Hours and Earnings in Anthracite and Bituminous Coal Mining, 1929," *Bulletin* No. 279 (Washington, DC: U.S. Government Printing Office, 1921), p. 64.

[a]Hourly earnings for hand loaders are based on hours in the mine, which includes travel time to and from the miner's place and time spent eating lunch at the face. Average travel time was about forty-eight minutes per day inside the mine. Hand loaders were chosen to represent piece rate workers because hand loaders represented approximately two-thirds of piece rate workers.

Regional Comparisons Within Coal Mining

The U.S. average for coal mining disguises substantial variation in coal hourly and annual earnings across states and coal districts. Table 6-5 contains the Bureau of Labor Statistics' (BLS) estimates of hourly earnings of loaders, who accounted for roughly 45 percent of coal workers and received earnings around the mean for all coal workers. The BLS estimates are the most accurate available for piece rate workers because they are compiled from payroll surveys where the time spent in the mine by piece rate workers was explicitly measured.

Throughout the early 1900s, coal workers consistently earned the most per hour in the Central Competitive Field states of Illinois, Indiana, and Ohio, where the UMWA was strongest. They earned the least in the southern, mostly nonunion states of Alabama, Tennessee, and Virginia. Colorado was the exceptional nonunion state with wages above the national average, at times ranking among the top three states. West Virginia's ranking is particularly interesting. West Virginia was the site of several major struggles between the miners' union and coal employers, including all-out warfare in 1912–13 and 1919–21. UMWA rhetoric described West Virginia miners as virtual slaves, while coal operators claimed that their miners earned as much as union miners. Neither side was very accurate. West Virginia miners earned less per hour than miners in the Central Competitive Field, but they fared well relative to manufacturing workers. During the 1920s hand loaders in West Virginia earned about the national coal average per hour, and therefore more per hour than

TABLE 6-6. Average Earnings per Start for Tonnage Men and per Eight-Hour Day for Daymen in 1921

Area	*Union Status*	*Tonnage*	*Daymen*
Wyoming	Union	10.13	7.72
Illinois	Union	n.a.	7.46
Indiana	Union	8.35	7.38
Colorado	Nonunion	8.11	7.19
Ohio	Union	7.86	7.20
West Virginia	Union	7.85	6.92
West Virginia	Nonunion	7.76	6.03
Iowa	Union	7.46	7.15
E. Kentucky	Nonunion	7.44	5.71
Maryland	Nonunion	7.31	7.02
Northwest Pennsylvania and Pittsburgh	Union	7.26	7.15
Pennsylvania	Union	7.15	7.09
Kansas	Union	7.12	7.63
Virginia	Nonunion	6.82	5.30
Pennsylvania	Nonunion	6.54	5.57
Alabama	Nonunion	5.17	3.90

Source: From Coal Commission's sample of 1177 union and 751 nonunion firms in 1921 and sample of 145 union and 140 nonunion firms in 1920. Edward Hunt, F. G. Tryon, and Joseph Willits, *What the Coal Commission Found* (Baltimore, MD: Williams and Wilkins Company, 1925), pp. 204–29.

Notes: The Coal Commission suggests that earnings per start for tonnage men may underestimate their average daily earnings slightly. A start was recorded when a miner was credited with a car of coal. It is possible for him to be credited in days when he was not in the mine. See U.S. Coal Commission, "Earnings of Bituminous Coal Miners," *Report*, pp. 1246–47.

the typical manufacturing worker. Earlier in 1902 and 1909, West Virginia miners earned less per hour than the national coal average but still more than the average U.S. manufacturing worker; see Table A-1 in Appendix A. The high hourly earnings help explain why so many miners stayed in West Virginia despite the wage cutting and labor strife of the 1920s.[17]

Within states containing both union and nonunion districts wage opportunities also varied. Table 6-6 shows the union status of major coal districts, which are ranked by the daily earnings in 1921 of tonnage men. In general, the union districts dominate the top of the list and the nonunion districts the bottom, although nonunion Colorado and West Virginia paid more per start than several of the union districts. Working in a union district benefitted daymen more than tonnage men. A reordering of the list based on daymen's wages puts union districts in eight of the first nine positions and nonunion districts in six of the lowest seven positions.

Despite lower daily earnings, coal employers in nonunion districts in West Virginia and Pennsylvania claimed that their workers were better off than union workers. They argued that nonunion workers, by avoiding collective action, had more work opportunities and earned more annually. Note the irony. Coal employers emphasized high hourly earnings in mining-manufacturing comparisons, but within the coal industry nonunion employers emphasized the advantages of greater work

TABLE 6-7. Median Annual Earnings of Full-Time Tonnage Men and Daymen and Estimates of Average Annual Earnings of All Tonnage Men and Daymen

	Full-Time Workers		*All Workers*		*Ratio No. of Full-Time No. on Payroll*	
Area	*Tonnage*	*Daymen*	*Tonnage*	*Daymen*	*Tonnage*	*Daymen*
Central Competitive Field—Union						
Illinois	1500	1610	n.a.[a]	1487	.399	.475
Indiana	1550	1800	1080	1322	.236	.457
Ohio	1475	1725	1080	1379	.161	.289
NW Penn. and Pittsburgh	1320	1630	925	1157	.172	.245
West Virginia						
Union	1360	1545	1017	1158	.153	.208
Nonunion	1460	1490	1158	1198	.169	.232
Pennsylvania						
Union	1235	1660	956	1280	.257	.396
Nonunion	1345	1530	1043	1139	.209	.293
Nonunion areas in the Southeast						
Alabama	930	800	755	706	.313	.307
E. Kentucky	1330	1415	1017	1066	.106	.145
Maryland	1545	1780	962	1188	.181	.199
Virginia	1200	1180	1030	1068	.283	.351
Union areas in the West						
Iowa	1275	1580	1135	1445	.275	.457
Kansas[b]			912	1468	.000	.000
Wyoming	1880	2125	1668	1896	.298	.415
Nonunion						
Colorado	1520	1780	1253	1537	.169	.282

Source: From Coal Commission's sample of 1177 union and 751 nonunion firms in 1921. Edward Hunt, F. G. Tryon, and Joseph Willits, *What the Coal Commission Found* (Baltimore, MD: Williams and Wilkins Company, 1925), pp. 204–29. The rough calculations of annual earnings for all workers takes the average earnings per start from Table 6-6 and multiplies them by the average number of starts per man found in Table 6 on pp. 1178–81 in U.S. Coal Commission, "Earnings of Bituminous Coal Mine Workers," *Report*. Where there were multiple districts in a region in Table 6, the average number of starts for the region was the weighted sum using the average number of men on the payroll in each of the districts as weights.

[a]n.a. = not available.

[b]There were no full-time men in Kansas in 1921.

opportunities in nonunion-union comparisons. We can examine the nonunion operators' claims with two measures of annual earnings for tonnage men and daymen reported in Table 6-7. The earnings for full-time workers are earnings of men who worked in all twenty-four payroll periods. Due to high turnover in 1921, full-time workers generally accounted for 10 to 50 percent of average employment, as shown in the far right-hand column. The annual earnings of the average worker is the product of earnings per start and average starts per man.

Annual earnings comparisons for daymen generally deny the nonunion operators' claims. Union daymen generally received both higher hourly earnings and higher annual earnings than nonunion daymen. This was true when comparing earnings in the union states of Illinois, Ohio, and Indiana with earnings in nonunion Pennsylvania and West Virginia. It was also true in three of four comparisons of annual earnings in union and nonunion districts within West Virginia and Pennsylvania.

The nonunion operators found mixed support for their claims of higher annual earnings among the different measures of annual earnings for tonnage workers. Consider full-time tonnage workers in the eastern United States. The highest full-time earnings are found in nonunion Maryland and the union districts in Illinois, Indiana, and Ohio. Relative to the top union districts, the nonunion areas of Pennsylvania and West Virginia fared poorly. However, within both states full-time earnings were higher in nonunion than in nonunion areas. Of course, full-time earnings focus only on workers who stayed at the same mine all year. The nonunion districts in West Virginia and Pennsylvania fare better in comparisons of the annual earnings estimates for the average worker. Annual earnings in nonunion West Virginia exceed annual earnings not only in union West Virginia but also in Indiana and Ohio. Earnings in the Pennsylvania nonunion districts were higher than in the Pennsylvania union districts, although still slightly below the earnings in Indiana and Ohio.

While Tables 6-5 and 6-6 show that union districts generally paid higher wages, a multivariate analysis shows more clearly how much of the wage differences across states are directly attributable to unionization. Collective action by miners helped to raise wages not only through union membership but also through strike activity. Labor demand theory and numerous wage studies show that hourly earnings are functions of the final price of the product and the productivity of workers. Wages also tend to rise to compensate workers for reductions in work opportunities, higher accident rates, and lower payments to injured workers in the absence of workers' compensation.

Table 6-8 contains the coefficients of a standard reduced-form wage equation.[18] The regression sample is a pool of state averages in twenty-three coal states for the years 1912 to 1923. The wage is the average hourly wage rate for inside daymen, deflated to 1967 dollars. A listing of the wages is in Table B-1 in Appendix B. Although most workers were tonnage men, the piece rates reported for them were not easily comparable, due to differences in mine conditions within and across states. Since both daymen and tonnage workers were hired in the same labor market, the hourly earnings for the two were generally highly correlated. However, the union effect may be stronger in this sample of daymen's wages than was actually the case for all coal workers. Tables 6-6 and 6-7 show that daymen fared relatively better than tonnage men in union districts. Working in the other direction, the union effect on real earnings might be understated slightly because the hourly earnings are not adjusted for regional differences in the cost of living, and evidence collected by the U.S. Coal Commission suggests that company store prices were lower in union districts.[19]

Table 6-8 reports both ordinary least squares (OLS) estimates and weighted least squares (WLS) estimates.[20] Both sets of estimates are from fixed-effects regressions, which include dummy variables for all states except Alabama and all years

TABLE 6-8. Fixed-Effects Wage Regressions on a Pooled Sample of Twenty-three Coal States for the Years 1912 to 1923 (Dependent Variable = Average Hourly Wage Rate for Inside Daymen, 1967$)

	Means (S.E.)	*Ordinary Least Squares*	*Weighted[a] Least Squares*
Mean of Dependent Variable	1.26		
	(0.33)		
Intercept		0.32*	0.12
		(2.54)	(0.90)
Coal Price	5.64	0.065*	0.073*
(1967 $)	(1.30)	(7.29)	(7.27)
Days Worked	206.4	−0.0006	−0.0003
	(45.1)	(1.69)	(0.87)
Output per Man Hour	0.42	0.17	0.51*
	(0.12)	(1.10)	(3.40)
Fatal Accidents per Million	2.04	0.003	0.004
Manhours	(2.09)	(0.89)	(0.73)
Workers' Compensation Law	1.32	−0.008*	−0.014*
Times Fatal Accident Rate	(2.09)	(2.05)	(2.38)
Strike Days per Employee	13.6	0.001*	0.002*
	(28.9)	(4.75)	(4.61)
Strike Days per Employee in	13.4	0.004*	0.005*
the Rest of the U.S.	(21.5)	(1.95)	(3.83)
Paid-up Members in UMWA	0.54	0.15*	0.08
as a % of Employment	(0.32)	(3.91)	(1.36)
State Effects		Included	Included
Year Effects		Included	Included
R^2		0.952	
N		276	276

Sources: See Appendix B. Average daymen's wage from Waldo Fisher and Anne Bezanson, *Wage Rates and Working Time in the Bituminous Coal Industry, 1912–1922* (Philadelphia: University of Pennsylvania Press, 1932) pp. 248–53, 338–43). The deflator was the CPI, series E135 in U.S. Bureau of the Census, *Historical Statistics of the United States, Colonial Times to 1970* (Washington, DC: U.S. Government Printing Office, 1975), p. 211. The union variable was reported in U.S. Coal Commission, *Report, Part III* (Washington, DC: U.S. Government Printing Office, 1925), p. 1052, with straight line interpolations to fill years not reported. Workers' Compensation Law was compiled in Price V. Fishback, "Workplace Safety during the Progressive Era: Fatal Accidnts in Bituminous Coal Mining, 1912–1923," *Explorations in Economic History* 23 (1986); 269–98. Data for the remaining variables were compiled from U.S. Bureau of Mines Bulletins titled, "Coal-Mine Fatalities in the year ———," and U.S. Geological Survey (after 1922 Bureau of Mines) publications titled, *Mineral Resources of the United States, Part II, Nonmetals,* various years. For more details on the sample, see Appendix B.

Notes: Absolute value of t-statistics in parentheses below coefficient estimates; standard error in parentheses below means. Coefficients of state and year dummies are available from the author. F-tests reject the hypothesis that the coefficients of the state and year dummies are simultaneously zero.

*Statistically significant at the 90 percent level.

[a]The weight is the square root of total employment.

except 1912. The state dummies control for state-related factors that influence earnings but are not included among the regression variables, for example, differences in the cost of living in various states. The year dummies capture time-related influences like the effect of government influence in the labor market during World War I that are not captured in the other regression variables.

Even after controlling for other influences, union representation and strike activity aided miners in obtaining higher wages. Coal workers in states with a higher percentage of paid-up membership in the UMWA received higher wages, although the union coefficient in the WLS regression is not statistically significant. In states where the UMWA percentage was 5.4 percent higher (10 percent of the mean union percentage), real hourly wages were higher by 0.3 to 0.6 percent.[21] Membership in the UMWA measures only part of the strength of collective action by miners. Union members and nonunion miners also exercised bargaining power through strikes. The coefficients in Table 6-8 imply that when strike days per employee rose 10 percent from a mean of 13.6 to 15, hourly wages rose by 0.1 to 0.2 percent. Actually, the miners in one state benefitted from spillover benefits when miners in the rest of the country struck. A 10 percent increase in strike days per employee in the rest of the United States raised hourly wages by 0.4 to 0.5 percent. A more detailed discussion of the costs and benefits of strikes follows in Chapter 11.

While collective action contributed to raising wages, the factors with the largest effects on coal workers' wages were the standard labor demand variables, the price of coal and output per man-hour. A 10 percent increase in coal prices raised the hourly wage by 2.9 to 3.3 percent, compared with unionization and strike effects well below 1 percent. A 10 percent increase in output per man-hour boosted hourly wages between 0.5 and 1.7 percent, although the OLS coefficient was not statistically significant.

Coal wages also adjusted to offset changes in nonwage aspects of coal employment. Miners experienced large drops in annual earnings when days the mines were open fell. The loss from fewer workdays was partially offset by an increase in hourly wages, although the WLS days coefficient was not statistically significant. In states that worked 10 percent fewer days the average hourly wages were 0.5 to 1 percent higher.[22]

During the sample period from 1912 to 1923, there were two alternative state legal systems under which coal workers could obtain direct compensation when injured in accidents. Under the negligence system, an employer was not required to compensate miners for accidents unless the accident had been caused by the employer's negligence. As a result, only about 50 percent of families of injured miners received some form of compensation for major injuries or deaths under the negligence system. When workers compensation was introduced in many states, payments to injured miners jumped markedly. All serious accidents were compensated, no matter who was at fault, and the amount of compensation jumped.[23] Two variables are used to examine the extent to which wages adjusted for greater risks of accidents and changes in post-injury compensation: the fatal accident rate and an interaction term, which is the fatal accident rate times a dummy variable with value one in states and years with a workers' compensation law. The workers' compensation law dummy is multiplied by the accident rate because workers' compensation does not come into play until after an accident occurs.

Higher wages at least partially offset the lower payments for injuries in states without workers' compensation. The coefficients imply that workers received 1.3 to 2.3 percent higher wages in states with no workers' compensation law. Workers also received higher wages in states with higher accident rates; however, it is not clear how much to trust the accident rate coefficient estimate. The estimate is not statistically significant in either equation, which means that we cannot reject the hypothesis that higher accident rates had no effect on the wage rate. Since the wage equation is a reduced form, the accident-rate coefficient may be disguising a compendium of labor market interactions. In an earlier study I tried to sort out these interactions by estimating a system of accident-rate, labor-demand, and labor-supply equations. The results implied that higher accident rates had offsetting effects on wages. Increases in accident rates reduced labor demand, driving wages down, while miners reacted to higher accident rates by reducing their labor supply, driving wages up. For more details on the study see Chapter 7 and Appendix C.[24]

Summary

When comparing coal mining and manufacturing earnings, a focus on only one measure of earnings is misleading. If we look only at annual earnings, it is hard to see why many workers chose coal mining. Coal miners earned about the same or in some years somewhat less over the course of the year than did manufacturing workers, but the miners often worked in a dangerous industry while living in isolated company towns. In contrast, a focus on hourly earnings makes coal mining look better than any other industry, since workers earned substantially more per hour in coal mining than in manufacturing. By examining both hourly and annual earnings together, it becomes obvious that employers paid coal workers high hourly earnings in compensation for limits on their work year. On the plus side, coal workers worked substantially fewer days and still earned an average of between 92 and 104 percent of manufacturing annual earnings. Higher hourly earnings also compensated miners for working under more dangerous conditions and for living in isolated communities. Even within the industry, hourly earnings were higher in states where mines were open fewer days and where workers' compensation laws had not yet passed.

While collective bargaining helped to raise coal wages, other contributors were equally if not more important. The development of the United Mine Workers certainly helped raise miners' earnings around the turn of the century, and the demise of the union in the late 1920s contributed to a fall in real earnings. However, over the entire period from 1890 to 1929 coal wages rose in large part to keep pace with a long-term rise in the opportunity cost wage in manufacturing. Within the coal industry, collective action by miners led to higher hourly earnings in states where miners joined the union or struck. But again, other factors were as important, as earnings rose even more in response to similar percentage increases in coal prices and productivity.

NOTES

1. The coal hourly earnings, compiled by the Bureau of Labor Statistics, are based on total time spent in the mine, including time spent at lunch and time spent travelling in the mine. The coal earnings were roughly 4 percent higher when time at lunch is excluded. The National Industrial Conference Board (NICB) collected manufacturing earnings for both males and females; therefore, it offers a more accurate measure of male manufacturing earnings than the estimates in Table 6-1, which are interpolations based on earnings for all workers. See Appendix I for details. The NICB earnings may overstate the true national averages in each industry because the NICB surveyed primarily larger than average firms in the Northeast.

2. Edwards listed 52 percent of coal operatives in 1910 as unskilled workers; the remaining 48 percent as semiskilled workers. The only way he could have counted 52 percent as unskilled was to class loaders (who accounted for 45 percent of the work force) as unskilled. Edwards considered an occupation to be skilled if it required a long period of training or apprenticeship and its pursuance called for a relatively high degree of judgment and manual dexterity. Semiskilled occupations required a shorter training period and only a moderate degree of judgment and manual dexterity. Laborers required no special training, judgment or manual dexterity, but supplied mainly muscular strength for the performance of coarse, heavy work. Alba Edwards, "Social-Economic Groups of the United States," *Journal of the American Statistical Association* (June 1917): 646–47. When categorizing all occupations Edwards focused on broader socio-economic occupational categories. He only placed workers in skilled, semiskilled, and laborer categories for jobs requiring muscular activity.

3. Keith Dix, *Work Relations in the Coal Industry: The Hand-Loading Era, 1880–1930*, West Virginia University Bulletin Series 78 No. 7–2, 1977, pp. 34–36.

4. The statements about the Depression are based on comparisons of full-time equivalent earnings from the National Income Accounts in Stanley Lebergott, *Manpower in Economic Growth: The American Record Since 1800* (New York: McGraw-Hill Book Company, 1964), pp. 525–27. The manufacturing earnings in Lebergott's volume were multiplied by the 1.10 scalar to obtain male manufacturing earnings.

5. For more evidence of the impact of strikes on the number of days worked during the year, see Chapter 11.

6. For the comparison of nominal annual earnings, I multiplied the annual coal earnings in Table 6-1 by the ratio of hourly earnings for outside laborers to all workers in mining from Table 6-2 for 1926. This may understate the true annual earnings for outside laborers, who tended to work more days than many underground workers. The estimate of annual earnings for farm laborers is average monthly earnings of farm laborers multiplied by 12 from Paul Douglass, *Real Wages in the United States, 1890–1926* (Boston, MA: Houghton-Mifflin Company, 1930), p. 186. I made a rough adjustment for differences in farm prices and coal mines based on adjustments suggested by Lee Alston and T.J. Hatton, "The Wage Gap Between Farm and Factory: Labor Market Integration in the Interwar Years," unpublished working paper, University of Illinois, 1990.

7. West Virginia Bureau of Negro Welfare and Statistics, *Second Biennial Report, 1922–3*, p. 39.

8. Albert Rees, *Real Wages in Manufacturing, 1890–1914*, National Bureau of Economic Research Number 70 (Princeton, NJ: Princeton University Press, 1961), p. 33.

9. See David Corbin, *Life, Work, and Rebellion in the Coal Fields: The Southern West Virginia Miners 1880–1922* (Chicago: University of Illinois Press, 1981), pp. 30–31, quoting a letter from L.C. Anderson to *Outlook* 82 (April 28, 1906): 861–62.

10. The comparisons in Table 6-3 show that coal mining was in many ways an outlier. Most of the industries were within a relatively narrow band with respect to weekly hours and accident risk with coal mining well outside that band. To examine the entire sample more fully, I also ran regressions using the data in Table 6-3. The regressions control for skill differences by using the hourly earnings of unskilled males as the dependent variable. The ordinary least squares regression estimates (with absolute values of t-statistics below) are:

$$\underset{}{WAGE} = \underset{(3.47)}{0.65} - \underset{(1.16)}{0.004}\ \textit{Weekly Hours} + \underset{(1.22)}{0.033}\ \textit{Premium}, \quad R^2 = 0.24,\ N = 18$$

$$WAGE = \underset{(0.93)}{0.26} + \underset{(0.80)}{0.004}\ \textit{Weekly Hours} + \underset{(2.40),}{0.098}\ \textit{Fatal}, \quad R^2 = 0.42,\ N = 16$$

where *Premium* is the West Virginia Worker's Compensation Premium and *Fatal* is the fatality rate per million man-hours. The coefficient of the accident variables seem to support the hypothesis that wages were higher in more dangerous industries although wages did not change much to adjust for differences in weekly hours.

11. The 1.7 percent difference in the cost of living comes from the following assumptions. Roughly 65 percent of the coal miners in the United States were employed in areas like Illinois, Ohio, and Pennsylvania where the cost of living for miners and manufacturing workers was the same or lower. From Table 8-1 in Chapter 8, I averaged the gap between the mining wage and the manufacturing wage for the seven districts in Ohio, Pennsylvania, and Illinois, which came to −1 percent. The remaining 35 percent were in nonunion states like Alabama, Colorado, Kentucky, Tennessee, Virginia, and West Virginia. For this group of miners I assumed that they all paid 8 percent more than did manufacturing workers for food and other store purchases. The 8 percent overstates the true difference because the average of the Alabama and West Virginia prices in Table 8-1 was only 5.6 percent. Food and other store purchases together accounted for roughly 80 percent of the miners' expenditures. For the remaining expenditures—10 percent on rent, electricity, and fuel, and another 10 percent on other services—I assumed the miners paid the same prices as manufacturing workers. The cost of living for the miners in the southern and nonunion regions relative to manufacturing workers in those areas was $0.8 \times 1.08 + 0.1 \times 1 + 0.1 \times 1 = 1.064$, which reflects that 80 percent of expenditures were spent on food and store purchases, which cost miners 8 percent more than they did manufacturing workers, 10 percent was spent on rent and electricity and fuel, which cost miners the same as manufacturing workers, and 10 percent was spent on other services, which cost the same for miners. In the rest of the country the coal miners' relative cost of living was $0.8 \times 0.99 + 0.1 \times 1 + 0.1 \times 1 = 0.992$. The weighted average relative cost of living for miners in the United States as a whole was $0.35 \times 1.064 + 0.65 \times 0.992 = 1.0172$, where 0.35 means that 35 percent of the miners lived in southern and nonunion states where their average cost of living was 6.4 percent higher and 65 percent lived in states where their cost of living was 0.8 percent lower. The overall national average implies that in the United States as a whole coal miners faced a cost of living that was 1.72 percent higher. This comparison is biased toward finding high coal prices because the miners' relative food prices in the South are biased upward. Further, in all cases I assumed miners paid the same rents as manufacturing workers, when in fact they generally paid lower rents and lower fuel charges. U.S. Coal Commission, "Bituminous Workers and Their Homes," *Report of the U.S. Coal Commission*, 68th Cong., 2nd sess. (Washington, DC: U.S. Government Printing Office, 1925), pp. 1456–60. See also Chapter 8.

12. Rush V. Greenslade, "The Economic Effects of Collective Bargaining in Bituminous Coal Mining," Ph.D. dissertation, University of Chicago, 1952, pp. 71–91.

13. The earnings were deflated with the BLS consumer price index for all goods, which is listed in Table A-4 in Appendix A. Because many miners lived in company towns, the CPI may be an imperfect deflator. Table 8-1 shows that company store food prices ranged from 5 percent below to 11 percent above prices in urban districts, but rent and fuel charges were lower in company towns than in urban areas. However, company store food prices followed a similar trend to the BLS's food CPI. If there is any bias in the trend in real earnings from using the CPI, it is probably against finding that real earnings rose. As transportation improved, it is likely that the difference between company prices and urban prices narrowed. See Chapter 8 for more details.

14. The rise from 1890 to 1923 was 135 percent using Paul Douglas's cost-of-living deflator. Douglas found a relatively lower cost of living in the 1890s than either the BLS or Albert Rees. Comparisons of real earnings deflated by the BLS CPI, Douglas's cost-of-living index, and Rees's cost-of-living index are found in Table A-4 in Appendix A.

15. *COALEARN* is coal miners' hourly earnings in Table 6-1 deflated by the CPI. The pattern of coal hourly earnings can be seen in Figure 6-2 and Table A-3 in Appendix A. *MANUEARN* is male manufacturing earnings from Table 6-1 deflated by the CPI. *UNION* is a rough estimate of the percentage of miners who were members of the United Mine Workers by H. Gregg Lewis, based on Greenslade's accounts of fluctuations in union membership from H.G. Lewis, *Unionism and Relative Wages in the United States*, (Chicago: University of Chicago Press, Midway Reprint, 1963), pp. 75–76, and Greenslade, "The Economic Effects," pp. 19–26. The coal price and *DAYS* the mines were open are found in Table 3-1. The coal price is then deflated by the CPI to get the real coal *PRICE*.

16. Dickey-Fuller tests for unit roots did not reject the hypothesis that a unit root was present in the levels of coal earnings, coal price, percent union and manufacturing earnings. The same test rejected the presence of a unit root in the days the mines were open. When a time series has a unit root, it implies it has an infinite variance which creates problems in estimating time-series relationships. The analysis here follows the time-series analyst's practice of differencing the variables with unit roots while leaving variables without unit roots in level form. Theoretically, the equation estimated with the level of days and differences for the remaining variables still makes sense because increases (decreases) in days the mines were open would cause the change in the wage to fall (rise). Additional tests could not reject the null hypothesis of no cointegration between coal earnings, the coal price, manufacturing earnings, and the percent union. Ken Kroner at the University of Arizona helped me develop the analysis. The tests for unit roots and cointegration are discussed in Robert Engle and C. Granger, "Co-Integration and Error Correction: Representation, Estimation, and Testing," *Econometrica* 55 (March 1987): 251–77, and Robert Engle and B.S. Yoo, "Forecasting and Testing in Co-integrated Systems," *Journal of Econometrics* 35 (1987): 152–59.

17. Within West Virginia, there was a nonunion-union differential of about 5 percent in daily earnings in 1921. The difference was not high enough to offset the large differential between West Virginia hourly earnings and the U.S. manufacturing average.

18. The coefficients of a reduced-form equation summarize a combination of a number of relationships between wages and other variables. The variables in the equation might affect the wage by shifting labor demand, shifting labor supply, or through other relationships. Appendix C offers an example of a set of structural equations that attempt to measure the extent to which the variables cause changes in labor supply and labor demand. It also shows how a reduced-form accident equation can be derived from the set of structural equations.

19. See Chapter 8, Table 8-1.

20. Regression equations include an error term to capture random fluctuations and other

influences that are not measured by the variables included in the equations. We would prefer to have individual observations on the wages paid to coal workers, but the regression sample is averages at the state level. If the error term for each individual worker has the same mean and variance, state averages create some statistical problems when the averages come from states with different numbers of workers. The mean wage in each state is the sum of all individual wages divided by the number of workers. The error term at the state level is therefore the sum of all the error terms for each worker in the state divided by the number of workers, and the variance of the error term for each state is inversely correlated with the number of workers in the state. When the variance is not the same for each error term, the statistical problem is called heteroskedasticity, which causes the OLS regression to calculate biased estimates of the standard errors that are used to calculate the t-statistics in Table 6-8. A Glejser test confirmed the presence of this type of heteroskedasticity. J. Johnston, *Econometric Methods*, 2nd. edition (New York: McGraw-Hill Book Company, 1972), p. 220. The analysis corrects for this type of heteroskedasticity by estimated the equation with weighted least squares, where each variable for each state observation is multiplied by the square root of employment in the state. Potluri Rao and Roger LeRoy Miller, *Applied Econometrics* (Belmont, CA: Wadsworth Publishing Co., 1971), pp. 79–80, 116–21. The same reasoning underlies the use of weighted least squares to estimate the elasticities in Table 5-1 and later models in Chapters 7 and 11.

21. In this section the calculations of percentage changes are based on the means and coefficients in Table 6-8 and are calculated in manner described below for the union effect. A 10 percent rise in the UMWA percentage is 10 percent of the mean of 0.54, which is 0.054. Multiply 0.054 times the OLS coefficient for the UMWA percentage of 0.15 in Table 6-8 and the effect on wages is to raise them by 0.0081 (0.81 cents per hour), which is 0.6 percent of the mean wage of $1.26.

22. In the analysis in this chapter, days worked is treated as an exogenous variable to examine the extent to which wages adjusted in the labor market in response to changes in days. Days and wages may be simultaneously determined in the labor market; therefore, the days coefficient may be affected by simultaneity bias. The analysis in Chapter 11 treats the days variable as an endogenous variable and examines the effect on days of changes in coal prices, strikes, unionization and other variables.

23. For more details see Chapter 7 and Price V. Fishback, "Liability Rules and Accident Prevention in the Workplace: Empirical Evidence from the Early Twentieth Century," *Journal of Legal Studies* 16 (June 1987): 305–28.

24. Price V. Fishback, "Workplace Safety During the Progressive Era: Fatal Accidents in Bituminous Coal Mining, 1912–1923," *Explorations in Economic History* 23 (1986): 269–98.

7

Death's Taken a Mighty Toll for Coal, Coal, Coal

The coal miner performed one of the most dangerous jobs known. Tons of rock often shifted overhead with only timbers for propping. Encompassed by darkness with limited lighting, the miners worked with explosives, sometimes in mines with ignitable gases. Cars heavily laden with coal were pulled through the mines and could crush men who were not careful.[1] While sawmills and some other industries presented similar threats to limbs, coal mining differed by offering greater threats to lives. Fatalities per million man-hours in coal mining more than quadrupled the levels seen in any other major industry. This chapter tries to answer a series of questions about how miners and employers responded to the dangers in the mines. How great was the danger? Did it vary by region or change over time? What steps did miners and employers take to reduce the risk of accidents? Was accident prevention affected by changes in wage rates and to what extent did workers demand wage premiums to accept more danger? How much did the United Mine Workers enhance safety in the mines? Were state mine safety laws effective at reducing accident rates? And what impact did the introduction of workers' compensation have on the safety decisions of workers and employers?

The Extent and Nature of Coal Accidents

In the early 1900s coal mining was nearly four times as dangerous as it is today.[2] Prior to the drop in employment in the late 1920s, between 1500 and 2000 miners were killed in U.S. coal mines each year. The fatal accident rates in Table 7-1 show that in the United States before 1930 slightly more than two deaths occurred for every million man-hours worked, or roughly three to four fatal accidents for every thousand workers each year. Accident rates varied across states. Fatality rates were highest in the western states of Utah, Colorado, and Oklahoma; lowest in Texas and Missouri. West Virginia held the dubious distinction of having the highest accident rate of states east of the Mississippi River. Fatal accidents represent only part of the

TABLE 7-1. Number of Accidents Underground and Accident Rates in the U.S. Bituminous Coal Industry, 1906–1930

	Number Killed in		*Accident Rates (per 10 million man-hours)*		
Year	*All Accidents*	*Large-Scale[a] Accidents*	*All Accidents*	*Small-Scale Accidents*	*Large Accidents*
1906	1431	211	19.28	16.44	2.84
1907	2364	899	26.60	16.48	10.12
1908	1637	319	22.60	18.20	4.40
1909	1965	476	23.50	17.81	5.69
1910	2068	471	22.75	17.57	5.18
1911	1840	318	20.83	17.23	3.60
1912	1683	248	18.34	15.64	2.70
1913	2039	445	20.64	16.14	4.50
1914	1714	284	20.12	16.79	3.33
1915	1553	249	18.36	15.42	2.94
1916	1553	142	16.44	14.94	1.50
1917	1908	257	18.84	16.30	2.54
1918	1839	54	18.23	17.70	0.54
1919	1537	101	19.17	17.91	1.26
1920	1627	53	17.34	16.78	0.56
1921	1340	29	19.68	19.25	0.43
1922	1546	269	23.17	19.14	4.03
1923	1825	286	21.03	17.73	3.30
1924	1805	444	24.55	18.51	6.04
1925	1727	253	21.61	18.44	3.17
1926	1953	327	22.00	18.32	3.68
1927	1632	153	20.63	18.70	1.93
1928	1662	316	22.43	18.17	4.26
1929	1615	150	20.97	19.02	1.95
1930	1517	214	23.72	20.37	3.35

Sources: U.S. Bureau of Mines (1932), *Bulletin* No. 355, "Coal-Mine Accidents in the United States, 1930," by W. W. Adams, L. E. Geyer, and L. Chenoweth (Washington, DC: U.S. Government Printing Office, 1930), pp. 94–100; Keith Dix, *Work Relations in the Coal Industry: The Hand-Loading Era, 1880–1930,* West Virginia University Bulletin, Series 78, No. 7-2, 1978, p. 79, with adjustments by Price V. Fishback, "Employment Conditions of Blacks in the Bituminous Coal Industry, 1900–1930," unpublished Ph.D. dissertation, University of Washington, 1983, p. 185.
[a]Accidents killing five or more people.

danger, however. In 1930, there were 1.5 times as many permanently disabling accidents as fatal accidents, while nearly forty-two times as many less serious accidents caused miners to lose one or more days of work.[3]

The specter of black lung disease also loomed. Constant inhalation of microscopic coal dust particles helped cause pneumoconiosis, a disabling lung disease in which excessive fibrous tissue developed in the lungs. The symptoms showed up as "the miner's asthma," marked by coughing, coal dust in spit, and breathlessness. In various studies between 1924 and 1960 X-rays showed the build-up of fibrous tissue in 10 to 40 percent of the miners studied. Black lung received relatively little attention at the time. Medical opinion failed to link coal dust and black lung in the United States prior to the 1960s. Most reform movements and miners' activities focused on eliminating mine accidents. Before the 1960s miners received no com-

TABLE 7-2. Average Underground Fatal Accident Rates for Major Coal Mining States, 1903–1930[a]

State	*Total*	*Small-scale*
Alabama	26.1	19.4
Arkansas	26.8	25.5
Colorado	38.4	29.5
Illinois	16.8	14.4
Indiana	17.9	16.4
Iowa	13.1	13.1
Kansas	16.8	16.1
Kentucky	16.0	14.1
Maryland	11.9	11.4
Michigan	11.0	11.0
Missouri	10.6	10.4
Montana	23.5	22.1
New Mexico	47.1	26.6
Ohio	21.0	19.8
Oklahoma	43.9	24.2
Pennsylvania	16.1	14.0
Tennessee	17.0	14.2
Texas	5.1	5.1
Utah	49.4	34.3
Virginia	22.2	21.4
Washington	32.9	25.0
West Virginia	28.6	23.5
Wyoming	37.4	27.9
United States	20.91	17.6

Source: Reprinted from Price V. Fishback, "Workplace Safety during the Progressive Era: Fatal Accidents in Bituminous Coal Mining, 1912–1923," *Explorations in Economic History* 23 (1986): 272, with the permission of Academic Press, Inc. Copyright © 1986 by Academic Press, Inc. All rights of reproduction in any form reserved. For sources for the United States see Table 7-1, for the remaining states see Appendix B.

Notes: Accident rates are fatalities per 10 million man hours. The small-scale accident rate excludes workers killed in accidents killing more than four people.

[a]All means span 1903–1930 except Arkansas (1906–1930), Texas (1909–1930), Virginia (1909–1930), Wyoming (1908–1930), and United States (1906–1930).

pensation for black lung through workers' compensation or in the courts.[4] The only compensation to miners came indirectly through higher hourly earnings in coal mines than in other industries.

The overall fatal accident rate in the United States stayed surprisingly constant before 1930. This constancy hides diverging trends for two major accident categories. Rates for large-scale accidents—gas and dust explosions and other accidents killing five or more people—declined. Graebner argues that this decline was aided by the increased focus of state mining legislation and the U.S. Bureau of Mines (formed in 1910) on larger accidents, which received much publicity but accounted for only about 16 percent of mining fatalities.[5] In contrast, there was a rise in the rates for small-scale accidents—roof falls (about 50 percent of all underground deaths), haulage accidents (18 percent), misuse of small explosives (4 percent), and electrocutions (4 percent).[6]

Pat Crorkin of O'Fallon, Illinois summarized the variety of ways men were killed in his song "All for Coal."

Tho' tall and young and "strong as a mule,"
  A simple coal miner am I;
When I think of the years that have gone
  I lay down my fiddle and sigh.
From the ranks of the true-hearted mates I have known
  Death's taken a mighty big toll
As, down in the mine, sweat-grimed they did dig
  For coal, coal, coal.

Take my pal, Jimmie Donnelly, a blithe Irish lad.
  (An explosion had just taken place),
His mates, overcome by the deadly gas fumes,
  To rescue brave Jimmie did face!
His own life poor Jimmie could easily have saved,
  But greater than life was his soul;
Brave Jimmie! dear pal! never more will he dig
  For coal, coal, coal!

I think of the mightiest man I have known,
  He was Irish, was "Mathy" Gazan;
A shot had misfired; after waiting some time,
  He went back with his fuse and his can.
Poor Mathy, no doubt, had just reached "the face"
  When the spark to the old charge did roll.
He was blown to bits! His remains were picked up
  In the coal, coal, coal.

I sadly remember the fate of "wee Tim,"
  A boy just two days in the mine.
A race of coal cars caught his mother-made blouse;
  He was dragged 'twixt the coal and the line.
His frail little body was squeezed and was rolled
  For yards 'tween the cars and the coal;
Oh, such is the price oft a coal miner's wife
  Pays for coal, coal, coal!

I think of another poor dead mate of mine,
  Bill Wilson, who worked out in Troy;
To clean a rock-fall in a room he did go
  In the Donk mine in old Illinois.
A deadly big piece just hung overhead,
  The risk he did take, poor brave soul,
But down came the rock! he was buried and smashed
  In the coal, coal, coal!

In Scotland was the fire at the Mauricewood pit,
  Oh, sad was that terrible day!
Four hundred and more were entombed down below,
  And the flames we on top could not stay.
The mine, after burning for three days, was flooded,
  In the village was mournful dole;
Four hundred men perished, on their buckets were scrawled
  Their farewells to dear ones—and coal!

Oh, now, my dear friends, please don't think too hardly
  Of those who toil down in the ground;
'Midst hundreds of men, thro' the years I have worked
  A rich miner I never have found!
Facing death without fear, thro' year after year
  And still forty years from their goal,
Brave, gray-headed fathers have still got to dig
  For coal, coal, coal![7]

The vast majority of deaths occurred one at a time, receiving attention mostly from family and friends before joining the long roll of fatalities in state mining reports. The typical accident occurred in the miner's room when the roof fell or explosives misfired. Operators paid the miners piece rates and gave them a great deal of independence. The miner therefore explicitly saw the trade-off between income and safety while he made nearly all of the accident prevention decisions within his own workplace. He decided how often to timber the roof to prevent roof falls, and how large a blast to use in dislodging the coal.

John Brophy aptly describes the nature of these decisions for miners pulling pillars in his autobiography:

> The miner says, "The damn roof is getting heavy," and he keeps one eye cocked for the signs that show he has gotten all the coal he is going to get out of that workplace. As the roof gets heavier, it "softens" the pillar, making the coal easier to cut out. This is another sign to watch but it also tempts the miner to wait until the last minute and take advantage of the opportunity to get out a good run of coal.
>
> After a while the timbers begin to splinter and you can hear the roof "working." This means that the strata of slate in the roof are beginning to break. It makes a sound like thunder, which can go on for as long as two or three days. An experienced miner can tell from the way the roof is "working" and from the splintering of the timbers just about when the roof is ready to fall. Then he gets his mine car and himself out of there, fast. It is a matter of pride to get as much coal out as possible, but nobody gets any credit for foolhardiness.
>
> The roof breaks through with a tremendous roar. The miner then returns to his work, secure in the knowledge that the fall has reduced the weight on the coal he is digging. He might work for weeks before another fall of the roof occurs.
>
> An experienced miner would often work calmly on under conditions that would terrify a novice. This was not because he liked taking chances, but because he had to work steadily, with as little lost time as possible, to get out a good day's production. He had to develop something like a sixth sense that would tell him when the chances were going against him, and never miss that warning, or his career in mining would be a short one.[8]

Early in the period the miner constructed his own explosives with powder and squib—a wax-like fuse—inside the mine. Accidents occurred when a miner overloaded the explosives or "walked back on the shot." The miner generally lit the squib and quickly crawled around the nearest corner, hoping to avoid a spray of coal in the behind. Sometimes there was no explosion. Most miners then quit for the day. Others, after a seemingly interminable wait, walked back to check on the explosives just as the fuse began to work. Improvements in fuses and standardized explosives helped eliminate some of these problems.

Outside the rooms the loaders and miners had much less control over their accident environment. Miners and loaders were at times killed by runaway cars, when clothes were caught in cars, or when they fell off the "mantrip," the car transporting miners through the mine. Faulty car brakes or tracks caused some accidents, while speeding by drivers or motormen led to others. In the early days of mine electrification, electric wires that provided power to the cars and for lighting were left naked in some mines. Miners sitting in a mantrip sometimes accidentally brushed these wires and were killed.

The most publicized accidents were mine fires and gas and dust explosions. For example, the Monongah, West Virginia, disaster of 1908 killed 362 miners, and twin explosions killed 117 at the Lick Branch mine in Switchback, West Virginia. Even the most careful miners were killed in the disasters because of an "externality" problem. The miscalculations of a single individual in the mine sometimes caused accidents that killed large numbers of people, regardless of their skill. A fire boss may have missed the presence of flammable gases in the mine, an individual miner may have set off too large an explosive and caused a chain reaction with the coal dust in the air, or mine management may not have "dusted" the mine with fine rock to keep coal dust down and minimize the spread of mine fires.

The division of safety tasks between miners and operators typically assigned responsibilities to the lower-cost preventer. While the miner was the primary preventer of accidents in his own room, the operator was primarily responsible for providing safety-related "public goods" and services for which there were economies of scale.[9] This led management to take responsibility for ventilation, mine gas inspections, watering of coal dust to prevent the spread of mine fires and explosions, and provision of precut timbers to use as roof props.[10] In several ways the operators' and miners' safety responsibilities overlapped. State laws and many mines' safety rules assigned the mine foreman the role of safety supervisor. On visits to a workplace, the foreman often examined the mine roof and could force the workman to make his workplace safe before he resumed mining. Yet the foreman visited at most once a day, leaving the miner alone to make nearly all the decisions about safety in his workplace. The operator also provided the large capital equipment, such as track and motors for haulage and cutting machines. Both the operator's choice of safety features on such equipment and the worker's care in handling it determined the probability of equipment-related accidents.

Early in the period much of the blame for accidents was placed on the miners' work habits and safety attitudes.[11] More recently, a historical backlash has sought to assign operators most of the blame. Unfortunately, both miners and operators at times ignored or relaxed safety precautions. State mine inspectors regularly complained that miners inadequately timbered their workplaces, rode illegally on mine cars, brought too much powder into the mine, overcharged their shots, and ignored many of the rules for "shooting off the solid," blasting the coal without making an undercut at the base of the wall. Ignorance of proper techniques was an often-cited cause, especially in areas where there were many new immigrants, who lacked mining experience and often the ability to speak English.[12] Miners also cut corners when they thought that the precautions unnecessarily hindered their earning power. Government mine officials also blamed coal operators, who failed at times to provide enough mine timbers, or meet state requirements with respect to ventilation, training in proper mining techniques, and supervision of miners.[13]

Wages and Accident Rates

Why would someone undertake such dangerous tasks? Dangerous work paid better. Miners received higher hourly wages than in other industries in part because they did more dangerous jobs. Within the coal industry, workers in the more dangerous jobs inside the mines received wages up to 14 percent higher than similarly skilled workers outside the mines.[14] The regression analysis summarized in Table 6-8 of Chapter 6 shows that miners received higher wages when they received less compensation for injuries under the negligence liability system. Since neither workers' compensation nor negligence lawsuits paid miners the full value of lost working time, miners still sought higher wages in areas with higher accident rates. Although the accident rate coefficient was positive in Table 6-8, we could not reject the hypothesis that there was no direct relationship between wages and accident rates across states. One reason wages did not appear to adjust may be that cross-state differences in coal mining fatality rates were not large enough to be obvious to the miners. Thus workers sought and obtained higher wages for obvious differences in accident rates between coal mining and other industries. But miners were less successful at getting wages fine-tuned to less obvious differences across states in coal mining accident rates.

Another reason the results in Table 6-8 might not show a relationship between safety and earnings is that it is a reduced-form equation that fails to fully illuminate several offsetting relationships between wages and accident rates. Accident rates were higher at mines where the natural conditions of the mine were more dangerous or the employer offered inadequate safeguards. Accident rates increased when more accident-prone (typically less-experienced) workers were hired. And higher accident rates may have reflected decisions by workers or employers to work with less regard for safety when wages changed.

Each cause of higher accident rates influenced different aspects of the wage-accident relationship. If a mine was more dangerous, either naturally or because the employer skimped on safeguards, miners would adjust their supply of labor to the mine, requiring higher wages before agreeing to work there. Thus, in labor-supply relationships, wages and accident rates were likely to be positively correlated.

If the cause of higher accident rates was more accident-prone workers, the employers' demand for labor was likely to be reduced, implying a negative relationship between the wage and accident rates in labor demand. The wage-accident relationship in labor demand might also be negative if the higher accident rate reflected more unsafe geological conditions, as coal operators sought to combine more labor with natural resources of higher quality.[15]

Changes in wage rates caused by factors beyond the control of miners and coal employers also affected accident prevention by employers and workers. An increase in the wage rate had offsetting effects on accident prevention by employers. The wage increase might have caused employers to cut costs by spending less on safety. However, higher wages also gave employers more incentive to prevent accidents because higher wages raised the compensation employers paid to each injured worker and the risk premium they paid in wages.[16]

The miners' response to exogenous wage changes depended on how well they could adjust their incomes across time periods. Some writers argue that miners had such low incomes and so few opportunities to save or borrow that they were forced to maximize income in each year to survive. When wage rates were cut, accident rates rose as miners "gambled" their lives more to maintain their meager standard of living.[17] However, the earnings evidence in Chapter 6 suggest that the miners' incomes were generally above the subsistence level. Miners actually saved during upturns and dissaved, sometimes accumulating debts, during downturns. Thus they were able to shift income over a longer time horizon. If miners maximized their "permanent" (long-term) income, they faced some incentive to increase safety efforts when wages fell. Since they were paid piece rates, the opportunity cost of time spent preventing accidents was the earnings lost from producing less coal. When piece rates fell, miners gave up less in earnings when they devoted more time to safety, leading them to increase accident prevention at the expense of earnings. This implication is derived from a formal model describing the actions of a risk-neutral miner who maximizes permanent income. Generally, miners were risk-averse and the effect of a wage cut was ambiguous. A miner's aversion to risk reduced his willingness to accept higher risk despite the fall in the opportunity cost of accident prevention.[18]

To examine each of these relationships between wages and accident rates, I estimated a system of simultaneous equations—an accident prevention equation, a labor-demand equation, and a labor-supply equation—using evidence from the twenty-three major coal mining states for the years 1912–1914, 1917, 1919–1923. Table 7-3 lists the estimated relationships between wages and accident rates from those equations.[19] The estimates marked by an asterisk are ones where statistical tests reject the hypothesis that there was no relationship.[20]

Only the labor-supply relationship where miners required higher wages to work at more dangerous mines consistently passes statistical significance tests. Holding union membership, hours worked, and strike activity constant in the equation for small-scale underground accidents, coal workers were willing to accept an added risk of one death for every 10 million man-hours for a wage increase of 1.5 cents (in 1967 dollars) per hour. This wage premium offers an implicit estimate of the value miners attached to their lives. If the miner was risk-neutral, the wage premium of 1.5 cents is equal to the additional expected loss from a small-scale fatal accident (the change in probability of a fatal accident (1/10,000,000) multiplied by the value

TABLE 7-3. Relationships Between Fatal Accident Rates per 10 Million Man-hours, Wage Rates, and Union Membership From Structural Equations[a]

	Type of Accident Rate		
	Total	*Small-Scale*	*Roof Falls*
From Labor-Supply Equation with Wage as Dependent Variable			
Accident Rate Coefficient	0.006*	0.015*	0.02*
(t-statistic)	(1.69)	(3.50)	(2.28)
Union Coefficient	0.40*	0.44*	0.43*
(t-statistic)	(4.92)	(5.37)	(4.86)
Strike Coefficient	0.14*	0.11	0.11
(t-statistic)	(1.70)	(1.38)	(1.25)
From Labor-Demand Equation with Wage as Dependent Variable			
Accident Rate Coefficient	0.0002	−0.004	−0.01*
(t-statistic)	(0.09)	(−0.97)	(−1.89)
From Accident Prevention Equation with Accident Rate as Dependent Variable			
Wage Coefficient	44.67	−3.98	−21.76
	(0.55)	(−0.21)	−(1.07)
Union Coefficient	10.13	−0.14	−4.59
	(0.37)	(−0.02)	(−0.79)

Source: See Table C-1 in Appendix C.

[a]Estimated with pooled annual data for twenty-three coal mining states for the years 1912–1914, 1917, 1919–1923; N = 198. See Table C-1 in Appendix C for the full description of the model, all other coefficients, and sources.

*Estimate is statistically different from zero at the 90 percent level in a two-tailed t-test.

the miner attaches to his life). The value of life implied by the accident rate coefficient in the small-scale–fatality rate equation is $150,000, by the coefficient in the total fatality rate equation $60,000, and by the coefficient in the roof-fall equation $200,000 (all in 1967 dollars).[21] The estimates are similar to the range of $140,000 to $260,000 estimated by Thaler and Rosen with labor market evidence from the late 1960s.[22] The lowest estimate of $60,000 is approximately equal to the discounted present value of lifetime earnings of a coal miner in the 1920s. Miners in 1920 earned roughly $2000 in 1967 dollars each year. Assuming a real interest rate of 2 percent and a working life of fifty years, the present value of that stream of earnings is $62,847 in 1967 dollars.[23]

To the extent that the fluctuations in accident rates reflected differences in accident proneness or inexperience, the labor demand results suggest that employers paid less for more accident-prone workers. However, we cannot reject the hypothesis in most of the estimates that higher accident rates had no effect on labor demand.

The gambling hypothesis is tested in the relationship between wages and accident rates in the accident rate equation. We cannot reject the hypothesis that accident rates were not affected by changes in the wage rate. The results seem inconsistent with the gambling hypothesis in that lower wages were not associated with higher accident rates. However, the test does not fully refute the gambling hypothesis. Mixed in with the workers' responses to higher wages are the responses of employers, which economic theory predicts would be indeterminant. Further, the analysis could not hold the mining experience (and accident proneness) of the work force constant. When wages were cut, less experienced miners were less likely to enter mining, causing accident rates to fall. Therefore our estimate of the relationship in the accident rate equation was biased against the gambling hypothesis.

Unions and Safety

Chapter 3 shows that miners and operators made their safety decisions in settings characterized by disparate degrees of union strength. The UMWA could have enhanced the miners' economic welfare with respect to accidents in two ways. One was to raise the wage rate paid, holding accident rates constant. The regression results in Table 6-8 of Chapter 6 show that the unions met that challenge. The union coefficient in the reduced-form wage equation shows that a shift in the work force from fully nonunion to fully union, would have caused hourly earnings to rise between 8 and 15 cents per hour (in 1967 dollars), or roughly 6.3 and 10.1 percent (based on the mean). Collective action by miners was also effective. Had all workers in the state gone on strike for ten days, the hourly wage would have risen by 0.8 to 1.6 percent.

The union coefficient in the reduced-form wage equation in Chapter 6 mixes labor-demand and labor-supply effects. The union coefficient from the labor-supply equation in Table 7-3 shows that the union had a much stronger effect on wages within the labor-supply equation than it did on the overall wage. Figure 7-1 shows the relationships between the union effect on wages from the labor supply equation and the union effect estimated in Table 6-8 of Chapter 6. Full unionization shifted the labor supply curve such that wages would have risen 40 to 44 cents per hour (see Table 7-3) had the union been able to force the employers to continue to hire the same number of workers (H_N). However, the higher wage demands of the union pushed employers back along their labor-demand curve, causing them to hire fewer workers for fewer hours (H_U). Therefore, the overall impact of the union on the wage was the 8-to-15-cent rise found in Table 6-8 in Chapter 6.

The second way unions might have enhanced the miners' welfare was to lower accident rates directly. Unions potentially offered the miners an effective voice for negotiating improvements in safety, particularly for safety public goods, like ventilation or keeping coal dust down to prevent the spread of explosions.[24] Public goods like ventilation benefitted all miners, but there were free rider problems if miners negotiated individually. Each individual miner received only a small part of the overall benefits of ventilation and the benefits would have come to him if someone else successfully negotiated for ventilation. Thus each miner faced incentives to let other miners negotiate for ventilation while he focused on negotiating for his own wage and workplace. The union might have negotiated better for ventilation because it represented all miners and could get the miners to pay union dues to cover the costs of negotiating for ventilation.

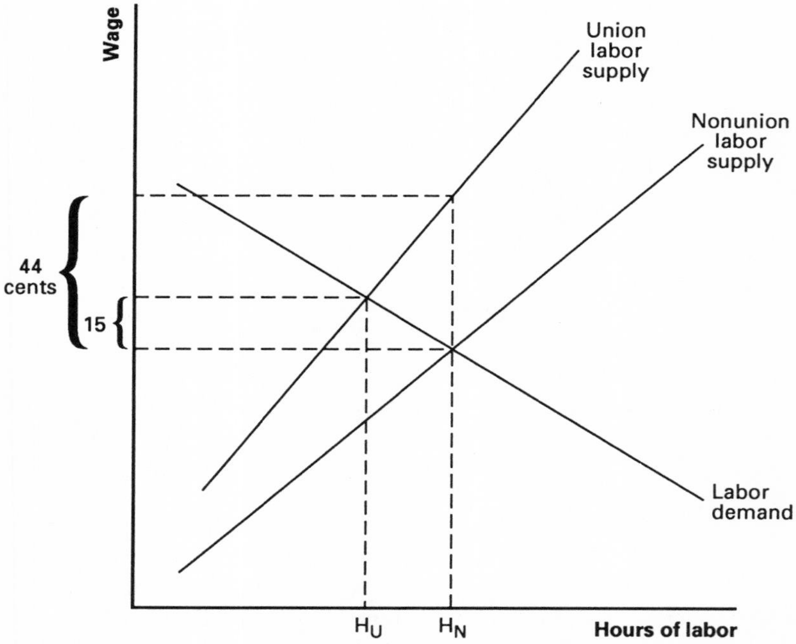

FIGURE 7-1. Union Effects on Wages Through Shifts in Labor Supply.

In fact, the UMWA did not have much effect on accident rates. The statistical tests for a relationship between UMWA membership and fatal accident rates shown in Table 7-3 cannot reject the hypothesis that the UMWA had no impact on accident rates.[25] Graebner suggests that mine safety was a secondary goal of the UMWA.[26] Most of its energies were devoted to organizing drives in nonunion states, where expansions in coal production threatened the strength of the union. The UMWA seemed ambivalent toward mine safety legislation. It sought certification of miners to reduce the number of inexperienced workmen, but this may have been an attempt to obtain more control over the labor supply. In fact, results later in the chapter show that accident rates were no lower and possibly higher in the states where state boards certified miners. Union pit committees might have promoted safety by providing a grievance mechanism that protected workers from dismissal when they complained of unsafe conditions. Graebner notes, however, that few of the grievances adjudicated by pit committees were related to safety. Miners were less likely to use the grievance mechanism to protest unsafe conditions than to seek reinstatement of a miner fired for violating safety provisions in the contract.[27]

Government Regulation of Safety

The major federal agency for mine safety, the U.S. Bureau of Mines, was established in 1910. Graebner describes the overall impact of the Bureau on mine safety as disappointing, primarily because the Bureau shifted its main focus away from coal mining safety and toward promotion of western metal mines within three years of its beginning. The Bureau had no coercive power, so it became an informational agency. It conducted experiments to discover better safety techniques, focusing in its early years on the elimination of large-scale explosions. Probably more importantly, the Bureau consistently publicized better mine safety techniques. In 1912 the Bureau distributed nearly 352,000 *Miner's Circulars* to coal workers, as well as another 150,000 technical papers.[28] The Bureau also tested cutting machines, safety lamps, explosives, and other mining equipment to provide information on whether they met the Bureau's noncompulsory safety standards.

The states were the primary regulators of mine safety. Nearly all of the coal mining states had passed some form of coal mining regulation by 1900, but the regulations were incomplete and often vaguely worded. According to Graebner, the best safety statutes in 1900 were found in Pennsylvania and Ilinois, while West Virginia's laws ranked among the worst.[29] Between 1905 and 1915, most states revised and updated their mining codes in response to public outcry over a series of major mine explosions, killing 1700 miners from 1907 to 1909. Table 7-4 shows the variation across states in coverage of several technical mining regulations between 1901 and 1930. Most states eventually expanded the codes to require state licensing of foremen, although only three directly licensed miners. Nearly every state code established means of enforcing the law: budgets for state mine inspectors, fines, guidelines for closing mines for violations, and minimum requirements for inspectors to prevent pure patronage appointments. Most laws required between one and six mine inspections per year, but the actual number of inspections per mine rarely met the required minimum.[30] Small inspection budgets meant low pay for an already inadequate number of inspectors.

When the mine inspector discovered violations, his enforcement options often were limited. In most states for most offenses, a court order was required before the inspector could close the mine. Some inspectors complained that they got little support from the courts and in some cases direct opposition.[31] State inspectors faced additional incentives to turn a blind eye to violations. Most were poorly paid with few chances for advancement within the bureaucratic hierarchy. Many had left mine management jobs and did not wish to jeopardize a return to such jobs.[32] Aside from individual incentives, Graebner argues that the department's zeal for enforcing costly safety regulations was often dampened by the substantial coal price competition among mines across state lines.[33] Imposing costly safety improvements with uncertain effects on safety could put a state's mines at a disadvantage when competing with mines in states without such requirements. Mine operators, directly and through the state legislature, pressured the inspectors not to put their mines at a cost disadvantage.

The problems with enforcing the law led Graebner and Lewis-Beck and Alford to believe that state safety regulations were a Progressive Era disappointment.[34] Quantitative analysis of the question suggests that in most cases they were correct, although some specific laws enhanced safety.[35] Table 7-5 shows the coefficient estimates from weighted least squares regressions of underground accident rates on safety laws and other determinants of accident rates.[36] The regressions are run over

TABLE 7-4a. State Mine Safety Laws in Place in 1901 or Date Law Passed After 1901

State	*DUST*	*FIREBOSS*	*TIMBER*	*ELECTRIC*	*NORIDE*	*SAFEXPL*	*WORCOMP*
Alabama	1911	1901	1901	1911	1911	—	1919
Arkansas	—	—	1901	—	—	—	—
Colorado	1901	1901	1901	1913	1913	—	1915
Illinois	1901	—	1901	1911	1911	—	1911
Indiana	1905	1901	1901	1923	—	—	1915
Iowa	1911	—	1902	—	—	—	1913
Kansas	1901	1901	1901	—	—	—	1911
Kentucky	1914	1901	1908	—	—	—	1916
Maryland	1922	1922	1901	1922	1902	1922	1910[c]
Michigan	—	1901–12	1901	1913	—	—	1912
Missouri	—	1901	1901	—	—	—	1926
Montana	1911	1901	1911	—	1911	—	1915[d]
N. Mexico	1901–11	1901	1912	—	1915	—	1917
Ohio	1906	1905	1910	1910	1910	—	1911
Oklahoma	1901	1901	1908	1908	1929	—	1915
Pennsylvania	1901	1901	1901	1901	1901	1911	1915
Tennessee	1903	1903[a]	1903	—	1903[b]	—	1919
Texas	—	—	1907	1911	—	—	1913
Utah	1901	1901	1901	—	—	—	1917
Virginia	1912	1912	1912	1924	1912	—	1918
Washington	1917	1917	1901	1917	1917	—	1911
W. Virginia	1901	1901	1901	1915	1915	—	1913
Wyoming	1910	1901	1901	1919	—	—	1915

Source: See Appendix B. Reprinted from Price V. Fishback, "Workplace Safety During the Progressive Era: Fatal Accidents in Bituminous Coal Mining, 1912–1923," *Explorations in Economic History* 23 (1986): 284–85 with the permission of Academic Press, Inc. Copyright © 1986 by Academic Press, Inc. All rights of reproduction in any form reserved.

Notes: 1901 means law was passed in 1901 or earlier. If only one date is listed the law was in effect through 1930 or beyond. If two dates are listed, the first date is the date of passage and the second date is the year the law was retracted.

[a]Law dropped temporarily in 1906.

[b]Law dropped temporarily in 1910.

[c]Law passed in 1902 but declared unconstitutional soon after.

[d]Law also in effect from January through October of 1910.

DUST	Must sprinkle or rock dust the mine to keep coal dust down.
FIREBOSS	Fire boss must examine mine for gas daily in gaseous mines.
TIMBER	Mine management must provide adequate timbers to prop roof.
ELECTRIC	Underground electric wires must be insulated.
NORIDE	Miners cannot ride on coal cars underground.
SAFEXPL	Permissible explosives, stringently defined, must be used.
WORCOMP	Workmen's compensation law.

a sample of the twenty-three largest coal mining states from 1903 to 1930; thirty-four observations in the sample were lost to missing values. See Appendix C for a fuller discussion of the equation.

Table 7-5 shows results for three types of accident rates. All the rates exclude surface accidents and workers because most of the dangers were underground; inclusion of surface accidents and workers in the accident rates changes the results very little. The total accident rate includes large-scale accidents abetted by the

TABLE 7-4b. State Mine Safety Laws in Place in 1901 or Date Law Passed After 1901

State	*INSTEST*	*CLOSE*	*POLICE*	*FORELIC*	*SBLICMIN*	*FLICMIN*	*FVISIT*
Alabama	1911	1911	—	1911	—	—	—
Arkansas	1919	—	1917	1919	—	—	—
Colorado	1901	1913	—	1913	—	—	1913–30: 1.0
Illinois	1901	1901	—	1901	1908	1901–07	1911–30: 0.1
Indiana	1901–22	1901	1907	1901	1911	—	1901–30: 0.5
Iowa	1901	1901	—	1901	—	—	1911–30: 1.0
Kansas	—	1901	—	1917	—	—	—
Kentucky	1908	—	—	1908	—	—	1914–30: 0.3
Maryland	—	—	—	1922	—	—	1922–30: 1.0
Michigan	—	1901	1913	—	—	—	1901–30: 0.3
Missouri	1903–28	1915	—	1900–28	1901	—	—
Montana	1901	—	—	1901	—	—	1911–30: 0.1
N. Mexico	1912	—	—	—	—	—	—
Ohio	—	—	—	1927	—	1908	1910–30: 0.5
Oklahoma	1913	1908	1900–28	1908	—	—	1908–30: 1.0
Pennsylvania	1901	1911	—	1901	—	—	1911–30: 1.0
Tennessee	1903	—	—	1903	—	—	—
Texas	1907	—	—	—	—	—	—
Utah	1901	—	—	1901	—	—	—
Virginia	—	—	—	—	—	—	1912–18: 0.5 1919–30: 1.0
Washington	1901	1912	—	1917	—	—	1912–30: 1.0
W. Virginia	—	1907	—	1915	—	—	1915–30: 1.0
Wyoming	1911	1910	—	1901	—	—	1901–24: 0.5 1925–30: 1.0

Source: See Table 7-4a.

INSTEST	State inspectors must pass a qualifying exam.
CLOSE	Inspector can close mine immediately for some violations, most often for poor ventilation.
POLICE	Inspector has power to make arrests for safety violations.
FORELIC	Mine foremen must be licensed by a state board.
SBLICMIN	All miners must be licensed by state board.
FLICMIN	Foreman must ensure that all workers have training.
FVISIT	Minimum number of visits foreman must make to workplace each day.

absence of such precautions as dusting the mine, inspecting for gas, and other measures that affect the mine as a whole. Since large-scale accidents were relatively uncommon but killed large numbers, the variance of the total accident rate is relatively large. The small-scale accident rate (which eliminates accidents killing more than four people) therefore is more useful for examining attempts by miners and operators to prevent small-scale accidents, which account for 84 percent of mining fatalities, and 99% of all accidents. The small-scale accident rate also eliminates worries about externality effects in large explosions where a mistake by one miner negated the efforts of all other miners to prevent them. The roof fall fatal accident rate allows examination of accident prevention by miners alone. The miner had the most control of roof fall prevention because 80 to 90 percent of all roof falls occurred in the miner's room, where he made nearly all the safety decisions.[37]

Most of the mine safety laws were disappointments, particularly the licensing

TABLE 7-5. Coefficient Estimates of Reduced-form Accident Rate Equation Weighted Least Squares Estimates from Pooled Annual Data for Twenty-three Coal Mining States from 1903 to 1930

		Underground Deaths per Million Man-hours Worked Underground		
	Mean (Std. Dev.)	*Total*	*Small-scale Accidents*	*Roof Fall Accidents*
Constant		2.40* (2.80)	2.07* (8.52)	1.17* (6.69)
Coal Price (1967$)	5.26 (1.38)[a]	−0.02 (0.28)	0.019 (1.07)	−0.02* (1.68)
Percent of Coal Produced by Cutting Machines	38.9 (29.4)	0.0004 (0.07)	0.003* (1.51)	0.001 (1.08)
Average Number of Days Mines Were Open	204.8 (40.7)	−0.002 (1.03)	−0.002* (3.70)	−0.001* (3.82)
Men on Strike/Men Employed	0.195 (0.26)	−0.351* (1.73)	0.025 (0.40)	0.054 (1.14)
Technical Laws				
Management must dust the mine	0.66 (0.48)	−0.379 (1.50)		
Fire boss must inspect mine daily	0.73 (0.44)	0.194 (0.38)		
Management must provide timbers	0.93 (0.26)	0.81 (2.38)	−0.132 (1.28)	−0.010 (0.14)
Insulated electric wires required	0.36 (0.48)	0.41 (1.28)	−0.121 (1.25)	
Miners must not ride on coal cars	0.39 (0.49)	−1.38* (3.91)	−0.185* (1.71)	
Must use permissible explosives	0.04 (0.21)	−0.12 (0.34)	−0.230* (2.23)	
Minimum number of visits to workplaces by foreman	0.32 (0.40)	0.059 (0.15)	−0.043 (0.37)	−0.215* (3.41)
Laws Determining Power and Competence of Inspectors				
Safety inspectors must pass test	0.64 (0.48)	0.20 (0.62)	−0.07 (0.74)	—
Inspector can close mine immediately	0.50 (0.25)	−0.28 (1.13)	0.015 (0.20)	—
Inspector can arrest for violations	0.12 (0.33)	−0.51 (1.02)	−0.097 (0.63)	—
Licensing Laws				
Foreman licensed by state board	0.62 (0.48)	0.24 (0.77)	0.357* (3.94)	0.164* (1.97)
All miners licensed by state board	0.11 (0.32)	0.90* (1.88)	0.231 (1.61)	0.052 (0.58)
Foreman must ensure miners are trained	0.08 (0.27)	0.34 (0.82)	0.346* (2.90)	0.164* (1.97)
Safety Inspection Budget per 1000 Tons of Coal (1967$)	2.60 (1.55)	0.009 (0.11)	−0.069* (2.77)	−0.057* (3.15)
Bureau of Mines	0.73 (0.44)	−0.13 (0.70)	−0.02 (0.34)	−0.038 (0.99)

(continued)

TABLE 7-5. *(Continued)*

	Mean (Std. Dev.)	*Underground Deaths per Million Man-hours Worked Underground* — *Total*	*Small-scale Accidents*	*Roof Fall Accidents*
Liability Laws				
Employer defenses limited by statute	0.34 (0.47)	0.454* (1.82)	0.256* (3.32)	0.218* (4.03)
Workers' compensation	0.53 (0.50	0.648* (2.56)	0.303* (3.88)	0.227* (4.01)
F-statistic		67.81	495.6	318.44
N	610	610	610	610
Means of Dependent Variable		2.28 (2.13)	1.85 (0.84)	1.00 (0.52)

Source: Data sources of variables are found in Appendix B.

[a]Absolute Value of t-statistics in parentheses. Dummy variable are included for all states except Alabama to capture geographical differences in the natural conditions of the mines. Sources of variables are described in Appendix C.

*Coefficient rejects the null hypothesis that the coefficient is zero in a two-tailed t-test at the 90 percent level.

laws. If the laws reduced accident rates, the coefficients in the table would be negative and the t-tests in parentheses would reject the hypothesis that the coefficients were zero. In each of the equations, the coefficients of the licensing laws—state licenses of foremen, licensing of miners by state boards, and requirements that foremen train miners—are positive. This does not necessarily imply that the licensing laws raised total accident rates and roof fall accident rates because the t-tests do not reject the hypothesis that there was no effect. Most of the remaining laws also lack much impact. Although some coefficients are negative, we generally cannot reject the hypothesis for most laws that their coefficients were zero.

There were some exceptions to this rule. States that passed laws preventing miners from riding on coal cars saw declines in both the overall accident rate and the small-scale underground accident rate. The coefficient of −0.213 in the equation for the small-scale accident rate implies that the law saved an extra life for every 2934 men who worked an average work year of 200 eight-hour days. Required use of permissible explosives served to lower small-scale accident rates a little more, saving an extra life for every 2551 men who worked an average work year. The U.S. Bureau of Mines claimed that closer supervision would reduce problems with roof falls.[38] Their claim is supported here by the negative and statistically significant coefficient on the law requiring a minimum number of daily visits to each workplace by the foreman. The coefficient of −0.219 implies that for an additional required daily visit by the foreman, an extra life was saved from a roof fall death for every 2854 men working an average work year.

There are two possible reasons why most of the laws had little or no impact on accident rates. First, many of these laws may have just codified practices followed by most mines already. Many mines, whether regulated or not, had daily inspections by fire bosses, provided mine timbers, and insulated electric wires. The laws preventing riding of coal cars and requiring use of permissible explosives probably had impact because they changed behavior in a major way. Second, the laws may not have been enforced very effectively.[39] The average state mining department spent $2.60 (in 1967 dollars) on mine inspections for every thousand tons of coal produced. The coefficients and t-tests in Table 7-5 imply that increased expenditures on inspections would have lowered small-scale and roof fall accident rates. Doubling the average mine inspection budget to $5.20 per thousand tons of coal would have lowered the small-scale accident rate per million man hours by 0.177, saving an extra life for every 3535 men working an average work year.

The state mining inspectors were more successful than the Occupational Safety and Health Administration (OSHA) is today. Numerous economic investigations of OSHA show that it has negligible impact on workplace safety,[40] partly because OSHA's enforcement resources, measured as real appropriations per worker covered, are even lower than those for the old state mining departments. Appropriations for the OSHA compliance budget in 1975 were roughly $0.54 per non-agricultural employee in the United States, adjusted for inflation in terms of 1967 dollars. In West Virginia in 1916 total appropriations for mine safety—inspectors' salaries plus travel, clerks' salaries, and equipment—were almost four times higher at $2.1 (in 1967 dollars) per coal worker.

The U.S. Bureau of Mines also had no statistically significant impact on mine safety. Lewis-Beck and Alford find that federal government intervention first lowered coal mining accident rates after 1941 when U.S. Bureau of Mines inspectors were allowed to inspect mines, although without coercive power. Accident rates were nearly halved from their 1930s level when appropriations for coal mine inspections and investigations by the Bureau reached approximately $7.85 (in 1967 dollars) per mine worker in 1949. Accident rates then fluctuated around a constant trend for two decades, despite additional increases in appropriations, rising to $65 (in 1967 dollars) per mine worker in 1969. The plateau ended with the passage of the stringent Coal Mine Health and Safety Act of 1969. The added costs of halving accident rates again were substantially higher than they were in the 1940s. The level of appropriations required rose to $173 (in 1967 dollars) per miner in 1972 before stabilizing at $137 (in 1967 dollars) per mine worker by 1975.[41] The resource costs to society were even greater, as coal mining productivity holding accident rates constant fell significantly.[42]

Changes in Liability Laws

The legal system also determined mine safety by assigning the liability for accidents. In the late 1800s, before workers' compensation, liability for workplace accidents was based on common law standards of negligence. If a worker was injured on the job, the employer was not expected to pay the injured worker's costs from the accident unless the employer had failed to exercise "due care." *Due care* under the law meant that the employer followed several practices: First, he offered and enforced reasonable safety rules, and posted warnings of dangers. Second, he hired enough qualified workers to handle the job. Even if the employer erred and hired an unqualified worker who caused an accident, the employer was not liable for that accident unless he knew the worker was unqualified.

Third, due care meant that the employer provided the tools customarily used by prudent people on the job. In a coal mine, for example, the employer provided adequate numbers of props to support the roof. The tools provided by the employer did not have to incorporate the latest safety advances unless they were in widespread use. Thus, when a new chainguard for a coal cutting machine was invented, the employer who did not provide it could still be exercising due care, as long as the chainguard was used in only a few mines. The employer also was not liable for accidents caused by the worker using a tool in uncustomary ways. So mine employers were not required to compensate miners injured while riding a mine car designed only to haul coal, particularly if the employer posted rules against it. In essence, under negligence liability the employer had only certain basic responsibilities in the workplace. He was not required to compensate an injured worker unless he failed to meet those responsibilities.[43]

The employer also was not required to compensate injured workers if he could successfully argue any of three legal defenses: assumption of risk by the worker, contributory negligence, and the fellow servant doctrine. Under the assumption of risk defense, the worker had to show that his or her accident was not caused by factors ordinary for that type of work or extraordinary but known and accepted. The common law presumed that he willingly accepted the risks when he accepted the job. Thus, employers were not required to compensate many of the miners killed in roof falls because such risks were known and accepted when miners took the job. Under the contributory negligence defense, the worker could not collect if he might have avoided the accident by exercising due care himself. The employer was probably not going to be liable for injuries to a motorman who slammed into a wall because he was driving too fast to make a turn. Finally, under the fellow servant doctrine, an injured worker was not compensated if the accident had been caused by the actions of another worker, unless the worker was an agent of the employer. A miner was not likely to be compensated by his employer when he was injured by a roof fall caused by his partner's failure to prop the roof correctly.

Clearly, injured workers had to overcome major obstacles to receive compensation for their injuries. Lawrence Friedman suggests that the courts favored entrepreneurs over workers in trying to stimulate economic growth.[44] Posner argues that the common law was not designed merely to favor the capitalists, but also aided in the prevention of accidents.[45] In his view, negligence liability with the three defenses was a means of reducing the sum of two costs: the costs of preventing accidents and the expected costs of the accident.[46]

Posner argues that negligence liability required that employers pay the costs of accidents in cases where their costs of prevention were lower than the expected cost of the accident. This gave employers incentives to prevent these accidents. Workers had incentives to prevent the remaining accidents because they would not be compensated if injured. But, there were some accidents that workers could prevent at lower cost than employers could, even though the employers' costs of prevention were lower than the expected cost of the accident. The doctrine of contributory negligence encouraged workers to prevent accidents in that category by ruling out compensation from the employer when their costs of preventing the accident were less than the expected harm from the accident. The fellow servant doctrine increased accident prevention by giving workers added incentive to report careless fellow workers who might cause them harm. The doctrine of assumption of risk allowed workers to choose jobs where they expected to be paid enough to offset the potential for injury.[47]

Employer liability legislation in many coal states modified and clarified the common law defenses in the late 1800s and early 1900s. Alabama, Colorado, Indiana, Missouri, Montana, and Wyoming passed general laws voiding contracts prior to injury that released the employer from liability for damages arising out of his negligence. Several states passed general laws altering the common law defenses. Alabama (1884–85), Colorado (1893 and 1901), Indiana (1893), Ohio (1902), Pennsylvania (1907) and Utah (1898) altered the fellow servant defense. Statutes in Ohio (1904) and Iowa (1907) affected the defense of assumption of risk. Laws altering the fellow servant defense only in mines were passed in Arkansas, Maryland, and Missouri. In addition, statutes in Arkansas, Colorado, Illinois, Indiana, Maryland, Missouri, New Mexico, Ohio, Pennsylvania, Utah, and Wyoming gave miners rights to court action for injury occasioned by the willful violation of or failure to comply with mine safety statutes.[48]

The largest changes in liability for workplace accidents came when workers' compensation laws were enacted. Early attempts to establish workers' compensation for miners in Maryland in 1902 and Montana in 1909 were declared unconstitutional within two years. Maryland passed another compensation statute in 1910 for two coal mining counties. Thereafter, with the support of many businesses and unions, most states passed laws covering most workmen.[49] Every coal mining state except Arkansas had enacted a law by 1930.

Under workers' compensation law employer negligence was no longer the criterion for compensation. Workers covered by workers' compensation were barred from pursuing negligence claims against their employers. Instead, the employer was obligated to pay employees or their heirs a set amount determined by the government for any accident "arising out of or in the course of employment."[50] The government limits on compensation typically meant that the worker received medical treatment for his injuries but was paid for lost working time at a rate two-thirds or less of his normal daily pay.[51]

Compensation and Accident Prevention

Miners partly insured against risk by demanding the wage premiums described in the section on wages and accident rates. Under both sets of liability rules miners also bought direct insurance by contributing to relief funds sponsored by workers and/or employers. Prior to 1910, miners and employers supplemented the negligence system with workers' insurance and benefit funds.[52] A noncomprehensive report by the Department of Labor in 1908 shows that at least 80,000 of the 680,000 anthracite and bituminous coal miners were members of relief funds established at local mines or groups of mines.[53] Most contributions to the funds came from employees, although only 10 percent of the funds were administered by employees alone. The typical establishment fund paid temporarily disabled miners roughly one-third of their daily wage for up to twenty-six weeks. Death benefits ranged from

$40 to $620 with an average of $277, 57 percent of annual earnings.[54] Although the United Mine Workers had no national relief fund in 1908, the Labor Department reported on sixty-two local union funds at mines employing 12,000 workers.[55] The average death benefit in these funds was only $70, and only 18 local union funds paid temporary disability benefits. The Labor Department also identified miscellaneous funds, like the Carnegie Fund, which paid death benefits of up to $1200, and more than 130 mining funds that paid hospital benefits in West Virginia.[56] Miners continued to join relief funds after the switch to workers' compensation. In Ohio 69 percent of families of coal mining fatalities received payment from a relief fund in 1916, five years after Ohio enacted a workers' compensation law.[57]

The change from negligence liability to workers' compensation led to two major changes in the extent of compensation of accident victims: the percentage of accident victims compensated rose and the amount that each compensated victim received rose. Prior to workers' compensation, employer negligence was the basis for compensation. Thus not all accident victims were compensated. Under the modified negligence system in Pennsylvania in 1915, fifty-eight of a sample of 137 families of fatal accident victims received settlements for damages on the average of $636, roughly 108 percent of a miner's average annual earnings.[58] The remaining seventy-nine families received no settlement during the period studied, although eighteen had hired lawyers and filed suit.[59] In contrast, under workers' compensation, employers were expected to compensate workers for all accidents "arising out of employment."[60] After Pennsylvania enacted workers' compensation, the average payments to heirs of fatal accident victims jumped to $2383 in 1916 and $2659 in 1918—about two to three times the miners' average annual income.

In Virginia, under common law negligence rules, the records of the Stonega Coke and Coal Company show forty-four fatal accidents and 210 serious nonfatal accidents from 1916 to 1918. Table 7-6 shows the distribution of damage payments made to the victims or their heirs from reports by Stonega's legal council.[61] At least 102 of the 210 victims of serious nonfatal accidents and thirty of the forty-four families of fatal accident victims received some compensation. The company typically settled quickly in accidents where it was potentially liable: roof falls where the company failed to provide an adequate number of timbers, roof falls where an inexperienced miner was working alone, roof falls in haulage ways where the company was responsible for propping the roof, equipment accidents where fault was hard to determine, and accidents caused by defective machinery. In general, the company would not settle when an experienced miner was injured in his own room, or it was a clear case where the miner did not follow the safety rules of the mine.[62] The average payment to families of fatal accident victims (excluding families that received no compensation) was under $560; the median was $250. When workers' compensation was introduced in Virginia, all victims received payments and the minimum payment jumped to $1500 with a maximum of $3000.[63] Similar jumps also occurred when workers' compensation was established in other states.[64]

The switch to workers' compensation also led to changes in the institutional features of accident compensation. Under negligence liability, the costs of using the legal system were high. Delays of two to five years between the date of the accident and a decision were common,[65] and the complexity of determining negligence led to

TABLE 7-6. Distribution of Settlement Payments to Accident Victims at Mines of the Stonega Coke and Coal Company, 1916–1918

	Fatal Accidents			*Nonfatal Accidents*		
	Lawyer's Assessment[a]			*Lawyer's Assessment*		
Amount	*No Comment*	*Potentially Liable*	*Not Liable*	*No Comment*	*Potentially Liable*	*Not Liable*
$3700		1				
2500		1				
2300					1	
2000		1				
1750				1		
1500					1	2
1300					1	
1200		1				
1000						
900–999		1		2	1	
800–899						1
700–799					2	2
600–699				1	1	
500–599		1			1	
400–499		1		1	1	
300–399		1	1		2	1
200–299	3	2	7		6	8
100–199		1	5	1	15	5
50–99				5	6	6
25–49				3	13	6
1–24				2	1	3
No Payment			1	4		46
Totals	3[b]	11	14	20	52	80

Source: Compiled from reports of the Legal Department covering thirty-four fatal accidents and up to 154 serious nonfatal accidents in the Annual Operating Reports of the Stonega Coke and Coal Company for the years 1916 to 1922. Boxes 210–212 in Records of the Stonega Coke and Coal Company at the Hagley Museum and Library, Wilmington, Delaware. Reprinted with the permission of the University of Chicago Press from Price V. Fishback, "Liability Rules and Accident Prevention in the Workplace: Empirical Evidence from the Early Twentieth Century," *Journal of Legal Studies* 16 (June 1987): 312 © 1987 by the University of Chicago. All rights reserved.

Notes: There were twelve additional nonfatal accidents listed in the reports that were reported as having caused slight injuries.

[a]The lawyer's assessment refers to the lawyer's opinion on whether Stonega was liable for negligence or not. Examples of accidents where the Stonega lawyers felt the company might be liable include roof falls where an inexperienced miner was working alone, roof falls in haulage ways where the company was responsible for propping the roof, equipment accidents where it was hard to determine who was at fault, and in cases where machinery was defective.

[b]In two more cases settlements were paid, but the payment was not reported.

great uncertainty about the final decisions.[66] The delays and uncertainty were avoided by settling nearly all of the negligence cases out of court, generally within six months of the accident. In a study of fatal accident cases for all workers in Minnesota in 1910, 88 percent were settled without the courts.[67] Only two of the Stonega miners who received compensation in Table 7-6 obtained the compensation from court decisions.[68]

Both sides used the threat of court delays to their advantage. There were numerous cases where employers were able to negotiate lower settlements with an injured miner who could not afford to wait several years for compensation. On the other side, employers compensated some injured miners even when the employer was not negligent. To avoid uncertain court decisions for serious injuries, Stonega's liability insurance company paid damages in 13 of 14 fatality cases and 34 of 80 nonfatal cases listed in Table 7-6 where Stonega's lawyers felt the company was not liable or the suit could be successfully defended. As Croyle found in Minnesota, accident victims used the threat of court cases to raise the gross settlement. The average award in the nonfatal cases listed in Table 7-6 was $355 higher when suit was filed against Stonega, $201 higher in fatal cases.

After the switch to workers' compensation, the new methods of administering compensation were much faster than use of the court system had been. But it is not clear that they were much faster than settling negligence suits out of court. Delays between the accident date and the first payment of damages were similar under workers' compensation and under negligence liability with settlements. Under Pennsylvania's modified negligence system in 1915, around 67 percent of the victims compensated were paid within three months of the injury.[69] The workers' compensation state insurance fund in Ohio compensated 72 percent of the cases within three months of injury.

Differences in the administrative structures of workers' compensation systems led to variations in the costs to workers and employers of working through the system. In states with exclusive state insurance funds, like Ohio, Washington, and West Virginia, the processing of claims was almost perfunctory. Administrative costs per worker were lower than in states with competitive state funds or insurance by private stock companies. State funds were more liberal with compensation and challenged fewer claims before industrial commissions.[70] This liberality lowered total legal fees for workmen in Ohio, where relatively few hired lawyers when going before the industrial commission.[71]

In Virginia, Colorado, Michigan, Pennsylvania, and Indiana, where private insurance was allowed, the injured miner and the company determined compensation through voluntary agreements. The state's industrial commission reviewed the agreements and used hearings to settle disputes. The process seems very similar to the de facto procedures under the negligence system where most claims were settled out of court. Stonega's lawyers considered each hearing to require "almost as much legal work done as would have been necessary if there had been a trial at law before a court."[72] Presumably the costs per settlement were similar under the two systems, but total administrative costs under workers' compensation were probably higher. There were more settlements to negotiate, and more disputed cases resulted in hearings under workers' compensation than in court under negligence liability. The Stonega Coke and Coal Company, which self-insured in Virginia, was involved in approximately 90 hearings of contested cases before the industrial commission between 1924 and 1926. Under the negligence system, Stonega's Annual Reports for 1916 to 1919 mention only 50 lawsuits of which 31 were settled out of court.[73]

Some observers predicted that accident rates would fall when workers' compensation was introduced. They expected that the increase in payments to injured workers would force employers to prevent more accidents. If they were right, the coefficients on the employer liability and workers' compensation law variables in Table 7-5 would be negative and statistically significant. In fact, the coefficients of both variables are positive and statistically significant for all three types of accident rates. Passage of the employer liability laws was associated with an increase of 0.454 accidents per million man-hours, or roughly a 20 percent increase relative to the mean accident rate. When the workers' compensation laws were passed later, accident rates rose 0.648 accidents per million man-hours. This 28 percent rise in accident rates when workers' compensation was introduced meant that an additional man died for every 965 men working an average work year of 200 eight-hour days.[74]

The rise in accident rates is in some ways a perplexing phenomenon. Coal employers faced plenty of incentives to enhance safety because the payments to injured miners were rising. Both state compensation funds and private insurance companies either inspected the mines or looked at their accident records and rewarded safer mines with lower premiums.[75] Employers responded by adopting safety measures, like first aid teams and more safety training, that led to lower insurance premiums. The emphasis on safety certainly increased in the operating reports of the Stonega Coke and Coal Company after the Virginia workers' compensation law was passed.[76]

Yet the rise in accident rates under workers' compensation shows that the employers' increased efforts were either cosmetic or insufficient to resolve a major accident problem. The rise in accident compensation created a "moral hazard" problem for accidents in each miner's workplace. Since loaders and pick miners were paid by the ton of coal, they saw that by working a little faster and taking more risks they could get higher earnings. All too often, a roof fall injured or sometimes killed a miner who tried to finish loading the car before he set new props for the roof. Under negligence liability, the miner had extra incentive to work more slowly and safely because if he was injured in a roof fall, he was likely to get little or no compensation. Under workers' compensation he could take more risks to increase his earnings because he was assured of injury compensation that was often higher than what he would have received under negligence liability.[77]

The resulting increase in risk taking led to more accidents like roof falls. The problem was that roof falls in the miner's workplace were the types of accidents that employers could not prevent at low cost. Effective prevention required constant attention to changing natural conditions; therefore the miner could prevent accidents in his room at much lower cost than the employer could. For the employer to be as effective at preventing roof falls as the miner, the employer had to hire large numbers of supervisors to check the rooms constantly. The costs of hiring supervisors to prevent the extra accidents caused by moral hazard appeared to be higher than the expected damage payments. Rather than take these costly steps, the employers chose instead to pay the extra damages.

The move to workers' compensation did not raise accident rates in every industry. Chelius found that the fatality rates for machinery accidents in industry fell with the introduction of workers' compensation.[78] It appears that the efforts of manufacturing employers to reduce accident rates more than offset moral hazard problems. The difference between the results for small-scale accidents in coal mining and in manufacturing probably can be traced to the difference in the cost to the employers of preventing accidents. Supervisors could monitor the workers' use of machinery more easily in manufacturing than in coal mining. Instead of tramping long distances through a mine to visit sixty men in a day, the manufacturing foreman could probably meet with sixty men in two hours and still had the option, unavailable in a mine, of standing on catwalks above the factory floor and observing overall activity. Further, companies discovered that they could eliminate many machinery accidents by putting more footguards and handguards near whirring blades and gears. In contrast, many of the accidents in the miner's room in a coal mine were a result of natural conditions that the employer could not fix at low cost.

Whether workers' compensation met its goal depends on how the goal is defined. If the goal was to enhance the welfare of workers, it succeeded. More workers were compensated for injuries and on average they received a larger amount in compensation. The gain was offset slightly because workers' compensation laws were associated with reductions in hourly earnings (see Chapter 6). Even though accident rates rose in coal mining, the rise appears to have been the result of the miners' own free choices, given more accident compensation. However, if the goal of workers' compensation legislation was to reduce accident rates, it failed in coal mining but may have succeeded in manufacturing.

Summary

While coal miners faced numerous dangers in the mine, they did receive some compensation for accepting those risks. Wages were higher in coal mining than in other industries and higher for jobs inside than for jobs outside the mines. Miners were sensitive to the risks and adjusted their labor supply to require higher wages before working at more dangerous mines. The United Mine Workers succeeded in improving the employment package for workers by raising wages holding the accident rate constant. However, the states where the UMWA was strong were not associated with lower accident rates.

Progressive Era safety legislation in many areas was a disappointment although some specific laws may have enhanced safety. The U.S. Bureau of Mines offered large amounts of information about improving mine safety, but the information seemed to have little impact on accident rates. The federal government generally had little impact on coal mining accident rates until the federal agency began inspecting mines in the 1940s with a budget roughly four times the level per worker of the budgets of state mining departments. State laws to license miners and foremen failed to reduce accident rates. In fact, the only specific laws that lowered accident rates were rules against riding coal cars and requiring the use of permissible explosives. Increases in the required number of visits by foremen to the workplace also lowered the roof fall accident rate. Most of the remaining laws either codified existing practices or were not enforced. Giving more resources to state mining departments for inspections, however, would have lowered accident rates such that doubling the typical budget would have reduced fatal accident rates by roughly 10 percent.

Incentives for accident prevention were also established by the liability rules for compensation of accidents. Prior to 1910, liability in most states was established by common law rules of negligence. The rules imposed most of the costs of accidents on the miners. Thus the employer often was not required to compensate miners for accidents in their rooms, although the employer typically paid compensation for accidents where he was the least-cost preventer. With the passage of workers' compensation legislation, miners were compensated for all serious injuries and received on average more compensation than they did under negligence liability. Miners benefitted because they now received much more compensation for their injuries. The extra compensation provided more of a safety net that allowed them to raise earnings by working with less regard to safety. Unfortunately, this meant higher accident rates because employers faced high costs of trying to prevent the extra accidents that resulted. The employers thus chose to pay the compensation instead of the extra costs of preventing the accidents.

NOTES

Some material in this chapter is reprinted with the permission of Academic Press, Inc. from Price V. Fishback, "Workplace Safety during the Progressive Era: Fatal Accidents in Bituminous Coal Mining, 1912–1923," *Explorations in Economic History* 23 (1986): 269–98. Some material on changes in liability rules is reprinted with the permission of the University of Chicago Press from Price V. Fishback, "Liability Rules and Accident Prevention in the Workplace: Empirical Evidence from the Early Twentieth Century," *Journal of Legal Studies* 16 (June 1987): 312. The quote from John Brophy, *A Miner's Life: An Autobiography* © 1964 (Madison: The University of Wisconsin Press) is used by permission of the publisher.

1. The workers' compensation premiums in West Virginia suggest that a few narrowly defined occupations were more dangerous: making explosives, constructing large edifices, working on logging railroads, fire, and police work. West Virginia, *Report of the State Compensation Commissioner*, 1925, pp. 35–37.

2. Michael Lewis-Beck and John Alford, "Can Government Regulate Safety?: The Coal Mine Example," *The American Political Science Review* 74 (1980): 749.

3. U.S. Bureau of Mines (1932), *Bulletin* No. 355, "Coal-Mine Accidents in the United States, 1930," by W. W. Adams, L.E. Geyer, and L. Chenoweth (Washington, DC: U.S. Government Printing Office, 1930), p. 5.

4. For a more extended discussion of black lung, see Curtis Seltzer, *Fire in the Hole: Miners and Managers in the American Coal Industry* (Lexington: University of Kentucky Press, 1985), pp. 93–104.

5. William Graebner, *Coal-Mining Safety in the Progressive Period* (Lexington: University of Kentucky Press, 1976), p. 6; Keith Dix, *Work Relations in the Coal Industry: The Hand-Loading Era, 1880–1930*, West Virginia University Bulletin, Series 78, No. 7-2, 1978, p. 72.

6. Dix, *Work Relations*, p. 72.

7. *United Mine Workers Journal*, September 15, 1923, printed in George Korson, *Coal Dust on the Fiddle* (Philadelphia: University of Pennsylvania Press, 1943), pp. 244–45.

8. John Brophy, *A Miner's Life* (Madison: University of Wisconsin Press, 1964), pp. 40–41. Brophy was president of District 2 of the UMWA in Pennsylvania in 1917 and in the 1920s was a leader of the opposition to John L. Lewis.

9. In economics a public good is a good that many people can use simultaneously without preventing other people from using it. For example, keeping coal dust down in the mine is a public good because all miners benefit from eliminating a means for explosions to spread, and it is hard to exclude miners from the benefits. Public goods typically lead to free-rider problems where some people get the benefits without paying their share of the costs.

10. Hugh Archbald, *The Four Hour Day in Coal* (New York: Wilson, 1922); Carter Goodrich, *The Miner's Freedom* (Boston, MA: Marshall Jones, 1925).

11. Dix, *Work Relations*, pp. 73–85.

12. Doris Drury, *The Accident Records in Coal Mines of the United States* (Bloomington: Indiana University Department of Economics, 1964), p. 125, citing the number of accidents among miners with experience, suggests that greater experience did not effectively reduce accident rates. However, Price V. Fishback ("Discrimination on Nonwage Margins: Safety in the West Virginia Coal Industry, 1906–1925," *Economic Inquiry* 23 [October 1985]) shows that miners with greater experience had lower accident rates. Further, as immigrants gained experience relative to their native counterparts, their accident rates declined to similar levels.

13. See Colorado Inspector of Mines, *15th Biennial Report*, 1911–1912, p. 6; Kentucky, *Report of Inspectors of Mines*, 1920; U.S. Bureau of Mines, *Bulletin* No. 115, "Coal-Mine Fatalities in the United States, 1870–1914," by Albert Fay (Washington, DC: U.S. Government Printing Office, 1916), p. 4; and Graebner, *Coal-Mining Safety*, pp. 3, 95.

14. See Chapter 4.

15. Wage rates might also rise in labor-demand equations when accident rates rise if coal workers were risk lovers and thus willing to accept more risks. See Richard Thaler and Sherwin Rosen, "The Value of Saving a Life: Evidence from the Labor Market," in N. E. Terlecky (Ed.) *Household Production and Consumption*, Studies in Income and Wealth Volume 40, National Bureau of Economic Research (New York: Columbia University Press, 1975), pp. 281–82.

16. Compensation and risk premiums will rise with increases in wage rates in situations where injury compensation and risk premiums are specific percentages of the wage. See Appendix D for a mathematical discussion of how accident prevention might change when economic variables change.

17. Graebner, *Coal-Mining Safety*, pp. 10, 112; Curtis Seltzer, *Fire in the Hole: Miners and Managers in the American Coal Industry* (Lexington: University of Kentucky Press, 1985), p. 10. Graebner presents this case, but it is not clear whether he accepts it. The discussion of gambling miners, although not fully developed in an economic model, seems similar to Wright and Kunreuther's description of "gambler" farmers in the post-bellum South. Gavin Wright and Howard Kunreuther, "Cotton, Corn, and Risk in the 19th Century," *Journal of Economic History* 35 (1975): 526–51.

18. See Appendix D. The following example illustrates definitions of risk-neutral and risk-averse. A risk-neutral person would be indifferent between two choices: $100 with certainty or a situation where there was a 50 percent chance of receiving $150 and a 50 percent chance of receiving $50. Given the same choice, a risk-averse person would choose the $100 with certainty. A risk-loving person would choose the gamble.

19. Appendix C contains a full description of the system.

20. One caveat in examining the relationships: The discussion suggests that in each equation the wage is related to a specific aspect of the accident rate—accident-proneness of workers, dangers in the mine, decisions by workers and employers. When we estimate the relationships, we are forced to use a single accident rate that is influenced by all three aspects at once. Thus, in any of the equations there is some measurement error in estimating the relationship between wages and that specific aspect of accident rate.

21. The $150,000 figure was calculated in the following way. In the text the wage premium of 1.5 cents is equal to the value of life (V) multiplied by the added probability of a

fatal accident (1/10,000,000). Dividing both sides by 1/10,000,000 implies that the value the miner placed on the life was

$$V = 1.5 \text{ cents} \times 10{,}000{,}000 = \$150{,}000.$$

For the other two estimates replace the 1.5 cents with 0.6 cents and 2 cents, respectively.

22. See Thaler and Rosen, "The Value of Saving a Life," pp. 265–98 for estimates of value of a human life. For other estimates, see W. Kip Viscusi, *Employment Hazards: An Investigation of Market Performance* (Cambridge, MA: Harvard University Press, 1979) and Viscusi, "Wealth Effects and Earnings Premiums for Job Hazards, *Review of Economic Statistics* 60 (1978): 408–16.

23. The estimate of the miners' evaluation of their lives may be understated. Modern evidence shows that omitting the level of workers' compensation benefits biases the measure of risk premiums downward in nonunion situations and has mixed effects in union situations. Stuart Dorsey and Norman Walzer, "Worker's Compensation, Job Hazards, and Wages," *Industrial and Labor Relations Review* 36 (July 1983): 642–54.

24. Richard B. Freeman and James L. Medoff, *What Do Unions Do?* (New York: Basic Books, Inc., 1984), pp. 8–9.

25. The lack of a statistically significant effect is present in both reduced-form and structural tests of the relationship between union membership and accident rates. For more information on union effects, see Appendix C. 26. Graebner, *Coal-Mining Safety*, pp. 3, 28, 127, and 130–35.

27. Ibid., pp. 132–33.

28. Ibid., p. 59.

29. Ibid., p. 72.

30. Between 1909 and 1928, Colorado mines were typically inspected only 3.2 times per year; the statutory minimum was four times a year. Colorado, *Report of the State Mine Inspector*, for the years 1909 through 1928. Between 1909 and 1912, Ohio inspectors averaged 2.7 inspections per mine; more dangerous mines were supposed to be inspected 4 times a year: Ohio, *Annual Report of the Chief Inspector of Mines*, for the years 1909 to 1912. Kentucky's chief of inspectors complained in 1914 that it was impossible to inspect each mine the required three times. By 1920 and 1921, he faced a situation where some inspectors' seats were vacant for six to eight months. Kentucky, *Report of Inspector of Mines*, for the years 1914–15, 1920, and 1921.

31. Pennsylvania, *Report of the Bureau of Mines*, 1906, p. xvii; and Graebner, *Coal-Mining Safety*, p. 97.

32. Graebner, *Coal-Mining Safety*, p. 90; Kentucky, *Report of Inspector of Mines*, 1912 and 1922.

33. Graebner, *Coal-Mining Safety*, p. 10.

34. Ibid., and Lewis-Beck and Alford, "Can Government Regulate Safety?".

35. The results reported here are somewhat different from those reported in Fishback, "Workplace Safety," pp. 289–93. The change results from expansion of the sample from nine to twenty-eight years (from 268 observations to 610 observations). A more detailed discussion of the differences is in Appendix C.

36. Weighted least squares was used to offset problems with heteroskedasticity. The weight was the square root of underground hours worked. The weights also have the advantage of giving more weight to states with more miners. The weighting procedure is similar to the procedure followed in Appendix C.

37. Dix, *Work Relations*, pp. 70–73.

38. U.S. Bureau of Mines (1930), *Technical Paper* No. 485, "Timbering Regulations in Certain Coal Mines of Pennsylvania, West Virginia, and Ohio," by J.W. Paul, J.G. Calverly,

and D.L. Sibray, (Washington, DC: U.S. Government Printing Office, 1930), p. 3; Drury, *Accident Records*, pp. 123–25.

39. Graebner, *Coal-Mining Safety*, and Lewis-Beck and Alford, "Can Government Regulate Safety," both argue that the laws were not well enforced.

40. Several studies suggest that OSHA has almost no effect on accident rates. For example, see Robert S. Smith, "Protecting Workers' Health and Safety," in Robert W. Poole (Ed.), *Instead of Regulation* (Lexington, MA: Lexington Books, 1982), pp. 311–38; Albert Nichols and Richard Zeckhauser, "Government Comes to the Workplace: An Assessment of OSHA," *The Public Interest* 49 (1977): 39–69; W. Kip Viscusi, "The Impact of Occupational Safety and Health Regulation," *The Bell Journal of Economics* 10 (1979): 117–40; David McCaffrey, "An Assessment of OSHA's Recent Effects on Injury Rates," *Journal of Human Resources* 18 (1983): 131–46; Ann Bartel and Lacy Thomas, "Direct and Indirect Effects of Regulation: A New Look at OSHA's Impact," *Journal of Law and Economics* 28 (1985): 1–25. OSHA inspects only one in fifty workplaces. Ostensibly OSHA has a sharp bite when it does inspect, although McCaffrey's work shows that its inspections may not lower accident rates in the workplaces inspected.

41. Sources for West Virginia calculations are in Appendix B. Fatal accident rates averaged about 1.5 per million man-hours in the 1930s, fell to 0.9 in 1948, levelled around 1.0 until 1969 and then fell to 0.4 in 1975 (Lewis-Beck and Alford, "Can Government Regulate Safety?" p. 749). Appropriations for OSHA's Compliance Budget and the budget for coal mine health and safety inspections are found in *Budget of the United States Government* for the fiscal years: 1977, pp. 465, 523; 1950, p. 581. Nonagricultural employment and the CPI are from *The Economic Report of the President*, 1982, pp. 266, 291. The number of miners is found in the National Coal Association's *Coal Facts*, 1978–79, p. 54.

42. Hal Sider, "Safety and Productivity in Underground Coal Mining," *Review of Economics and Statistics* 65 (May 1983): 225–33.

43. The liability system was similar for all workers. Lindley D. Clark, "The Legal Liability of Employers for Injuries to Their Employees in the United States," *U.S. Department of Labor Bulletin No. 74*, Vol. 16 (Washington, DC: U.S. Government Printing Office, 1908); Richard Epstein, "The Historical Origins and Economic Structure of Workers' Compensation Law," *Georgia Law Review* 16 (1982): 775; James R. Chelius, "Liability for Industrial Accidents: A Comparison of Negligence and Strict Liability," *Journal of Legal Studies* 5 (1976): 293.

44. Lawrence Friedman, *A History of American Law*, 2nd. ed. (New York: Simon and Schuster, 1985), pp. 467–73.

45. Richard Posner, "A Theory of Negligence," *Journal of Legal Studies* 1 (1972): 4, 74–76.

46. Expected costs are the costs of the accident multiplied by the probability that the accident will occur. We factor in the probability that the accident will occur so that we do not waste resources trying to prevent accidents that are not likely to happen even though they might cause horrendous damage.

47. Posner, "Theory of Negligence," pp. 44, 74–76.

48. Clark, "Legal Liability," pp. 94–120.

49. Roy Lubove, "Workmen's Compensation and the Prerogatives of Voluntarism," *Labor History* 8 (Fall 1967): 264–65; James Weinstein, "Big Business and the Origins of Workmen's Compensation," *Labor History* 8 (1967): 156.

50. In most states, workers' injuries that were intentionally self-inflicted or resulted from intoxication were excepted from compensation.

51. Since employees bore some of the accident costs, Chelius describes workers' compensation as shared strict liability (Chelius, "Legal Liability," p. 300). This form of strict

liability for workplace accidents differs somewhat from Epstein's descriptions of strict liability under the common law. See Richard Epstein, "A Theory of Strict Liability," *Journal of Legal Studies* 2 (1973): 151. The worker does not receive full compensation for his injury, and the coverage differs. For example, an employer who injured himself with his own tools might be covered under workers' compensation. But because the injury is self-inflicted, he would be unable to recover damages under common-law strict liability.

52. These benefit funds apparently supplemented negligence liability but did not replace it with shared strict liability. Representative by-laws and announcements of relief funds in West Virginia and Pennsylvania in 1908 and 1906 do not mention clauses requiring the employee prior to injury to trade away his rights to a negligence suit to become a member of the fund. See U.S. Immigration Commission, *Report on Immigrants in Industries: Bituminous Coal Mining, Volume 2*, Senate Document, 61st Cong., 2nd sess. (Washington, DC: U.S. Government Printing Office, 1911) pp. 206–07 and Pennsylvania Department of Mines, *Report Part II: Bituminous*, 1906, pp. 12–21. This does not necessarily imply that workers would not have traded their rights to negligence suits for compensation insurance prior to injury if allowed to do so. Although neither West Virginia nor Pennsylvania had statutes that voided such contracts, Clark ("Legal Liability," p. 15) cites a Pennsylvania Supreme Court decision that suggests that such contracts would be void. Contracts were allowed that stipulated a bar to action if the worker chose to accept the benefits of the fund.

53. At the mines studied another 28,000 workers chose not to join the funds, which were not compulsory.

54. Calculations are based on evidence from the U.S. Commissioner of Labor, "Workmen's Insurance and Benefit Funds in the United States," *Twenty-Third Annual Report* (Washington, DC: U.S. Government Printing Office, 1908) pp. 430–537 and from Paul Douglass, *Real Wages in the United States, 1890–1926* (Boston: Houghton Mifflin, 1966), pp. 143, 161, and 350.

55. This may include miners of other ores (except copper) because the funds were not specifically designated as coal mining funds. U.S. Commissioner of Labor, "Workmen's Insurance," pp. 223–66.

56. Ibid., pp. 623 and 637–39.

57. Table in Mary Conyngton, "Effect of Workmen's Compensation Laws in Diminishing the Necessity of Industrial Employment of Women and Children," *U.S. Bureau of Labor Statistics Bulletin No. 217* (Washington, DC: U.S. Government Printing Office, 1917), pp. 125–45.

58. The average annual wage is for all U.S. bituminous workers from Paul Douglas, *Real Wages*, p. 350. Even if all eighteen families who filed suit in the sample received substantial sums, the median payment did not exceed $1000, and the conclusion that most victims compensated received substantially less under negligence liability than under workers' compensation is unchanged. Conyngton, "Effect of Workmen's Compensation Laws," p. 102.

59. Approximately 80 percent of the families in the study were coal mining families, although some were anthracite miners. Conyngton, "Effect of Workmen's Compensation Laws," p. 102.

60. The move to workers' compensation probably altered the percentage of slight injuries compensated very little because most states required the miner to be disabled longer than a week before he was eligible for workers' compensation.

61. The Stonega Company employed 1400 men at seven mines in Virginia and Kentucky in 1917. Contemporary sources suggest that the Stonega mines were representative of the larger nonunion operations in West Virginia, Kentucky, and Virginia. See notes to Chapter 8.

62. Reports of the Legal Department in the Annual Operating Reports of the Stonega Coke and Coal Co. for the years 1916–1922, boxes 210–212 in Records of the Stonega Coke

and Coal Company, Westmoreland Collection at the Hagley Museum and Library, Wilmington, Delaware.

63. *Acts and Joint Resolutions of the General Assembly of the State of Virginia, Session which Commenced at the State Capital on Wednesday, January 9, 1918* (Richmond, 1918), p. 647.

64. Willard Fisher, "American Experience with Workmen's Compensation," *American Economic Review* 10 (1920): 26. Similar results occurred when Ohio shifted to workers' compensation. Under employer liability in 1911 the median settlement for fatal accidents was under $600, about one year's income for a miner, with one-fourth of the amount spent on legal fees. In 1916 the present value of workers' compensation payments ranged from roughly $1301 to $3200, 1.7 to 4.3 times the miner's annual income in 1916. Conyngton, "Effect of Workmen's Compensation Laws," pp. 71 and 125–45; Douglas, *Real Wages*, p. 350. There were similar ranges of workers' compensation in other states. Lindley Clark, "Workmen's Compensation Laws of the United States and Foreign Countries," *Bureau of Labor Statistics Bulletin No. 126* (Washington, DC: U.S. Government Printing Office, 1913), pp. 49–70.

65. E. H. Downey, *History of Work Accident Indemnity in Iowa* (Iowa City: State Historical Society of Iowa, 1912), p. 79; Annual Operating Reports of the Stonega Coke and Coal Company.

66. Some charge that judicial decisions were biased against workers, but Croyle found no antiworker bias in court decisions. James L. Croyle, "Industrial Accident Policy of the Early Twentieth Century," *Journal of Legal Studies* 7 (1978): 279.

67. Ibid., p. 295.

68. There were several cases where after a settlement was made with the parents of a minor a friendly suit was brought and disposed of quickly. Operating Reports of the Stonega Coke and Coal Company for the years 1916 to 1922.

69. The 67 percent figure in Pennsylvania assumes that half of the extra eighteen who filed suit eventually received compensation. Based on information in Conyngton, "The Effect of Workmen's Compensation," pp. 69 and 103.

70. Hookstadt's measure of administrative expenses summed the expenses of state funds, industrial commissions, and stock insurance companies. I then divided the expenses by the number of workers covered. Carl Hookstadt, "Comparison of Workmen's Compensation Insurance and Administration," in U.S. Department of Labor, *Bureau of Labor Statistics Bulletin Number 301*, (Washington, DC: U.S. Government Printing Office, 1922), pp. 4, 6 and 7.

71. Conyngton, "The Effect of Workmen's Compensation," pp. 70–71.

72. Stonega Coke and Coal Company Annual Operating Reports, Report of the Legal Division for 1921, p. 225.

73. The descriptions of the fifty suits suggest that the lawyers made *at most* sixty-four court presentations under the assumption that all thirty-one cases settled were finalized with a friendly suit (only ten were directly mentioned). Included in visits were five continuations, five dismissals of cases, and two cases where the plaintiff filed writs of error. The records show only twenty-one cases (including appeals) where the court decided for the plaintiff or the defendant. Stonega Coke and Coal Company Operating Reports, Report of the Legal Division for the years 1916 to 1926. The Virginia workers' compensation law went into effect in 1919. The years 1924 to 1926 were chosen for comparison to avoid inclusion of compensation hearings where Stonega sought to test the extent to which negligence liability still applied.

74. There are some slight differences between the results reported here and those reported in Price V. Fishback, "Liability Rules and Accident Prevention in the Workplace:

Empirical Evidence from the Early Twentieth Century," *Journal of Legal Studies* 16 (June 1987): 305–28. In the analysis in this chapter all the safety laws were included, and I combined all three types of workers' compensation systems into a single workers' compensation variable. Table 7-5 looks at underground accident rates, but a regression on total accident rates (including surface accidents and workers) offers very similar coefficient estimates and t-statistics. The workers' compensation variable can be divided into three systems: systems with no state fund, systems with a state fund that competes with private insurance, and systems where employers must insure in the state fund. The Liability Rules paper shows that the states where employers were required to insure in the state fund had the largest jump in accident rates.

75. The inspections followed schedule ratings which checked the mine against the "ideal" mine. Graebner, *Coal-Mining Safety*, pp. 149–51; Hookstadt, "Comparison of Workmen's Compensation Insurance and Administration," p. 53.

76. Graebner, *Coal-Mining Safety*, pp. 151–52. Operating Reports of the Stonega Coke and Coal Company, 1916 through 1925.

77. Since dead miners received no income, there might not be a moral hazard problem for fatal accidents. However, the moral hazard problem arose because miners did not expect each accident to result in death. Only 1 in 50 to 100 accidents were fatal. The regression analysis focused on fatal accidents as a random sample from the list of all accidents. Focusing on fatal accidents rather than severe accidents is useful because all fatal accidents were reported both before and after workers' compensation laws were passed. Increases in the number of severe accidents *reported* after the introduction of workers' compensation might have arisen even with no change in the actual number of accidents when miners *reported* a higher percentage of accidents. Workers might not have reported accidents under negligence liability when they saw no possibility of being compensated.

78. Chelius, "Liability for Industrial Accidents."

8

Did Coal Miners "Owe Their Souls to the Company Store"?

The company store is one of the most reviled and misunderstood of economic institutions. In song, folktale, and union rhetoric the company store was often cast as a villain, a collector of souls through perpetual debt peonage. Nicknames, like the "pluck me" and more obscene versions that cannot appear in a family newspaper, seem to point to exploitation. The attitudes carry over into the scholarly literature, which emphasizes that the company store was a monopoly.[1] David Corbin summarizes the common view of the company store in his study of southern West Virginia coal miners.

> If a coal miner survived a month of work in the mines, he was paid not in U.S. currency but in metals and paper (called coal scrip), which was printed by the coal company. Because only the company that printed the coal scrip honored it, or would redeem it, the coal miner had to purchase all his goods—his food, clothing, and tools—from the company store. Hence, the miner paid monopolistic prices for his goods. Journalists and U.S. senatorial investigating committees repeatedly revealed that the region's coal company store prices were substantially higher, sometimes three times higher, than the local trade stores. . . . To the miners, it meant, as they later sang, that they "owed their souls to the company store." For some miners, it meant being held in peonage.[2]

Corbin and others suggest that company stores had a local monopoly because the company only issued scrip or kept miners in debt. Economic theory and evidence from government reports and archival sources are used here to investigate these claims. The company store's monopoly power in nonunion districts was limited because store prices were part of an employment package offered to geographically mobile miners in a labor market with hundreds of mines. Alternative reasons for company ownership of stores exist, and those based on transactions-costs theories of the firm are offered. Claims of high store prices based on scattered evidence are compared with the conclusions of the U.S. Coal Commission in 1922 and the Immigration Commission in 1909. Finally, the use of scrip and the extent of the miners' indebtedness are examined with evidence from archival sources and government investigations.

The Limits on Store Monopoly

Those who view the company store as a monopolist argue that the store's monopoly power stemmed from the geographic isolation of the coal towns. They further assert that when independent stores began to compete nearby, the company store maintained its monopoly power by forcing miners to purchase goods by threats of dismissal, issuance of scrip, or debt peonage. The union, in this interpretation, is the only countervailing force to prevent the company from using its monopoly power. Yet, even had the company been able to maintain a local store monopoly in a nonunion area, there were limits on the prices it could charge. These limits were imposed by competition among the mines to attract laborers to their towns.

The store and its prices were only part of the employment package offered by the coal companies in a relatively competitive labor market.[3] In nonunion areas, like southern West Virginia in the early 1900s, hundreds of mines competed to attract miners, who moved quite often.[4] If the labor market had been perfectly competitive with homogeneous miners and zero transaction, transportation, and information costs, each miner would have received an employment package with value equal to the value of his marginal product. A mine charging higher store prices would have to compensate by paying higher wages or improving other aspects of the package. Variations in employment packages would arise in response to differences in the costs of providing parts of the package and the tastes of miners.[5] Isolated mines, for example, faced higher transport costs for store goods and would therefore be expected to charge higher store prices that were offset by higher wages. Miners' evaluations of parts of the package varied with respect to factors including age, ethnicity, and the size of their families. Miners with lower propensities to purchase goods, like immigrants saving to bring families from Europe, were more likely to select mines with higher wages and higher store prices.

To the extent that information and transportation costs were high or employers obtained labor market power, employers could potentially "exploit" miners by providing employment packages valued at less than their marginal product. Several hypotheses about changes in the value of employment packages follow from consideration of these possibilities. First, to the extent that moving to another mine was costly, differences in local store competition become more important in determining company store prices. We should expect lower store prices at mines where workers could buy from nearby independents. Second, we should expect less exploitation over time in the coal labor market as information and transport costs declined. As the demand for coal boomed, previously isolated areas became dotted with mines—in West Virginia the number of commercial mines rose from 35 in 1870 to 325 in 1900 to a peak of 1702 in 1923—and transportation costs fell with improved railroad connections and, later, the paving of highways.[6] Further, the miners' ability to assimilate information improved with increasing literacy and after 1907 the immigrants' improved knowledge of English.[7] Third, the value of employment packages would be expected to decline during coal downturns when labor markets loosened and increase during upturns when labor markets tightened. Declines in the value of the package during downturns do not necessarily imply increased exploitation because the value of the marginal product also declines with the price of coal. Fourth, miners who faced higher moving costs, illiterate miners or miners with families, were more likely to be exploited by higher store prices. Fifth, if there were higher costs of gathering information about store prices than about wages, the coal employer would have more ability to charge higher store prices, given the wage, than to pay lower wages, given store prices. When the operator raised store prices, the miner was less likely to move than if nominal wages had been lowered because it was more costly to compare store prices than wages.[8] Sixth, employment packages would have higher value in union than in nonunion mines, as successful collective action gives workers the market power to raise the value of the employment package.

Why Did Companies Own Stores?

Miners and operators agreed that during the mines' initial stages, company provision of stores and housing was close to a necessity.[9] Population density in the mining regions was generally very low, with few if any existing stores or homes. Opening a mine was a risky proposition; mines expanded, contracted, and closed with fluctuations in coal demand. But opening an independent store was even riskier because determining the future actions of the mine company was costly. Further, most early mining towns were small, probably below the size for it to be profitable to open an independent store. One would expect most of the independents to locate in areas with several mines, where the extent of the demand for their product was greater and uncertainty could be reduced by a more balanced portfolio of customers.[10] The location of stores in the Kanawha and New River districts in West Virginia confirms this logic. Nearly all independent stores were located on the major thoroughfares in the region, where they could be reached by workers from several mines.[11]

This explains why the companies established stores in the first place, but why did they continue to operate them? The Corbin quote in the introduction suggests that companies owned the store and issued scrip to obtain monopoly profits. Yet gains from store monopoly were limited to the extent that the mines hired in a competitive labor market. George Hilton offers two reasons for company ownership of stores in Great Britain. First, store prices could be adjusted to alter real wages when nominal wages are fixed by collective bargaining. This hypothesis is consistent with the continuation of company stores at mines with union contracts. But it does not explain the large number of company stores in nonunion areas where wages were more flexible.[12] Second, Hilton suggests that scrip was a sumptuary device used to ensure labor productivity through control of drinking. This could not be a dominant explanation. Some saloons provided credit; stores and scrip existed throughout Prohibition; and miners in Appalachia often made their own liquor, sometimes with the encouragement of the mine owners.[13] Some argue that company stores were part of a broader strategy to limit miners' collective power. Yet this may only partially explain company ownership of stores, because employers had more effective means of limiting collective power: firing union sympathizers or bringing in replacements for striking miners.

The literature on transactions and information costs provides alternative explanations for the persistence of company stores. Company ownership of stores lowered the information and enforcement costs of providing credit. Because the company paid the miners their wage, it had nearly complete income information and could deduct the credit provided directly from wages. Supplying credit to miners was much riskier for the independent store. The independent had far less information about the miner's earnings, especially for miners new to the area, and the options for forcing repayment were costly, requiring a law suit to garnish wages. Further, denial of continued credit when debts got too large during downturns often meant the loss of trade during upturns from that miner and his friends.[14] In isolated regions with relatively few banks, the issuance of scrip saved on costs of obtaining and holding currency. In particular, the company's interest income increased, and the costs of police protection of the payroll fell.

A final implication of the transactions cost literature is that companies ran stores to prevent opportunistic behavior by an independent. Running a store on company land through the store payroll gave the store operator locational and administrative advantages at that mine. These advantages were also specific to a single store because at many mines the population was probably not large enough to support more than one store profitably. Once established, an independent storeowner had incentives to exploit these advantages by charging higher prices than the company would like. The independent then earned monopoly profits at the expense of the coal company, as the coal company was forced by labor market competition to pay higher wages to workers to offset the high prices at the store. Company ownership of the store saved on the costs of negotiating and enforcing contracts that would prevent the store owner from exploiting the monopoly at the coal company's expense.[15]

Store Prices

Ideally, store prices should be discussed in the context of the entire employment package at the various mines. Unfortunately, such information for each mine is unavailable. One can, however, examine claims that company store prices were "substantially higher, sometimes three times higher than at the local trade stores." Because pricing practices varied across stores and across goods within stores, scattered evidence on a few prices at a few stores can be highly misleading when used to describe the price differentials faced by most miners. The evidence brought forth by the major Senate investigations of violent conflict in the mining regions is especially problematic.[16] Evidence was gathered only through testimony in hearings before the Senate subcommittee. Testimony was often emotional, the evidence provided was adversarial, and miners offered contradictory testimony.[17] Given the evidence presented, these investigating committees could hardly reach accurate conclusions about the norm for company store prices.

TABLE 8-1. Price Comparisons of Stores in Coal Areas with Stores in Manufacturing Areas of Nearby Cities, December 1922

Coal District[a]	*Nearby City*	*Price Differential Percentage*[c]	*District Type*
New River District, WV	Charleston, WV	11.8%	Nonunion[d]
Kanawha District, WV	Charleston, WV	4.9	Mixed
Alabama District	Birmingham, AL	0.0	Nonunion
Connellsville Region, PA[b]	Uniontown and Connellsville, PA	−0.5	Nonunion
Westmoreland District, PA	Greensburg, PA	5.4	Nonunion
Barnesboro Region, PA	Pittsburgh, PA	−5.0	Union
Belmont County, OH	Zanesville, OH & Wheeling, WV	−2.2	Union
Central & southern Illinois	Springfield, IL	−2.0	Union
Southern Ohio	Zanesville, OH & Wheeling, WV	−1.0	Union
Windbar District, PA	Pittsburgh, PA	−1.8	Nonunion

Source: Reprinted from Price V. Fishback, "Did Miners 'Owe Their Souls to the Company Store'? Theory and Evidence from the Early 1900s," *Journal of Economic History* 46 (December 1986): 1017 with the permission of Cambridge University Press and the Economic History Association. United States Coal Commission, *Report*, 68th Cong., 2nd Sess. (Washington, DC, 1925), p. 1457.

[a]Includes both company stores and independent stores in the mining regions.

[b]In Pennsylvania, company-owned stores were illegal, but stores in mining areas were often affiliated with the mines indirectly.

[c]The percentage represents the percentage by which the prices at coal district stores exceed the prices in stores in the manufacturing district in the nearby city listed.

[d]This district was traditionally nonunion but was unionized briefly from 1918 to 1921.

An effective investigation of store prices requires systematic collection of evidence, budget studies to determine weights for a price index, and widespread coverage of the mining fields. The investigation that best meets these requirements was performed by the U.S. Coal Commission in December 1922. By analyzing store purchases and interviewing miners' families, the Commission determined the average miner's consumption bundle. Prices of food items in the bundle were collected in December 1922 from coal company stores and independent stores in the mining and manufacturing districts in Table 8-1. The commission held other conditions of demand constant by comparing goods of the same quality and by comparing stores in areas where incomes and tastes of the workers were similar to those of miners. The results show that in six of the ten comparisons the stores in mining districts—including independent and company stores—charged less than stores in manufacturing districts. As expected, the price differentials were lowest in the four union districts, where workers had effectively obtained market power. The price differentials were also generally low in nonunion districts, less than 2 percent in three of the five comparisons of manufacturing and nonunion coal districts. The largest differential appears between store prices in the New River district and in Charleston, West Virginia.

The differentials in the two southern West Virginia districts, the Kanawha district near Charleston and the more isolated New River district, merit further discussion. With a weak union but a mobile work force, this area provides an excellent testing ground for the ability of labor market competition among mines to limit store prices. Since the union often asserted that West Virginia was the site of the worst abuses, price differentials there should establish an upper bound for price differences between company and independent stores in general.

The price differentials between the two districts and Charleston are consistent with the hypothesis that store prices and wages would be higher in more isolated districts. Up to half of the price differential between the New River district and Charleston is due to transportation costs.[18] Further, the 6.6 percent difference in prices between the New River and Kanawha districts was offset at least partially by differences in wages. Average earnings per day listed on the payroll in the New River district were about 2.8 percent higher than in the Kanawha district in 1921.[19]

The Coal Commission also compared company store prices with prices at nearby independent stores within the Alabama, New River, and Kanawha districts. Again, these comparisons hold the quality of goods, and incomes and tastes of consumers constant. In both West Virginia mining districts, the company stores charged 4.2 percent more for food; in Alabama they charged 7 percent more. These differences represent the maximum monopoly profit from the company stores' more convenient locations within mining towns. The actual monopoly profit may have been lower because the company provided more services by offering more credit through issuance of scrip. Further, transport costs to many company stores were probably higher than to most independents, which were located more often along major thoroughfares. By examining the range of prices, one can see how scattered evidence can be misleading. On many foods the highest price at company stores was double the lowest price at independent stores. On those same foods, however, the highest price at independent stores was double the lowest price at company stores.

Although the Coal Commission data for 1922 are the most comprehensive and scientifically collected evidence on store prices in the early 1900s, they may present a biased picture of the entire period. The two potential biases, however, produce opposite effects. Price differentials may have been lower than in earlier periods due to the long-term trend toward lesser isolation of mines; automobiles and paved roads had reached these regions by 1922. Alternatively, if company store prices were adjusted upward during downturns, the price differentials during the down year of 1922 may have been higher than normal.

Evidence from comprehensive but less quantitative field investigations by the Immigration Commission in 1908 and 1909 portrays conditions similar to those found by the Coal Commission. In its general conclusion the Immigration Commission stated that

> In isolated communities . . . it has been charged that the prices at the store were too high and that stock of an inferior quality was carried. In the majority of cases, however, the reverse is true, the employee being able to secure from the company store as good, if not better, articles for the same or a less price than would be charged by an independent store.[20]

In Alabama "a careful investigation of prices in several of these commissaries, as compared with market prices in workingmen's districts in Birmingham, reveals very slight differences."[21] In West Virginia

> Prices varied at different stores and in some isolated communities are excessive. In many locales there are independent stores in nearby towns and in stores so located they usually meet the prices of competitors. Many companies offer better quality at the same or lower prices. Stocks at company stores in many instances are larger, more varied, and of better quality.[22]

Investigators in Pennsylvania found that "many company stores handle first-class goods throughout and charge prices no higher than in the best-managed town and city stores," but at the other extreme were stores "marketing poor-quality merchandise and charging higher prices for the same brand as elsewhere."[23] In sum, the Immigration Commission's impressions suggest that at most company stores the prices were similar and sometimes even lower than those at nearby independent stores. Store prices were higher at more isolated mines. But the Immigration Commission pointed out that "in many of these isolated communities it costs more to get provisions laid down at the stores because of their inconvenient location, and this accounts, at least in part for the higher prices."[24]

Evidence collected from an earlier period also shows similar patterns. In 1885 the Illinois State Bureau of Labor Statistics enumerated "all the stores in the State, operated by mine owners or their representatives, for the use of their employees."[25] Since Illinois was a more settled region, 75 mines, or roughly one-fourth of the major mines in Illinois were equipped with stores. Of the 75 stores, 48 faced direct competition from independents, while 27 were without local competition. To illustrate the typical situation in the larger fields, the Bureau reported the statements of a miner "familiar with the facts" about 13 mines. During a period when travel was more costly, the role of local competition was important. At nine mines the companies clearly faced local competition, of which seven had the same or lower prices as the competition with two charging prices a little bit higher. At three mines with no local competition, the company store prices were somewhat higher to higher than at nearby towns. One mine appeared to meet the prices of a store 1.5 miles away, but charged higher prices than at a larger town 5 miles away.[26] The principle of compensating differences also seemed to be at work. After examining wages, powder fees, rents, seam sizes, and other components of the miners' earnings and expenses, the Bureau noted: "Wide as the differences in all these details seem, they in some cases offset each other so as to make the average condition in one place about as good as another."[27]

The range of store prices apparently widened as coal demand plunged during the Great Depression. Homer Lawrence Morris of the American Friends Service Committee presented price comparisons from an independent investigation in 1932. Two price lists comparing a company store to a nearby independent selected "at random" showed company store prices that were typically double those at nearby chain stores. At the other extreme, Consolidation Coal Company, which owned numerous mines in Kentucky and West Virginia, charged prices similar to those the Salvation Army paid in purchasing large lots from independent storekeepers.[28] With numerous operations failing and others working sporadically at a loss, the companies may have tried to use the store to offset their losses. But owning the store was not

TABLE 8-2. Food Price Indices and Wage Rates at the Stonega Coke and Coal Mines, 1918–1932 (Price Indices 1922 = 100)

Year	*U.S. Food CPI*	*Stonega Food CPI*	*Stonega Hourly Wage Machine Miners*	*Stonega Piece Rate Wage Loaders*
1918	1.12	1.33	55 cents	90 cents
1919	1.25	1.55	59	94
1920	1.41	1.24	77	122
1921	1.07	1.02	78	126
1922	1.00	1.00	71	108
1923	1.03	1.04	95	150
1924	1.02	1.10	65	101
1925	1.11	1.37	55	85
1926	1.14	1.17	62	89
1927	1.10	1.13	55	85
1928	1.09	1.08	55	85
1929	1.11	1.15	55	85
1930	1.05	0.86	55	85
1931	0.86	0.75	55	85
1932	0.72	0.66	51	.

Sources: U.S. consumer price index for food is from Bureau of the Census, *Historical Statistics of the United States: Colonial Times to 1970* (Washington, 1975), Series E137. The hourly rate paid machine miners and the piece rate paid loaders are from the Annual Operating Reports of the Stonega Coke and Coal Company for various years, Boxes 212 to 215 from the Stonega Coke and Coal Collection, Accession 1765, Series II within the Westmoreland Coal Collection at the Hagley Museum and Library, Wilmington, Delaware. The retail price index is the product of a Stonega wholesale price index and an index of the average markup on goods at the Stonega stores. The Stonega wholesale price index was based on the following information. The U.S. Coal Commission studied the expenditures by mine workers' families in the New River district in 1922 (see pp. 1514–1531 in U.S. Coal Commission Report, vol. III, 1925), providing a detailed set of weights for foodstuffs purchased at stores (U.S. Coal Commission, pp. 1526–1527). A weighting scheme within the food category was developed from this information. The Stonega store department reported wholesale prices on fifty-three food items, of which twenty-five could be matched with items composing 77.8 percent of the food purchases made by miners in the Coal Commission study. For each food item I created a wholesale price index based in the year 1922 for the year 1918 to 1932 from the Annual Operating Reports of the Stonega Coke and Coal Company for 1925, 1926, 1928, 1930, and 1932 (Boxes 212–215). I assumed that the prices of the remaining items listed in the Stonega data, which composed 22.2 percent of the purchased bundle, followed the same price path as the included items. This index for the food category is a measure of the wholesale price of food at the Stonega company stores. In most cases the goods described for Stonega matched directly with goods listed in the Coal Commission Reports. The Coal Commission weights were used for those goods. In addition the Coal Commission weight for navy beans was used for white beans in Stonega, because in the three years when Stonega information was listed for both navy and white beans their prices moved together. The Coal Commission weight for chuck roast (not mentioned in the Stonega list) was used for chop (not mentioned in the Coal Commission list). The Coal Commission weight for cabbage (not mentioned in the Stonega list) was used for lettuce (not mentioned in the Coal Commission list). The total coal commission weight for round steak, loin steak, flank, and rib roast was matched with meat. And the weight of yeast in the Stonega list was matched with the weight for bread in the Coal Commission list. To obtain prices for all the commodities, some special assumptions had to be made in cases where brands changed or prices were missing: For the years 1918 to 1925 no specific brands were listed for canned corn. From 1926 to 1930, two or more brands were listed. I averaged the prices for the various brands to get a single canned corn price. For 1931 and 1932 three brands were listed, one of which appeared to be a lower quality brand. I averaged only the prices of the two higher quality brands. From 1918 to 1928, the price on coffee was for Arbuckles; afterward it was the price for Pilot Knob. I treated this as a continuous series. Prices for several different brands of flour were listed each year. I averaged the prices reported for each year to obtain a single price. A similar technique was used for muslin prices. Canned tomato prices were for #3 through 1926 and for #2 1/2 for the remainder of the period.

The average markup was based on the Stonega stores' total sales and gross profits in each year from the Comparative Statements of the Store Department, Stonega Coke and Coal Company, 1911–1947, Boxes 253–255 in Series II of the Westmoreland Collection, Accession 1765 at the Hagley Museum and Library, Wilmington, DE). The cost of goods sold is approximated (within 0.3 percent) by deducting gross profits from total sales; therefore, the ratio of total store sales to the measure of the cost of goods can be multiplied by the wholesale price index to obtain a retail food price index.

necessarily a good hedge against coal losses. At the Stonega mines in Virginia, where the sale price of coal fell from 7.5 percent more than the cost of production in 1929 to 12.4 percent less in 1933, net store profits also fell from 8 to −1 percent of sales.[29]

Although most discussions of company stores focus on cross-sectional comparisons, Corbin also discussed intertemporal price changes at particular mines. He claimed that company stores had enough market power in southern West Virginia so that "wage advances were always absorbed, 'in whole or in part,' by price increases at the company store."[30] The miners he quotes may have mistaken price increases caused by inflation as attempts by operators to reduce real wages. Table 8-2 shows the path over time of a retail food price index for the Stonega mines in the nonunion district in southwest Virginia, nominal wage rates in Stonega, and the food portion of the consumer price index. The Stonega food price index is strongly correlated (0.797) with the U.S. consumer price index for foods for the years 1918 to 1932, while showing almost no correlation (0.036 or −0.089) with nominal wage rates at these mines.

Generally, it appears that in normal or tight labor markets, company store prices were at most slightly higher than prices at nearby independent stores. Store prices at more isolated mines were higher, in part due to higher costs of transporting goods, but wages there may also have been higher. The overall employment package therefore may look less exploitative than store prices alone. During severe downturns, as in the Depression, the range of prices appears to have broadened. In sum, even had the miners been forced to purchase at the store, it appears that the miners' market power in union districts and the competition among mines for labor in nonunion districts limited the degree to which high store prices were used to lower real incomes.

Were Miners Forced to Buy at the Store?

Company stores were charged with maintaining a monopoly by three techniques: forcing miners to buy at the store, issuing scrip, or imposing debt peonage. Reported cases of forced buying included delivery of unwanted goods to the miner's door, threats of dismissal for not buying at the store, and placement of recalcitrants in the worst workplaces.[31] Yet these practices were not universal, and were more common in earlier periods. In their 1885 study of company stores the Illinois Bureau of Labor Statistics received 34 replies to a questionnaire on company stores from lodges of the Miners' Protective Association. There were no company stores at 17 of the lodges. Of the 17 lodges at mines with company stores, 10 reported no compulsion was used, in 2 cases companies openly demanded the miners trade at the store, and in 5 cases it was understood. In another sample of stores discussed by a miner "familiar with the facts," seven of eleven stores faced with competition expected their miners to trade at the store, although most of the companies charged prices that were the same as at other stores. The Bureau noted that there was "rarely any open solicitation of trade, or threat made for failure to trade, but the employee who does not [trade] is regarded as an undesirable man to retain."[32] In later years the compulsion to buy lessened. The Immigration Commission reported that Alabama and Virginia miners in 1908 were not forced to buy at the company store, although several cases of coerced buying were found in Pennsylvania.[33] The Coal Commission in 1925 reported that "the system of openly forcing employees to buy at commissaries is said to be no longer in practice." They noted that attempts to solicit trade by an energetic store manager might be misconstrued as coercion and lead to ill feelings toward the company when not proposed congenially.[34] Some abuses did occur. Some companies tried to keep peddlers and nearby independents from delivering goods. Other companies allowed peddlers but carefully checked that they transacted only their stated purpose.[35]

The most frequently misunderstood practice of the company store was the issuance of scrip to the miners. The quotation that opens the chapter suggests that miners were paid almost entirely in scrip. In reality, miners were paid in cash monthly or every two weeks. Scrip was an advance on wages due the following payday, which was negotiable at full value at the company store.[36] Given that periodic paydays were and still are an institutional feature of employment that save on bookkeeping costs and interests costs from having to constantly have cash on hand, scrip was a convenience that offered the miner the opportunity to draw his wages as he earned them. Relatively few firms today provide the service of advances on payday in any form.

The Immigration Commission described scrip as a convenience in some parts of its report, but they also suggest that the practice made store "patronage practically compulsory," because only scrip was available between infrequent paydays.[37] The extent to which scrip raised the percentage of miners' earnings spent at the store may have been small. Given the small differences in the prices of company stores and nearby independents and the company store's more convenient location, miners might have spent similar amounts at the store had they been paid entirely in cash. Any compulsion through scrip was lessened further with the shift toward biweekly paydays, which were almost universal by the early 1920s. By then, the Coal Commission, which also recognized scrip as a convenience, was criticizing issuance of scrip for relieving the miner's wife of all responsibility for planning a household budget, allowing her to avoid close examination of goods and prices, and dulling her sense of the value of money. They recommended a switch to a pure cash system, in essence, to give the miners the "responsibility of adults."[38] One wonders how the miners would have responded to the removal of this service, if this were the reason given.

Debt peonage at the mines was unusual. It certainly is not implied merely by the existence of scrip. Debt peonage could only have existed if the miner owed the company money on payday. Even then it cannot be confirmed without greater knowledge of the circumstances of the loan. Both the Immigration Commission and the Coal Commission suggested that scrip was rarely extended beyond the amount due the employee on payday.[39] The records of the Stonega Coke and Coal Company agree. Between 1910 and 1947, outstanding accounts at the stores averaged about 1.9 percent of store sales with a range of 0.45 to 4.68 percent. Store correspondence during the 1930s shows that the store owners carefully monitored these accounts and sought quick repayment.[40] The coal companies saw little reason to give miners scrip in excess of what they had earned because there was always the risk that the miner would leave without repaying the scrip or working off the debt.

The companies allowed miners to incur debts in three ways. To keep a skeletal work force when the mine was not working, rent and fixed charges at times were allowed to accumulate; at some mines in severe downturns these charges were waived. To attract workers from distant locations, the company advanced the cost of transportation to the mine. Finally, the company loaned funds to better workers to purchase durable goods like furniture, automobiles, and later, houses and washing machines.[41] Debt peonage was not the primary motivation for these loans because the possibility that miners would repudiate their debts was enhanced by the lack of attachment to the mines of workers owing transport costs, and the adversarial attitudes that developed during strikes. In fact, between 1910 and 1923 the Stonega company records show that 16 to 37 percent of the men who came in on transportation left, often for other mines, without working for Stonega.[42]

Evidence from government reports and archival sources shows that miners received a significant proportion of their earnings in cash, that these proportions varied widely for individual miners, and that relatively few miners were in debt. Table 8-3 summarizes frequency distributions of the percentage of earnings paid to the entire workforce in cash on payday. The percentages paid in cash ranged widely from mine to mine and over time. In West Virginia the Stevens and Cabin Creek Consolidated companies in the early 1900s typically paid 30 to 50 percent of their payroll in cash on payday. The Cabin Creek data show that the percent paid in cash varied by type of worker; coalmen, paid piece rates, generally received less of their earnings in cash than daymen. The normal cash percentage may have been higher in 1910 in West Virginia, where the Immigration Commission found percentages of 51 and 62 at "representative" mines. Representative companies in Pennsylvania, where the Immigration Commission's descriptions of stores were harshest, paid 60 to 80 percent of their payroll in cash on payday.[43] After 1924, the Stonega mines in Virginia typically paid out 50 to 70 percent of their payrolls in cash despite sharp drops in income during the Depression that might cause miners to rely more on scrip prior to payday.

The payments above are in cash after deductions for the miner's rent, doctor fee, fuel, blacksmithing, powder, and store purchases before payday. The Coal Commission's description of family spending in the New River and Kanawha districts in 1922 suggests that the miner spent about 5 percent of his income on rent and another 6 to 7 percent on doctors, fuel, blacksmiths, schools, and insurance. About 75 to 80 percent of his income was spent on items that might be obtained at the store.[44] The extent of store deductions from earnings is summarized in Table 8-4. The highest percentages for store deductions are found in the monthly pay periods at the Acme mine prior to 1900. After 1900 store deductions accounted for 30 to 50 percent of the mine payroll in West Virginia and Virginia, 20 to 30 percent in Pennsylvania. These percentages suggest that miners purchased about 40 to 70 percent of their store goods in cash at company or independent stores. The bulk of these goods were probably purchased from independents because most of the business at stores was conducted in scrip.[45]

At least part of the cash income on payday was used for savings. Stories of

TABLE 8-3. Frequency Distributions of Percentages of Earnings Paid on Payday, Payroll Summaries

% of Earnings Paid on Payday	*Cabin Creek Consolidated Coal Company 9 mines Jan. 1912–June 1912*		*Stonega Coke & Coal Average All Mines 1925–1947*	*Pennsylvania Representative Mines Averages 1/06 to 12/08*	*Stevens Coal Company*		
	Coalmen	*Daymen*			*Keystone, Halfmonths, Nov. 1905–Jan. 1907*	*Empire, Half-months, Oct. 1905–Jan. 1907*	*Acme, Months, Dec. 1895–Oct. 1897*
10–20	13.0	0	0	0	0	3.1	0
20–30	33.3	0	0	0	3.3	40.6	30.4
30–40	38.9	42.6	0	0	43.3	53.1	60.9
40–50	14.8	42.6	21.7	0	50.0	3.1	8.7
50–60	0	13.0	47.8	0	3.3	0	0
60–70	0	1.9	30.4	44.4	0	0	0
70–80	0	0	0	56.6	0	0	0
Number of Payrolls	54	54	23	36	30	32	23

Source: Reprinted from Price V. Fishback, "Did Miners 'Owe Their Souls to the Company Store'? Theory and Evidence from the Early 1900s," *Journal of Economic History* 46 (December 1986): 1024 with the permission of Cambridge University Press and the Economic History Association.

Cabin Creek Consolidated Coal Company, West Virginia, nine Mines for months of January through June 1912, *Conditions in Paint Creek District*, pp. 1236–41. Stonega Coke and Coal Company: Comparative Statements of Store Departments, Boxes 253–255, Stonega Coke and Coal Company Records, Westmoreland Collection, Hagley Museum and Library. Representative Mines for Pennsylvania (seven mines in 1906, twelve mines in 1907–1908): U.S. Immigration Commission, *Immigrants in Bituminous Mining*, vol. 1, p. 316. Stevens Coal Company, West Virginia: Payroll of Keystone Mines for Half-months between Nov. 1905 and Jan. 1907; Payroll of Empire Mines for Half-months between Oct. 1905 and Jan. 1907. Payroll of Acme Mine, for months between Dec. 1895 and Oct. 1897. Stevens Coal Company Records. West Virginia, Regional and History Collection, West Virginia University Library.

[a]This should be read as greater than or equal to 10 and less than 20 percent.

TABLE 8-4. Frequency Distributions of Percentage of Payrolls Deducted for Store Purchases, Payroll Summaries

% of Payroll Spent at Store	*Stonega Coke and Coal Co.—All Mines Annual Average 1910–1947*	*Pennsylvania Representative Mines, Monthly Averages Jan. 1906–Dec. 1908*	*Stevens Coal Company*		
			Keystone, Half-months, Nov. 1905–Jan. 1907	*Empire, Half-months, Oct. 1905–Jan. 1907*	*Acme, Months, Dec. 1895–Oct. 1897*
20–30[a]	7.9	86.1	0	0	0
30–40	47.4	13.9	36.7	25.0	4.3
40–50	39.4	0	56.6	68.8	52.2
50–60	5.3	0	6.7	6.2	43.5
Number of Payrolls	38	36	30	32	23

Source: Reprinted from Price V. Fishback, "Did Miners 'Owe Their Souls to the Company Store'? Theory and Evidence from the Early 1900s," *Journal of Economic History* 46 (December 1986): 1026, with the permission of Cambridge University Press and the Economic History Association.
See also source notes in Table 8-3.

[a]Read as greater than or equal to 20 and less than 30 percent.

immigrants saving to send money home, to bring their families to America, or to return and buy property in their native land are legion. A number of black and white migrants from the South used West Virginia as a way station, where they earned enough to move north. Others saved enough to purchase farms or homes in nearby towns.[46] Finally, miners saved during booms and dissaved during downturns and strikes. Mining families in the Kanawha district accumulated savings during the coal boom in the late teens but ran them down during the 1921 downturn and the strike year of 1922.[47] Morris gives examples of miners who accumulated savings during the 1920s but, like most workers, saw them dissipate quickly during the Depression.[48] The miners may have suffered more than most workers during the 1930s because opportunities to save were limited while the coal industry stagnated during most of the 1920s.

The payroll summaries in Tables 8-3 and 8-4 hide the wide divergence in the cash percentages received by individuals at each mine. At the Raleigh and Coalburg mines in West Virginia and the representative Pennsylvania mines, none of the miners was in debt and the range of cash percentages was large. At the Stevens Keystone mine in December 1906, nearly 12 percent of the miners owed the company on payday, yet nearly 20 percent received 80 to 100 percent of their earnings in cash. The differences in percentages were not purely random. At the Cabin Creek mines the cash percentages received by industrious individuals with high earnings in Table 8-5 were substantially higher than the payroll percentages in Table 8-3. The Immigration Commission found that immigrants drew much higher percentages of their earnings in cash than did native white and black miners, in part because a greater percentage of native workers had families.[49] The wide range of cash percentages suggests that miners were a diverse group with varying demands for store goods and savings. The range in percentages also seems inconsistent with the notion

TABLE 8-5. Frequency Distributions for Percentage of Earnings Received on Payday, Individual Miners

	Percentage of All Employees				*Percentage of Selected "Industrious" Individuals*	
% of Earnings Paid on Payday	*Keystone, Stevens Dec. 1–16, 1906*	*12 Mines Pennsylvania Apr.–June 1909*	*Raleigh Coal & Coke February 1903*	*Coalburg Apr., Jul. 1912*	*West Virginia Colliery Co., Jan., Feb., Mar., Aug. 1912*	*Cabin Creek Consolidated Con. Co. 1912*
Less than 0	11.6	0	0	0	0	0
0–20[a]	24.1	7.2	28.6	26.4	4.7	5.4
20–40	21.4	38.2	12.1	23.7	9.3	16.1
40–60	15.2	43.4	15.9	22.0	30.2	35.7
60–80	8.0	7.9	17.9	13.7	32.6	23.2
80–100	19.7	3.3	17.1	14.1	23.3	19.6
Number of Workers	112	152	280	227	78	56
Mean Percentage of earnings paid in cash	28.0	43.0	41.6	44.0	60.4	57.4
Mean gross earnings per month	$51.08[b]	$61.22[c]	$35.71	$53.63	$95.26	$105.49

Source: Reprinted from Price V. Fishback, "Did Miners 'Owe Their Souls to the Company Store'? Theory and Evidence from the Early 1900s," *Journal of Economic History* 46 (December 1986): 1026, with the permission of Cambridge University Press and Economic History Association.

Keystone Mine: Payroll Book, Stevens Coal Company Records, West Virginia Regional and History Collection, West Virginia University Library. Pennsylvania Mines: U.S. Immigration Commission, *Immigrants in Bituminous Mining*, vol. 1, pp. 316–20. Raleigh Coal and Coke: Payroll Book on Display at Beckley Exhibition Mine, Beckley, West Virginia. Coalburg, West Virginia Colliery, and Cabin Creek Mines: *Conditions in the Paint Creek District*, pp. 1220–25, 1499–528, 2284–98.

[a]Read as greater than or equal to zero and less than 20 percent.

[b]These workers were paid half-monthly. Figure was obtained by multiplying by two.

[c]Information was provided for three-month period. Figure was obtained by dividing by three.

that the mines in Table 8-5 had a consistent policy of forcing workers to spend a minimum percentage of their earnings at the company store.

Conclusions

Economic theory and empirical evidence offer several reasons to doubt the monopoly view of company stores. First, company stores faced competition not only from local stores but also from other mines to the extent that mine employers hired in a competitive labor market. In nonunion areas like West Virginia, company store prices were part of an employment package, including wages and housing, offered to mobile miners in a labor market with hundreds of mines. The theory of compensating differences suggests that the gain from charging high store prices would be offset by the higher wages the mine would be forced to offer to attract workers. Second, extension of this analysis suggests that the value of employment packages would have fluctuated cyclically within a long-term trend toward less opportunities for exploitation as information and transportation costs fell. Third, one reason company ownership of stores persisted was that it lowered transactions costs, reducing the costs of holding currency in isolated areas, lowering the risks of extending credit for store purchases, and preventing the costs of contracting to minimize opportunistic behavior. Fourth, comprehensive studies by the Immigration Commission in 1908 and the Coal Commission in 1922 show that prices at most company stores were similar to prices at nearby independent stores. Prices apparently were higher at isolated mines, in part due to higher transport costs, but scattered evidence suggests that higher prices were offset partially by higher wages. Finally, miners were typically not in debt to the stores nor paid entirely in scrip. Scrip was offered as an advance on payday, when miners, on average, received 30 to 80 percent of their earnings in cash after deductions for rent, fuel, doctors, and store purchases between paydays.

NOTES

Most of the material in this chapter appeared in Price V. Fishback, "Did Miners 'Owe Their Souls to the Company Store'? Theory and Evidence from the Early 1900s," *Journal of Economic History* 46 (December 1986): 1011–1029. It is reprinted here with the permission of Cambridge University Press and the Economic History Association.

1. See Curtis Seltzer, *Fire in the Hole: Miners and Managers in the American Coal Industry* (Lexington, KY: University of Kentucky Press, 1985), p. 19; David Corbin, *Life, Work, and Rebellion in the Coal Fields: The Southern West Virginia Miners, 1880–1922* (Chicago: University of Illinois Press, 1981); and Anna Rochester, *Labor and Coal* (New York: International Publishers, 1931).

2. Corbin, *Life, Work, and Rebellion*, p. 10.

3. There is evidence that miners moved in response to changing store prices. For example, Jairus Collins, a nonunion operator, attracted workers during one upturn by cutting store prices "to the bone." Letter from George Wolfe to Justus Collins, September 20, 1916,

Justin Collins Papers, West Virginia Regional and History Collection at the West Virginia University Library, Morgantown, West Virginia. Miners also moved for other parts of the package. See Chapter 3 and Corbin, *Life, Work, and Rebellion*, p. 42; James T. Laing, "The Negro Miner in West Virginia," Ph.D. dissertation, Ohio State University, 1933, pp. 146–51; Marlene Hunt Rikard, "An Experiment in Welfare Capitalism: The Health Care Services of the Tennessee, Coal, Iron, and Railroad Company," Ph.D. dissertation, University of Alabama, 1983.

4. See Chapter 3. There was substantial movement in and out of coal mining as well. United States Senate, United States Coal Commission, "The Bituminous Mine Workers and Their Homes," *Report of the United States Coal Commission*, part 3, 68th Cong., 2d sess. (Washington, DC: 1925), p. 1522; West Virginia Bureau of Negro Welfare and Statistics, *Report*, 1923–24, p. 39; Margaret Ripley Wolfe, "Aliens in Southern Appalachia: Catholics in Coal Camps, 1900–1940," *Appalachian Heritage* 6 (Winter 1978): 43–56.

5. Sherwin Rosen, "Hedonic Prices and Implicit Markets: Product Differentiation in Pure Competition," 82 (Jan. 1974): 34–55. For another discussion of the impact of compensating wage differences on the employer's decisions, see Chapter 9.

6. James T. Laing, "Negro Miner," pp. 39–52; West Virginia Department of Mines, *Annual Report* for the years 1901 (p. 2) and 1923 (p. 265).

7. Illiteracy rates for males of voting age in the five leading mining counties in West Virginia fell by more than one-third between 1900 and 1920. U.S. Bureau of the Census, *Twelfth Census of the United States, Population, 1900*, Part 2, p. 487; U.S. Bureau of the Census, *Fourteenth Census of the United States, Population, 1920*, vol. 3, part 2, pp. 1105–09. The percentage of miners who did not speak English in West Virginia fell from approximately 10 percent in 1908 to 2.9 percent in 1920. U.S. Coal Commission, "Bituminous Workers," p. 1424 and U.S. Immigration Commission, *Immigrants in Mining*, vol. 2, pp. 249, 276.

8. Another way companies could take advantage of the higher information costs for store prices would be to raise store prices before lowering wages during downturns and raise wages before lowering store prices during upturns.

9. The term necessity is misleading. For further discussion of these issues see Chapter 9 on company housing.

10. Coal demand fluctuations did not affect all mines equally. See Fishback, "Employment Conditions," pp. 49–50.

11. U.S. Coal Commission, "Bituminous Workers," pp. 1513–14, 1531–32.

12. George Hilton, "The British Truck System in the Nineteenth Century," *Journal of Political Economy* 65 (June 1957): 237–56. For evidence on greater wage flexibility in nonunion than in union areas, see U.S. Coal Commission, "Wage Rates in the Bituminous Coal Industry," *Report of the U.S. Coal Commission*, part 3, p. 1098.

13. U.S. Immigration Commission, *Immigrants in Mining*, vol. 1, pp. 225–28; Charles K. Sullivan, "Coal Men and Coal Towns: Development of the Smokeless Coalfields of Southern West Virginia, 1873–1921," Ph.D. dissertation, University of Pittsburgh, 1979, pp. 195–96; Corbin, *Life, Work, and Rebellion*, pp. 35–38; A. F. Hinrichs, *The United Mine Workers of America and the Non-Union Coal Fields* (New York: Longmens, Green and Company, 1923), pp. 41–42.

14. U.S. Coal Commission, "Bituminous Workers," p. 1514.

15. Oliver Williamson, "The Modern Corporation: Origins, Evolution, Attributes," *Journal of Economic Literature* 19 (Dec. 1981): 1548–49. Benjamin Klein, Robert G. Crawford, and Armen Alchian, "Vertical Integration, Appropriable Rents, and the Competitive Contracting Process," *Journal of Law and Economics* 21 (October 1978): 297–326. Pennsylvania mine officials made statements consistent with this argument. U.S. Immigration Commission, *Immigrants in Mining*, vol. 1, p. 325.

16. U.S. Senate, Subcommittee of the Committee on Education and Labor, *Hearings on Conditions in the Paint Creek District, West Virginia*, 3 vols. 63rd Cong., 1st sess. (Washington, DC: 1913); idem, Committee on Education and Labor, *Hearings on West Virginia Coal Fields*, 2 vols., 67th Cong., 2d sess. (Washington, DC: 1921–22); idem, Committee on Interstate Commerce, *Hearings on Conditions in the Coalfields of Pennsylvania, West Virginia, and Ohio*, 2 vols., 70th Cong., 1st sess. (Washington, DC: 1928).

17. For evidence of conflicting testimony by miners, see *Conditions in Paint Creek District*, pp. 440, 442, 476, 572, 998, 1013. One analyst at the time suggested that the miners made far-reaching accusations often based on negligible evidence. A. F. Hinrichs, *The UMWA and the Non-Union Coal Fields*, pp. 42–45.

18. According to the Coal Commission, the additional freight rates on flour from Charleston to Mount Hope in the New River district accounted for about 50 percent of the price differentials on flour, 22 percent on oats. U.S. Coal Commission, "Bituminous Workers and Homes," p. 1518.

19. The relative wage rates in the two districts were the same in 1921 as they were in December 1922. The comparison was made for earnings per day rather than wage rates because wage rates for daymen, paid time rates, and tonnage men, who were paid piece rates, are not comparable. There were differences in the relative pay of daymen and tonnage men in the two districts. Tonnage men earned 8.96 percent more more per start in the New River district than in the Kanawha district. Daymen earned 2.2 percent more per day in the New River district. Evidence suggests that hours per day were similar in the two districts. Hours per day may even have been higher in the Kanawha district since inside daymen in the two districts were paid very similar hourly wages. See Waldo Fisher and Anne Bezanson, *Wage Rates and Working Time in the Bituminous Coal Industry 1912–1922*, pp. 248–51. Calculations of earnings per day for daymen and per start for tonnage men are based on tables of the average number of starts for each income category in U.S. Coal Commission, "Atlas of Statistical Tables," *Report*, Part 5, pp. 308, 457–58, 472–73. To calculate earnings per start for each income category, the midpoint income was divided by the average number of starts by workers in that category. Mean earnings per start for all workers was calculated as a weighted mean with the earnings per start in each category weighted by the total number of starts for workers in that category. Earnings per appearance on the payroll was calculated by a weighted sum of earnings per appearance by daymen and tonnage men, with the weights being the total number of appearances listed in the tables.

20. U.S. Immigration Commission, *Immigrants in Mining*, vol. 2, p. 95. In part to determine the extent of exploitation of immigrants in industry, researchers were sent into the field to collect micro-level evidence on the earnings and living conditions of immigrants. Researchers in the coal regions recorded their impressions of store prices but reported no data.

21. Ibid., vol. 2, p. 199.

22. A similar description was given of the nearby Virginia field. Ibid., vol. 2, pp. 201, 213.

23. Ibid., vol. 1, p. 327.

24. Ibid., vol. 2, p. 204.

25. Illinois State Bureau of Labor Statistics, *Statistics of Coal in Illinois* (1885), p. xxii. I thank Gerald Friedman for making me aware of this evidence.

26. Ibid., pp. xxii–xxv. The miner discussed sixteen mines but at three of the mines he either did not mention the store prices or did not discuss the competition.

27. Ibid., p. xxix.

28. Homer Lawrence Morris, *The Plight of the Bituminous Miner* (Philadelphia: University of Pennsylvania Press, 1934), pp. 166–69.

29. Net store profits at the Stonega mines were between 10 and 15 percent of sales from

1910 to 1915 and then averaged about 6 percent both from 1916 to 1929 and from 1937 to 1947. Compiled from Comparative Statements of Annual Store Reports, 1911–1947 in Boxes 253–55. Data on coal prices and production costs are from Annual Operating Statements, 1929–1933, Box 248 from the Stonega Coke and Coal Collection, Series II, within the Westmoreland Coal Collection at the Hagley Museum and Library, Wilmington, Delaware.

The Stonega Coke and Coal operations, which employed about 1400 men in 1915, seem representative of the average coal community. In the Coal Commission's rankings of 349 company communities, the Stonega communities of Osaka and Dunbar were ranked 67th and 210th. U.S. Coal Commission, "Bituminous Workers," pp. 1489–94 and Individual Community Ratings Schedules for Osaka and Dunbar, Boxes 24–32, U.S. Coal Commission Records, Record Group 68, National Archives, Suitland, Maryland.

Stonega's reputation varied from source to source. According to Margaret Ripley in "Putting Them in Their Places: Industrial Housing in Southern Appalachia, 1900–1932," *Appalachian Heritage* 7 (Summer 1979): 27–36, the Stonega operations were among the better ones in the area. However, Stonega is mentioned prominently in Justice Department Affadavits (see the testimony of Hy Young, Percy Jemison, James Jemison, Will Henry, Willie Parker, Earnest Randolph, Nathan Burton, and Ed Hardaway in File 182363, part 2, Record Group 60 at the National Archives, Washington, DC). Apparently Stonega's labor agent misrepresented the pay at Stonega when seeking men for employment in Alabama. Stonega stationed men at the train depot to stop disgruntled men from leaving without paying transport costs. At various times the Stonega operations tried to stop delivery of goods by independents to company houses, in part because the company was strongly opposed to efforts to unionize its mines.

30. Corbin, *Life, Work, and Rebellion*, p. 32.

31. Morris, *Plight of Bituminous Miner*, p. 166; Hinrichs, *The UMWA and Non-Union Fields*, pp. 42–43.

32. Illinois Bureau of Labor Statistics, *Coal Report* (1885), pp. xxiv–xxv.

33. U.S. Immigration Commission, *Immigrants in Mining*, vol. 1, pp. 95, 327; vol. 2, pp. 66, 199, 212, 213.

34. U.S. Coal Commission, "Bituminous Workers," p. 1462.

35. U.S. Immigration Commission, *Immigrants in Mining*, vol. 1, p. 326; Letters between George Wolfe and Justus Collins, December 26, 1915, December 27, 1915, December 28, 1915, Justus Collins Papers; Sullivan, "Coal Men and Coal Towns," pp. 182–83; Testimony of C.A. Cabell, *Conditions in Paint Creek*, pp. 1497–98.

36. U.S. Immigration Commission, *Immigrants in Mining*, vol. 1, p. 95; vol. II, pp. 65, 199, 202, 212–13; U.S. Coal Commission, "Bituminous Workers," pp. 1462–63. At some mines miners could get cash advances, but these were carefully doled out only to better workers. Testimony of C.A. Cabell, *Conditions in Paint Creek*, p. 1499. In West Virginia in 1908 some "individuals, saloons, and independent storekeepers buy the scrip at from 65 to 85 percent of its face value and use it in buying provisions from the company store." A majority of companies disallowed the selling of scrip to stop such practices. U.S. Immigration Commission, *Immigrants in Mining*, vol. 2, p. 202. The discounts do not reflect differences between the company and independent store prices because the miners often sold scrip to obtain cash to buy services not available from the company.

37. Ibid., vol. 1, p. 95; the Illinois Bureau of Labor Statistics, *Coal Report*, 1885, p. xxvi, also emphasized the problems arising from long intervals between paydays.

38. U.S. Coal Commission, "Bituminous Workers," pp. 1462–63.

39. Ibid.; U.S. Immigration Commission, *Immigrants in Mining*, vol. 1, pp. 95, 326; vol. 2, pp. 204, 212–13.

40. Comparative Statements of the Store Department (Boxes 253–55) and Store Files 5–7, Box 347, Stonega Records.

41. Ibid.; U.S. Coal Commission, "Bituminous Workers," pp. 1517–22, 1536–37, 1438; Laing, "Negro Miner," pp. 297–98.

42. Annual Operating Report, 1923, p. 6, Stonega Records.

43. U.S. Immigration Commission, *Immigrants in Mining*, vol. 1, p. 317 and vol. 2, pp. 202–03.

44. The items in the budget considered as purchasable at the company store were food, clothing and dry goods, house furnishings, drugs and toiletries, hardware and mine supplies, and other miscellaneous items. U.S. Coal Commission, "Bituminous Workers and Homes," p. 1456. Examination of the payrolls summarized in Tables 8-3 through 8-5 suggests similar breakdowns of expenditures in the early 1900s.

45. Since scrip prices were the same as cash prices, the miner had little incentive to buy goods with cash if he could draw scrip. Between 85 and 97 percent of the Stonega stores' business was paid for with coupons or on a charge account. The Stonega data overestimate deductions for store purchases by 3 to 15 percent in Tables 8-3 and 8-4, because the data were calculated as total store sales as a percentage of the payroll. Comparative Statements of Store Department, Box 253, Stonega Records.

46. West Virginia Bureau of Negro Welfare, *Second Biennial Report, 1922–23*, p. 39. Laing, "Negro Miner," pp. 292–300.

47. U.S. Coal Commission, "Bituminous Workers and Homes," pp. 1454, 1456, 1534.

48. Morris, *Plight of Bituminous Miner*, pp. 169–72; U.S. Coal Commission, "Bituminous Workers," pp. 1454–58.

49. U.S. Immigration Commission, *Immigrants in Mining*, vol. 2, p. 202.

9

The Company Town

The essence of the company town was the coal company's ownership of housing. Company housing is often cited as the textbook example of a monopolist charging high rents. To many scholars of labor history, company housing was a classic means of busting unions and preventing collective action. The companies claimed that company housing was a necessity because no one else would build houses in remote mine locations. Others who study the development of model towns suggest that the companies were seeking to enhance productivity. Closer examination of these views of housing offers several insights. The monopoly view is inconsistent with evidence on rents and wages, and the productivity view is at best a partial explanation. The most complete explanation emphasizes the isolation of mines in conjunction with some elements of the anti-collective action view. In isolated areas the coal company often faced lower costs than independents of providing the housing and wished to avoid giving miners control of the town when they struck. Most workers sought to rent rather than own housing to avoid being stuck in a town with only one employer with all their wealth in houses whose value depended heavily on the fluctuating fortunes of the coal industry.

Employers in company towns also provided services, like sanitation, that in most places were provided by local governments. Although company towns bore reputations as horrible places to live, the quality of sanitation in company towns varied from town to town, often in response to differences in the costs of providing sanitation. The quality of sanitation in company towns was roughly the same as in independent towns of similar size.

The Nature of Company Housing

In the early 1920s the percentage of miners living in company housing varied across regions. Company towns were found in less settled regions where mines were in more remote locations. In the coal fields of Southern Appalachia (West Virginia, eastern Kentucky, Tennessee, Virginia, Maryland, and Alabama) and in the Rocky Mountains, the mines were remote from normal settlements, and roughly 65 to 80 percent of the coal miners lived in company towns. In the Midwest (Illinois, Indiana, Kansas, Missouri, and Iowa), where prior development in agriculture and industry had led to self-governing towns and cities with ample transportation connections, less than 20 percent of the workers were housed in company towns. In Pennsylvania and Ohio, where there were mixtures of already settled areas and some isolated areas, over 50 percent and roughly 25 percent, respectively, of the miners lived in company towns.[1]

The quality of company housing was never palatial. The homes ranged from comfortable to shoddy, a function of both the miner's desires and the company's policy. Enough commonality existed that the United States Immigration Commission constructed the following description of the miner's options in West Virginia in 1909:

> There are three general types of houses found in the coal-mining villages of the State, and it is not uncommon to find all of them represented in the same village. The most general type found, especially in the older established villages, gives every appearance of cheapness and lack of permanence. This is a one-story structure of from two to four or sometimes five or six rooms. They are usually boxed on the outside with 10 or 12 inch boards nailed on vertically with 3-inch strips over the cracks. They are either ceiled with good dressed and matched lumber, or plastered. They are usually two rooms long, and if there are more than two rooms, the additional rooms are usually built as a wing running back from the front part. A rather narrow porch is built on the front of the house, and in some cases in the rear. The double houses are two stories high, two rooms wide, and two long. If they contain six rooms, the rear ones are only one story high; and if there are eight rooms, the front and rear are both two stories. The houses are divided by a main wall running from front to rear, each section or side accommodating one family. Double chimneys are usually constructed in the front rooms, with open fires as sources of heat. These houses have narrow porches at the front running the width of the house, with railings, or in some instances, an outside continuation of the dividing wall, which cuts the porch into two sections. The houses are either ceiled or plastered and in some cases, papered. They are always painted on the outside and while not attractive are usually comfortable and kept in a very good state of repair. The third type of house found in mining villages is better in quality and general appearance, and occurs less frequently than the other. This type of house is a single one-story building of four or five rooms and hall, and finished both inside and out with better material than that usually found in the types above described.[2]

The standard houses in Alabama were built of wood but not weatherboarded. Each of the four or five rooms averaged about $10' \times 12'$ with a front and sometimes a back porch. Interiors were sealed or whitewashed, with unpainted floors and ample chimneys for heating and cooking. Housing in Pennsylvania at this time was considered inferior to Alabama housing, which was inferior to much of the housing in midwestern and southwestern coal communities, where a significant number of miners owned their own homes.[3]

In the thirteen-year span following the Immigration Commission Report, the basic housing changed little, although electric lighting became more common in miners' homes. Nearly all houses surveyed by the U.S. Coal Commission in 1923 were built of wood. Weatherboard was used to finish the outside of the houses in two-thirds of the dwellings, while two-thirds of the houses were roofed with composition paper. Running water was found in 13 percent of the houses, but tubs, showers, and flush toilets were highly unusual. Hydrants and wells shared with other families were the primary sources of water. As in the earlier period, the state of repair ranged from good to terrible. Conditions varied across communities and within the same community. The miners blamed the coal operators for poor conditions, while the operators blamed their tenants for their lack of concern.[4] Although the basic house did not change much during the 1910s, a number of companies tried to improve conditions in their towns by fixing and rebuilding housing, offering more recreation facilities, and providing incentives for the miners' families to garden and spruce up the housing. Corbin suggests that the improvements were designed primarily as defenses against unions.[5] Even had unions not been an issue, coal operators might well have been forced by increased competition for labor inside and outside the coal industry to improve the quality of housing at the mines.[6]

The leases on company houses were more restrictive than the terms in the typical landlord-tenant lease, providing for termination by either party, ordinarily with five days notice. At many mines the miner's lease was also contingent on employment at the mine.[7] In representative leases from West Virginia, when the mine worker quit or was dismissed by the company, his lease for the company house also was terminated.[8] The courts in West Virginia supported the leases as valid on the basis that the miner and his employer had primarily an employment relationship with housing as part of the relationship.[9] The legal term for an employment relationship with contingent housing was a "master-servant" relationship, referring to situations where servants were housed in the homes where they worked. The use of the term by the West Virginia court in deciding the case *Wilhelmina Coal Company* v. *B. H. Young* in the circuit court of Mingo County in 1921 has led to flights of rhetoric by the UMWA and later scholars that miners were "serfs" or only a step away from indentured servitude.[10]

In contrast to the company leases, under West Virginia state law the landlord-tenant relationship required notice of termination of the lease based on how often the rent was due. Weekly rent implied a week's notice was required; monthly rent implied a month's notice.[11] Since most mines collected rent twice a month, a half-month's notice would have been required for eviction under the landlord-tenant relationship. However, had the companies been required to write landlord-tenant leases, they might have reduced the notice time by requiring rent payments more often.

In many company towns housing leases prevented nonemployees from living in or trespassing upon company housing. According to some leases, the mine worker could not entertain or harbor persons objectionable to the company.[12] Some leases stipulated that lodgers or boarders had to be employees of the company. Other leases provided that the mine worker's right of entering and leaving the premises was restricted to himself and members of his families. Some explicitly stipulated that the relationship was not one of landlord and tenant, and committed the tenant to waiving laws covering tenants rights. In some leases the company reserved the right of entry into the property and the right to make and enforce regulations affecting the streets or roads upon which the premises abutted.[13]

In the Coal Commission Reports the coal companies claimed that the provisions were mere forms and were rarely enforced.[14] A number of companies allowed families to stay in houses during slack times or in sickness, often allowing rent to run until the men could catch up with expenses. Families of mine workers killed in the mines were sometimes allowed to live on indefinitely in company houses.[15] However, such treatment generally depended on the continued goodwill between the company and the miner. Coal operators wanted the restrictive clauses so that when relations with miners broke down, they had the legal right to remove discharged miners, striking miners, or quitting miners quickly from the premises.[16]

More evidence is needed to determine how often companies evicted miners without notice. In the U.S. Coal Commission reports, the coal operators claimed to have been considerably more tolerant and slower to evict than the dictates of justice and humanity required. David Corbin in his study of southern West Virginia miners displays an eviction notice giving more than a month's notice, while also citing another dismissal notice that said purely "I want my house."[17] However, Corbin goes on to say that in southern West Virginia "notification was *exceptional*; the coal companies *usually* sent mine guards to the miner's house and without warning dumped him, his family, and the furniture onto the company road [my italics]."[18] He then cites examples of mine guard behavior during the Paint Creek–Cabin Creek strike of 1912–1913. This is probably a misleading citation as to the norm in company towns. That particular strike was an extraordinarily violent confrontation with egregious actions by all parties involved. It is not clear that Corbin's description of evictions was commonplace during normal operations, or necessarily commonplace during all strikes. Evictions were more common during long strikes; in the Paint Creek strike the evictions did not occur until a month and a half into the strike.[19] Evictions were often avoided because most strikes were settled peacefully within a week or two. However, the incidents in major strikes show that the restrictive nature of the housing leases were put to use and sometimes abuse by the companies.

Why Did Companies Own Housing?

The contingent nature of rental contracts and other restrictive clauses lead many to describe company housing as a means of busting unions and limiting collective action. Others see company housing as economic exploitation of a local monopoly on housing. The companies themselves argued that the company town was a necessity because no one else would have provided housing or services. Yet another view sees company towns as means of enhancing the workers' productivity, reducing turnover and absenteeism. Each view offers some insight into the nature of company housing, but the most compelling view focuses on the isolation of the towns and the nature of bargaining between miners and employer.

Monopoly Ownership?

At first look many company towns seem to be examples of employers exploiting a local monopoly on housing. Companies often owned much of the land around the mines, and some required employees to live in company housing. However, it is instructive to apply the same analysis to housing that was applied to store prices in Chapter 8. The companies' success at charging monopoly rents was determined by the mobility of miners between towns and the extent of competition in the labor market. If the worker's wages adjusted fully to offset higher rents, the company could not exploit their local monopoly.

Evidence on rental charges by companies in coal mining and in other industries during the 1910s and 1920s shows that employers generally were not charging monopoly-level rents for housing. In Magnusson's survey of more than 200 employers providing housing (sixty-four were coal employers) during the 1910s, he found that the rents of company housing appeared reasonable, with no attempt to overcharge the tenants.[20] The U.S. Coal Commission found in the early 1920s that rents for company-owned houses were lower than for all others, as were charges for fuel, light, and water. The rents in West Virginia company towns were substantially lower than the rents in Charleston, West Virginia in the 1920s, but Charleston homes and apartments had more modern conveniences.[21]

A. F. Hinrichs used Magnusson's evidence from coal towns in West Virginia and Pennsylvania to examine the direct returns to housing on the company books.[22] He calculated that the average cost of building a house was $687, while the average house rent was $7.78 a month or $93.36 over the year. The gross return from rents was therefore 13.7 percent per year on the investment in building the house (not including the cost of the land or any apportioned cost of town improvements).[23] The net return is determined by subtracting from the gross return the annual costs of providing the housing, which included general repairs, maintenance of town roads, street lighting and improvements, insurance, taxes and depreciation of the housing. Four Pennsylvania companies that included general repairs to housing, cleaning, street cleaning, and lighting and drainage in maintenance costs spent roughly 38 percent of their rent receipts on such costs.[24] Two other companies who included taxes and insurance among their costs, spent roughly 63 percent of rent receipts on annual maintenance costs. Based on these figures, an upper-bound estimate of the net returns to housing was 8.4 percent. When taxes and insurance are included as annual costs, the net return was 5 percent, which was close to the opportunity cost return on other investments. Magnusson's evidence for coal towns in Ohio, Indiana, Kentucky, Tennessee, and Alabama suggests similar results.[25] The net returns were even lower if the initial cost of building roads and other town improvements were prorated across the houses.

In the calculations of the net rates of return above, we assumed that the companies receive the return each year forever. The assumption overstates the profitability of company housing because it ignores the short life of the mine. Using the figures above, the annual net rent from the houses each year was $34.35 (5 percent of $687). Using a discount rate of 5 percent for a mine lasting twenty-five years, the present value of the stream of net rents at the time the house was built was $493.18 compared with the initial cost of building the housing of $687. To raise the twenty-five-year stream of rents to a level covering the initial cost of building the house requires an annual net rent of $47.79 (6.9 percent of the $687 building cost).

Why did the companies keep rents low and not exploit their local monopoly?

Miners were mobile enough across towns that there was little gain to charging monopoly rents. In a study of sanitation in coal towns, Dieter Lauszus and I found that miners demanded dollar-for-dollar increases in monthly wages in areas with higher rents.[26] When compared with the wage compensations for higher store prices in Chapter 8, it appears that miners were more effective at demanding higher compensation for higher rents than they were for higher store prices.

The "Necessity" of Company Housing

Many observers claim that company housing was necessary because the coal mines were located in isolated and sparsely settled regions.[27] Leifur Magnusson, who surveyed over seventy mine operators (in coal, copper, and iron mining) offering company housing, found that "(t)he first and practically only reason assigned by many mine operators for housing their men is that there are no houses available or likely to be provided. The mine is the only reason why community life has developed in the particular locality."[28] Claims of necessity are misleading because they imply no alternative to company housing. Independent investors or the miners themselves might have provided housing, but few did. Thus we need to explore the key elements that made it more economical for the employer than for an independent investor to provide housing.

Contemporaries were right to emphasize the isolation of the mine and prior lack of settlement around it, but many failed to clarify why the isolation was so important. Isolation forced all investments in housing to be specific to that one mine. The success of investments in the mine and in housing were therefore strongly intertwined. Such "asset specificity" gave the coal employer several cost advantages and other incentives for building and owning the housing that an independent did not have. The employer's costs of discovering and surveying housing sites were generally lower because he had already investigated the area for mining purposes. The success of the housing investment was also determined by effective forecasting of the fluctuations in the coal industry. The employer had two advantages there. First, since he produced coal, he already forecasted coal fluctuations. Second, he decided the number and type of workers he expected to house. The independent, on the other hand, not only had to forecast coal fluctuations but also the employer's response to them.

The interdependence of the mining and housing investments also created situations where the joint mining-housing investment was profitable, but an independent's investment in housing was not. Such situations may have arisen because most mines only lasted for twenty to twenty-five years. Reconsider the example where the cost of building the house was $687 and annual net rents were $34.35 (or 5 percent of $687). At an opportunity cost rate of return of 5 percent, the present value of the stream of net rental receipts for twenty-five years was $493.18.[29] An independent faced with these net rental receipts would not build the house. The coal employer might still build the housing because the success of his mining investment depended on his ability to hire workers, who would not come without housing. The employer would build the house as long as building the house increased his expected stream of profits from the mining investment by more than $193.82.[30]

Employers also sought to avoid bargaining problems arising from independents exploiting a local housing monopoly. The small number of houses in most towns, the short life of the mine, and the startup costs of building in an isolated area made it hard to attract more than one or two independents to build housing. An independent builder was therefore in a position to charge higher rents. High rents raised the wage bill to the employer who was forced to pay a higher wage to attract miners despite the higher rent. The employer might have contracted with the independent to prevent this behavior. However, the employer saved the costs of negotiating and enforcing the contract by owning the housing himself.[31]

Rather than dealing with an independent, another alternative was for the miners to own the housing themselves. Some argue that economies of scale in home building and the inability to obtain credit were obstacles to the miners owning their own homes.[32] Such obstacles were easily overcome. Given economies of scale, the employer could build the homes and then sell them to miners. Further, the miners' lack of credit could have been overcome by establishing rent-to-own plans. A more important obstacle to the ownership of homes by the miners was the strong ties of housing to the mine in an isolated region. Since the employer had the larger investment in the area, the strong ties created incentives for both miners and employers to have the employer own the housing.

The worker's demand for home ownership diminished when there was only one employer within commuting range. The situation gave the employer a monopsony over the services of a home-owning worker.[33] If the employer cut wages, the home-owning worker faced the choice of working at the mine or being unemployed. The worker might have sold his house, but buyers would offer a lower price to offset the employers' monopsony position.[34] The transactions costs of buying and selling houses also inhibited the home-owning miner's long-run mobility. Such mobility was useful to the miner because he could maintain his earnings by moving to other mines when the mine where he worked shut down.[35]

Further, the miner faced substantial risk of capital losses on his house. He most wanted to leave when the mine closed and the value of his house was at its lowest. The risk of a capital loss on housing in a coal mining town was greater than in most urban areas, because the value of housing was so dependent on the success of the mine in a risky industry. The typical miner, with relatively small wealth, had less opportunity than the typical employer to diversify and limit the impact of capital losses on his wealth holdings.

The U.S. Immigration Commission noted that the miners' lack of home ownership was also a function of company policy.[36] Although the company potentially had monopsony power over home-owning miners, miner-owned housing limited the mine employers' flexibility in replacing workers. When the employer fired an unproductive worker who owned his home, the worker might be able to appropriate income from the company, because the company had to offer housing to his replacement. The company could choose to build a new house or purchase the fired miner's house. The fired miner's bargaining position was enhanced to the extent that the costs of building a new house exceeded the value of the fired miner's house. As discussed in the next section, the employer's problem of replacing intransigent workers was more acute when the miners struck. The striking miners' goal was to prevent the employer from hiring alternative workers. If the miners owned the housing near the mine, the mine operators' costs of housing replacement workers rose substantially, enhancing the strikers' bargaining position.

In a brief theoretical discussion of the company town, Oliver Williamson suggests that miners would not have built or purchased housing in a mining town without some form of contractual safeguard (buy-back clauses, long-term employment guarantees at an agreed-upon wage, lump-sum severance payments) or price reduction to offset the employers' monopsony position.[37] Absent such safeguards workers would demand a wage premium or sign-on bonus. The companies could avoid the costs of negotiating the safeguards, the payment of wage premiums, and the greater inflexibility of replacing workers by owning the homes and renting to miners.

Magnusson found that only 33 of 213 employers in the 1910s had actually sold houses to workers. Nearly all these employers were manufacturing concerns in or near cities. Some manufacturing employers who sold housing to their workers included repurchase options.[38] In the coal industry, it seems that in most cases where miners purchased company homes, the purchases came when the region became more settled, or when companies sold the housing cheaply when the mine closed down. A number of oral histories have discovered that miners near the end of their working lives purchased company houses in these close-out sales. In general, it appears that most working miners who purchased housing or lots bought farms or houses in independent towns.[39]

A Device to Prevent Collective Action

Corbin sees company housing as a form of power, a valuable control for the operator against agitators, complaints, and strikes. Brandes sees anti-unionism as one of several reasons why employers maintained company housing.[40] There are two elements of housing leases that might be seen as anti-collective action devices.[41] First, since the company town was on private property, the companies had the right to prevent trespassers. Second, most housing leases were incident to employment. When the worker separated from the firm, his housing lease was also terminated.

Anti-unionism and worker control clearly played a role in the clauses that allowed the companies to prevent trespassing by anybody aside from miners and their immediate families. Companies may have inserted the clauses to eliminate gambling and forms of criminal activity. However, there were a number of instances where the clauses were used to keep union organizers and other "agitators" off company property.

In one sense, making housing contingent on employment was a device to control workers and prevent collective action. The clause raised the expected costs of complaining if a miner thought he might be fired. If the worker was fired, he not only incurred the costs of finding a new job but also the costs of finding new housing. But how much was the cost raised? Given that the mine was the only source of employment nearby, if the worker was fired, he had to move anyway to find employment. Most of the cost incurred therefore resulted from the location of the mine in an isolated area. The employment contingency clause raised the cost of being fired because the time horizon for leaving the house was shorter than in a standard housing lease. Typical landlord-tenant leases in West Virginia in 1920 gave tenants two to four weeks notice. The typical mine house lease provided for five days' notice, although if the worker's employment was terminated, the company could put him out immediately. Since many miners moved on relatively short notice even when not fired, the added costs of moving with five days as opposed to two weeks might not have been large.

The employment-contingency clause became most important during strikes. At some stage during a strike, companies sought to restart production. Long-term housing leases enhanced the striking workers' bargaining position. When strikers occupied mine housing, the company could not hire replacement workers without establishing new quarters, and strikers could more effectively use moral suasion and/or intimidation to prevent workers from returning to work.[42] With leases contingent on employment, the companies could evict striking workers with little notice. In addition to eliminating the bargaining advantage of the striking workers, the evictions imposed additional costs of finding and moving to new housing away from the mine. In major disputes strikers moved into tent colonies off company property. The evictions at times backfired by angering the miners, further convincing them that they were right to strike. Clearly, evictions were emotional events and missteps on either side sometimes brought fierce and violent responses.

In examining the employment contingency of housing leases, the anti-collective action and the isolation arguments are strongly intertwined from the employers' point of view. Under either argument, the employer sought to avoid giving the miners or their union an enhanced bargaining position. The arguments differ in that the isolation argument recognizes that workers also had incentives to rent rather than own in isolated mining towns. By renting and remaining mobile the worker avoided giving the employer monopsony power over his labor as well as investing in housing with significant risk of capital losses.

Was the desire to limit collective action the decisive determinant of company ownership of housing? Probably not. Problems with collective action were ubiquitous throughout the coal industry, so companies seeking to limit the miners' bargaining power would have provided company housing everywhere. Yet the U.S. Coal Commission in the early 1920s found that large numbers of miners did not live in company houses. Company housing was highly correlated with the isolation of the mine and lack of prior settlement in the area. Further, the decline of company housing coincided with increased density of settlement and better transportation. The decisive factor seems to be the effect of greater isolation on the workers' demands to own housing and the independents' costs of building it. Company towns were more common in more isolated areas because the miners themselves sought to avoid owning housing in a one-employer setting in an uncertain industry. In more settled areas, the miners sought to own their own housing and independents faced no cost disadvantage, overcoming any desire by the company to maintain a company town.

Model Towns

Some coal employers saw company housing as a means of practicing "welfare capitalism" in the 1910s and into the 1920s. By providing better housing the company hoped to increase productivity through enhanced health and work attitudes of workers; reduced absenteeism, particularly from liquor problems; by attracting a better quality of worker, often with families; and/or by reducing turnover and its associated costs. Welfare capitalism was not a universal goal of company housing. In Magnusson's 1920 survey of employers' reasons for owning housing, securing a better class of men and maintaining greater employment stability were only the third and fourth most common reasons given for providing housing.[43] If all coal operators had been surveyed, the percentage giving productivity explanations probably would have been smaller, because Magnusson's survey was skewed toward larger firms. During the peak of the model town movement in West Virginia in the 1910s, Robert Munn found that roughly half of the *major* bituminous coal companies engaged in some form of welfare capitalism. The welfare work included improving housing, building YMCAs and other recreational facilities, garden competitions, improved health care, better schools, and the hiring of welfare workers. In general, larger companies were more likely to have a formal and fairly extensive welfare program.[44]

Enhancing productivity may not have been the only reason for welfare capitalism. Based on quotes from *Coal Age* and various operators in West Virginia, Corbin and Munn to some extent saw the model towns as attempts to prevent strikes and unionization.[45] Brandes, although recognizing other reasons for the development of welfare capitalism, states that at its heart, welfare capitalism was a defensive strategy aimed at trade unionism.[46]

The model town movement also may have been a response to increased competition for workers, who had experienced a rise in their standard of living in other industries. Brandes notes that welfare capitalism waxed with prosperity and waned with depression. Within West Virginia coal mining, Munn notes that the model town movement peaked during World War I, when the demand for coal had expanded enormously while unemployment fell.[47] During the 1920s, interest in model towns in the coal industry declined, as the demand for miners slackened relative to the available supply. By the Great Depression, interest in welfare capitalism in coal mining and in other industries appears to have been eliminated.[48] The timing of the rise and fall of the model town also coincides with the decline in the UMWA's strength, making it hard to determine to what extent the model town was an anti-union device as opposed to a response to changing demand and supply conditions in the labor market.

Sanitation in Coal Towns During the 1920s

One important aspect of company housing that has been described briefly in many studies but not fully analyzed is the quality of sanitation. Straightforward descriptions of sanitation in coal towns in the early 1900s generally leaves the modern reader aghast that people could live in such conditions. However, such descriptions need to be placed in the context of their times. Although large metropolitan cities led the way in offering better sanitation, most small towns lagged behind. The methods for protecting the water supply and disposing of waste in coal towns appear roughly comparable with those in other small cities and better than in many rural areas. Further, the quality of sanitation varied widely among coal company towns. At one extreme were towns described as squalid pits with coal dust covering every surface, trash strewn about, unkept surface privies with excreta oozing into the water supply, and a pervasive and foul stench in the air. At the other extreme were carefully planned communities with regular cleanups, a well-protected water supply, and either flush toilets or well protected, watertight pail privies. Why the wide variation? The coal companies responded to differences in the costs and benefits of providing sanitation caused by differences in town age, location, and population. Since the company towns generally competed in regional labor markets, they paid penalties for offering worse sanitation. To attract workers, they had to raise wages despite the lower productivity caused by worse sanitation.

In the 1920s public health programs focused most on protection of the water supply and sewage control and disposal. The most advanced controls of the water supply were found in major cities with public water supplies that were treated, filtered, and tested consistently for bacteria. By 1920 slightly more than one-third of urban residents in the United States were drinking filtered water.[49] The percentages for coal communities were similar. In a 1922 study of 123 coal communities (including both independent and company towns) the U.S. Public Health Service found that the prevailing source of water in 38.2 percent of the towns was a public water supply. In 19.5 percent of the towns, including 50 percent of the population in the study, the water was chlorinated, coagulated, or filtered. In 39 percent of the towns, there was some form of laboratory testing for bacteria, although much of the testing was perfunctory.[50]

The sources of water and the ease with which families could obtain it were important considerations.[51] Unlike major cities, most coal towns relied on wells because they were not near large rivers or lakes. Deep, driven wells and impounded waters, prevailing in under 22 percent of the coal communities, were the safest water sources because they were more easily protected from soil contamination and surface waters. About 53 percent of the towns relied on shallow wells, which were more adversely affected by the environment. Sources in the remaining towns were rivers, springs, or combinations of the above. Miners generally obtained water at hydrants or pumps, one for each two to six families, as running water was found in only 15 percent of the family dwellings in mining towns.[52]

The Public Health Service considered waste and sewage disposal in the coal communities much less satisfactory than the water supply. Since sewage disposal was more effective in areas with rivers, lakes, or oceans, most major cities had a locational advantage over the coal towns. Advanced practices in major cities combined indoor flush toilets with sewer systems and sewage treatment. In part because they lacked access to larger bodies of water, most coal communities' facilities did not match these practices. Inside flush toilets were found in only about 3 percent of the miners' homes.[53] However, the percent of nonfarm households with flush toilets in towns with fewer than 2500 people was probably similar.[54] Although sewers were found in 37 of the 123 coal towns surveyed by the Public Health Service, they were the primary form of disposal in only 10, and sewage was treated in only four communities. The vast majority of miners disposed of human waste in privies of various types: sanitary pail privies that protected against contamination of ground water (prevailing in 8 percent of the towns); vault and pit privies (50 percent), which reduced odors and protected against flies but contaminated the ground water; and surface privies (24 percent), which often failed to protect the waste from flies. The sanitation provided by privies was heavily dependent on their maintenance, which often was inadequate.[55] As backward as these conditions seem, they were probably better than those in rural areas. The Public Health Service, in a study of rural sanitation from 1914 to 1916, found that prior to their educational programs in 15 counties, over 91 percent of country homes had "grossly insanitary disposal of human excrement."[56]

Sanitation in Company Towns

Although descriptions focus on the "representative" company town, the quality of sanitation varied from town to town. In 1922 the U.S. Coal Commission sent agents out to rate a large number of company towns, and Table 9-1 shows the frequency of the ratings. The variation in the quality of sanitation provided can be attributed in large part to differences in the costs and benefits of sanitation faced by the coal companies. The companies clearly did not provide sanitation for altruistic reasons. The U.S. Bureau of Mines claimed that the companies' primary consideration was profitability.[57] Even paternalistic employers generally saw that providing better sanitation was a means of increasing profits. They generally charged no explicit price for better sanitation but might have recovered some of the costs by attracting better workers, raising worker productivity, or through compensating reductions in wages. In an econometric study based on sanitation ratings by the U.S. Coal Commission, Dieter Lauszus and I found that workers were willing to accept lower

TABLE 9-1. Frequency Distribution of Community Ratings Collected by the United States Coal Commission, 1922[a]

	0–25	*25–40*	*40–50*	*50–60*	*60–75*	*75–100*
Housing	1	23	38	81	101	20
Water	8	21	31	47	72	83
Sanitation	22	55	66	55	42	24
Layout and Upkeep	77	78	34	36	24	15
Food and Merchandise	1	2	6	12	60	183
Medical and Health	5	6	37	73	105	38
Education	2	3	13	32	98	115
Religion and Recreation	36	52	36	54	50	36

Source: United States Coal Commission, "Bituminous Workers and Their Homes," *Report of the U.S. Coal Commission,* vol. 3 (Washington, DC: U.S. Government Printing Office, 1925), p. 1495.

[a]There were a total of 264 communities in this sample, information was not reported for the water rating of two communities or for the education rating of one community.

wages to work in towns with better quality sanitation.[58] Workers in West Virginia were willing to accept about three dollars less per month (roughly 3.4 percent of their monthly wage) in towns that shifted the sewage control from outdoor vault privies protected from flies to sanitary sewage control with clean indoor flush toilets (in the U.S. Coal Commission ratings this was a change of about one standard deviation). When we used a sample of towns from several states, workers were willing to accept $17.80 less per month (17 percent) for such an improvement in sewage control.

Companies balanced the gains from better sanitation against the costs of improved sanitation. In the Fishback-Lauszus study of sanitation ratings, larger populations allowed companies to take advantage of economies of scale in installing public water supplies, sewer systems, and hiring health inspectors. An increase in the town's population by roughly 1000 people (almost two standard deviations in the sample) was associated with an overall community rating that was typically eleven points (or almost one standard deviation) higher. Older company towns generally had worse community and sanitation ratings. Many relied on the sanitation technologies that they originally installed when they built the town. The older towns had less incentive than new towns to install new sanitation technologies. Both faced similar costs of installing the new technology. With no technology already in place, the new towns compared those costs with the full benefits of the new technology. The older towns with an existing technology compared their costs with the difference in sanitation benefits from the old and new technologies. Finally, company towns blessed with better locations, more space and less mountainous terrain, generally took advantage of those locations to offer better sanitation and nicer towns. The reverse side of the coin was that less fortunate towns were unwilling to sacrifice profits and overcome disadvantages from age, smaller size, and poor natural locations. A number of company towns deserved their reputation for dirt, stench, and unhealthy practices.

Sanitation in Company versus Independent Towns

Not all bituminous miners lived in company towns. A substantial percentage lived in independent towns in 1922, ranging from about one-third in southern Appalachia to 90 percent in Illinois and Indiana.[59] A commonly held opinion is that conditions were better in independent towns, because company towns sacrificed sanitation for higher profits. The impression may be flawed for three reasons. First, hundreds of employers, some in company towns and others in nearby independent towns, competed in the same coal labor market. In fact, in the Fishback-Lauszus study of sanitation, we found that miners did not demand higher wages to come to more remote company towns, suggesting that the coal labor market was truly a regional market in which miners could reach both remote and accessible company towns with similar ease.[60] In a company town the employer might have owned all the land and exercised autocratic authority, but if he provided too low a level of sanitation, ceteris paribus, miners "voted with their feet" and moved to another community where conditions were better.

Second, better sanitation potentially enhanced company profits. As shown in the previous section, workers were willing to accept lower wages to live in towns with better living conditions. Better sanitation led to lower turnover and thus lower costs of training workers in skills specific to that mine. Further, better sanitation contributed to lower absenteeism. The Bureau of Mines found that better sanitation led to as much as an 18 percent reduction in the number of miners carried on the payroll without a loss of output.[61]

Third, differences in the structure of decision making might have enabled company towns to improve sanitation more easily than independent towns. Lawrence Veillor, secretary of the National Housing Association in 1911, argued that "strangely enough democracy itself seems to be an obstacle to sanitary progress." Small property owners often were unwilling to vote tax increases for sanitary improvements, even though the improvements would have produced positive externalities and raised the general welfare.[62] In the company town, the employer's ownership of all property allowed him to internalize such external benefits more easily. It is possible that the external beneficiaries of better sanitation in an independent town might have negotiated with property owners to alter the incidence of taxation and thus get the town to build the improvement. Yet the costs of negotiation were higher than in the company town. In independent towns, each voter had some voice in altering tax schedules and institutional arrangements, while in the company town the employer could unilaterally decide to build projects and alter the "tax" incidence.

In 1922 the U.S. Public Health Service rated the public health practices in a number of company towns and independent coal communities. The Fishback-Lauszus study used econometric analysis to examine the effects of population and the type of town on the provision of sanitation. As in the study of company towns, we found that towns with larger populations had better sanitation. Further, controlling for population size, the sanitation ratings in company towns were roughly the same as in independent communities.

Conclusions

The widely held view of company towns is that they were uniformly dismal. Coal employers maintained a local monopoly on housing, stores, and other services, and little prevented employers from exploiting this position aside from collective action by the miners. Combined with the results in earlier chapters on wages, safety, and company stores, the results here revise this dismal view. Even in the absence of unions, competition among company towns for labor constrained the employers' ability to exploit their local monopoly on town services. The key factor causing the development of the company town was the isolation of mines and the lack of prior settlement. Company housing was not necessary, but in these isolated areas the employer had cost advantages over independents in providing housing. Given that housing was specific to the mine in an highly uncertain industry, part of the reason companies sought to own housing was to limit collective action. However, in more isolated areas workers also had incentives to leave the ownership of the housing in the company's hands. In more settled areas, the demands of workers to own their own housing overcame the companies's desire to limit collective action, and companies generally left the housing business.

Living in a company town was no picnic. Often, the housing had a dull sameness, coal dust hung in the air, and few had indoor plumbing. This was caused less by monopoly than by the higher costs of providing housing and store goods in isolated regions. Companies who faced lower costs generally offered better services, while workers demanded higher wages from lower-quality towns. During the coal boom numerous workers chose coal mining because the material conditions of life there were similar to those offered in other industries. There were negative aspects to mining, including dangerous work and living in an isolated area. But these were offset in part by higher hourly wages, more leisure, and lower rents.

The negative image of the company town stems in part from nonmaterial factors. In a larger city, workers might become angered with their employer over working conditions, their landlord over rent, the local merchant for price gouging, and the local politician for lousy garbage or police service. Thus, the workers' dissatisfactions were diffused over several independent entities. In the company town, the employer was landlord, merchant, and politician rolled into one. The employer therefore became the focal point of discontent over any and all aspects of life. Further, since the company town was private property, employers could prevent trespassers and maintain political control over the town. Workers feared the abuse of this power and the violation of their personal freedom. When these fears were realized in some situations where miners struck for higher wages or better conditions, violence erupted. In consequence, all aspects of the company town, material and nonmaterial, stood indicted.

NOTES

Parts of this chapter are reprinted with the permission of the *Journal of Law, Economics, and Organization* and Oxford University Press from Price Fishback, "The Economics of Company Housing: Historical Perspectives from the Coal Fields," *Journal of Law, Economics, and Organization* 8 (Spring 1992). © Oxford University Press. All rights reserved. The section on sanitation reprints some material that first appeared in Price V. Fishback and Dieter Lauszus, "The Quality of Services in Company Towns: Sanitation in Coal Towns During the 1920s," *Journal of Economic History* 49 (March 1989): 125–44. The material is reprinted with the permission of Dieter Lauszus, the Economic History Association, and the Cambridge University Press. © The Economic History Association. All rights reserved.

1. United States Coal Commission, "The Bituminous Mine Workers and Their Homes," *Report of the United States Coal Commission*, part 3, 68th Cong., 2d sess., (Washington, DC: U.S. Government Printing Office, 1925), pp. 1426–28, 1465–67.

2. United States Immigration Commission, *Report on Immigrants in Industries, Part I: Bituminous Coal Mining*, 61st Cong., 2d sess., (Washington, DC: U.S. Government Printing Office, 1911), vol. 2, p. 204.

3. Ibid., pp. 197–98.

4. U.S. Coal Commission, "Bituminous Mine Workers," pp. 1429–31.

5. David Corbin, *Life, Work and Rebellion in the Coal Fields: The Southern West Virginia Miners, 1880–1922* (Chicago: University of Illinois Press, 1981), pp. 117–22.

6. Robert Munn, "The Development of Model Towns in the Bituminous Coal Fields, *West Virginia History* 40 (Spring 1979): 243–53.

7. The U.S. Coal Commission collected a number of leases from various companies in West Virginia, Pennsylvania, and Ohio and published seven representative leases in its report. The clause making the lease contingent on employment appeared in all of the representative leases from West Virginia, but did not appear in the Ohio lease or in two of the three leases in Pennsylvania. U.S. Coal Commission, "Bituminous Mine Workers," pp. 1579–87.

8. Albert Hinrichs, *The United Mine Workers of America and the Non-Union Coal Fields* (New York: Longmans, Green and Co., 1923), pp. 63–69; U.S. Coal Commission, "Bituminous Mine Workers," pp. 1437–39, 1579–1587.

9. For a discussion of court cases concerning such relationships, see Hinrichs, *The United Mine Workers*, pp. 63–69.

10. See Winthrop Lane, *Civil War in West Virginia*, (New York: B. W. Huebsch, Inc., 1921), p. 51; Curtis Seltzer, *Fire in the Hole: Miners and Managers in the American Coal Industry* (Lexington, KY: University of Kentucky Press, 1985), p. 16.

11. Lane, *Civil War*, p. 49.

12. One example of such a clause comes from the Island Creek Coal Company of Logan, West Virginia. It states

> That the said lessee shall not permit any gambling or gaming of any description for money or anything of intrinsic value, or permit *any improper or suspicious person* to come upon or remain on the said demised premises, and the lessor shall at all times have the right to enter upon the demised premises for the purpose of ejecting any and all such persons.

Quoted in Hinrichs, *The United Mine Workers*, p. 63 (his italics).

13. U.S. Coal Commission, "Bituminous Mine Workers," pp. 1438, 1579–87.

14. Ibid., p. 1438.

15. In a study by Leifur Magnusson in West Virginia and Pennsylvania all thirty-two companies studied deferred rental payments during times of sickness or shutdown of the mine. Five of thirty-two companies reported rebates on rent during sickness or unemployment. Several others had no specific policy in that respect but judged each case on its merits. There were also several instances where pensioners or widows of former employees lived rent-free. Leifur Magnusson, "Housing by Employers in the United States," *Bureau of Labor Statistics Bulletin No. 263* (Washington, DC: U.S. Government Printing Office, 1920), pp. 65–66.

16. The Coal Commission also noted several other clauses found in the leases of some companies. At some companies, the company legally could put the mine worker and family out of the house at the termination of the lease without prejudicing its claim for any rental arrears and without incurring liability for damage resulting to the mine workers' belongings after eviction. The company had clauses allowing it to pay itself out of mine workers' wages for rent due and also for damage to property. In a lease used by certain companies in West Virginia, the company could also withhold all unpaid wages at the termination of a lease, until the premises were surrendered. Also, the company could retain permanently $2 for each day the premises were occupied by the mine worker or his family after termination of the lease. U.S. Coal Commission, "Bituminous Mine Workers," 1925, pp. 1438–39, 1579–87.

17. Corbin, *Life, Work, and Rebellion*, pp. 9–10.

18. Ibid.

19. Howard B. Lee, *Bloodletting in Appalachia* (Morgantown, WV: West Virginia University Press, 1969), p. 20–21).

20. Magnusson, "Housing by Employers," p. 49. The sample of employers may not be fully representative. Magnusson (p. 9) states that the object of the investigation was to study "the best and most representative" work being done by employers. The sample was skewed toward larger housing enterprises, but, "in many instances, smaller enterprises were included

in the survey because of their representative character, or because they illustrated points of special interest."

21. U.S. Coal Commission, "Bituminous Mine Workers," p. 1437. In studying rentals, the Coal Commission (1925, pp. 1519, 1533) found that in West Virginia miners paid significantly lower rents but had fewer conveniences than workers in nearby manufacturing districts. In Charleston, a three- or four-room apartment in a tenement building, equipped with electricity and gas hookups and running water, rented for $9 to $14 a month. A four-room house in Charleston with more modern conveniences than in company houses rented for at least $14, but rent of $25 was more common. Mining houses in the New River district, without electricity or inside running water rented for $8 to $9 a month. In its comparisons, the Coal Commission concluded that the miner in the New River and Kanawha districts paid "less rent than city wage earners even though his home ha[d] less equipment." Company house occupants often got their fuel and light at much lower cost than other wage earners, generally paid nothing for water, and medical service was much cheaper than the expense of the same service was in town. In budget studies, the U.S. Coal Commission (p. 1456) found that in West Virginia, Pennsylvania, and Ohio, rent accounted for only 4.2 to 5.8 percent of the miners' expenditures. Michael Haines's analysis of budgets for workers in various industries in the 1890s shows that rent was a smaller share of expenditures for coal miners than for other workers. Michael Haines, "Consumer Behavior and Immigrant Assimilation: A Comparison of the United States, Britain, and Germany, 1889–1890," NBER Working Paper Series on Historical Factors in Long-Run Growth, Working Paper No. 6, August 1989.

22. Hinrichs, *The United Mine Workers*, pp. 61–62.

23. Magnusson argued that the land cost could be left out of the calculation because the company had purchased the land primarily for mining purposes. Magnusson, "Housing by Employers," p. 86. That depends on whether the company had the option to buy just the mineral rights to the land. The cost of surface rights might reasonably be included as part of the initial investment in the house.

24. Ibid., p. 67.

25. Ibid., pp. 83–5, 89. There is one exception. A company in Alabama estimated a gross return of 20 percent on the value of their housing (pp. 86–87). However, their methods of calculation appear to underestimate the value of housing and thus overestimate the gross return on the investment.

26. Price V. Fishback and Dieter Lauszus, "The Quality of Services in Company Towns: Sanitation in Coal Towns During the 1920s," *Journal of Economic History* 49 (March 1989): 136.

27. Among the people who describe isolation and sparse settlement as a major reason for employer housing are: Hinrichs, *United Mine Workers*, p. 54; Magnusson, "Housing by Employers," pp. 19–21; James B. Allen, *The Company Town in the American West*, (Norman: University of Oklahoma Press, 1966), p. 7; Stuart Brandes, *American Welfare Capitalism, 1880–1940* (Chicago: University of Chicago Press, 1976), p. 43; U.S. Coal Commission, "Bituminous Coal Miners," pp. 1426–28; U.S. Immigration Commission, *Immigrants: Bituminous Coal Mining*, vol. 2, p. 206.

28. Magnusson, "Housing by Employers," p. 21.

29. The example presumes that when the mine closes few people will wish to remain in the housing with no work available.

30. The mine operator might subsidize an independent to build and own the housing. However, if the costs of building for employer and independent were the same, the employer had no incentive to incur the transactions costs of bringing in an independent. The only reason for hiring the independent was if the independent built and managed the property more cheaply.

31. The asset-specificity of the housing and land to the mine is important for another

reason. The coal company might have allowed independents to own the surface rights to the land while retaining the mineral rights beneath it. However, mining decisions also involved destroying housing to create a new mine opening, tipple, railroad spur, or slag heap. Unless previously negotiated, the surface owner was in a position to extract extra compensation from the company for these actions. Once again, contractual stipulations might be included in the housing and land deeds to allow the company to exercise these options. The costs of negotiating these stipulations and enforcing them were avoided when the company maintained control of both the surface and mineral rights to the land.

32. Brandes, *American Welfare Capitalism*, p. 43.

33. Monopsony means single buyer, analogous to the monopoly as a single seller. Magnusson ("Housing by Employers," p. 211) recognized the impact of owning housing in isolated towns on the miners' bargaining position, while the U.S. Immigration Commission (*Immigrants: Bituminous Coal Mining*, vol. 2, p. 206) noted the impact of the close ties between the house and the mines on the value of the miner's home when the mine closed.

34. At this point I have ignored "reputation" effects. If the employer cuts wages after miners buy homes, he may have trouble attracting new miners to the town in the future, unless he offers a bonus to guard against wage cuts. However, if the miners had not established safeguards, the damage to the employer's reputation was borne by the home-owning miners as new miners purchased the homes at a low price, reflecting the employers' monopsony position. The reputation effect may be diminished if there is a constant stream of new workers coming into the labor market without full information on the reputations of different mines.

35. Not all mines were hit equally by fluctuations in coal demand. See Chapter 3.

36. U.S. Immigration Commission, *Immigrants: Bituminous Coal Mining*, vol. 2, p. 206.

37. Oliver Williamson, *The Economic Institutions of Capitalism* (New York: The Free Press, 1985), pp. 35–38.

38. Magnusson, "Housing by Employers," pp. 205–23.

39. In a survey of black miners in the early 1930s in West Virginia, Laing found that despite the Great Depression, at least 20 percent owned real estate. Most who owned real estate owned farms, or lots and houses in independent towns. James T. Laing, "The Negro Miner in West Virginia," Ph.D. dissertation, Ohio State University, 1933, pp. 292–300.

40. Corbin, *Life, Work, and Rebellion*, pp. 122–23; Brandes, *American Welfare Capitalism*, p. 48.

41. Hinrichs, *United Mine Workers*, p. 63.

42. Brandes, *American Welfare Capitalism*, p. 49.

43. Magnusson, "Housing by Employers," p. 20.

44. Munn, "Model Towns," p. 247.

45. Corbin, *Life, Work, and Rebellion*, pp. 117–22; Munn, "Model Towns."

46. Brandes, "American Welfare Capitalism," p. 32.

47. Ibid., pp. 18–19, 26; Munn, "Model Towns," p. 251.

48. Brody, David, "The Rise and Decline of Welfare Capitalism," *Workers in Industrial America: Essays on the 20th Century Struggle* (New York: Oxford University Press, 1980).

49. G. Whipple, "Fifty Years of Water Purification," in M. Ravenel, ed., *A Half Century of Public Health* (American Public Health Association, 1921) p. 166.

50. U.S. Public Health Service, "Sanitation of 123 Communities in the Bituminous Coal Districts of 9 States," *Report of the U.S. Coal Commission*, 68th Cong., 2nd sess. (Washington, DC: U.S. Government Printing Office, 1925), pp. 1625–29. The source is considered prevailing if more than 60 percent of the population in the community used it.

51. The importance of the water source to sanitation choice in major cities is discussed in Louis Cain, "An Economic History of Urban Location and Sanitation," *Research in Economic History* 2 (1977): 337–89.

52. U.S. Coal Commission, "The Bituminous Mine Workers and Their Homes," *Report of the U.S. Coal Commission*, pp. 1439, 1474.

53. Ibid., pp. 1473, 1445.

54. Stanley Lebergott, *The American Economy: Income, Wealth, and Want* (Princeton, NJ: Princeton University Press: 1976), pp. 271–72, estimated that, in 1930, 51 percent of American households had inside flush toilets, 85 percent of urban households had flush toilets and 8 percent of farm households had flush toilets. Using Lebergott's figures and data on the number of households from U.S. Bureau of the Census, *Historical Statistics of the United States: Colonial Times to 1970* (Washington, DC: U.S. Government Printing Office, 1975), pp. 11 and 43, we calculated that about 6.7 percent of rural nonfarm households had inside flush toilets in 1930. Since only 20 percent of all U.S. households had flush toilets in 1920, the percentage of households with flush toilets was probably similar in company towns and other towns of similar size in 1922.

55. U.S. Public Health Service, "Sanitation of 123," pp. 1616, 1630–35.

56. L. L. Lumsden, "Rural Sanitation, a Report on Special Studies Made in 15 Countries in 1914, 1915, and 1916," U.S. Public Health Service *Bulletin* No. 94 (Washington, DC: 1918), p. 43.

57. Joseph H. White, "Houses for Mining Towns," U.S. Bureau of Mines, *Bulletin* No. 87, (Washington DC: 1914), p. 6.

58. Fishback and Lauszus, "Quality of Services," p. 136.

59. U.S. Coal Commission, "Bituminous Workers," p. 1427.

60. Fishback and Lauszus, "Quality of Services," p. 136.

61. Dwight E. Woodbridge, "Sanitation at Mining Villages in the Birmingham District, Alabama," U.S. Bureau of Mines, *Technical Paper* No. 33 (Washington, DC: 1913), p. 21.

62. Lawrence Veillor, "Housing and Health," *The Annals of the American Academy of Political and Social Science* 37 (March 1911): 260.

10

Coal Mines as Melting Pots

The rapid expansion of the coal industry from the 1890s into the 1920s opened coal mining opportunities for workers from a wide variety of ethnic backgrounds. European immigrants poured into the coal fields at the turn of the century. By 1910 they accounted for almost half of the coal mining labor force. Their percentages dropped in the late teens and early 1920s when immigration controls were established. A significant number of black workers also entered the coal fields. The percentage of black workers in U.S. mines peaked at 9.2 percent in 1930 before declining dramatically during the Great Depression and afterward. The mix of immigrants, blacks, and native whites varied greatly by region. Black workers were located primarily in the South, while immigrants tended to locate in Pennsylvania, the Midwest, and the West. Southern West Virginia was the area with the greatest mixture of ethnicities with a work force mixing Appalachian whites, other native whites, blacks from the South, and European immigrants.

A number of excellent studies describe the cultural interactions and clashes among these groups. Nearly every modern labor history describes the immigrant experience. Lewis, Corbin, and Trotter describe how black workers were ostracized or assimilated into the coal towns.[1] Lewis discusses the black experience in each region as examples of different theories. In Alabama he sees Marxist class struggle theory as the basis of discussion, in the northern fields he uses the theory of split labor markets, and he sees West Virginia as a combination of the two.[2] We needn't rely on multiple theories. The black experience in different regions can be explained just as easily using standard labor economics and emphasizing the tightness or looseness of labor markets and the extent of unionization. Blacks did better in tight labor markets where employers were constantly seeking new workers. They migrated to the higher wage fields, so that there was some integration of the Alabama and West Virginia labor markets. But black migration further north was constrained by the limits on employment growth and race barriers stemming from the unionization of the northern fields.

The tools of modern labor economics can be used to examine how blacks and immigrants fared relative to native whites in the workplace. Were they paid lower wages, denied upward mobility in the job hierarchy, placed in more unsafe parts of the mine, housed differently, or charged different prices at the company store? Economists who study discrimination offer several insights into the study of ethnic workers. First, some differences in pay or in treatment may reflect differences in the productivity of workers. A number of immigrants were less productive because they had little mining experience, could not speak English, and had little formal schooling. Similarly, most blacks received only limited schooling in the highly unequal school systems of the deep South. These differences may not fully account for ethnic differences in earnings, but it is important to control for them before charging that employers were practicing pure discrimination. Some of the worst discrimination was practiced by local school systems against blacks long before they ever reached the workplace. Second, the more competition among employers to hire workers, the less likely that employers will discriminate effectively against workers. When the coal industry expanded in unpopulated areas, even employers who disliked blacks and immigrants found it too costly to indulge their taste for discrimination, because they could not have attracted enough able workers to fill their mines. On the workers' side of the market, tight labor markets offered black workers (and immigrants) more opportunities to avoid working for discriminating employers. Unfortunately, during downturns the impact of discrimination was likely to be greater. Third, employment packages were complex, such that discrimination may have been more common on nonwage aspects of employment, such as limits on advancement in the job hierarchy, or assignments to worse workplaces. Therefore, the researcher cannot stop at examining just wages and earnings when searching for discrimination.[3] Fourth, employers were not the only discriminators in the labor market. Blacks and immigrants at times suffered the prejudices of fellow workers, who saw other ethnic groups as primary competitors for their jobs. The impact of discrimination by fellow workers was most obvious in union areas where workers had obtained some labor market power. As with employers, when there were higher costs to discriminating, fellow workers practiced less discrimination. In situations where workers unionized a work force without black workers, the local union often continued to prevent blacks from joining the union. On the other hand, where blacks were a significant part of the work force before unionization, they were incorporated as important partners in the union efforts.[4]

The Geographic Location of Blacks and Immigrants

Immigrants from the British Isles and northern European countries played major roles in the early development of the U.S. coal industry in the mid 1800s. Most British immigrants came with coal mining experience and helped train American workers. Some eventually became foremen and mine supervisors. By 1890 the origins of migration had begun to shift. In the 1880s the Pennsylvania and Midwestern mining regions began to hire Italians, Hungarians, Czechs, Poles, and other nationalities in southern and eastern Europe. As the coal industry boomed after the depression of the 1890s, the number of immigrants in the coal industry expanded rapidly.[5] Table 10-1 shows the enormous increase in immigrants between 1890 and 1900 and again between 1900 and 1910. In Pennsylvania the number of immigrants

TABLE 10-1. Black, Immigrant and Native White Mine Operatives in Coal States, All Mining, 1890–1900, Bituminous Coal Mining, 1910–1930

State	*All Mining*		*Coal Mining*		
	1890[a]	*1900*[a]	*1910*	*1920*	*1930*
Alabama					
Black	3,687	9,735	11,189	14,097	12,742
Immigrants	1,492	1,573	1,381	819	371
Native Whites	2,787	6,590	8,208	11,288	10,843
West Virginia[b]					
Black	2,016	4,620	11,237	17,799	22,089
Immigrants	1,375	2,968	16,485	17,943	13,551
Native Whites	6,314	13,209	27,161	51,985	61,749
Virginia					
Black	1,700	2,651	1,719	2,450	1,511
Immigrants	375	479	1,310	797	276
Native Whites	1,848	4,239	4,261	10,071	10,840
Kentucky					
Black	976	2,206	3,888	7,407	7,346
Immigrants	581	471	577	2,212	1,212
Native Whites	3,534	6,622	13,845	34,648	45,719
Pennsylvania[c]					
Black	849	1,616	1,773	2,930	7,574
Immigrants	67,790	105,845	195,798	164,826	113,350
Native Whites	48,117	73,013	94,158	129,588	146,648
Tennessee					
Black	769	3,092	1,609	913	578
Immigrants	500	300	348	120	49
Native Whites	3,620	7,498	9,137	11,193	8,135
Missouri					
Black	915	1,422	1,066	1,132	657
Immigrants	2,404	2,488	1,874	1,480	580
Native Whites	9,629	16,673	5,257	6,887	3,629
Illinois					
Black	556	1,368	1,512	2,194	1,242
Immigrants	12,720	18,487	28,424	32,192	18,919
Native Whites	8,919	18,329	28,802	47,917	33,967
Iowa					
Black	542	1,065	1,600	1,103	485
Immigrants	4,063	4,400	5,460	4,277	2,042
Native Whites	3,133	5,613	6,930	7,427	4,550
Ohio					
Black	578	780	1,004	1,389	1,261
Immigrants	7,770	8,978	14,141	14,705	7,790
Native Whites	16,087	23,451	25,241	31,693	18,561
Indiana					
Black	172	399	376	614	314
Immigrants	2,184	2,678	4,183	4,933	2,371
Native Whites	4,121	9,498	14,625	23,601	12,716
Colorado					
Black	142	137	297	328	267
Immigrants	9,968	13,545	7,751	6,622	3,429
Native Whites	9,950	14,634	3,388	5,456	4,853

(*continued*)

TABLE 10-1. *(Continued)*

State	All Mining		Coal Mining		
	1890[a]	1900[a]	1910	1920	1930
United States					
Black			40,584	54,432	57,291
Immigrants			323,669	278,091	175,898
Native Whites			304,602	398,942	383,839

Sources: U.S. Department of Commerce, Bureau of the Census, *Eleventh Census of the United States, Populaiton, 1890,* part II, Table 116; idem, *Occupations at the Twelfth Census (Special Report)* (Washington, DC: U.S. Government Printing Office, 1904), Table 41; idem, *Thirteenth Census of the United States, Population, 1910,* vol. IV, Table VII; idem, *Fourteenth Census of the United States, Population, 1920,* vol. 4, pp. 874ff.; idem, *Fifteenth Census of the United States, Population, 1930,* vol. IV, Table 11.

[a]Data for 1890 and 1900 are for miners and quarrymen for all minerals and metals. The states with significant amounts of other types of mining are Colorado, Misouri and Virginia. Data for 1910, 1920, and 1930 are specifically for coal mines.

[b]The census figures in West Virginia from 1920 may be underestimated. A *McDowell Times* reporter followed the census enumerators in one area and found he had missed a large group of miners. The paper estimated an undercount of about 2000 black miners in West Virginia for that year. West Virginia Bureau of Negro Welfare and Statistics, *Report,* 1921–1922, p. 12.

[c]Includes anthracite miners in every year.

in coal mining (including anthracite) nearly tripled between 1890 and 1910. In West Virginia the number rose from less than 1400 in 1890 to over 16,000 in 1910. Around World War I the number of immigrant miners began to tail off. Many left coal mining for other employment, as the War and then import quotas curtailed the flow of new immigrants.

Immigrant coal workers were not evenly dispersed across the United States. In 1910 immigrants accounted for roughly two-thirds of the work force in Pennsylvania, over 70 percent of the Colorado workforce, and roughly 50 percent in Illinois. The southern states of Kentucky, Alabama, and Tennessee, which offered among the lowest coal wages in the country, attracted relatively few immigrants.

In contrast, black coal miners were concentrated in the low-wage south. Slaves worked in the coal mines in Virginia prior to the Civil War, and black workers helped open the coalfields near Birmingham, Alabama and in West Virginia.[6] As late as 1900 most blacks in the coal industry had located in the southern Appalachian regions that dipped down into Birmingham. Blacks represented over 20 percent of the mine workers in Alabama (54.3 percent), West Virginia (22.2), Virginia (35.9), Kentucky (23.7), and Tennessee (28.4). After 1890, these areas were paying the lowest wages in the industry.[7] Table 10-2 shows the average daily earnings of coal miners by region and ethnic group from surveys collected by the United States Immigration Commission in 1909. The U.S. average earnings for blacks were much lower largely because blacks were located in the south. Within regions the black-white wage gaps were smaller. One caveat: the differences caused by regional wage gaps probably overstate the real differences in wages because studies that adjust for regional cost-of-living differences generally show smaller differences.

As coal mining experienced a long-term boom into the 1920s, black workers

TABLE 10-2. Average Earning per Day by Ethnic Group, 1909 (Current $)

	Native White Native Parents	*Native Black*	*Native White Foreign Parents*	*Foreign Born*
Survey Average	2.31	1.98	2.38	2.16
Pennsylvania	2.18	2.02	2.20	2.04
Midwest	2.46	2.43	2.65	2.45
Southwest	2.60	2.48	2.57	2.66
South	2.16	1.87	2.16	2.12
West Virginia	2.16	2.10		2.14
Alabama and Virginia	2.14	1.85		2.06

Source: U.S. Immigration Commission, *Report on Immigrants in Industries, Part I: VBituminous Coal Mining,* vol. II, 61st Cong., 2nd Sess. (Washington, DC: U.S. Government Printing Office, 1911), pp. 180, 301, 374, 434, 479, 528, 529. Alabama and Virginia wages were calculated as a residual from the southern wages after West Virginia wages were calculated. Since other evidence suggests that Virginia and West Virginia wages were similar, it is likely that most of the workers in the Virginia and Alabama group were from Alabama.

began shifting into the higher wage regions. Initially the shift was out of Alabama toward West Virginia. Then in the late teens and the 1920s more opportunities opened in Pennsylvania and Northern West Virginia. In 1900 Alabama employed nearly 33 percent of the black miners in the twelve states listed in Table 10-1, while West Virginia employed only 16 percent. Numerous Alabamans left the Birmingham fields for West Virginia during the teens.[8] By 1930, West Virginia employed 38.6 percent of the black coal miners, Alabama only 22.2 percent.

Most black migrants initially settled in the southern fields of West Virginia. Until World War I it seemed like there was a wall preventing black migration into the coalfields in the Midwest, northern West Virginia and Pennsylvania. During World War I, the wall began to crack, releasing a trickle of black migrants into the more northern fields. During the mid 1920s, when the coal industry stagnated and the operators in the northern fields began repudiating their contracts with the United Mine Workers, black migration into northern West Virginia and Pennsylvania increased. Pennsylvania's share of black coal miners in the United States rose from 5.4 percent in 1920 to 13.2 percent in 1930. Previously unionized northern West Virginia saw a sharp jump in the number of black coal miners. Spero and Harris saw the increases as primarily the result of black strikebreaking in areas where the union locals had kept a predominantly white work force. But at least part of the trend had been established before the union struggles began.[9]

The late 1920s was a watershed for black employment in the coal industry. With coal employment dropping dramatically, the potential for effective discrimination increased since blacks had fewer opportunities to avoid discriminating employers. Some scholars blame the introduction of the hand loader.[10] By 1932, blacks were concentrated in hand-loading jobs. When hand loading was replaced by machine loaders, they claim that few blacks were given machine loader jobs and consequently they left the industry. Other factors also contributed to the decline in black employment. The 1930s saw significant outmigration of blacks and whites from Appalachia, as a number were pushed out by the loss of jobs or were pulled north by higher wages in industrial cities. Whatever the reason, the percentage of black miners in southern Appalachia fell from 22.5 percent in 1930 to 16.3 percent in 1940, falling again to 10.7 percent in 1950.[11]

The Limited Nature of Discrimination in West Virginia

The greatest melting pot of ethnic groups was West Virginia during the hand-loading era. From 1890 through the early 1920s the West Virginia coal industry experienced an enormous boom in an isolated area with a small local population. West Virginia coal operators constantly sought new workers and brought blacks from the south, immigrants from Europe, and native whites from near and far. Aside from short-term slowdowns in the boom, West Virginia seems to be an excellent example of a tight labor market, where employers competed actively to hire laborers. A series of studies of discrimination show that strong competition among employers led to the elimination of many common forms of discrimination, although the refusal of whites to work for black supervisors withstood the competitive onslaught. Amazingly, competition among employers chipped away at some forms of societal discrimination. In a handful of mining towns, housing was integrated, while West Virginia coal employers acted to reduce the inequality of the West Virginia segregated school system.

Wage Rates and Earnings

Of the geographic areas in Table 10-2, West Virginia displayed the smallest range in daily earnings. Black workers earned about 6 cents less than native white workers with native parents and only 4 cents less than foreign-born workers. Why the difference?

The differentials probably did not arise due to direct differences in the piece rates paid to different ethnic groups.[12] James Laing in his extensive study of black miners in West Virginia in the early 1930s stated: "With very few exceptions the principal jobs of coal mining pay the same wage to all employees regardless of color or nationality, a condition which does not exist in all industry."[13] Evidence from other sources confirm his statements. Payrolls from the Raleigh Coal and Coke Company for 1903, which hired a number of black and white miners, show that nearly every miner was paid the same 67 cents per ton.[14] Information published by George Surface on Appalachian mines suggests that in most cases black workers were paid the same piece rates as whites.[15] In nearby Virginia, evidence on black and white wages collected by the Department of Labor and Industry shows that in most jobs blacks were paid the same or higher average rates as whites.[16]

In the absence of wage-rate differentials, the difference in daily earnings might have been caused by several factors: differences in the average productivity of ethnic groups, differences in the locations of ethnic groups, differences in the assignments of workplaces, and differences in the positioning in the job hierarchy.

Although we have no direct measures of the productivity of workers, some of the wage differences may reflect productivity and mobility differences arising from the relative lack of literacy of black and immigrant workers.[17] In the major coal mining counties of West Virginia in 1910, the native white literacy rates were typically 14 percent higher than the literacy rates for blacks and immigrant workers.[18] Literacy had some relevance for coal mining because it was a sign of at least minimal schooling with some mathematical training, which would have aided workers in learning the intricacies of coal extraction. Immigrants faced an added disadvantage when they could not speak English, raising the supervisory costs to employers and limiting their movement to mines where there were other immigrants who spoke their language.

Some of the wage differences might also reflect differences in location in 1909. I estimated regressions using evidence from counties in West Virginia of the average piece rate on the price of coal, differences in output per man-hour, the black percentage of employment, and the percent of Southern European immigrants for the years 1907, 1910, 1914, 1915, 1918, and 1923. The regressions were run for two sets of piece rates: pick mining rates and rates paid to loaders. After 1910 Southern European immigrants, who were spread throughout the state, did not appear to be located in low-wage areas after controlling for the other factors either in the pick mining or the loader regressions. The story for black workers was more complicated. In the years from 1907 to 1914, blacks were found in areas with lower pick mining rates. During the boom of World War I there was no evidence that blacks were located in low-wage areas. However, in 1923 they again were located in low-wage regions. In contrast, in the loader piece rate regressions, blacks did not appear to be located in low-wage regions in any of the years. The results seem to suggest that location affected black pick miners to a small extent and helps account for the differences in wages seen in Table 10-2. But blacks seemed to have benefitted from the spread of the machine cutter technology, since they were not located in counties that paid low piece rates to loaders.[19]

Given that the earnings differences were small, the differences in literacy and geographic location seem to more than account for the ethnic differences in West Virginia wages seen in Table 10-2. Wage-rate differences are not the only aspects of employment where discrimination might appear. James Laing found:

> In the assignment of "place" in the mine the foreman is likely to give the pet pension drawers to other than Negro loaders. A comment of a former superintendent from Alabama, now selling insurance to the miners is of interest here. . . he remarked concerning [Laing's] study of payrolls: "But that won't show the efficiency of the Negro because he don't get a fair show. The Negro is not apt to get a fair show in the matter of places to work. He cannot load as large an amount of coal under such conditions." He says that always some clique controls the mine due to a favored position with the mine boss. He says further "The Negro is not apt to be in such a position, but does not complain, he takes what he is given."[20]

Unlike discrimination on wage rates, nonwage discrimination often is not easily discovered before arriving at the mine. Since black workers find such discrimination harder to avoid, nonwage discrimination probably persists more than wage discrimination in competitive environments.[21]

TABLE 10-3. Fatal Accidents per Million Man-Days and Mean Experience for Inside Workers Killed in Accidents from West Virginia Counties with Over One Hundred Black Coal Workers

	Fatal Accidents per Million Man-Days			*Mean Experience of Fatal Accident Victims*		
Half Decade	*American White*	*Black*	*Southern European*	*American White*	*Black*	*Southern European*
1906–1910	28.38	31.28	51.83	7.4	6.7	3.2
1911–1915	25.21	27.25	39.53	8.6	7.3	4.8
1916–1920	22.22	23.04	28.68	9.6	8.8	7.0
1921–1925	28.80	23.15	27.16	9.9	10.6	10.5

Source: Fatality samples from the West Virginia Department of Mines, *Annual Reports,* 1906–1925. See also Price V. Fishback, "Discrimination on Nonwage Margins: Safety in the West Virginia Coal Industry, 1906–1925," *Economic Inquiry* 23 (October 1985): 651–69.

Note: The number of men killed can also be treated as the number of man-days in which a worker was killed; therefore accident rates can be treated as the percentage of man-days in which a worker was killed. Differences-in-percentages tests who that the black and native white accident rates are not statistically significantly different until the last period. The Southern European death rates are statistically significantly different from those for native whites in the first three periods but not in the last period.

Differences in Workplace Safety

One potential area for nonwage discrimination is in the assignments to workplaces or jobs. In mines where all workers were paid similar piece rates, a foreman might have discriminated by assigning blacks and/or immigrants to more dangerous workplaces, like areas with faulty roofs. Or he might give blacks and immigrants more dangerous jobs. Discrimination would then appear in the form of higher accident rates. Table 10-3 shows comparisons of the fatal accident rates of American whites, blacks, and immigrants from southern and eastern Europe. The fatal accident rates for blacks and American whites are roughly the same. Statistical tests show that the only period when there is a significant difference between the two accident rates is the early 1920s, when the black accident rate was lower. On the other hand, the accident rates for Southern Europeans were substantially higher than for American whites and blacks until the early 1920s.

A major cause for differences in accident rates was differences in the mining experience of blacks, native whites, and immigrants. Table 10-3 also shows the mean experience of workers killed in fatal accidents in West Virginia. Black and native white workers had roughly the same accident rates largely because their levels of experience were similar. The high accident rates for southern and eastern Europeans prior to 1921 stemmed largely from their relative lack of experience. The flood of new immigrants prior to 1910 meant that immigrants had less than half the mining experience of American whites and blacks. As the number of new immigrants slowed to a trickle, the average mining experience of southern and eastern Europeans caught up with that of the native miners, and the immigrants' accident rates fell to the same level as accident rates of native-born workers in the early 1920s. Although there may have been some safety discrimination against southern and eastern Europeans, it is clearly not the major cause of accident rate differences.

Had discrimination been the cause of higher accident rates, it would have had to lessen tremendously over the period from 1905 to 1925. In fact, the discriminatory atmosphere against immigrants was becoming increasingly virulent during World War I and gained enough strength to cause the exclusion of immigrant workers in the early 1920s.[22]

Positioning in the Job Hierarchy

Histories of black workers in the early twentieth century suggest four basic tenets about their job prospects: Blacks were generally denied management jobs, kept out of machine jobs, stuck primarily in low-wage occupations, and given the dirtiest, most dangerous jobs.[23] Job prospects for immigrants were also often described in the same way. The four tenets are based on observations across all industries in the United States. How well do these basic tenets fit the distribution of ethnic workers in the job hierarchy in coal mining?

Tables 10-4 and 10-5 summarize evidence presented in Appendix E on the distribution of blacks, native whites, and southern and eastern European immigrants. The evidence from 1932 comes from a survey conducted by James T. Laing for his study of black workers. The evidence prior to 1930 comes from the occupa-

TABLE 10-4. Classification of Black, Open, and Nonblack Jobs, 1906–1932

	1906–1910	*1911–1915*	*1916–1920*	*1921–1925*	*1932*
Black Jobs					
Driver	Black	Black	Black	Black	Black
Miner	Black	Black	Black	Black	?
Slateman	Open	Black	Black	Black	?
Nonblack Jobs					
Motorman	Nonblack	Nonblack	Open	Nonblack	Nonblack
Boss	Nonblack	Nonblack	Nonblack	Nonblack	Nonblack
Bratticeman & Timberman	?	Nonblack	?	Nonblack	?
Tippleman	Open	Nonblack	?	?	Nonblack
Open Jobs					
Machine runner	Open[N]	Nonblack	Open	Open	Nonblack
Brakeman	Nonblack	Open	Open	Black	Open
Loader	Nonblack	Nonblack	Open	Open[B]	Black
Trackman	Nonblack	Open[N]	Open[N]	Nonblack	Open
Laborer	Black	Open	Open	Open	?
Machine Helper	Open	Open	Open	Open	?

Source: Information from James T. Laing, "The Negro Miner in West Virginia," Ph.D. dissertation, Ohio State University, 1933, pp. 193–97 for 1932. For the earlier years from the lists of accident victims, West Virginia Department of Mines, *Annual Reports* for the years 1906 to 1925. For the percentages of workers in each job, see Appendix E. A version of this table appeared in Price V. Fishback, "Segregation in Job Hierarchies: West Virginia Coal Mining, 1906–1932," *Journal of Economic History* 44 (September 1984): 763. It is reprinted here with the permission of The Economic History Association and Cambridge University Press.

Notes: The question mark suggests unknown. For the periods prior to 1932 there were less than twenty-five workers in the job sample. for 1932, it is not measured.

[N]Job would be defined as nonblack if the significance level of the chi-square test was 10 percent.

[B]Job would be defined as black of the significance level of the chi-square test was 10 percent.

TABLE 10-5. Classification of Southern European, Open, and Non-Southern European Jobs, 1906–1932

	1906–1910	*1911–1915*	*1916–1920*	*1921–1925*	*1932*
Southern European Jobs					
Miner	S. Eur.	S. Eur.	S. Eur.	S. Eur.	?
Loader	S. Eur.	S. Eur.	S. Eur.	S. Eur.	S. Eur.
Non-Southern European Jobs					
Motorman	NonSE	NonSE	NonSE	NonSE	NonSE
Brakeman	NonSE	NonSE	NonSE	NonSE	NonSE
Boss	NonSE	NonSE	NonSE	NonSE	?
Driver	NonSE	NonSE	Open	NonSE	?
Machine helper	NonSE	Open	NonSE	NonSE	?
Tippleman	Open[N]	NonSE	?	?	NonSE
Open Jobs					
Machine runner	NonSE	NonSE	Open	Open	NonSE
Bratticeman & timberman	?	Open	?	Open	?
Slateman	S. Eur.	S. Eur.	Open	Open	?
Laborer	S. Eur.	Open	Open	Open	?
Trackman	Open[N]	NonSE	Open[N]	Open	Open

Source: Information from James T. Laing, "The Negro Miner in West Virginia," Ph.D. dissertation, Ohio State University, 1933, pp. 193–97 for 1932. For the earlier years from the lists of accident victims, West Virginia Department of Mines, *Annual Reports* for the years 1906 to 1925. For the percentages of workers in each job, see Appendix E. A version of this table appeared in Price V. Fishback, "Segregation in Job Hierarchies: West Virginia Coal Mining, 1906–1932," *Journal of Economic History* 44 (September 1984): 764. It is reprinted here with the permission of The Economic History Association and Cambridge University Press.

Notes: The question mark suggests unknown. For the periods prior to 1932 there were less than twenty-five workers in the job sample. for 1932, it is not measured.

[N]Job would be defined as nonsouthern European if the significance level of the chi-square test was 10 percent.

tions listed for workers killed or seriously injured in the West Virginia mines. The tables are designed to answer the question of whether blacks (southern Europeans) were underrepresented in jobs when compared with the employment of whites and northern Europeans, who were typically not victims of discrimination.

Each entry of Table 10-4 describes whether the job can be classified as a black job, an open job or a nonblack job. The bases for these definitions come from statistical procedures testing whether the distribution of ethnic groups within the jobs was similar to the ethnic composition of the work force. Consider the entry for the motorman position. If the statistical test could not reject the hypothesis that the ethnic distribution of workers in the motorman job came from random assignments of workers, the job is defined as open. If the test rejected the hypothesis of randomness and blacks were overrepresented in the job, it was a black job, if blacks were underrepresented it was a nonblack job. The entries for Table 10-5 were determined using the same procedure but focusing on southern and eastern Europeans rather than blacks. Appendix E gives a fuller description of the sources, the division of immigrants into southern and northern European, and the tests. Further it contains tables showing the percentages of workers from each ethnic group in each job.

Segregation in the job hierarchy might have arisen for several reasons: differences in experience, education, or other factors related to productivity; different attitudes toward piece rate and day jobs; or from discrimination by employers or other workers. Blacks and immigrants faced some disadvantages because they were typically less educated. Blacks and whites had similar distributions of work experience, while in the early periods southern Europeans typically had much less mining experience. Different types of discrimination imply different patterns in the job hierarchy. If employers disliked working with blacks, we might expect to see black employment focused in the mines owned by nondiscriminating employers. If other workers disliked working alongside blacks, we would to see attempts at physical separation, which were relatively easily to achieve since miners were spread singly or in pairs in rooms throughout the mines. Dewey describes yet another taste for discrimination in the refusal by whites to work for black bosses.[24]

Differences in the distribution of workers across jobs had little impact on the average wages of black and southern Europeans. In three of the four periods prior to 1930 the highest-paying job, machine runner, was open to blacks. Southern Europeans had similar access to the machine runner job after 1916 when their average experience became more similar to that of native workers. Further, both blacks and southern Europeans were present in the mining and loading jobs, which paid higher wages per hour and per start and gave workers greater freedom over labor-leisure choices. To give a fuller view of the impact of segregation on average wages, Table 10-6 shows ratios of average wages constructed by assuming that all workers in the same job received the same wage; the ratios differ from one only because of differences in the distributions of ethnic groups across jobs. The constructed hourly wage and earnings per start ratios in the table are close to one throughout, implying that earnings differences caused by the job distribution were small. The gap in half-monthly earnings ranges from 2 to 4 percent, but differences in the miners' and loaders' labor-leisure decisions play a more important role at this level. As expected, when labor markets loosened, black workers did not fare as well. The largest segregation gaps in wages are found during the Great Depression, while the next largest gaps occur during the slowdown in the coal boom that occurred from 1911 to 1915. The situation for southern Europeans was quite similar. They earned slightly higher hourly earnings but lower earnings per start and half-month as a result of job segregation.

Blacks and southern Europeans more often than native whites worked inside the mines, where jobs were dirtier and more dangerous. The percentage of native white workers employed inside the mines exceeded 80 percent only once between 1907 and 1925. The percentage of black workers inside the mines stayed within a range of 85 to 91 percent, while the inside percentage of southern Europeans fell below 92 percent only twice.[25] The concentration of blacks and southern Europeans inside the mine probably did not stem from discrimination forcing them into dirtier and more dangerous jobs. Most blacksmiths and carpenters working outside the mines were trained elsewhere, and relatively few blacks and southern Europeans in West Virginia were trained in these crafts.[26] Further, the inside jobs paid higher wages than the outside jobs. Laing argued that both groups sought the piece rate jobs of loading and pick mining, because of the greater independence from supervision, and such jobs were only available inside.[27] Inside the mines blacks and southern Europeans

TABLE 10-6. The Impact of Segregation in the Job Hierarchy on Average Earnings and Accident Rates of Inside Workers, 1906–1932

	Ratios of Constructed Earnings and Accident Rates Assuming No Ethnic Differences Within a Job Category				
	1906–1910	*1911–1915*	*1916–1920*	*1921–1925*	*1932*
Black/Native White Ratios					
Earnings					
Hourly	0.998	0.993	1.001	1.014	0.989
Per start	0.991	0.981	0.993	0.994	0.961
Half-monthly	0.958	0.960	0.979	0.978	0.953
Accident Rates	0.983	1.006	1.006	1.002	0.982
Southern European/Native White Ratios					
Earnings					
Hourly	1.038	1.036	1.058	1.056	1.014
Per start	0.980	0.984	1.011	1.003	0.971
Half-monthly	0.958	0.962	0.993	0.991	0.959
Accident Rates	0.967	0.976	0.988	0.978	0.964

Sources: The average wages and accident rates underlying these ratios were constructed in the following way for each ethnic group:

$$\text{Average Wage} = \left[\sum_{j=1,8} WI_j \times PS_j \times N_j \right] \Big/ \left[\sum_{j=1,8} PS_j \times N_j \right],$$

where WI_j is the wage index from job category j from Tables 4-3 through 4-5 in Chapter 4. PS_j is the percentage of workers in job category j in that ethnic group from tables in Appendix E. N_j is the number of workers in job category j from a complete mine job structure. The employment figures in Tables E-1 through E-4 in Appendix E were not used because more dangerous jobs are overrepresented in the accident samples. The numbers used are the number of workers sampled by the Department of Labor in their 1924 earnings survey of more than 140 West Virginia Mines. U.S. Bureau of Labor Statistics, "Hours and Earnings in Bituminous and Anthracite Coal Mining, 1922 and 1924," *BLS Bulletin No. 416*, pp. 44–48. The 1924 job structure had more specialization and machine mining than in earlier periods. If the distribution of employees is adjusted to include more pick miners and drivers, the earnings ratios rise, implying that the black-white ratios prior to 1920 in the tavble understate the true ratio. The job categories for the comparisons from 1906 to 1925 are machine runner, loader, miner, driver, motorman, brakeman, trackman, and laborer. Pumpman, brattice-man, and timberman were excluded because the samples in the accident statistics wer too small to determine the number of ethnic workers in thos jobs. For 1932 the job information was used from Table E-5 in Appendix E, with only five job categories: machine runner, loader, motorman, brakeman, and trackman. The accident-rate ratios were calculated using the same procedures and the accident rates in Table 4-6 of Chapter 4. Laborers were excluded from the comparisons because no accident rate was available for them, leaving only seven jobs in the sample.

were not overrepresented in more dangerous jobs. Table 10-6 shows average relative accident rates for the groups based on their distribution among the inside jobs. Native whites were slightly more likely to be found in more dangerous jobs than southern Europeans, and faced the same relative dangers as black workers.

Blacks generally had access to the high-paying machine cutter job in most time periods, particularly in periods of expansion in the coal industry. When black employment and coal employment was growing, the job was open, as in 1906–10 and 1916–20. When the demand for coal was stagnant and black employment fell, the machine job closed, as in 1911–15 and the Great Depression. Even when the job appeared closed in 1911–15, blacks were about 14 percent of the machine miners compared with 19 percent of all workers. The one anomaly was the period 1921–25 when coal demand was stagnant, but opportunities for blacks opened more in northern West Virginia during strikes. For southern Europeans the key problem was lack of experience during the peak phase of migration prior to 1910. As the immigrants gained experience, first the machine helper job opened in 1911–15 and then the machine runner job opened from 1916 to 1925. The machine helper job became nonsouthern European again, as the influx of new immigrants slowed down. As happened to black workers, the machine cutter job became nonsouthern European again during the Depression, as workers competed for fewer coal jobs.

Where discrimination seems to have been the primary cause of segregation was at the management level. From 1906 to 1925 only nine black bosses out of 248 were found in the accident sample. Of 9000 black workers in Laing's 1932 survey, there were "only eleven cases of Negroes in positions which, even by the most liberal stretch of the term, could be called positions of authority."[28] The West Virginia Bureau of Negro Welfare and Statistics found only seven bosses among 6483 black workers surveyed in 1922, and only one fire boss among more than 7000 black workers surveyed in 1927.[29]

Since blacks and whites had similar mean experience levels, two important factors help explain the lack of black managers: discrimination in education outside the mines and discrimination based on white refusal to work for black bosses. Management jobs were the only jobs requiring at least a common school education and possibly a high school education.[30] The separate and unequal schools in the South, where most blacks were schooled, gave whites an added advantage in 1910, when foremen and fire bosses were required to pass written examinations.[31] Whites gained an extra advantage when the white state universities started mining extension courses around World War I.[32] In West Virginia, blacks were not offered the same training until 1937 when U.G. Carter started an extension course for blacks at West Virginia State College. Prior to 1937 only nine blacks had received their foreman papers. Even obtaining the foreman papers was no guarantee of a foreman job. Carter found that after five years of operation, only about 46 percent of his graduates who passed the foreman's exam were in positions reflecting their competency.[33]

Dewey's finding of white refusal to work for blacks probably best explains the almost total absence of black managers. The following is one of a number of quotations from Laing's interviews with West Virginia operators that makes this point:

> I have seen but very few Negroes whom I felt inclined to give positions of responsibility to and if I felt so inclined to place them in a position of authority this act would be resented by other employees. This same reason prevents the Negro from getting a job on motor runs, plans runs, fire bosses or other positions of the nature. The management cannot afford to incur the displeasure of all other employees by appointing a Negro to a responsible position.[34]

Where blacks were in a position of authority in Laing's job sample, they generally gave orders to other blacks.[35] An ex-maintenance man for one company in the 1920s told me that the Raleigh Coal and Coke Company had once set up its No. 7 mine as an all-black mine to reward its harder working blacks with positions of authority. U.G. Carter claims that one technique of giving a black a position of authority was to make him a contractor and allow him to hire his own work force to work a mine section. Black contractors found few whites who would work for them. In other cases, Carter asserted a black may have had the authority of a foreman without the title and sometimes without the pay.[36]

Although the distribution of blacks and whites in transport jobs seems at first to fit the machine tenet, mule driver was a black job and motorman was a white job, the overall pattern of the haulage jobs fits better Dewey's finding that whites refused to work for black bosses. Motormen gave orders to their brakemen and also typically took charge of hooking up the cars brought by the driver from the rooms to the main line. The motorman job was a nonblack job, while the brakeman and driver jobs were typically open or black. Where there were black motormen, the brakeman and the driver were likely to be black. Further, Laing found that blacks who became motormen more often drove the small gathering motors that brought cars to the mainline where they were picked up by mainline motors.[37]

The Impact of Competition on Segregated Schools

The relatively small impact of discrimination on the wages and working conditions of black workers also carried over into the school systems. West Virginia was similar to the southern states in that its constitution of 1872 required segregated schools for blacks and whites. But West Virginia differed greatly from the southern states because expenditures per pupil in black and white schools were more equal than in the remaining southern states. David Corbin suggests that the coal companies, responding to the demands of black workers, helped push the public schools toward separate-but-equal expenditures.[38]

The West Virginia coal companies stood to gain from reducing inequality for two reasons.[39] First, coal companies during the boom often sought to hire new workers, and black workers were an integral part of the mine work force. In competing for labor, coal companies that spent money on education felt they could attract more workers, particularly more productive and more stable ones with families. Extra school spending was likely to be more effective at attracting black than white workers to the West Virginia coal fields. Black schools in the rest of the South were woefully underfunded, while white schools elsewhere were likely to be similar to the white schools in West Virginia.

Second, many mines were in company towns; therefore, the company faced less political competition for the gains from enhanced spending on education in its town. In company towns the employer obtained full benefits from better schooling, avoiding free-rider situations where other employers obtained the benefits from more spending on education without spending themselves.

Corbin suggests that the coal companies aided black education at the state and local levels. At the state level, Corbin credits the West Virginia coal companies with securing "the passage of progressive educational legislation. Largely because of the efforts of the coal industry teachers' salaries became based on qualifications, not color."[40] The coal companies were a powerful force in the Republican party, which dominated West Virginia state government from the 1890s into the early 1930s. Their interests and those of their black workers were strongly intertwined, as coal mining employed 42 percent of black male workers in West Virginia in 1910, 55 percent by 1920.[41] Further, by working at the state level, the coal companies could potentially shift some of burden of spending on black schools onto noncoal counties.

Locally, companies could influence education in three ways. First, the company might make general contributions to the local public school system and influence the school board's allocation of funds among schools. As the primary local employer, coal company officials wielded considerable influence, sometimes as members of the school board. Yet making general contributions was the least promising means of elevating the company's own school above those at other mines. An individual company's ability to appropriate more than its share of the school board's funds was constrained by political competition from other companies in the same school district. The political competition increased the risk that a company's donations were used to benefit another mine's workers.[42] Second, the company could work within the school system and maintain some control over its contributions by donating land and buildings, which could be used only in its community. Numerous companies donated school houses, built the school house at cost, and/or deeded land to the school board.[43] Third, the company could also ensure that its donations benefited only its workers by offering external supplements at its mine's school. Various companies contributed external funds to lengthen school terms by up to three months, to increase teachers' salaries by up to 50 percent, and to provide better housing for teachers.[44]

The relative expenditures on black and white schools in West Virginia differed enormously from those in Virginia, Alabama, and North Carolina, the primary areas where the coal companies recruited. In 1910 West Virginia spent slightly *more* per black child aged 6 to 14 ($11.64) than they spent per white child ($11). In contrast, Virginia ($2.66 per black child), Alabama ($1.58), and North Carolina ($2.01) respectively spent 3.4, 5.7, and 2.6 times as much per white child as they did per black child.[45] Comparisons of student-teacher ratios show similar results. The only other state where expenditures per black child and per white child were similar was Kentucky, another state where coal mining was booming in isolated areas and blacks accounted for over 20 percent of the work force.[46]

The cross-state differences in relative expenditures on black and white schooling are probably not all due to the coal companies' influence in West Virginia. There may have been less racial hostility in West Virginia than in the deep South. The area that became West Virginia had few slaves and remained in the union when Virginia seceded in 1861. West Virginia did not disfranchise black voters to the same extent as did other southern states.[47] Yet don't underestimate the importance of coal employers, who maintained enough power at the state level and a strong enough association with black workers that equal education policies could not have succeeded without their support.

A stronger test of the impact of the coal companies on segregated schools is to compare the spending on public schools in coal and noncoal counties within West Virginia. At the local level school boards made the decisions on how to allocate local tax funds and state funds between black and white schools. The school board's allocation decisions were affected by the demands of white voters, black voters, and the coal companies. In many southern states where black voters were disfranchised, school boards responded to white demands by appropriating the lion's share of state funds for spending on white schools.[48] Although blacks were not disfranchised in West Virginia, they typically accounted for a small percentage of any county's voters and so they wielded limited political power. Therefore, white voters controlled the ballot box and gained when school funds were allocated more for white than for blacks schools. The white voters' dominance was countered by the actions of black voters, who sometimes acted as swing voters in elections, and their primary employers the coal companies.

In an econometric study summarized in Appendix F, I examined this tug-of-war between the interest groups by estimating the black-white ratio of expenditures per pupil on the percentage black children, the ratio of coal miners to the adult male population, the average wealth in the county, and the population density of the county. The results suggest that school boards did try to reallocate funds from black schools to white schools as the number of black pupils increased. An increase of 5.6 percent in the percentage of black students (one standard deviation in the sample) would have lowered the black-white ratio of school expenditures per child from 1 to 0.78. Coal mining employers acted as a countervailing force. If the increase in the percentage of black students above was associated with a comparable increase in the extent of mining, the coal companies' pressure would have raised the black-white ratio in teachers' expenditures per pupil from 0.78 back to 0.87.

The analysis focuses on the influence the coal companies wielded within the public school system on expenditures. It may underestimate how much the coal companies reduced inequality because it doesn't show the extent to which companies promoted equal schooling at the state level. Further, evidence on public school budgets focuses on only one form of company influence at the local level, their impact *within* the local school system on expenditures on black and white teachers' salaries. The results do not reflect the extent to which companies made company-specific contributions of land and buildings or worked outside the school system by offering teachers' bonuses. The companies used these alternatives because they could retain more control over how the gifts were used.

Table 10-7 gives a sample of the companies' involvement in 1922 in the provision of school land and buildings for blacks and whites at 114 representative mines in West Virginia. In 99 of the 114 mines the companies were involved in some way in providing school facilities. Many of these efforts were devoted to black education. In 51 of the 114 mining towns in Table 10-7, the company owned the colored school building and land, in another four it owned just the land, and in fifteen more it had donated the land for the school. At one mine the company was paying the black teacher's entire salary. The data show that the coal companies were more likely to give the land to the school districts for white schools but maintain control of it for black schools. Given that whites were expropriating school funds for use in their schools, the companies may have maintained control of land for black schools to ensure that the land was actually used for black schools.

Housing Segregation

Miners of all ethnic groups generally were offered the same type of housing, rental rates, and conditions of tenancy. The primary differences in housing opportunities

TABLE 10-7. Number of Companies Contributing Buildings and Land for Black and White Schools, 1922[a]

Company Action	Type of School				Total Number[b] in Sample
	Black	*Both Black & White*	*White*	*Not Listed*	
Company Owns School Buildings	44[c]	7	4	7	114
Company Owns School Land	42	14	4	16	114
Company Gave Land for Schools	4	11	23	11	114
Company Controls Appointment of Teachers				10	108
Cases Where Company Involved				99	114

Sources: Unrated Mining Camp Schedules for West Virginia Entry 62, Record Group 68 Boxes 29–32. Records of the U.S. Coal Commission, National Archives, Suitland, Maryland. For a copy of the schedule and the questions asked, see the Mining Community Schedule A in the U.S. Coal Commisssion, Report, 68th Congress, 2nd Session 1591 (1925). The table appeared in Price V. Fishback, "Can Competition Among Employers Reduce Governmental Discrimination? Coal Companies and Segregated Schools in West Virginia in the Early 1900s," *Journal of Law and Economics* 32 (October 1989): 323. Reprinted with the permission of the University of Chicago. © 1989 by the University of Chicago. All rights reserved.

[a]These companies were considered by the Coal Commission to be among the median group of company communities. The number of companies in each county were: Kanawha, 18; Boone, 4; Fayette, 26; Logan, 19; Raleigh, 25; Putnam, 1; Mingo, 12; McDowell, 1; Mercer, 3; Wyoming, 12.

[b]Includes companies taking the action and those companies not taking the action.

[c]Five of these schools are actually in black churches owned by the company.

came from the separation of ethnic groups. Residential segregation was the rule in urban areas in the North and South. Segregation arose in part because people preferred to live near others from the same group and partly due to discrimination by other groups already settled in the areas. In either case, it is not surprising that the predominant societal patterns of segregation at the time were also common in company towns. Blacks were generally found in one area of town, at the top of the hollow or separated by natural barriers such as hilltops or different hollows. There were some exceptions to this rule in southern West Virginia.

In Alabama segregation was the rule in the coal towns of 1909 and often took the form of lower quality housing in black sections than in other areas. The Immigration Commission's rule of thumb for housing conditions in this regions was

> that the type of company house varie(d) more with the company than with the race of the tenant with two exceptions: (1) The housing conditions of the Italian, Greek, and Macedonian (were) better than those of the negro; (2) in most instances the English, Irish, Scotch, and Welsh live(d) in better houses than did any other race except the native white.[49]

Part of the difference in housing was accounted for by differences in income suggested by the daily earnings in Table 10-2. Blacks sometimes reduced their rental payments further by crowding more than one family into a single-family dwelling. Native whites tended to put only one family into a dwelling unit, while immigrants were often found in boarding houses on a group plan.[50]

West Virginia housing patterns varied from town to town. In interviews with miners in the West Virginia towns of Keystone, Anawalt, and Alpoca, David Corbin discovered that residential segregation either was not practiced or was not effective at separating the races.[51] He argues that black and white miners distrusted each other less because they shared a common experience in isolated company towns. A company's policy toward segregation could change with changes in ownership and management personnel. At one town in West Virginia blacks and whites lived intermingled until the company hired a new man to assign rooms to the miners.[52] At the mine in Tams, West Virginia the town was segregated because Mr. Tams, the owner, ordered it.[53] In boom times, when companies were hiring large numbers of workers, coal towns were sometimes integrated temporarily, as workers were put into whatever houses became available. When new houses in their ethnic section became available, the worker was then moved, if the town was segregated.[54]

Segregation remained the rule in many towns in southern West Virginia. U.G. Carter, who grew up in mining towns in McDowell County, stated that he lived in a segregated community where the whites stayed in the bottom of the hollow and the blacks on the hill.[55] There was also some overcrowding of black houses in West Virginia. In Tams, West Virginia, there was an average of seven persons per house in the black section, five per house in the white American section, and ten per house in the foreign section.[56] In the early 1930s Laing discovered overcrowding in many black homes. About 15 percent of the black homes he studied had more than two people per room; roughly 50 percent of the homes had one or fewer people per room. Experts at the time considered more than one person per room to be overcrowded and more than two persons grossly overcrowded.[57]

In towns where there were large numbers of black miners, opportunities for black doctors arose. Most black doctors were in urban areas in West Virginia but twenty-four of the fifty-eight resident black physicians practiced in the coal regions. A number of black doctors had practices contracted with the coal companies in the coal fields of McDowell, Mercer, Logan, and Raleigh counties.[58]

A number of companies also offered recreational facilities, which were usually racially segregated. There were separate churches, YMCAs, baseball teams, and even mine safety competitions. Movie theaters had black and white sections. The segregated facilities were probably better where the black population density was greater. The larger population allowed some aspects of the black group economy to take hold, and provision of recreation probably was characterized by economies of scale. Further, operators who hired large numbers of black workers were less likely to have strong preferences for discrimination and may have been more willing to offer more equal treatment.

Segregation Across Mines

Some scholars consider the hiring of a mixture of immigrants, blacks, and native whites as a judicious practice where mine owners hired a variety of workers so that cultural differences among the workers would inhibit the growth of unionism.[59] Anti-unionism certainly played a role in the diversity of the work force, but other forces were also at work that led to ethnic mixtures in the work force. Employers may have hired a mixture of ethnic groups because they grabbed any available labor during shortages. Word-of-mouth networks were important in determining where

TABLE 10-8. Number of Mines with Percents Black and Immigrant in the Range Listed in the Five West Virginia Counties Employing the Most Black Miners in 1910

Range of Percentages	*Number of Mines with*	
	Percent Black	*Percent Immigrant*
0	71	83
$0 < p \leq 5$	15	21
$5 < p \leq 10$	21	22
$10 < p \leq 15$	34	23
$15 < p \leq 20$	38	22
$20 < p \leq 25$	33	21
$25 < p \leq 30$	21	19
$30 < p \leq 35$	31	31
$35 < p \leq 40$	8	17
$40 < p \leq 45$	20	11
$45 < p \leq 50$	13	16
$50 < p \leq 55$	8	8
$55 < p \leq 60$	5	12
$60 < p \leq 65$	3	10
$65 < p \leq 70$	3	6
$70 < p \leq 75$	5	5
$75 < p \leq 80$	1	1
$80 < p \leq 85$	0	0
$85 < p \leq 90$	0	3
$90 < p \leq 95$	0	1
$95 < p \leq 100$	0	3
Total	331	331

Source: West Virginia Department of Mines, *Annual Report for the Year Ending June 30, 1910,* pp. 84–103, 118–210. Counties include McDowell, Fayette, Mercer, Kanawha, and Raleigh. Of known miners in the five counties in 1910 the percent black was 27.7, percent native white 45.7, and percent immigrant 26.6.

miners from various ethnic groups migrated, as might have been differences in the extent of discriminatory policies at various mines.

The racial mix looks more judicious when examining data at the county level than it does at the mine level. Table 10-8 shows the number of mines in which the percents black and immigrant were in the ranges listed in the table in the five West Virginia counties employing the most black miners in 1910. In the five counties, 45.7 percent of the miners whose nationality was reported were native whites, 27.7 percent blacks, and 26.6 percent immigrants. Of the 331 mines, 21 percent had no blacks working underground, 31 percent had work forces with less than 10 percent black; and 12 percent had only native whites. The distribution of blacks across mines does not appear to be random. Given the percentages of blacks, whites, and immigrants in the county, if a company had chosen twenty workers at random, the odds of having no blacks in the mine would only have been 0.15 percent. The absence of blacks in 21 percent of the mines may reflect discriminatory attitudes of employers or workers already employed at those mines. If so, even though blacks in West Virginia generally did not receive lower wages due to discrimination, they and immigrants still faced one disadvantage that whites did not. There remained some mines where they were not welcome. So even in an area where working conditions were relatively equal, blacks and immigrants faced extra costs in searching for employment to avoid working at discriminatory mines.

Black Workers in Alabama

In many ways West Virginia was a haven for black workers. The black miners who left Alabama for West Virginia found they had moved to an area of much greater equality. As shown in Table 10-2, the black-white gap in daily earnings in Alabama was nearly 30 cents in 1909, compared with almost no gap in West Virginia. Part of the gap was a result of literacy differences. The separate but highly unequal school system in Alabama left blacks with much less literacy than whites in the Alabama mines. Black workers probably suffered from more problems with discrimination because the Alabama mine employers did not face the same strong competition for workers seen in West Virginia. The Alabama mines drew from a much larger population of workers near the mines. Most of the mines were near Birmingham. Farm laborers in Alabama could easily migrate in and out of the mines in response to seasonal changes in coal demand or to the cyclical coal booms and coal busts. Finally, the Alabama state government leased convicts to several mines. In fact, a number of free black miners obtained their initial training as convicts.[60]

Black Workers and the UMWA

Part of the concentration of black workers developed because of the stronger presence of the UMWA in northern and western fields than in the southern fields. The concentration of blacks in nonunion areas does not necessarily imply racial discrimination by the union. Employers in those areas may have been the discriminators, although many owners in unionized areas willingly opened their mines to black workers during strikes. The black share of employment in Pennsylvania more than doubled during the strikes of the 1920s.[61] Even if black employment was halted by UMWA restrictions, the restrictions might not have been racially motivated. The union raised wages by controlling the number of workers hired by the firms, leading to limits on the number of new workers whether black or white. If this was the policy, the lack of blacks in the Central Competitive Field was explained by the small number of blacks in nearby areas during the booms of the late 1890s and early 1900s. As the nonunion fields grew relative to the union fields, larger numbers of blacks were located in West Virginia, closer to the Pennsylvania fields. However, by that time employment opportunities in the Central Competitive Field were growing more slowly and black workers saw opportunities in other industries.

At the time the UMWA was a paragon of racial equality. It was one of the few unions to organize blacks and whites into the same union.[62] A handful of blacks actually attained higher offices at the regional and national level.[63] The UMWA constitution contained a clause calling for its members "to unite in one organization, regardless of creed, color or nationality, all workmen employed in and around the coal mines."[64] In some situations the national union enforced the policy with fines and threats of expulsion.[65]

The national union's stance on racial equality was grounded in economic reality as much as in the virtue of its leaders. A successful union required the organization of all the producing coalfields, and the South remained unorganized. The problem worsened as the nonunion southern fields expanded production relative to the unionized fields. As the southern mines already employed large numbers of black workers, the union could never have organized successfully without including blacks. If excluded from the union, black miners willingly broke strikes that were likely to reduce their opportunities. When allowed to join the union, blacks were among its more fervent supporters.[66]

The national union's attempts to maintain an egalitarian policy were not always sustained by the locals. Abram Harris found several instances of discrimination in his studies of the northern West Virginia coal fields in the mid-1920s. He ascribed some of the blame to the unions and some to the operators in the offending mines.[67] Foner cites several complaints by black workers about union-enforced segregation.[68] Boris Emmet found that in the Fairmont district in northern West Virginia whites disliked serving on mine committees with blacks and refused to follow orders given by black committeemen.[69] Ron Lewis compiled a number of examples of attempts to keep black workers out of the coalfields in Illinois and Ohio, in part because of earlier incidents where black workers were brought in as strikebreakers.[70] These instances point out the hard reality that the union membership consisted of thousands of men, some of whom held deeply felt prejudices. The mixture of good intentions and racial hostility sometimes resulted in situations where blacks felt that the "union's purpose is good but the functioning awful."[71] All told, the UMWA's attitude toward blacks appears to have been similar to the attitudes held by employers. Treat them well when you need them, toss them aside when you don't. This became all the more obvious after 1930, when neither employer nor union protected the interest of black miners.[72]

Summary

During the early 1900s there was a substantial black and immigrant population in the coal industry. The relative status of black workers was largely determined by the degree of tightness in the labor market, their original location in the South, and limits on their movement into northern mines stemming in part from unionization. In situations where labor demand expanded faster than labor supply, black workers were likely to receive more equal treatment. At the turn of the century most blacks were located in the low-wage southern mines but over time an increasing percentage of black coal workers had moved into higher wage areas. Many blacks started in the South because the vast majority of the black population lived in the South. To some extent their movement into more northern mines was limited by a union barrier, although the barrier was not always racially motivated. In Alabama, racial wage differentials were quite large in part due to a relative large number of workers available to the industry near the coalfields.

In contrast, in West Virginia, which was relatively sparsely settled, strong competition among employers for labor led to greater equality than in many other areas. Blacks received the same piece rates and generally were assigned similar workplaces. When their average experience was similar, blacks, whites, and immigrants had similar mean accident rates. In the job hierarchy most jobs were open during expansions in coal demand, including the high-wage machine runner's job, although the jobs closed during coal recessions. The primary form of discrimination was the denial of management jobs to black workers. Competition for labor could not overcome the bedrock refusal of most whites to take orders from a black manager. Coal towns often followed the same societal strictures—segregated schools, segregated recreation, segregated housing—practiced in the rest of society at the time. However, the competition among employers for workers did nibble away at such societal strictures. The UMWA in southern states encouraged the interaction of black and white workers for the common cause of unionization. In West Virginia, the coal companies helped to equalize spending in segregated schools. In some coal towns, the lines of segregation were blurred when employers found it expedient.

NOTES

Some material in the section on segregation in job hierarchies was first published in Price V. Fishback, "Segregation in Job Hierarchies: West Virginia Coal Mining, 1906–1932," *Journal of Economic History* 44 (September 1984): 755–74. It is reprinted here with the permission of The Economic History Association and Cambridge University Press. © The Economic History Association. All rights reserved. Much of the discussion in the section on competition and segregated schools was first published in Price V. Fishback, "Can Competition Among Employers Reduce Governmental Discrimination? Coal Companies and Segregated Schools in West Virginia in the Early 1900s," *Journal of Law and Economics* 32 (October 1989): 311–28. Reprinted with the permission of the University of Chicago. © 1989 by the University of Chicago. All rights reserved.

1. Ronald Lewis, *Black Coal Miners in America: Race, Class, and Community Conflict 1780–1890* (Lexington: University of Kentucky Press, 1987); David Corbin, *Life, Work, and Rebellion in the Coal Fields: The Southern West Virginia Miners 1880–1922* (Urbana: University of Illinois Press, 1981); Joseph Trotter, Coal, Class, and Color (Urbana: University of Illinois Press, 1990).

2. Lewis, *Black Coal Miners*, pp. ix–xv.

3. Price V. Fishback and Donald C. Keenan, "Discrimination, Worker Search, and Multiple Attributes of Employment Contracts," University of Georgia College of Business working paper.

4. For a discussion of this general pattern of relationships between black workers and unions, see William Sundstrom, "Understanding the History of Racial Exclusion by American Labor Unions," working paper, Economics Department, Santa Clara University, 1990. A version is summarized in the *Cliometrics Society Newsletter* 5 (October 1990).

5. U.S. Immigration Commission, *Immigrants in Industry, Part I: Bituminous Coal Mining*, 61st Cong., 2nd Sess. (Washington, DC: U.S. Government Printing Office, 1911), vol. 1, pp. 21–25.

6. Price V. Fishback, "Employment Conditions of Blacks in the Coal Industry, 1900–

1930," Ph.D. dissertation, University of Washington, 1983, pp. 72–77 and footnote 57. See Lewis, *Black Coal Miners*, pp. 1–12.

7. The 1889 census statistics suggest that Alabama was paying historically high wages, so that blacks did not appear to be stuck in low-wage regions in 1890. See Fishback, "Employment Conditions, pp. 110–20.

8. James T. Laing, "The Negro Miner in West Virginia," Ph.D. dissertation, Ohio State University, 1933, pp. 104–12. The share of the West Virginia population born in Alabama rose sharply from 0.3 percent in 1910 to 6 percent in 1920 to 9.2 percent in 1930. U.S. Bureau of the Census, *Thirteenth Census of the United States, 1910, Population*, Vol. I (Washington, DC: U.S. Government Printing Office, 1913), pp. 740–43; idem, *Fourteenth Census of the United States, 1920, Population* (Washington, DC: U.S. Government Printing Office, 1922), Vol. II, pp. 637–38; idem, *Negroes in the United States, 1910–1932* (Washington, DC: U.S. Government Printing Office, 1935), pp. 27–30.

9. Fishback, "Employment Conditions," p. 68; Sterling Spero and Abram Harris, *The Black Worker* (New York: New York University Press, 1931), pp. 210–26.

10. Donald Barnum, "The Negro in Bituminous Coal," *Negro Employment in Southern Industry: A Study of Racial Policies in Five Industries*, edited by Herbert Northrup and Richard Rowan (Philadelphia, Pennsylvania: Wharton School of Finance and Commerce, Industrial Research Unit, 1970); Paul Nyden, *Black Coal Miners in the United States*, Occasional Paper No. 15 (New York: American Institute for Marxist Studies, 1974); Herbert Northrup, *Organized Labor and the Negro* (New York: Harper and Brothers Publishers, 1944).

11. Barnum, "The Negro in Bituminous Coal," p. 26.

12. Fishback, "Employment Conditions," pp. 160–66.

13. Laing, "The Negro Miner," p. 209.

14. Raleigh Coal and Coke Company Payroll, 1903. Beckley Exhibition Mine, Beckley, West Virginia. Fishback, "Employment Conditions," p. 161.

15. George Surface, "The Negro Mine Laborer: Central Appalachian Coal Field," *Annals of the American Academy of Political and Social Science* 33 (March 1909): 114–28. One caveat about Surface's data. His evidence on daily wages and daily productivity implies that foreign workers were paid higher piece rates. For further discussion, see Fishback, "Employment Conditions," pp. 161–63.

16. The differences in wage rates are relatively small with one exception. The average pick miner rates in 1929 were much higher for white miners than for black miners, although it may have been caused by some extreme outliers. In contrast, the average pick miner rates in 1931 were higher for blacks than for whites. See *Thirty Third Annual Report of the Department of Labor and Industry of the State of Virginia, for the Year Ending September 30, 1930*, p. 32; *Thirty-Fifth Annual Report of the Department of Labor and Industry of the State of Virginia, for the Year Ending September 30, 1932*; or Fishback, "Employment Conditions," Tables 26 and 27, pp. 164–65.

17. A number of studies of the Immigration Commission evidence have shown that indirect measures of productivity like literacy, age, and for immigrants the ability to speak English were important determinants of ethnic wage differences. See Robert Higgs, "Race, Skills, and Earnings: American Immigrants in 1909," *Journal of Economic History* 31 (June 1971): 420–28; Paul McGouldrick, and Michael Tannen, "Did American Manufacturers Discriminate Against Immigrants Before 1914?" *Journal of Economic History* 37 (September 1977): 723–46; Francine Blau, "Imigration and Labor Earnings in Early Twentieth Century America," *Research in Population Economics*, vol. 2 (New York: JAI Press, 1980), pp. 21–41. My own results using the coal evidence were mixed. When I estimated coefficients for all the workers without specific coefficients for regions, the English speaking variable had a

statistically significant effect, but literacy did not. When I estimated specific region coefficients the literacy variable was statistically significant in the South, but English speaking was not. Fishback, "Employment Conditions," pp. 120–48.

18. Fishback, "Employment Conditions," p. 150; U.S. Bureau of the Census, *Thirteenth Census of the United States, Vol. III, Population, 1910* (Washington, DC: U.S. Government Printing Office, 1913), pp. 1032–41.

19. See Appendix G for a complete description of these regressions. The regressions discussed here are the same as the ones underlying the elasticities in Table 5-1.

20. Laing, "The Negro Miner," p. 230.

21. For a formal discussion of these ideas, see Fishback and Keenan, "Discrimination, Worker Search, and Multiple Margins of the Employment Contract."

22. The mean experience of fatality victims offers a biased estimate of the average experience of all workers because less experienced workers are more likely to be killed. Although the discussion here focuses on the means in Table 10-3, I have done a more sophisticated analysis using the sample from which the evidence on means in Table 10-3 was collected. See Price V. Fishback, "Discrimination on Nonwage Margins: Safety in the West Virginia Coal Industry, 1906–1925," *Economic Inquiry* 23 (October 1985): 651–69. I examined the frequency distributions of the number of workers killed at each experience level (fatality-experience profile) for each ethnic group. The fatality-experience profile can be seen as a function of the death rate at each experience level, discrimination in the assignment of jobs and workplaces, and the distribution of experience of the entire work force. The basic story told in the text follows from the statistical hypothesis testing for differences in fatality-experience profiles and additional evidence on the age distributions of black and white miners in West Virginia. Between 1906 and 1925 blacks and native whites had statistically similar fatality-experience profiles and evidence from the census suggests that their age distributions were roughly the same, implying that there was no discrimination. The southern European fatality-experience profiles were skewed toward less experience until the early 1920s.

23. For example, see Gunnar Myrdal, *An American Dilemma: The Negro Problem and Modern Democracy*, 2 vols. (New York: Pantheon Books, 1972); Lorenzo Greene and Carter Woodson, *The Negro Wage Earner* (Washington, DC: The Association for the Study of Negro Life and History, Inc., 1930); Charles Johnson, *The Negro in American Civilization* (New York: Harper and Brothers Publisher, 1930); and Spero and Harris, *The Black Worker*. More recently researchers have revised these beliefs, using census data showing that blacks obtained skilled jobs increasingly more often over time. See Gary Becker, *The Economics of Discrimination*, 2nd. ed. (Chicago, IL: University of Chicago Press, 1971) and Edward Meeker and James Kau, "Racial Discrimination and Occupational Attainment at the Turn of the Century," *Explorations in Economic History* 14 (July 1977): 250–76.

24. For seminal work on the economics of discrimination, see Gary Becker, *Economics of Discrimination*. For discussions of the patterns of discrimination in the South in the 1950s, see Donald Dewey, "Negro Employment in Southern Industry," *Journal of Political Economy* 60 (August 1952): 283. For more discussion of segregation in the job hierarchy see Price V. Fishback, "Segregation in Job Hierarchies: West Virginia Coal Mining, 1906–1932," *Journal of Economic History* 44 (September 1984): 755–74.

25. Figures were compiled from tables titled "Nationalities of Mine Employees Summarized," West Virginia Department of Mines, *Annual Reports* for the years from 1907 to 1925. For information on the percentage for specific years see Fishback, "Employment Conditions," p. 315.

26. Fishback, "Employment Conditions," p. 315.

27. Laing, "The Negro Miner," pp. 194, 202–07.

28. Ibid., p. 182.

29. West Virginia Bureau of Negro Welfare and Statistics, *Report*, 1921–1922, p. 58; 1927–1928, p. 16. There were several black owners of small mines in the late 1800s. Charles Simmons, John Rankin, and U.G. Carter, "Negro Coal Miners in West Virginia, 1875–1925," *Midwest Journal* 6 (Spring 1954): 6–7.

30. United States Bureau of Mines, prepared for the Department of Labor, *Descriptions of Occupations: Mines and Mining* (Washington, DC: U.S. Bureau of Mines, 1918), p. 20.

31. The next section shows that West Virginia schools were segregated but relatively equal, but this benefitted the children of miners more than their parents.

32. Interview conducted by Keith Dix with U.G. Carter, West Virginia Oral History Project. West Virginia Regional and History Collection at the West Virginia University Library.

33. Ibid. "Report to the West Virginia State College Mining Extension Course for 1942–43," U.G. Carter Collection at the West Virginia Regional and History Collection at the West Virginia University Library.

34. Laing, "Negro Miner," pp. 212–18.

35. Ibid., p. 182.

36. Interview with U.G. Carter, West Virginia Oral History Project.

37. Laing, "Negro Miner," p. 242.

38. Corbin, *Life, Work, and Rebellion*, pp. 70–72.

39. For further information on competition and segregated schools see Appendix F and Price V. Fishback, "Can Competition Among Employers Reduce Governmental Discrimination? Coal Companies and Segregated Schools in West Virginia in the Early 1900s," *Journal of Law and Economics* 32 (October 1989): 311–28.

40. Corbin, *Life, Work, and Rebellion*, p. 70. Progressive legislation specific to black schools included requiring a black school in subdistricts with ten black children (1901, down from fifteen after 1881), hiring a state supervisor of Negro schools (1919), and requiring equal salaries for black and white teachers with the same training, credentials, and experience in the same district (1929). The state also established black colleges in 1891 and 1895. Although not specifically provided in state law, black and white schools were subject to the same minimums for school terms and teacher salaries at each certificate level. The coal companies were potentially influential in assuring that such provisions were enforced for black schools in their districts. In many cases, black and white teachers received equal salaries and school terms. See State Superintendent of Free Schools, *History of Education in West Virginia* (Charleston, WV: The Tribune Printing Company, 1904), p. 295. Laing, "The Negro Miner," pp. 375–77. Enforcement was not uniform, however. In some counties, typically noncoal, with small black populations, the state supervisor of Negro Schools reported that boards of education were slow to provide black schools and there was discrimination in teachers' salaries. See State Superintendent of Free Schools of West Virginia, *Biennial Report* for the Two Years Ending June 30, 1922, pp. 77, 79.

41. U.S. Bureau of the Census, *Thirteenth Census of the United States, Population, 1910*, vol. 4, p. 529. U.S. Bureau of the Census, *Fourteenth Census of the United States, Population, 1920*, vol. 4, p. 1039.

42. The coal companies devoted most of their efforts concerning teachers' salaries *within* the school system to influencing the use of tax dollars and not to making donations. Receipts of the teachers' fund from miscellaneous sources, including company contributions, were not on average any larger in coal counties than in noncoal counties. See West Virginia State Superintendent of Free Schools, *Biennial Report* for 1910, p. 131.

43. U.S. Coal Commission, "Bituminous Mine Workers and Their Homes," *Report of the U.S. Coal Commission, vol. III*, 68th Cong., 2nd. sess. (Washington, DC: U.S. Government Printing Office, 1925), p. 1479.

44. U. S. Immigration Commission, *Immigrants in Bituminous Coal Mining*, vol. 2, pp. 197, 210. Corbin, *Life, Work, and Rebellion*, p. 71; A. F. Hinrichs, *The United Mine Workers and the Non-Union Coal Fields* (New York: Longmans, Green and Company, 1923), pp. 71–73; Winthrop Lane, *Civil War in West Virginia* (New York: B.W. Huebsch Inc., 1921), p. 34.

45. Jonathon Pritchett, "The Racial Division of Education Expenditures in the South, 1910," unpublished Ph.D. dissertation, University of Chicago, 1986, p. 2. All the black-white expenditure comparisons in the paper are based on expenditures on teachers, the predominant item in school budgets. Some states, including West Virginia, did not report expenditures on other school budget items separately for blacks and whites.

46. Fishback, "Employment Conditions, p. 75.

47. Paul Lewinson, *Race, Class, and Party* (New York: Oxford University Press, 1932), pp. 21, 104, 120, 153, 185.

48. Robert Margo, "Race Differences in Public School Expenditures," Social Science History 6 (1982): 9–33.

49. U.S.Immigration Commission, *Immigrants in Bituminous Mining*, vol.2, p. 198.

50. Ibid. 197–99.

51. Corbin, *Life, Work, and Rebellion*, pp. 66,67, 82.

52. Oral History Interview with C.E. Bradshaw and Jim Dillard (misspelled Dillon in the Archives), and Thelma Cosby, conducted by Bill Taft, West Virginia Oral History Project, West Virginia Regional and History Collection.

53. Sullivan, "Coal Men and Coal Towns," pp. 162–63.

54. Corbin, *Life, Work, and Rebellion*, pp. 66–67.

55. Interview with U.G. Carter, conducted by Keith Dix, West Virginia Oral History Project, West Virginia Regional and History Collection.

56. Mack Gillenwater, "Cultural and Historical Geography of Mining Settlements in the Pocahontas Coal Field of Southern West Virginia, 1880–1930," Ph.D. dissertation, University of Tennessee, 1972, p. 135.

57. Laing, "The Negro Miner," pp. 349–52.

58. West Virginia Bureau of Negro Welfare and Statistics, *Second Biennial Report, 1923–4*, p. 29.

59. Lewis, *Black Coal Miners*, pp. 122–42; Kenneth Bailey, "A Judicious Mixture: Negroes and Immigrants in the West Virginia Coal Mines," *West Virginia History* 34 (January 1973): 141–63.

60. Robert D. Ward and William W. Rogers, *Convicts, Coal, and the Banner Mine Tragedy* (Tuscaloosa: University of Alabama Press, 1987); Lewis, *Black Coal Miners*; U.S. Immigration Commission, *Immigrants in Bituminous Coal Mining*, vol. II, p. 218.

61. Spero and Harris, *The Black Worker*, pp. 224–30.

62. Ira Reid, *Negro Membership in American Labor Unions* (1930; reprinted New York: Negro Universities Press, 1969); Herbert Northrup, *Organized Labor and the Negro* (New York: Harper and Brothers Publishers, 1944); Spero and Harris, *The Black Worker*; Phillip S. Foner, *Organized Labor and the Black Worker, 1619–1973* (New York: International Publishers, 1974).

63. Herbert Gutman found that several blacks held high positions in the UMWA. Richard C. Davis was a founder of the union, a delegate at the first convention, and served on two National Executive boards. At the district and local level, W. Riley was secretary treasurer of District 19 in Tennessee in the 1890s, F. A. Bannister was vice president of the West Virginia district, Henry Rector was vice president in an Illinois district with a constituency that was only one quarter black, and Tom Rollins was the unanimous vice president of the predominately white Saginaw, Michigan district. Herbert Gutman, "The Negro and the United Mine Workers," in *The Negro and the American Labor Movement*, edited by Julius Jacobson

(Garden City, NY: Anchor Books, 1968), pp. 81–83. In some areas where blacks and immigrants were the largest group, blacks were elected to local mine committees to meet the requirement that members speak English and show their intentions of becoming citizens. Boris Emmet, "Labor Relations in the Fairmont, West Virginia Bituminous Coal Field," *U.S. Department of Labor Bulletin No. 361* (Washington, DC: U.S. Government Printing Office, 1924), p. 4.

64. The wording of the clause was changed slightly as the constitution was revised, but the meaning remained the same. Barnum, "Negro in Bituminous Coal," p. 22.

65. Foner, *Organized Labor*, pp. 95–100, 169–70.

66. Foner, among others, has given similar reasons for the UMWA's racial policies. Ibid., p. 83.

67. Spero and Harris, *The Black Worker*, pp. 369–75; West Virginia Bureau of Negro Welfare and Statistics, *Report* 1925–1926, pp. 24–41.

68. Foner, *Organized Labor*, pp. 95–97.

69. Emmet, "Labor Relations in Fairmont," p. 4.

70. Lewis, *Black Coal Miners*, pp. 98–118.

71. Quote from C.W., a miner working one day a week, Reid, *Negro Membership in American Labor Unions*, p. 173.

72. Lewis, *Black Coal Miners*, 167–89; Barnum, "Negro in Bituminous Coal."

11

What Did Miners Gain from Strikes?

STRIKE!!! The word conjured up fears of lost output, lost profits, and possible violence for most mine operators. To the miners involved, it meant sacrifices in hopes of obtaining higher wages and better working conditions. Strikes often were a defining moment for the people involved. The humdrum everyday rhythms of rising early to enter the mines, working through the day, and returning home were suddenly disrupted. An aura of excitement developed, as miners picketed and held meetings in spite of the company's efforts to prevent them. Miners and families united in a common cause. Sometimes tempers flared as some miners sought to return to work or replacement workers were hired. As the strike continued, the operators were more likely to take damaging actions, like evicting strikers from housing, and violence was more likely to flare. The excitement and fears generated by strikes caused them to stand out in the memories of miners interviewed in oral histories and in the newspapers of the period. Since miners struck more often than workers in other industries, strikes and the advancing path of unionization draw much of the attention in histories of coal mining.

Strike activity was the primary means available to miners to exercise their voice. The common labor history view of strikes is that they were necessary to raise wages and improve working conditions, implying that workers gained from strikes. Neoclassical economists have a quite different view. Sir John Hicks argues that strikes were generally costly propositions for both sides. Workers lose paydays and management loses profits while coming to an agreement that both could have reached without the strike. He therefore saw strikes as the result of two possibilities: workers wielding the strike occasionally to show management that they were willing to carry through the threat of a strike, or a result of "faulty negotiations."[1] Others have extended the emphasis on "faulty negotiations" to suggest that one or both sides lacks complete information about the other side's willingness to settle for less than the original stated demands. Empirical studies show that when there is greater uncertainty about profits in an industry, strike activity is greater. Other economists emphasize differences in the costs of strikes, finding that strikes are more common in situations where companies can easily make up for lost working time.[2]

Although economists emphasize that strikes are costly, relatively few have tried to estimate the costs and benefits of strikes to workers. In the late 1800s and early 1900s, the Bureau of Labor Statistics and similar bureaus in other countries picked wins, losses, and compromises based on the terms of the final settlement. Although often based on impressions, the wins and losses give some information about whether workers gained or lost in the final settlement.[3] However, the results tell us only about the benefit side of the strikes, either the workers saw an improvement in conditions or they didn't. The wins or losses tell us nothing about the losses incurred in the course of the strike before they reached the final terms. In this chapter we make a start toward estimating both the benefits and the costs of strikes by estimating the pecuniary costs and benefits of a strike: the lost earnings from working fewer days and the wage increase generated by a strike.[4]

Strike Activity in Bituminous Coal Mining

Coal miners struck more than the average for workers in United States industry. Tables 11-1, 11-2, and 11-3 depict the number of men on strike as a percentage of the work force in bituminous coal mining and in United States Industry (including mining, manufacturing, contract construction, transportation, and public utilities).[5] In all but one year shown in the tables, the percentage of men on strike in bituminous coal mining was greater than the average for U.S. industry. In most years the percentage of workers on strike in coal mining was more than double that in U.S. industry. The difference is even larger than the figures show because the figures on U.S. industry include bituminous coal mining and thus overstate the strike activity in the remaining industries. Mining (including other types of mining) continued to be more strike prone than any other industry in the 1940s and the 1950s, before falling behind transportation equipment and contract construction in the 1960s.[6]

Evidence on strikes collected by the U.S. Commissioner of Labor from 1881 to 1905 shows that coal strikes were generally longer and involved more workers than the average strike in U.S. industry. The average number of days per establishment until strikers were reemployed or their places filled by others in coal mining was 50.9 compared with 25.4 in U.S. industry. The typical coal strike threw 94 percent of the workers in the establishment out of work compared with 58 percent in U.S. industry. The greater intensity of the coal strikes did not necessarily lead to greater success (subjectively measured by the Commissioner of Labor). Coal strikes failed in 49.5 percent of the establishments struck, partially succeeded 28 percent, and succeeded in 22.5 percent. In U.S. industry strikes failed at only 36.7 percent of the establishments, partly succeeded at 15.2 percent, and succeeded at 47.8 percent.[7] When the BLS started collecting comprehensive strike data again in the late 1920s and the early 1930s, coal strikes continued to be longer. Over the period from 1927 to 1936, bituminous coal mining averaged 40.97 man-days idle per striking worker, compared with an U.S. industry average of 20.6 days.[8]

Coal mining may have experienced greater strike activity for several reasons. First, the cost in terms of lost days of output may have been lower than in other industries. The mine capacity in the United States was large enough that coal mines

TABLE 11-1. Work-Stoppage Activity in Bituminous Coal Mining, Coal and Coke, U.S. Industry, 1900–1905, Workers on Strike or Locked Out as a Percentage of Employees

Year	*Bituminous Coal Mining*[a]	*Coal and Coke*[b]	*U.S. Industry*[c]
1900	10.5		4.7
1901	6.1	14.2	4.0
1902	15.0	39.8	5.2
1903	11.4	12.9	5.8
1904	17.2	8.3	3.8
1905	7.1	9.5	2.1
Average for			
1901–1905	11.43	15.4	4.2
1881–1905		21.1	3.7

[a]Number of men on strike as a percentage of the average number of men employed in bituminous coal mining from various issues of U.S. Geological Survey, *Mineral Resources in the United States, Part II, Nonmetals* (Washington, DC: U.S. Government Printing Office, various years).

[b]Coal and coke employees on strike or locked out divided by total coke and coal employees. The strikers are from U.S. Commissioner of Labor, *Twenty-First Annual Report, 1906, Strikes and Lockouts* (Washington, DC: U.S. Government Printing Office, 1907), pp. 432–435, 712–15. Total coal employees include anthracite and bituminous coal miners listed in various issues of the U.S. Geological Survey, *Minerals in the United States, Part II, Nonmetals* (Washington, DC: U.S. Government Printing Office, various years). The number of coke employees is listed in Bureau of Census, *Manufactures, 1905, Part IV, Special Reports on Selected Industries* (Washington, DC: U.S. Government Printing Office, 1908), p. 515.

[c]The number of strikers and workers locked out is divided by the number of employees on payrolls in mining, contract construction, manufacturing, and transportation and public utilities. Agriculture, wholesale and retail trade, finance, insurance and real estate, services, and government employment were left out of the denominator because with the exception of agriculture there were no listings in the strikers' table that seemed to fit those forms of employment. The number of strikers and workers locked out is from U.S. Commissioner of Labor, *Twenty-first Annual Report, 1906, Strikes and Lockouts* (Washington, DC: U.S. Government Printing Office, 1907), pp. 478–79, 736–37. The number of workers is from series D127–D141 in Bureau of the Census, *Historical Statistics of the United States, Colonial Times to 1970* (Washington, DC: U.S. Government Printing Office, 1975), p. 137.

generally operated an average of only 210 days per year, compared to 290 to 300 in most other industries. Short strikes were not as damaging in coal mining when production time could be shifted to normally slack times. In a number of years when United Mine Workers contracts expired on March 31, mines operated overtime prior to the expiration date, as both miners and mine owners prepared for a possible strike.[9]

Second, coal mining experienced more fluctuations and profit variability than many other industries. Thus, miners had more trouble than most workers in discerning their employer's willingness and ability to pay for wage increases. Economic theorists argue that with greater uncertainty the bargaining process will take longer before both sides reveal enough information about their positions to come to a

TABLE 11-2. Work-Stoppage Activity in Bituminous Coal Mining and U.S. Industry, 1906–1926, Workers on Strike or Locked Out as a Percentage of Employees

Year	*Bituminous Coal Mining*	*U.S. Industry*
1906	44.2	
1907	6.3	
1908	28.1	
1909	4.6	
1910	38.8	
1911	6.5	
1912	29.0	
1913	12.5	
1914	23.2	
1915	6.6	
1916	16.2	10.0
1917	20.9	7.7
1918	9.8	7.6
1919	67.2	24.4
1920	29.0	8.6
1921	14.9	7.8
1922	67.0	10.6
1923	8.7	4.4
1924	9.4	4.0
1925	6.5	2.6
1926	4.9	1.9

Sources: Number of men on strike as a percentage of the average number of men employed in bituminous coal mining from various issues of U.S. Geological Survey, *Mineral Resources in the United States, Part II, Nonmetals* (Washington, DC: U.S. Government Printing Office, various years). The number of strikers and workers locked out in U.S. industry is divided by the number of employees on payrolls in mining, contract construction, manufacturing, and transportation and public utilities. Agriculture, wholesale and retail trade, finance, insurance and real estate, services, and government employment were left out of the denominator because with the exception of agriculture there were no listings in the strikers' table that seemed to fit those forms of employment. The number of employees on payrolls in mining, construction, and so on, is from series D128–D133 in Bureau of the Census, *Historical Statistics of the United States, Colonial Times to 1970* (Washington, DC: U.S. Government Printing Office, 1975), p. 137. The number of strikers and workers locked out is from Florence Peterson, "Strikes in the United States, 1880–1936," *U.S. Bureau of Labor Statistics Bulletin No. 651* (Washington, DC: U.S. Government Printing Office, 1938), pp. 35–40. According to Peterson (pp. 36, 39), although the number of workers involved in work stoppages was obtained for only about two-thirds of the total number of strikes, the missing information is for the smaller disputes. The unknown number of the smaller strkes is probably offset by the 'generous' figure used in large strikes. Information on the latter was usually taken from newspaper reports, which are likely to give slightly exaggerated figures. The strike information differs from the pre-1906 and post-1926 Bureau of Labor strike data in that they include strikes and lockouts with fewer than six persons and lasting less than one day.

TABLE 11-3. Work-Stoppage Activity in Bituminous Coal Mining and U.S. Industry, 1927–1936, Workers Involved as a Percentage of Total Employees in Industry and Number of Man-Days Idle/Total Employees in Industry[a]

	On Strike/Total Employees (%)			*Man-Days Idle/Total Employees*		
	Bituminous Coal			*Bituminous Coal*		
Year	*BuMines*	*BLS*	*U.S. Industry*	*BuMines*	*BLS*	*U.S. Industry*
1927	29.1	29.6	2.0	44.6	130.8	1.6
1928	9.7	12.1	1.9	8.1	11.4	0.8
1929	3.6	3.6	1.7	0.4	0.3	0.3
1930	4.6	5.4	1.2	2.0	1.8	0.2
1931	9.9	11.6	2.5	3.5	3.4	0.5
1932		15.6	2.8		14.6	0.9
1933		34.0	10.1		5.3	1.5
1934		24.0	11.3		3.4	1.5
1935		90.9	8.2		6.2	1.1
1936		4.1	5.3		1.1	0.9

Source: Total employment in bituminous coal and the number of men on strike and days idle for bituminous coal mining under BuMines are from various issues of U.S. Bureau of Mines, *Mineral Resources in the United States, Part II, Nonmetals* (Washington, DC: U.S. Government Printing Office, various years). The number of workers involved in strikes and days idle for bituminous coal mining under BLS and for U.S. industry are from Florence Peterson, "Strikes in the United States, 1880–1936," *U.S. Bureau of Labor Statistics Bulletin No. 651* (Washington, DC: U.S. Government Printing Office, 1938), pp. 41, 152. For U.S. industry, the number of strikers and workers locked out is divided by the number of employees on payrolls in mining, contract construction, manufacturing, transportation and public utilities. Agriculture, wholesale and retail trade, finance, insurance and real estate, services, and government employment were left out of the denominator because with the exception of agriculture there were no listings in the strikers' table that seemed to fit those forms of employment. The number of employees on payrolls in mining, construction, and so on, is from series D128–D133 in Bureau of the Census, *Historical Statistics of the United States, Colonial Times to 1970* (Washington, DC: U.S. Government Printing Office, 1975), p. 137.

[a]U.S. Industry includes bituminous coal mining.

solution. By striking, workers raise the costs of extended bargaining, leading to a quicker solution. Using modern data, economists have found that greater variability of profits is associated with greater strike activity.[10]

Third, if strikes are caused by greater uncertainty, the workers' attitudes toward risk may influence strike activity. Economic studies of modern workers show that more dangerous industries are more strike prone, possibly by attracting workers with less aversion to taking risks.[11] As Chapter 7 shows, coal mining was among the most dangerous industries of the period.

Fourth, bituminous coal mining was more unionized than most manufacturing industries. The United Mine Workers of America was the leading union in the United States in the early 1900. Friedman's empirical studies at the turn of the century show that greater unionization was associated with greater strike activity. Once they were already in place, unions faced lower costs in getting workers to join a strike. Further, Friedman found that the success rates (as determined by the Commissioner of Labor) for union strikes were higher.[12] To the extent that miners struck occasionally to show that strike threats were serious in later negotiations, union members were more likely to strike than nonunion men because they were more likely to stay with the same company. A union miner was more likely to be still working at the same mine in the next negotiating period when the threat of the strike might become effective.

Finally, a much larger percentage of coal workers lived in company towns than in other industries. In the company town the employer not only hired the worker but also rented him housing, sold him goods, determined his recreation, and often had a large hand in local law enforcement. In a city, different people served each of these functions, and when the worker was frustrated with housing or store prices, he was angered at the landlord or the corner store owner. In the company town, his grievances were all centered on his employer. Thus, workers struck over a whole range of nonjob issues in company towns that they did not strike over in cities.

Differences in Strike Activity Within the Coal Industry

At first glance, strike activity within the coal industry seems strongly associated with the UMWA. Table 11-4 shows the average number of man-days idle per employee on the payroll and the average percentage of workers with paid-up mem-

TABLE 11-4. Strike Activity in Major Bituminous Coal States

State	*Man-Days Idle per Employee*	*UMWA Membership/ Employees*	*Union Designation*
Ohio	24.3	79.8%	Union
Kansas	20.7	68.9	Union
Illinois	20.3	94.1	Union
Arkansas	18.6	72.0	Union
Missouri	16.7	74.5	Union
Oklahoma	16.0	71.9	Union
Michigan	15.8	79.0	Union
Indiana	15.5	81.8	Union
Colorado	12.3	10.4	NonUnion
Iowa	11.9	87.5	Union
Maryland	10.8	12.6	NonUnion
Pennsylvania	8.5	36.6	Mixed
Montana	7.8	96.9	Union
Washington	6.7	61.3	Union
Tennessee	5.8	18.9	NonUnion
Wyoming	5.4	65.5	Union
West Virginia	5.2	12.6	NonUnion
Kentucky	4.6	18.8	NonUnion
Alabama	4.5	13.0	NonUnion
Texas	2.9	72.0	Union
New Mexico	2.8	10.4	NonUnion
Utah	2.3	65.3	Union
Virginia	0.2	18.9	NonUnion

Source: Average man-days idle per employee is the state average for 1901 to 1930 from U.S. Geological Survey (U.S. Bureau of Mines for issues after 1922), *Mineral Resources of the United States, Part II, Nonmetals* (Washington, DC: U.S. Government Printing Office, various issues). UMWA paid-up membership as a percentage of employees on the payroll for 1902 to 1023 is from U.S. Coal Commmission, *Report, Part III* (Washington, DC: U.S. Government Printing Office, 1925), p. 1052. For more details on both variables see Appendix B.

bership in the United Mine Workers during the hand-loading era for the major bituminous coal states. Man-days idle is an imperfect measure of the time spent on strike. It was collected from surveys of employers, who might have seen a strike as ended when replacements were hired, while the strikers saw the strike as continuing. Thus days idle might understate the number of days in which strikers were on strike. Since paid-up membership is an imperfect measure of the UMWA's strength, a union designation was inserted for all states where the paid-up percentage of employees exceeded 50 percent. Pennsylvania received a mixed designation because part of the state was in the Central Competitive Field stronghold of the union. Nonunion states are ones where the membership percentage was less than 20 percent.

The union states in the eastern United States dominate the top eight positions in terms of strike activity. The Central Competitive Field (Illinois, Indiana, Ohio, and western Pennsylvania) generally was the leader in negotiations with coal operators, while other eastern union states generally followed the same negotiating and strike patterns. Out west the union states with relatively small coal production (Utah, New Mexico, Texas, Wyoming, Washington, and Montana) tended to go their own way in negotiations and displayed strike activity similar to that in the nonunion coal states.

Union strength was not the only factor influencing strike activity and may not have even been the most important one. In addition to union membership (UNION), the number of strike days idle per coal worker (STRIKE) also was influenced by major factors influencing the quantity demanded of coal, like the coal price (PRICE), which is deflated to 1967 dollars, the growth rate of real GNP (RGNP%), and years in which a new contract was to be negotiated (CONTRACT).[13] The following equation shows Weighted Least Squares estimates of the effect of these variables on strike activity on the panel of twenty-three leading coal states for the years 1902 to 1923 used in Chapters 6 and 7 and described in Appendix B.[14] Absolute values of t-statistics are in parentheses.

$$\begin{aligned} &STRIKE = \qquad\qquad\qquad\qquad\qquad\qquad\qquad\qquad\qquad\qquad\qquad\qquad\qquad\qquad (11\text{-}1)\\ &-8.74 + 15.30\,UNION + 2.27\,PRICE + 56.84\,RGNP\% + 4.07\,UNION \times CONTRACT\\ &\ \ (1.72)\quad\ (3.05)\qquad\qquad\ \ (2.20)\qquad\qquad\quad (3.50)\qquad\qquad\quad (0.89) \end{aligned}$$

Evaluating these effects at the means for the sample suggests that a 10 percent increase in paid-up UMWA membership from 52.0 to 57.0 percent of the coal workers in the state increased strike days idle per coal worker from 12.38 to 13.1 days or 6.2 percent.[15] Unionized states may have been more likely to strike in periods when there was a new contract. UMWA agreements were made in every year from 1898 to 1912, and then two-year contracts went into effect. The two-year contract continued to be the custom until 1924, when a three-year contract went into effect.[16] Thus contracts were scheduled to end each year from 1899 to 1912, then 1914, 1916, 1918, 1920, 1922, 1924, and 1927. The coefficient above suggests that the end of contracts was positively associated with strikes in more unionized states, but we cannot reject the hypothesis that strike activity was no greater when contracts were under negotiation.

The effects of industry demands and general economic growth on strike activity in bituminous coal are similar to the patterns in many modern studies of strike activity. Strike activity was associated with higher coal prices, although it is not clear whether higher coal prices led to the strike or were a result of coal shortages caused by the strike. A 10 percent increase in the real price of coal (in 1967 dollars) of 53.9 cents increased strike activity by 1.2 days, or nearly 9.9 percent. Strike activity in bituminous coal was also procyclical. When the growth rate of real GNP rose by 10 percent, strike days rose by 0.2 or roughly 1.5 percent. These results suggest that at least prior to 1923, miners struck to share in the gains of growth in the coal industry. Inclusion of the years after 1923, however, might show a different situation as the coal industry began to decline and miners struck to prevent reductions in wages.

The Pecuniary Gains and Losses from Strikes

Striking workers hoped to gain improvements in wages, working conditions, or the overall employment package. The gains to the worker might have come directly through a wage increase above what would have been paid without the strike. Where union recognition was at issue, the gains might have come indirectly through increased wages associated with unionization. The gains from the strike might be longer-term in the Hicksian sense that by striking at one time, the miners could wield the threat of the strike to gain concessions in later negotiations. Since a large number of workers often switched mines or left the industry, such deferred benefits would have accrued to the union or to miners who stayed in the industry longer. Striking workers at times received strike benefits from the UMWA, but most of the benefits had come from the miners' own contributions earlier. The only strikers who received a net gain from the strike benefits were miners in nonunion districts who received strike funds donated by collections from union miners. Not all the gains are easily measured. Union recognition strikes often sought a goal of increased voice in the day-to-day matters in the workplace. Further, strikes carried an ideological component. To the extent that the individual miner defined his identity in relationship to other miners, he may have received psychic benefits from banding with other miners in seeking to improve conditions for all miners.

Yet the strikes also imposed economic costs on the miners (and the employers). The most obvious costs were the lost earnings while on strike, which were diminished to the extent that production could be shifted to other periods. The pecuniary costs may overstate the true costs of the strike to the extent that miners valued a short-term vacation from the rigors of working in the mines. Yet the costs of the strike went beyond lost earnings. If men were evicted from company housing, there were the added costs of dislocation of families and furniture. The possibility of violence during the strike meant that resources were devoted to self-defense. When strikes continued for several months, there were additional hardships from living in tent colonies with lower rations, and the problems with disease from bad sanitation.

Although many of the costs and benefits described above are not easily measured, we can at least assess the wage gains and the losses in days worked from strikes. A focus on wage gains captures most of the gains that workers sought in bituminous coal mining. During the period from 1927 to 1936, wages and hours were the primary issue in 87.5 percent of the 44.8 million days that miners were idle due to strikes. The hours issue was often a wage issue because the demands for reduced hours often did not include a desire for a matching cut in the daily wage. Another 10.7 percent of total days on strike were over union organization, which often indirectly affected wages.[17]

Using the panel of state level data from the twenty-three leading coal states from 1912 to 1923, the reduced-form wage equation in Table 6-8 in Chapter 6 is reestimated without the days-worked variable and with more attention to strike activity. Further, a reduced-form days-worked equation is estimated.[18] The coefficients from the two equations show the impact of each day on strike per employee on the number of work days lost and the increase in hourly earnings. Since union recognition was an issue in a number of strikes, we also determine the effect of union membership on hourly earnings and the number of workdays. Strikers faced a great deal of uncertainty about the length and success of the strike when it started. The state level estimates are average measures of the impact of strikes and unions on wages and days worked, and thus give us an idea of what a striker who faced the mean labor market conditions might expect to gain or lose. The averages clearly do not tell the whole story. Some short strikes were associated with relatively large wage gains. On the other hand, there were several long and violent strikes, like those in the Paint Creek and Cabin Creek districts of West Virginia in 1912 and 1913, in Mingo County in 1920 and 1921, and in Colorado in 1913 and 1914 that imposed huge losses on the striking workers and the coal companies with marginal gains on each side. Although information on a large number of strikes at the mine level would avoid the aggregation problems with the state level evidence above, I have been unable to obtain information on wages at the mine level. The state panel has an advantage over single case studies of strikes because with more observations we can more effectively control for a variety of other factors that influenced wages and working time.

The average days worked at the mines and hourly earnings were simultaneously determined by the actions of employers and workers in the labor market. Since we are interested in the overall effects of strikes and unions after all the shifts in labor demand and supply have occurred, reduced-form days and hourly earnings equations are estimated. The reduced-form coefficients from the wage (and days worked) equations are an estimate of a compendium of interactions. For example, a strike reduced the supply of labor (both the number of men and the number of days they were willing to work). The strike effect does not end there because reduced labor supply moved employers back along their labor demand curve. So the final effect on wages was determined by a combination of coefficients representing the strike effects on the supply of labor, its interaction with labor demand and with the choices determining days worked.[19] Appendix C shows one example of how reduced-form coefficients summarize labor demand and supply effects.

As in Chapter 6, the measure of the wage is the average hourly wage of daymen deflated by the consumer price index (1967 = 100).[20] The days variable is the average number of days the mines were open during the year. Both the wage and days-worked equations are estimated with fixed effects using weighted least

TABLE 11-5. Coefficients of Reduced-Form Wage and Days Equations, Weighted Least Squares, Panel of Twenty-Three Leading Coal Mining States for Years 1912–1923

	Coefficient Estimates				
Variables	*Wage*	*Days*	*Wage*	*Days*	*Unweighted Means*
Hourly Wage of Inside Daymen $1967	Dependent Variable		Dependent Variable		1.258 (0.33)
Days the Mines Were Open		Dependent Variable		Dependent Variable	206.4 (45.1)
Weight	0.026 (0.45)	350.8* (32.79)	0.044 (0.75)	351.6* (32.2)	
Fatal Accident per Million Man Hours	0.0037 (0.66)	0.957 (0.91)	0.0038 (0.67)	0.958 (0.91)	2.04 (2.09)
Coal Price in $1967	0.076* (8.30)	−11.080 (6.54)	0.076* (8.30)	−11.09* (6.54)	5.64 (1.30)
Workers' Compensation Law Times Fatal Accident Rate	−0.013* (2.15)	−2.32 (2.16)	−0.012* (2.07)	−2.30* (2.13)	0.66 (0.48)
Output per Man Hour	0.530* (3.70)	−110.10* (4.16)	0.517* (3.62)	−110.64* (4.17)	0.42 (0.12)
Days Idle on Strike per Employee	0.00176* (5.77)	−0.490* (8.68)	0.00068 (0.94)	−0.535* (3.95)	13.64 (28.88)
Days Idle on Strike per Employee Squared			0.000008 (1.63)	0.00034 (0.36)	1017.2 (3545.2)
Days Idle on Strike per Employee Lagged One Year	0.00043* (1.78)	−0.063 (1.44)	0.00047* (1.97)	−0.062 (1.38)	12.91 (28.05)
Strike Days per Employee in Other Fields	0.0047* (4.26)	−1.60* (7.92)	0.00396* (3.39)	−1.63* (7.50)	13.41 (21.5)
Paid-Up Members in UMWA as a Percent of Employment	0.105* (1.70)	−1.73 (0.15)	0.109* (1.78)	−1.54 (0.13)	0.535 (0.32)
State Effects	Included	Included	Included	Included	
Year Effects	Included	Included	Included	Included	
N	276	276	276	276	

Sources: See Appendix B.

Notes: Absolute values of t-statistics are in parenthesis below the coefficients, standard deviations are below the means in parentheses. The weight is the square root of total employment in each state. Ordinary least squares estimates and different weights gave similar results.

*Statistically significant at the 90 percent level in a two-tailed test.

squares.[21] The fixed effects are dummy variables for all states except Alabama and all years except 1912. The state dummies capture state-specific differences not measured by the remaining variables in the equation, such as geological differences or differences in regional costs of living. Similarly, the year dummies capture year-specific effects, such as the effect of government intervention into the economy during World War I. The results of the estimation are reported in Table 11-5.

Although we are primarily interested in the strike and union effects, the two equations also contain a number of other variables that influence the labor market.

The results in the wage equation basically mirror those in Table 6-8. As predicted by labor-demand theory, wages rose with increases in the coal price (in 1967 dollars) and in output per man-hour. The wage may have risen to compensate miners for higher accident rates, but we cannot reject the hypothesis of no effect. Wages were higher in states with no workers' compensation law.

In the days-worked equation increases in the net coal price and output per man-hour were associated with reductions in days worked. To the extent that greater unionization was associated with higher coal prices and greater output per man-hour, their negative coefficients may be associated with the negative effects of unions on days worked.

Strike activity is measured as the total number of man-days idle on strike divided by the total number of men on the payroll. The measure is more comparable with the state averages of wages and days worked than a strike measure of man-days idle per worker on strike. Man-days idle per striking worker focuses only on the strikers, whereas the wage and days data are averages collected from nonstriking as well as striking workers. The impact of strikes on wages may be complex. The strike might lead to a wage increase that lasts for several years, or the wage increase might be temporary. The delayed effect of strikes is examined by including lagged values of the strike variable in the equation. Equations were estimated with strike variables lagged up to three years. For lags longer than one year the wage and days effects were very small and the hypothesis of a zero effect could not be rejected. In Table 11-5 the lagged effect of strikes on days worked is not statistically significant but is included for symmetry because the lagged effect in the wage equation is statistically significant.

Since mines may have been able to shift production given the short work year, the strike might have had a nonlinear effect, with stronger marginal effects on wages and days worked as the strike continued. The third and fourth columns of Table 11-5 show the results of including a squared strike term to try to capture this effect. Since the coefficient of the squared term is not statistically significant at the 90 percent level in either the days or the wage equations, the remainder of the discussion focuses on the equations in columns 1 and 2 with just the linear strike term and the lagged strike term.

The coefficients of the strike variables in Table 11-5 show the marginal effect on the hourly wage and days worked of an additional day on strike per employee in the state. Table 11-6 converts the coefficients into marginal effects on annual earnings based on an eight-hour day, 206.4 days worked, and a real hourly wage of $1.2584, which are the unweighted means from the regression sample. The strike raised wages in the year of the strike but the wage bump deteriorated and was much smaller in the year following the strike.[22] Each added day on strike raised the hourly wage in the current year by 0.176 cents per hour (based on the coefficient in Table 11-5). In the year following, the wage bump is only 0.04 cents per hour. Spread over an average work year of 206.4 eight-hour days, for each day on strike annual earnings were higher by $2.91 in the current year and $0.71 in the year following.

The strike coefficient in the days worked equation suggests the mines were able to do some production shifting, but not enough to prevent miners from losing earnings even as early as the first day of the strike. For each day on strike during the

TABLE 11-6. Pecuniary Gains and Losses for Each Day on Strike

Loss in Annual Earnings from Lost Days Worked[a]	
Year t	−$4.93
Year t + 1	−$0.63
Gain in Annual Earnings Due to Rise in Hourly Wage[b]	
Year t	+$2.91
Year t + 1	+$0.71
Net Gain in Annual Earnings for Each Day on Strike	
Year t	−$2.02
Yeat t + 1	+$0.08
Present Value of Stream of Changes in Annual Earnings (6% interest)	
	−$1.94

Source: All assumptions about hourly wage ($1.2584), days worked (206.4), and hours per day (8) are based on the means of the regression sample in Table 11-5. The values are based on the coefficients in the days worked and wage equations in the first two columns of Table 11-5.

[a]$1.2584 × 8 × Days Coefficient in Table 11-5.

[b]206.4 × 8 × Wage Coefficient in Table 11-5.

current year, the miners lost slightly less than half a day, which translates into a loss of $4.93 in earnings. Mines worked fewer days than manufacturing for a variety of reasons: seasonal shifts in demand, problems obtaining railroad cars, and substantial competition arising from coal mine capacity greatly exceeding annual production demands in most years. The strike could be damaging to individual mines because they lost contracts that could not easily be replaced. The loss in days worked may have continued into the following year. The coefficient on the lagged strike variable suggests an additional loss of 0.06 of a day for each day on strike in the previous year, valued at $0.63. However, we cannot reject the hypothesis that there was no effect in the following year.

If we add the marginal effects on the wage and days worked, the miner lost $2.02 for each day on strike in the current year, but gained back $0.08 in the following year. Discounting the gains in the following year by 6 percent, the miners experienced a net loss of $1.94 in annual earnings for each day on strike.[23]

The benefits of the strike are understated to the extent that we ignore the impact of strikes on unionization. In the 1890s miners in the Midwest and Pennsylvania struck to force the coal operators in the Central Competitive Field to recognize the union. At various times in the nonunion districts of the South miners struck for union recognition. In the union districts, particularly in the 1920s, miners struck for long periods of time when the coal operators threatened to return to nonunion status. To measure the effect of union status, the paid-up membership in the union as a percentage of total employment is included in both equations. The wage coefficient implies that a move from nonunion to fully unionized mines boosted wages by 10.5 cents per hour. The days coefficient suggests that union states worked on average

TABLE 11-7. Net Gains from Union Recognition Strike

Effects of Going from Fully Nonunion to Fully Union

Gain in hourly wage
$0.105

Loss in days worked per year
1.73 days

Yearly gain in annual earnings
$156.03

Discounted stream of gains from unionization if benefits last (6 percent discount rate).

Current year	$156.03
Current plus one year	$303.23
Current plus two years	$442.10
Current plus three years	$573.11

Net Losses in Earnings for Strikes of Differing Length

13.64 days	50 days	100 days
−$26.46	−$97.00	−$194.00

Source: All assumptions about wages, days worked, and hours per day are based on the means of the regressions samples. The values are based on the coefficients in the days worked and wage equations in the first two columns of Table 11-5. The gain in annual earnings from going union is evaluated around the sample means of an hourly wage of $1.2584, a level of unionization of 0.535 and total days worked of 206.4. For example, the union wage was $1.2584 + (0.465) × $0.119 = $1.31.37 and the nonunion wage was $1.2584 − (0.535) × $0.119 = $1.1947.

1.73 fewer days per year, but the coefficient is not statistically significant. Table 11-7 shows that annual earnings for the miner would have risen by $156.03 per year when moving from nonunion to fully union status. If the union status lasted the current year plus an additional year, which was the typical contract length between 1912 and 1923, the present value of gaining full union status at 6 percent interest would have been $303.23. If the union status lasted over two contract periods, the present value of gaining full union status would have been $573.11.

Miners did not achieve union recognition without a significant struggle. Many of the longest and most violent strikes were over union recognition. The typical strike over union recognition, particularly a shift from nonunion status to fully union status, might have lasted as much as one hundred days and sometimes more. The Colorado strike of 1913–14 started in late September and lasted through at least the following April. The Cabin Creek strike in 1912–13 in West Virginia lasted from August 1912 through at least April of 1912. An earlier strike over union recognition in West Virginia in 1902 led to the loss of a hundred or more working days in 55 of 120 mines.[24] Union repudiation strikes in northern West Virginia in 1924 lasted an average of 138 days per worker. When the Central Competitive Field contracts ended in 1927, the UMWA's survival was at stake as coal operators began

TABLE 11-8. Number of Establishments in Which Strikes Succeeded, Partially Succeeded, or Failed

Location of Strikes	*Number of Establishments in Which Strikes* Succeeded	Partially Succeeded	Failed	Total	*Expected*[a] *Success*
All Coal Strikes 1901–05 (includes anthracite)	719	580	1155	2454	
%	29.3	23.6	47.1	100.0	0.411
Union Recognition Strikes in All Industries in the 24 Leading Coal States for the Years from 1901 to 1905 in Which Coal Strikes Occurred in That State.					
All states	2997	1740	4158	8896	
%	33.7	19.6	46.7	100.0	0.435
Nine leading coal states	2519	1492	3334	7346	
%	34.2	20.3	45.4	100.0	0.443
Southern coal states	122	89	411	622	
%	19.6	14.3	66.1	100.0	0.268
All states with establishments weighted by number of strikers per establishment	67690	187406	188681	443795	
	15.3	42.2	42.5	100.0	0.364

Source: U.S. Commissioner of Labor, "Strikes and Lockouts, *Twenty-First Annual Report of the Commissioner of Labor* (Washington, DC: U.S. Government Printing Office, 1907), pp. 432–33, 472–73, 496–579. The union recognition strikes in all industries are from a table titled "Strikes for Each State, by Years and Causes, 1901–1905." Observations were groupings of strikes with the same specific cause listed, so there were usually several establishments included in an observation. To obtain the weighted measures we took the number of strikers per establishment in the observation and multiplied it by the number of establishments in each result category.

[a]*Expected Success* = *%succeeded* × 1 + *%partly succeeded* × ½ + *%failed* × 0.

operating their mines with nonunion workers. The average number of days idle per striker was 150 in Illinois, 136 in Indiana, 193 in Ohio, and 158 in Pennsylvania, and the union still lost most of its foothold in the Central Competitive Field. Table 11-7 shows that the lost earnings (at $1.94 per day on strike from Table 11-6) from a hundred-day strike for union recognition would have cost the miners $194 in annual earnings. If the miners could obtain full union status with certainty over a two-year contract the overall net gain was $109.23 (303.23 minus $194).

In fact, an union recognition strike was an uncertain proposition, particularly in the traditionally nonunion areas in the South and Colorado, where the operators avoided recognizing the UMWA as the miners' representatives in a number of situations even after yearlong strikes. Table 11-8 gives some rough indication of the probability of winning an union recognition strike in the period from 1901 to 1905. Treating partial successes as half a win, coal miners won around 41 percent of strikes. But those strikes included all causes. Workers in union recognition strikes (from all industries) in the twenty-four leading coal states won 43.5 percent of the strikes, but when the strikes are weighted by the number of workers involved, the average worker could expect a win rate of 36.4 percent. The win rate was even lower in the south at 26.8 percent.

Using the highest win rate above of 43.5 percent, the expected benefit of an union recognition strike where the union benefit lasted one two-year contract period would have been $131.91 (.435 × 303.23). The miner would have incurred an expected loss of $62. If the win rate were 43.5 percent, to equal the lost earnings from the strike of $194 would have required the gain from unionization to have been $446 ($194 = .435 × $446), implying that the union recognition would have had to have lasted for slightly more than two years beyond the year of the strike.[25] If we use the weighted estimate of the win rate of union recognition strikes of 36.5 percent, to offset the $194 loss required a union recognition gain of $532, which implies that the benefits from union recognition had to last almost three years beyond the current year before the expected gains from the strike offset the early loss.

Strikes in one state often had positive external effects on the earnings of workers in other states. A strike in the rest of the country benefited nonstriking workers in several ways, either by posing a threat of strikes in that state or by raising the demand for workers in the nonstriking state. Other strikes potentially had a dampening effect in that striking workers at times migrated to nonstriking regions, increasing the supply of labor in those regions. To capture the external effects of strikes in the rest of the country, the strike days per employee in other fields is included in the regression. The coefficient in Table 11-5 shows that strikes in other fields raised miners' wages by 0.47 cents per hour, although days worked were reduced by 1.6 days. Given that miners faced direct losses in nonrecognition strikes and potential losses even in the union recognition strikes, their best alternative may have been to free ride on strikes in the rest of the country. The external effects of strikes help explain why the UMWA devoted enormous efforts to trying to organize workers and develop solidarity across all coal fields. Without such solidarity they faced a substantial free rider problem in their strikes, where the primary gainers from the strikes were the miners and employers in nonstriking fields.

Violence During Strikes

The history of coal mining strikes is littered with explosions of violence, most often in struggles over union status.[26] The violence ranged from fistfights and name calling to full-scale warfare. Massacres occurred in the towns of Ludlow, Matewan, and Herrin, and several times between 1890 and 1930 the violence escalated to the point where state militia and even federal troops were called in to maintain order.[27] In fact, the coal mining industry has experienced more strike violence than most other industries prior to 1930. Jeffreys-Jones found that bituminous coal mining accounted for 71 of the 293 strike mortalities in the United States between 1890 and 1909.[28] Even after the number of strike deaths are adjusted for differences in the number of workers employed, strike mortality rates were substantially higher in bituminous coal mining than in steel, transportation, or manufacturing.

Violence in strikes was costly to both sides and often backfired. So why did the violence occur?

One view found in many popular treatments of the subject asserts that "deplorable living conditions, starvation wages, illegal, oppressive and often dishonest practices of early coal operators brought on bloody uprisings."[29] However, the rest of the book suggests that those living conditions and wages were on par with other sectors of the economy. Starvation was less a cause of strikes than the result of being on strike for several months, or being caught in a severe downturn. Strikes for better wages, union recognition, and/or better working conditions do not imply workers were destitute or exploited. Since strike activity rose when coal prices and economic growth rose, the strikes might also have been attempts to raise wages above wages elsewhere.

Mainstream newspapers and the general public at the time often blamed the workers. Edwin Witte, in his study of the government in labor disputes, stated:

> The public is shocked by violence in labor troubles but stops in its analysis of the problem with damning organized labor. There is little realization that it usually takes two to make a quarrel, and that employers by unintelligent action may provoke violence unthought of by their workmen.[30]

Former West Virginia Attorney General Howard Lee, who blamed both operators and miners for the violence in West Virginia, described the miners in the following way:

> The strikers acted upon the theory that it was their moral right to go to any extreme, even murder, to prevent coal from being mined in strike-bound mines by nonunion workers; and their leaders spared no effort to encourage that belief. No matter how unjustified and heartless were the crimes committed by union fanatics, no leader of the union, local or national, ever uttered a word of censure or condemnation. On the contrary, they attempted to justify every crime, supplied able counsel for defendants, and tried to block every effort of society to punish the criminals.[31]

In combatting this picture of miners, some have taken the workers' side, seeing all actions by the employers as suspect, particularly when workers fought hired guards. The mercenaries were protecting the employer's capital, his property, and his rights to ignore the union and hire whom he wished. In contrast, the workers were protecting themselves and their families from the depredations of the mine guard. They were underdogs, lacking the owner's wealth, in some cases dispossessed of housing, and facing a government that typically focused on protecting property and the peace, thus appearing to be on the side of the employer. The workers' story commonly was that of a stirring struggle against a superior force. However, it should be remembered that strikers directed the violence not only at the employer's property and mine guards, but also against fellow workers. Some violence was directed at the state militia and other neutrals.

In the final analysis, the operators' guards, the civil authorities, and the strikers at various times committed egregious acts of violence. Can we depict the violence in black and white: unsavory men willing to use violence in a calculated attempt to intimidate the other side into agreeing to their terms? Since both sides recognized that aggressive violence was a costly strategy that could backfire easily, the course of events seems better painted in unremitting shades of gray. Both sides were armed to deter violence by the other side, each side had problems in controlling all its members, and violence often occurred in the confusion accompanying strike events.

In studying strike violence, it would be a mistake to assume that intimidation and violence characterized all relationships in the coal industry. Most mines in most years experienced no strike activity, and the vast majority of strikes ended with no violence or property damage.[32] Thus any examination of violence has to consider that the normal strike pattern involved no violence at all. One explanation of this is that when miners and employers armed themselves in strikes, they saw it as self-defense.

At first blush, the path to violence seems to be like the prisoner's dilemma model of arms races. Both sides armed because no matter what the opponent did, they were better off armed than unarmed.[33] In many cases, the miners perceived that the government, which had a legal monopoly on the use of violence, was biased against them. Prior to strikes occurring in some areas where violence later broke out, mine guards had prevented union activity. State and local government, the courts, and militia sent into the strike zone all seemed to be controlled by the coal operators. Thus the miners felt that they had to set up their own defenses to protect themselves and their civil rights. On the other hand, the operators set up elaborate defenses because they feared destruction of property and attacks on men who continued to work. By 1900 miners and coal operators could point to an ample history of violent acts committed by the other side that suggested the need for self-protection. The prisoner's dilemma characterization has two advantages: First, it shows the "chicken-and-egg" dilemma in attempts to blame one side or the other for forcing the other side to arm. Second, it points out that lack of trust in communications between the two sides contributed to the problem. Union recognition strikes were more violent than strikes in union strongholds, in part because a history of negotiations developed more trust between the two parties in unionized mines.

With both sides armed, there was an initial deterrent against violence. Both sides probed each other, attempting to achieve an advantage without pushing the other side into violent action. The workers at times picketed the mines, held mass meetings, shouted insults at replacement workers, marched on the mine to close it down, surrounded trains of replacement workers, or sometimes took stronger measures to keep the mine from operating.[34] The operators at times brought in strike-breakers and evicted miners from their houses. Or, guards, often deputized by the county, at times tried to arrest a striker for illegal possession of firearms or to keep the miners from having a mass meeting. Other companies sought court injunctions to limit the miners' activities.

With both sides armed, confrontations on picket lines or at railroad stations where replacements disembarked, which might have ended with jearing and an occasional fistfight without arms became far more dangerous. A rock that found its mark, a guard stumbling under the pressure of the crowd, someone firing into the air, or an angry move in self defense could start a melee. In the confusion of the incident, both sides would charge the other with starting the violence. The violence might end there if both sides quickly settled, but this initial incident damaged relations, thus lowering the costs to both sides of aggressive retaliation. Both sides exacted revenge for prior acts, sometimes retaliating before the other side could act. The worst excesses of aggressive violence occurred during those periods of retaliation. The problems were further compounded by racial or ethnic differences between the strikers and replacement workers. When a strike heated up this way, an outside authority was required to end the violence. State militia were required. In some cases the state militia became involved in the struggle, and federal troops were required to prevent further bloodshed.

The two-sided model of strike violence is a useful starting concept, but it is too simplistic because of the wide assortment of personalities living among the miners, mine guards, and mine operators. The vast majority of people on all sides sought to avoid violence. Violent actions were enormously costly, hindering labor relations, reducing earnings and profits, and sometimes turning areas into war zones. The majority armed in self-defense and considered themselves reasonable people caught in unreasonable circumstances. However, there were subgroups on both sides who were either quick to anger or thought violence was useful strategically. The miners faced a "public bad" problem. When a striker covertly strafed a company town, the mine guards retaliated against all miners because it was hard to single out the culprit. The operators often faced problems reining in some hotheaded mine guards, who might beat a striker, causing retaliation against all the mine guards and the operators' property. Thus, senseless actions by individuals led to the involvement of large numbers of workers and employers who had not originally sought violence.

Conclusions

The decision to go on strike was a tough choice. It appears that the ideal situation was for miners in one state to hope that other coalfields struck so that they could obtain additional income as coal production shifted toward their state. When the miners struck, they usually obtained higher hourly earnings in the current year and the following year, but the gains in hourly earnings came at a substantial immediate cost. For every day on strike the miner lost roughly a half day of earnings. When the wage gains from a strike are compared with the lost days of earnings, the miners lost nearly two dollars for every day they struck. The strike was less onerous if the issue was union recognition, because winning an union recognition strike meant an average increase in annual earnings of $156 per year. But employers did not hand over that kind of increase without substantial resistance. Union recognition strikes were likely to last one hundred days or longer, costing the miners nearly $200 in lost earnings. Even then, there was probably no better than a 44 percent chance of winning the strike. Comparing the expected gains from winning the union recognition strike with the lost earnings during the strike, the expected increase in annual earnings from union recognition would have had to last almost three years before the strike losses were overcome. Thus in pecuniary terms, the strike was often a loser. When there was a net gain, the miner had to wait at least a couple of years for the expected gain from unionization to offset his early losses.

Given the likelihood of pecuniary losses, why did miners go on strike? Maybe the strikes were "mistakes" made with imperfect information. Many economists argue that strikes were breakdowns in negotiations when one or both sides could not accurately assess the other side's willingness to compromise.

Since all we have estimated here is average gains and losses from strikes, it is quite possible that a subset of miners gained from strikes while others lost. National union leaders may have used strikes in one region to gain concessions from employers in other regions of the country. Ashenfelter and Johnson suggest that union leaders at times call for strikes for internal political reasons even when it may not be in the best interest of the rank and file.[35] Workers with less mobility might have gained from strikes while more mobile workers did not, particularly when a strike aided miners by establishing the threat of strikes in future negotiations. More mobile miners gained less in these situations because they were likely to have moved on to other mines by the time the next negotiating round started. The division of interests among strikers was most prominent in situations where some strikers resorted to intimidation and social ostracism to prevent others from continuing to work.

Alternatively, miners may have struck because nonpecuniary gains may have offset the pecuniary losses. Although the vast majority of strike days were over wages and hours, we haven't measured all the gains from striking or unionization. Many short strikes dealt with disputes arising from hiring and firing decisions under the existing grievance mechanism. A major issue in union recognition strikes was often the establishment of such grievance mechanisms, to give miners freedom to voice their complaints without fear of injudicious firings. Further, a number of miners gained a sense of membership in a community of miners from joining in a strike against the operators. Certainly the extensive labor history studies of the development of solidarity among striking workers shows that this sense of community was an important part of the miners' decision to strike.

Strikes also meant the risk of violence. While living in company towns many miners did not trust the government at any level to protect their interests in a strike. On the other hand, employers feared that the existing police were inadequate for protecting both their property and those miners who continued working. With these fears fuelled by past incidents, both sides prepared for violence, largely to defend themselves against possible aggressive actions taken by the other side. On both sides most participants saw themselves as reasonable people caught in unreasonable circumstances. Yet both sides faced problems reining in their hotheaded members, and the operators faced problems in controlling the actions of their guards. While the vast majority of strikes ended with no violence, some exploded into full-scale warfare. The initial violent episode often came during marches or picketing, when someone had fired a shot in anger, and all hell broke loose. Since no one could identify who started the incident, both sides blamed the other. Relations between the two groups were then destroyed, and the situation turned to more aggressive use of violence by both sides.

NOTES

1. John R. Hicks, *The Theory of Wages*, 2d ed. (Gloucester, MA: Peter Smith Publishers, 1957), pp. 140–47.

2. For reviews of the economics literature on strikes see John Kennan, "The Economics of Strikes," *Handbook of Labor Economics*, vol. II, edited by O. Ashenfelter and J. Layard (Amsterdam: North-Holland, 1986), pp. 1091–1137 and Ronald Ehrenberg and Robert Smith, *Modern Labor Economics: Theory and Public Policy* (Glenview, IL: Scott Foresman Co., 1988), pp. 464–73.

3. For example, Florence Peterson, "Strikes in the United States, 1880–1936," *U.S. Bureau of Labor Statistics Bulletin No. 651* (Washington, DC: U.S. Government Printing Office, 1938), pp. 66–80; U.S. Commissioner of Labor, "Strikes and Lockouts," *Twenty-First Annual Report of the Commissioner of Labor, 1906* (Washington, DC: U.S. Government Printing Office, 1907). For an analysis of the strike results see Gerald Friedman, "Strike Success and Union Ideology: The United States and France, 1880–1914," *Journal of Economic History* 48 (March 1988): 1–26.

4. One attempt to estimate the costs and benefits of a strike was by Curtis Eaton, using evidence from twenty negotiations in Canada in the late 1960s. Curtis Eaton, "The Worker and the Profitability of the Strike," *Industrial and Labor Relations Review* 26 (October 1972): 670–79.

5. The division into three tables reflects differences in the coverage of strikes by the Bureau of Labor. The U.S. Commissioner of Labor published detailed information on strikes by industry from 1881 until 1905. In 1914 the Bureau of Labor Statistics again started collecting information from newspapers, supplemented with questionaires for larger strikes. The BLS began collecting strike information in a more systematic fashion in 1927. In bituminous coal mining, the U.S. Geological Survey collected information on the number of workers on strike and the number of days they were idle in questionaires that sought information about all aspects of mining.

6. In mining the percentage of estimated working time that miners were idle in work stoppages in 1942–50 was 4.08 percent, in 1951–60 was 0.85 percent, and in 1961–70 was 0.756 percent. Figures calculated from U.S. Bureau of the Census, *Historical Statistics of the United States, Colonial Times to 1970* (Washington, DC: U.S. Government Printing Office, 1975), series D986 to D1021, pp. 180–81.

7. Comparisons for the subperiod from 1901 to 1905 are similar. These figures are just for strikes and not for lockouts by employers as defined by the U.S. Commissioner of Labor. The number of lockouts was less than 4 percent of the number of strikes and lockouts tended to display similar characteristics, although coal lockouts tended to be shorter than the average lockout in U.S. industry. See U.S. Commissioner of Labor, *Twenty-First Annual Report, 1906, Strikes and Lockouts* (Washington, DC: U.S. Government Printing Office, 1907), pp. 432–35, 478–79, 712–15, 736–37.

8. Calculated from information in Peterson, "Strikes," pp. 41 and 152.

9. For discussions of output shifting in coal mining, see C. Lawrence Christenson, "The Theory of the Offset Factor: The Impact of Labor Disputes upon Coal Production," *American Economic Review* 43 (September 1953): 513–47. One example of output shifting occurred in 1919 when "the danger of a strike in the organized districts quickened the rate of production during September, so that in October, when a strike on November 1 became a practical certainty, the monthly total broke all previous records." F.G. Tryon and Sydney Hale, "Coal in 1919, 1920, and 1921," in U.S. Geological Survey, *Mineral Resources of the United States, 1921, Part II. Nonmetals* (Washington, DC: U.S. Government Pringing Office, 1924), p. 452. Similar events occurred in 1906, *Mineral Resources of the United States, 1906, Part II. Nonmetals*, p. 563. For general discussions of greater strike activity when production could be shifted more easily, see Melvin Reder and George Neumann, "Conflict and Contract: The Case of Strikes," *Journal of Political Economy* 88 (October 1988): 867–86.

10. See Beth Hayes, "Unions and Strikes with Assymetric Information," *Journal of*

Labor Economics 2 (January 1984): 57–83; Joseph Tracy, "An Empirical Test of an Assymetric Information Model of Strikes," *American Economic Review* 76 (June 1986): 423–36.

11. J. Paul Leigh, "Risk Preference and the Interindustry Propensity to Strike," *Industrial and Labor Relations Review* 36 (January 1983): 271–85.

12. Friedman, "Strike Success," pp. 11, 18.

13. The growth rate of real GNP and the CPI used to deflate the coal price are from U.S. Bureau of the Census, *Historical Statistics of the United States, Colonial Times to 1970* (Washington, DC: U.S. Government Printing Office, 1975), series F-3, p. 224 and series E135, 211. STRIKE and PRICE are from U.S. Geological Survey (after 1922 U.S. Bureau of Mines), *Mineral Resources of the United States, Part II, Nonmetals* (various years). The percent union is from U.S. Coal Commission, *Report, Part III* (Washington, DC: U.S. Government Printing Office, 1925), p. 1052. For more details on the evidence see Appendix B.

14. The weight is the square root of total coal employment in the state. Weighted least squares is used because I anticipated problems with heteroskedasticity arising from the use of state averages in states with different numbers of coal workers. A Glejser test confirmed that the variance of the error term was larger in areas with smaller coal populations. The data do not offer complete coverage of the period from 1902 to 1923 in each state. Some states had missing observations from the earlier years in the sample: Montana, nine years; Utah, two years; Virginia, two years; and Wyoming, two years.

15. The equation was also estimated with dummy variables for all states to try to capture state effects not measured by these variables. An F-test could not reject the hypothesis that the state effects were all simultaneously zero. I also experimented with dummy variables representing each year in the panel. Since the growth rate of real GNP is the same for each state in the panel, the year dummies are a linear combination of the growth rates of real GNP in that year, so we did not proceed further.

16. Charles Fowler, *Collective Bargaining in the Bituminous Coal Industry* (New York: Prentice-Hall, Inc., 1927), pp. 44–45. In 1909 E. W. Parker of the U.S. Geological Survey suggested that contracts tended to end in even-numbered years during the early 1900s. U.S. Geological Survey, *Mineral Resources of the United States, Part II, Nonmetals, 1909*, p. 38. I therefore tried an alternative description of years when contracts ended with value 1 in all even years through 1924 and 0 for odd years during that period (CONTRACT2). The results below imply that unionization still had strong effects, but that the effects were most pronounced in the even years.

$$\begin{aligned} STRIKE = {} & \\ & \underset{(1.38)}{-6.79} + \underset{(1.77)}{7.29}\, UNION + \underset{(1.89)}{1.88}\, PRICE + \underset{(3.54)}{53.84}\, RGNP\% + \underset{(5.74)}{22.52}\, UNION \times CONTRACT2 \end{aligned}$$

The coefficients show that fully unionized states struck on average on 7.29 days more than nonunion states in odd years, but struck almost thirty days more than nonunion states during even years when most contracts ended.

17. Calculated from information in Peterson, "Strikes," p. 152. The information in the text shows the breakdowns when the full intensity of strikes is considered. A different breakdown appears in information on just the number of strikes, because most strikes on other issues involved smaller numbers of workers and shorter periods of idleness. For the period from 1927 to 1936 only 39.7 percent out of the 522 bituminous coal strikes reported by the Bureau of Labor Statistics were over wages and hours; 24.7 percent over union organization. When the number of workers involved in the strikes are taken into account, 71.2 percent of the workers on strike were in wages and hours strikes, 20.3 percent in union organization strikes.

18. The analysis described by Table 6-8 in Chapter 6 treated days worked as an exogenous variable, one over which miners and employers had no control. In this section we treat it as an endogenous variable that is chosen simultaneously along with wages by the actions of employers and workers. When the days variable is an endogenous variable, it does not appear in reduced-form equations.

19. As one way of describing the structural relationships, consider each state to be a separate labor market, where the wage, the number of workers employed and the number of days worked by each worker are choice variables. The employers' demand for labor is characterized by an equation with the hourly wage as a function of the number of workers, the number of days worked by each worker, the price of coal, the productivity of workers, strikes in other coalfields, the accident rate, and the presence of workers' compensation. The number of workers who supply their labor is a function of the hourly wage, the number of days the worker can work, the degree of unionization, strike activity, strikes in other fields, the accident rate, and the presence of workers' compensation. The number of days worked in the mines is a function of the coal price, strike activity, unionization, the number of workers employed, the productivity of workers, and strikes in other coalfields. By estimating the structural equations above, we could examine the specific impact of strikes and unions on labor supply or on the days-worked decision. However, the full effect of strikes on wages and days worked is not determined until the labor supply and days variables interact with labor demand. Thus we estimate reduced form equations for days worked and wages as functions of all of the exogenous variables in the system. The coefficients of the reduced forms summarize the interactions of the coefficients from all three equations.

20. The wage data are state averages (aggregated from district information with the number of miners as weights) based on information from Waldo Fisher and Anne Bezanson, *Wage Rates and Working Time in the Bituminous Coal Industry, 1912–1922* (Philadelphia: University of Pennsylvania Press, 1932), pp. 248–53. The wages are averages of the wages on January 1 of the year, June 30, and December 31. For more detail on the aggregation procedures, see Appendix B.

21. Weighted least squares estimation is used because the data are averages from states with varying number of coal miners. Theoretically, the use of averages will lead to heteroskedasticity where the variances of the error term is smaller in states with greater employment. A Glejser test using the ordinary least squares residuals confirmed the presence of heteroskedasticity of this type in both equations. Therefore, the weight is the square root of coal employment.

22. Modern studies of strikes and wages find a mixture of positive and negative relationships. In modern collective bargaining situations economists have theorized that where employers have better information about profits than the union, there will be a negative relationship between wages and strikes. Unions use strikes as a means of determining the size of the employer's profits. Since the employer is likely to settle quickly with high wages when there are more profits, longer strikes will be associated with smaller wage gains. There is one major institutional difference between modern collective bargaining and bargaining prior to the passage of the National Labor Relations Act. In modern situations the workers already have collective bargaining and labor market power. Prior to the NLRA workers had to strike to gain market power. Therefore during the period covered in the book, wages would tend to rise in longer strikes, as miners struck to gain more market power. For estimates of modern relationships between strikes and wages, see Craig Riddell, "The Effects of Strikes and Strike Length on Negotiated Wage Settlements," University of British Columbia Discussion Paper No. 80–2, January 1980; Wayne Vroman, "Wage Contract Settlements in U.S. Manufacturing," *Review of Economics and Statistics* 66 (November 1984): 661–65. For estimates and modelling of negative strike-wage relationships, see David Card, "Strikes and Wages: A Test of an Assymetric Information Model," *Quarterly Journal of Economics* 105 (August 1990):

625–59; Sheena McConnell, "Strikes, Wages, and Private Information," *American Economic Review* 79 (November 1989): 801–15.

23. When calculating present values throughout this chapter all values in the current year are treated as being paid immediately, all values in year t + 1 are treated as being paid at the end of one year, values in year t + 2 at the end of two years, and so on.

24. West Virginia Inspector of Mines, *Annual Report for the Year Ending June 30, 1903*, pp. 90–94.

25. Using the coefficients in the third and fourth columns of Table 11-5, we find that a hundred-day strike would have cost the miners $287 in annual earnings during the strike year. The annual gain from full unionization was $164.59. The present value of unionization that lasted for the current year plus another year was $319.86, the current year plus two was $466.34, and the current year plus three years was $604.53. If the win rate for union recognition was 43.5 percent, the union recognition would have to last more than three years beyond the current year for the miners to see a net gain from the strike.

26. Philip Taft and Philip Ross, "American Labor Violence: Its Causes, Character, and Outcome," in Hugh Davis Graham and Ted Robert Gurr, eds., *The History of Violence in America, A Report to the National Commission on the Causes and Prevention of Violence* (New York: Bantam, 1969), p. 281. They claim that the introduction of the union or its survival was the issue in many of the violent strikes across all industries.

27. Book length considerations prevented the inclusion of a more extensive account of violence in the coal industry. The discussion here summarizes the analysis in Price V. Fishback, "Gun Thugs, Rednecks, and Scabs: Violence in the Bituminous Coal Industry, 1890–1930," University of Arizona, Department of Economics working paper. The working paper also includes a chronology of violent events during the period.

28. Rhodri Jeffreys-Jones, *Violence and Reform in American History* (New York: New Viewpoints, 1978), pp. 199–201.

29. Howard B. Lee, *Bloodletting in Appalachia: The Story of West Virginia's Four Major Mine Wars and Other Thrilling Incidents of its Coal Fields* (Morgantown: West Virginia University, 1969), p. ix.

30. Edwin E. Witte, *The Government in Labor Disputes* (New York: McGraw-Hill, 1932; reprinted by Arno and the New York Times, 1969), pp. 182–183.

31. Lee, *Bloodletting*, p. 31.

32. Taft and Ross, "American Labor Violence," pp. 281–395, p. 292; Edwin E. Witte, *The Government in Labor Disputes*, p. 177. Strike mortality paled in comparison with other types of homicides and the everyday dangers of working in a coal mine. Estimates from the Chicago Tribune from 1894 to 1900 found that homicides alleged to have occurred in strikes were 0.5 percent of all homicides in America. See Jeffreys-Jones, *Violence and Reform*, p. 26. The fatal accident rate in mines during this same period was 200 to 300 times the strike fatality rate. Roughly 12 deaths per million men employed per year occurred in strikes, compared with roughly 3,000 to 4,000 deaths in coal mining accidents for every million mine workers each year. See Fishback, "Gun Thugs," Table 1.

33. For a brief discussion of prisoner's dilemmas in arms races, see Peter Ordeshook, *Game Theory and Political Theory* (New York: Cambridge University Press, 1986), pp. 221–222.

34. In their study of labor violence in all industries, Taft and Ross, "American Labor Violence," p. 281, state that with "few exceptions the precipitating cause was attempts by pickets and sympathizers to prevent plant from reopening or attempts by mine guards, police, or militia to prevent interference."

35. Orley Ashenfelter and George Johnson "Bargaining Theory, Trade Unions, and Industrial Strike Activity," *American Economic Review*, 59 (March 1969): 35–49.

12

Conclusions

Consider the choices faced by any of the following persons in the early 1900s: an immigrant coming to the United States, a black agricultural laborer in the South, or a young native white worker who was just starting to work. They obtained their information about opportunities in the labor market through a combination of advice from parents and friends, information gathered from friends and relatives who had migrated to cities or the coalfields, handbills, newspaper ads, and labor agents.

Coal mining caught their interest because the hourly wages in the industry were substantially higher than in other industries. Further, the miner worked independently, free from no more than cursory supervision. However, coal mining did not look quite as good on closer inspection, because high hourly wages were in part compensation for limits on the number of days the miner could work, the greater dangers of working in a coal mine, and living in an isolated area with few of the lures of the big city. Rents in the isolated coal towns were cheaper than in many cities, but store prices were slightly higher. There were few opportunities to own housing, and frankly not much reason to want to own a house in an isolated area solely dependent on the fortunes of the mine.

So how did workers choose between farming, manufacturing, and coal mining? Since we have no way of measuring people's preferences, we cannot know how much weight people gave to high hourly earnings and independence relative to the negative features of more dangerous work or limits on working time. Various people reacted differently to the choices. Young males probably paid less attention to the dangers in the mine and living in isolated places and focused on the chances of earning big money quickly. Older men with families probably paid closer attention to the quality of life in the town.

We know that during the expansion of the coal industry large numbers of workers seemed to have found coal mining to be a favorable alternative. Many picked up stakes and moved to those isolated towns, when they could have moved with the same difficulty to manufacturing jobs in cities. Since few had complete information about life in a coal town, a number of migrants were disappointed and left quickly. Others stayed for a while, earning a stake before moving on. Still others settled into a longer career as a coal miner. A number of miners moved to new mines as they opened, or moved on when the mine where they worked closed. Others with families or in union districts were more likely to stay in one place longer.

Coal mining was not a superior choice in all times and at all places. The mines attracted large numbers of workers when coal mining boomed, raising coal earnings relative to earnings in other industries. The balance tilted in favor of other industries during short-term busts and then the long-term decline that started in the early 1920s. As relative coal earnings fell and mines closed, roughly 40 percent of coal workers either left or were pushed out of the industry. For experienced miners with skills specific to the coal industry, the coal bust was particularly devastating because they had to start again in a new industry at the entry level. Unskilled workers did not suffer as large a loss in income because they just moved from one entry-level job to another.

At all times, workers were faced with hard choices. At the turn of the century work environments were much harsher than today in every endeavor. In coal mining the workplace was far more dangerous than today and efforts by both the federal and state government to improve safety were often disappointing. Either regulations were not enforced or they failed to focus on the main causes of accidents. Even the introduction of workers' compensation, which increased the payments miners received when injured, had the unintended effect of raising accident rates.

To protect themselves against exploitation by coal employers, workers exercised both voice and exit. The voice came in the form of collective action either through the formation of unions or strikes. The United Mine Workers of America enhanced the welfare of their members in several ways. Within the coal industry miners obtained higher wages by joining the union and striking. The UMWA contributed to the long-term rise in coal wages and helped miners obtain the increases earlier. Company store prices in the union districts were somewhat lower. Union districts also set up grievance mechanisms, which helped limit injudicious firings. The union did not necessarily lead to a better situation in all phases of the job. Accident rates were no lower in union than in nonunion mines, nor was the quality of sanitation better, holding other factors constant. The union did not benefit all workers equally. Despite the emphasis on racial equality in the UMWA constitution, the union's treatment of black workers was schizophrenic. Blacks were welcomed into the union in the mining areas where they had long been located, but a number of union locals in the North treated blacks as pariahs.

The decision to strike was another of the hard choices faced by miners. Increases in hourly earnings from strike activity came at the cost of lost earnings from lost working time. When the the wage gains from strikes and unionization are weighed against the lost working time during strikes, it becomes evident that many strikes left miners with pecuniary losses. Further, costs rose during a number of strikes when violence erupted, even though both sides had armed in self-defense. Miners might have gained overall if we include the nonpecuniary gains of a greater voice in the workplace. However, the strikes may have reflected breakdowns in bargaining, where neither side had good information about what to expect from the other.

The movement of individual miners between competing mines and in and out of the industry also aided the miners in preventing exploitation. The impact of exit behavior has often been ignored because its effects are subtle and not easily identified. Exit has impact because of the individual decisions to quit or stay by thousands of workers, no one of which can be identified as the key action. The evidence here shows that exit was an important force. The long-term rise in coal earnings was largely driven by the requirement that earnings in coal mining keep pace with earnings in other industries. Miners, although not perfectly mobile, moved readily in response to new opportunities in other areas. Thus even in company towns with only one store and one source of housing, the companies faced limits on their ability to charge monopolistic prices. The importance of exit is shown indirectly by the interaction of wages and various parts of the employment package. Higher wages partially offset higher store prices in West Virginia. In comparisons of company towns, monthly wages rose dollar for dollar with increases in house rents, and they also were higher in areas with poorer quality sanitation. In comparisons across states hourly earnings were higher in states that offered fewer days of work per year and in states without workers' compensation. Strong competition among employers to hire workers helped protect black workers against discriminatory attitudes by both employers and other workers.

The major problem faced by both coal miner and employer was that they had no control over the coal product market. During the coal boom miners and employers flourished. However, conditions in the coal industry stagnated in the 1920s and then declined during the heart of the Great Depression. Exit was of little use to the miners who wanted to stay in coal mining, because the only way to avoid the decline in earnings was to move on to another industry. Nor was collective action effective at stemming the tide. The United Mine Workers were crushed along with the coal operators by the deterioration of the industry in the late 1920s and early 1930s.

APPENDIX A

Calculating Earnings for Workers in Coal Mining and Manufacturing

This appendix describes the basic methods for calculating hourly and annual earnings for coal miners and male manufacturing workers used in Table 6-1 and Tables A-1 and A-2. The data sources and methods of calculation are important to note because they may impart biases to comparisons of mining and manufacturing earnings.

Annual Earnings

The average annual earnings of full-time equivalent workers in Table 6-1 are roughly comparable for coal miners and manufacturing workers because they are constructed in a similar fashion. In several years, the Bureau of the Census published aggregate information on total wages paid to production workers and the number of workers on payrolls (including absentees) on or around the fifteenth of each month. Annual earnings per full-time equivalent worker are calculated by dividing total wages paid by the average number of workers on the payroll.[1] The earnings for the census years are treated as benchmarks, and estimates for other years are determined by interpolating with evidence from other sources.

The coal mining estimates are annual earnings after the cost of supplies to the miner are deducted. The benchmark estimates for total wages paid in 1929, 1919, 1909, 1902, and 1889 come from the 1939 mining census, which reports them on a comparable basis.[2] Table 6-1 shows two estimates for full-time annual earnings in coal mining based on substantially different estimates of average employment from surveys with similar, complete coverage of the coal industry.[3] The Greenslade estimates are based on employment figures from the U.S. Geological Survey, the Census estimates on employment from the mining Census. Interpolations between benchmarks for both series are based on Greenslade's work.

It is unclear which estimate is more accurate. The Census estimates for coal mining may be more comparable with the manufacturing estimates because the Census followed the same survey procedures in collecting employment data. Douglas and later Greenslade chose the Geological Survey employment estimates in their attempts to obtain time-series estimates of hourly earnings for three reasons.[4] First, an extended strike in 1919 meant that strikers did not appear on the payrolls for some months. The Census average employment estimate was lowered because the survey recorded only the number of workers who showed up for work in each month, while the number of miners on the payroll before and after the strikes was much greater.[5] Second, the 1902 Census reduced the employment figures to a 300 workday year, which makes them incomparable with later years. As a result, annual earnings based on Census employment in Table 6-1 begin in 1909. Third, they felt that the Geological Survey estimates were adequate because they were described as representing "the number of men commonly dependent on the mine for employment. They represent the number ordinarily reporting for work when the mine starts, plus the absentees."[6]

Greenslade's estimate of annual earnings based on Geological Survey employment is a lower bound. The U.S. Geological Survey's employment data overstates the relevant employment figure in two ways. The Geological Survey's employment estimates include supervisory personnel and technical people, while Census data on total wages paid do not. Subtracting the supervisory personnel and technical people raises the estimate of average annual earnings by around 2 percent.[7] Further, researchers for the Works Progress Administration in the 1930s discovered that when reporting to the U.S. Geological Survey, many mines reported the number of men on the payroll in December or January and not the average number for the year.[8] Since December or January are typically months of high employment, the number employed in December or January overstates the true average for the year. If all mines had reported December employment rather than average employment, the U.S. Geological Survey's estimates would have been roughly 4 percent too high in 1929, 8 percent too high in 1919, 9 percent in 1909, and 8 percent in 1902.[9]

Douglas calculated annual earnings per full-time equivalent worker for all manufacturing workers from Census data.[10] Since coal miners were nearly all males, Douglas's manufacturing earnings underestimate the manufacturing alternatives for miners by including the earnings of female workers. The manufacturing earnings in Table 6-1 are therefore Douglas's estimates multiplied by 1.10, which is a rough estimate of the ratio of male earnings in manufacturing to the earnings of all workers in manufacturing.[11] The annual earnings of farm laborers are based on the U.S. Department of Agriculture's series on monthly wages without board with straight-line interpolations by Douglas.[12]

Hourly Earnings

The estimates of hourly earnings for the United States in Table 6-1 are based on the work of Greenslade for coal mining and Albert Rees for manufacturing. Greenslade (and earlier Douglas) calculated coal earnings and Rees calculated manufacturing earnings for 1890 to 1919 using the same procedure. They started with average annual earnings per full-time equivalent worker in the census years and interpolated between census years with data from reports of the state labor bureaus. They transformed annual earnings into daily earnings with state data on the average number of days that establishments operated. The daily earnings are converted into hourly earnings with data on full-time hours from various sources.[13]

Rees's estimates for manufacturing workers include all workers, male and female. Nearly all coal miners were males, so their true opportunity cost wage in manufacturing was the wage for male workers. I calculated male annual earnings by multiplying Rees's estimate for all workers by 1.10. The 1.10 scalar is discussed more fully in note 11 and assumes that the ratio of female to male earnings was 0.558 and that females were 20 percent of the manufacturing work force. The resulting estimate of male manufacturing earnings is probably biased upward. Ratios of female to male hourly earnings from the National Industrial Conference Board range from 0.67 in 1914 to 0.59 in 1923, which would lower the male scalar to 1.07 and 1.089. A source of downward bias in the manufacturing estimates might be the use of full-time hours per day rather than actual hours per day. However, Rees found no downward bias when he checked his estimates against other benchmarks.[14]

TABLE A-1. Average Hourly Earnings for Male Manufacturing Workers Estimated from Census Data and Coal Wage Workers from Census and Geological Survey Data by States in Current Dollars

State	*1929*	*1919*	*1909*	*1904*	*1902*	*1899*
United States						
Manu.	58.7	52.5	20.5	18.6	18.2	16.1
Coal	64.5	69.7	27.7	26.7	24.2	18.5
Alabama						
Manu.	37.1	40.3	14.2	13.6		10.6
Coal	46.0	54.8	20.7		19.6	
Colorado						
Manu.	56.7	54.8	26.6	25.9		23.3
Coal	86.5	78.0	29.7		26.1	
Illinois						
Manu.	66.4	56.1	23.1	21.4		18.1
Coal	85.8	80.7	38.1		29.0	
Indiana						
Manu.	59.4	51.9	19.8	18.2		16.0
Coal	86.3	78.5	37.4		29.1	
Kentucky						
Manu.	50.4	43.6	16.6	16.1		13.5
Coal	57.0	64.7	22.8		17.1	
Ohio						
Manu.	65.6	58.2	21.6	19.6		16.7
Coal	59.7	73.2	31.5		26.7	
Pennsylvania						
Manu.	62.3	57.1	21.6	19.6		17.6
Coal	64.8	68.9	33.3		24.4	
Tennessee						
Manu.	42.4	39.6	14.7	14.7		12.0
Coal	41.9	46.0	20.2		17.0	
Virginia						
Manu.	45.5	46.0	14.2	13.9		12.0
Coal	49.2	56.1	19.8		11.0	
West Virginia						
Manu.	59.3	54.1	19.4	18.3		14.1
Coal	54.5	69.1	22.1		19.4	

Sources: Coal hourly earnings are average annual earnings from Table A-2 divided by average work hours, which are the product of average days worked at the mine and the average length of the work shift. Days worked and average length of work shift in each state are from U.S. Geological Survey (after 1922, U.S. Bureau of Mines), *Mineral Resources of the United States, Nonmetals,* various years. Male manufacturing hourly earnings are average annual earnings from Table A-2 divided by the national average for hours worked from Rees, "New Measures of Wage-Earner Compensation," pp. 3, 19; and Rees, *Real Wages,* p. 33. For 1929 I determined the national average for hours worked by dividing Rees's estimate of hourly earnings into the annual earnings reported by Rush Greenslade, "The Economic Effects of Collective Bargaining in Bituminous Coal Mining," (Ph.D. dissertation, University of Chicago, 1952, p. 49.

The hourly earnings of hired farm workers are based on U.S. Department of Agriculture surveys of farmers. The hired workers' earnings probably underestimate the coal worker's agricultural alternative. Hired workers represented less than one-fourth of the agricultural work force and included migrant workers and some women. However, Greenslade notes that hired workers are not clearly separate from farm operators and family workers. Farm operators at times worked for wages on other farms.[15] We know that some workers moved back

TABLE A-2. Average Annual Earnings for Male Manufacturing Workers Estimated from Census Data and Coal Wage Workers from Census and Geological Survey Data by States in Current Dollars

State	*1929*	*1919*	*1909*	*1904*	*1902*	*1899*
United States						
Manu.	1,433	1,257	563	534		478
Coal	1,142	1,097	498	464	490	379
Alabama						
Manu.	912	967	395	381		305
Coal	938	1,054	542		477	
Colorado						
Manu.	1,394	1,313	736	721		621
Coal	1,302	1,423	817		671	
Illinois						
Manu.	1,631	1,345	637	597		523
Coal	1,215	1,033	580		525	
Indiana						
Manu.	1,461	1,243	548	507		462
Coal	1,187	930	562		479	
Kentucky						
Manu.	1,239	1,046	459	448		390
Coal	1,026	1,000	404		329	
Ohio						
Manu.	1,612	1,394	597	547		483
Coal	963	962	526		428	
Pennsylvania						
Manu.	1,531	1,369	597	546		507
Coal	1,197	1,211	707		531	
Tennessee						
Manu.	1,041	950	406	409		347
Coal	787	755	454		367	

(*continued*)

and forth between the mines and their family farms. Comparisons of coal earnings and earnings for hired farm labor at worst show the relative opportunities for a farmer choosing supplemental employment.

Greenslade's estimates of coal hourly earnings in Table 6-1 start with his estimates of average annual earnings for full-time equivalent workers. He divided annual earnings by the U.S. Geological Survey's estimates of days the mine tipple operated to obtain daily earnings.[16] Hourly earnings are daily earnings divided by the standard length of the work shift. The resulting estimates of coal hourly earnings are biased in different directions at each stage of the calculation. First, as noted in the section on annual earnings, Greenslade's estimates of coal annual earnings are biased downward, possibly by as much as 10 percent. Second, hourly earnings might be slightly understated by an overstatement of days worked. The U.S. Geological Survey's inquiry about days worked concerned the number of days the mine tipple operated, which Greenslade felt understated days worked, because some maintenance work was performed when the tipple did not operate.[17] Although daymen, workers paid by the day, worked roughly 120 percent of tipple time in 1920 and 1921, tonnage men, who were paid piece rates, worked only about 85 to 90 percent of tipple time. Weighting the percent of tipple time worked by each group by their share of the work force (tonnage men were 65 percent of

TABLE A-2. *(Continued)*

State	*1929*	*1919*	*1909*	*1904*	*1902*	*1899*
Virginia						
Manu.	1,119	1,103	391	387		347
Coal	983	1,119	416		321	
West Virginia						
Manu.	1,458	1,296	537	512		407
Coal	1,204	1,117	509		381	

Sources: Manufacturing data for 1904 and 1899 are total wages paid to men sixteen and over divided by the average number of men employed sixteen and over from U.S. Bureau of the Census, *Census of Manufactures, 1905, Part I* (Washington, DC: U.S. Government Printing Office, 1907), pp. xxxv, lxxi–lxxiii. The census did not report the total wages paid to males and females separately after 1905. I estimated male earnings by calculating the ratio of earnings for all workers to earnings for males for 1909, 1919, and 1929 using the following formula: $W_t/W_m = (1-p) + p\ W_f/W_m$, where W_t, W_m, and W_f are the average annual earnings for all workers, male workers, and female workers and p is the percent of the manufacturing workforce that is female. I assumed that (W_f/W_m) was equal to the ratio of male to female wages in either 1904 or 1899, whichever resulted in a larger estimate of the male wage. Data for W_t (Wages total, divided by production workers) for the United States after 1904 come from U.S. Bureau of the Census, *Census of Manufacturers: 1947, Volume I, General Summary* (Washington, DC: U.S. Government Printing Office, 1950), p. 27. Data for p for the United States come from U.S. Bureau of the Census, *Fifteenth Census of the United States, Manufacturers: 1929, Volume I, General Report* (Washington, DC: U.S. Government Printing Office, 1933), p. 42. For the states after 1904, W_t and p are from U.S. Bureau of the Census, *Fifteenth Census of the United States, Manufactures: 1929, Volume III, Reports by States* (Washington, DC: U.S. Government Printing Office, 1933).

For coal mining annual earnings I followed Douglas and Greenslade and divided the total earnings paid to coal workers reported by the Bureau of the Census by the number of coal workers reported by the U.S. Bureau of Mines and the U.S. Geologic Survey. Total Wages in thousands for 1919, 1929 from Wages column, p. 256 in U.S. Bureau of the Census, *Fifteenth Census of the United States, Mines and Quarries, 1929: General Report and Reports for States and for Industries* (Washington, DC: U.S. Government Priting Office, 1933). Total Wages in thousands for 1909: Take gross wages column from U.S. Bureau of the Census, *Thirteenth Census of the United States, Mines and Quarries, 1909, Volume XI* (Washington, DC: U.S. Government Printing Office, 1911), p. 206, and multiply it by the ratio of Wages of production and development workers for 1909 from 1954 Census for the U.S. to the Wages for the U.S. from the 1909 Census (approx. 0.95). This eliminates miners' purchases of supplies, explosives, oil, and blacksmithing from the wages. Total Wages in thousands for 1902 are from U.S. Bureau of the Census, *Special Reports: Mines and Quarries, 1902* (Washington, DC: U.S. Government Printing Office, 1905), pp. 709–13. Employment for 1929, 1919, 1909, 1902 is from U.S. Geological Survey (after 1922 U.S. Bureau of Mines), *Mineral Resources of the United States, Part II, Nonmetals,* various years.

the work force in 1920), coal workers worked 97 percent to 100.5 percent of tipple time.[18] Earlier, when the percentage of daymen was lower, tipple time probably overstated working time more. Third, the standard length of shift may slightly understate the time miners spent working and travelling to workplaces in the mine, slightly overstating earnings per hour. During the 1920s the standard shift reported by the U.S. Geological Survey was 8.07 hours. The U.S. Bureau of Labor Statistics found that coal workers actually spent 8.1 hours in 1922 and 8.4 hours in 1929 in the mine either working or travelling to workplaces.[19]

After summing all the biases, comparisons of hourly earnings of coal miners and male manufacturing workers are likely to be biased against finding coal earnings to be high. The coal earnings series probably slightly underestimates coal hourly earnings, while the manufacturing series slightly overestimates male manufacturing earnings.

NOTES

1. The average number of workers for the year was calculated by summing the number of workers each month and dividing by 12.

TABLE A-3. Average Annual Earnings Per Full-Time Equivalent Worker and Hourly Earnings for Coal Workers in 1967 Dollars

	Annual Earnings		
Year	*Greenslade*	*Five-Year Average*	*Hourly*
1890	1504		0.667
1891	1396		0.626
1892	1456		0.663
1893	1419	1324	0.696
1894	1123		0.658
1895	1228		0.632
1896	1128		0.588
1897	1080		0.552
1898	1264	1348	0.680
1899	1516		0.740
1900	1752		0.852
1901	1860		0.948
1902	1885		0.931
1903	1922	1840	0.981
1904	1719		0.989
1905	1815		1.000
1906	1933		1.056
1907	2074		1.030
1908	1726	1896	1.041
1909	1844		1.026
1910	1904		1.021
1911	1896		1.046
1912	2045		1.066
1913	2061	1932	1.034
1914	1761		1.050
1915	1898		1.089
1916	2260		1.141
1917	2516		1.247
1918	2672	2466	1.322
1919	2118		1.346
1920	2765		1.560
1921	2056		1.713
1922	2060		1.799
1923	2593	2212	1.800
1924	2180		1.576
1925	2173		1.377
1926	2362		1.362
1927	2058		1.331
1928	2144	2145	1.310
1929	2226		1.277

Sources: See Table 6-1. Deflated to 1967 dollars with the BLS consumer price index for all goods, series E-135 from U.S. Bureau of the Census, *Historical Statistics of the United States, Colonial Times to 1970* (Washington, DC: U.S. Government Printing Office, 1975), p. 211.

TABLE A-4. Index of Greenslade Estimate of Coal Hourly Earnings Deflated by Different Measures of the Cost of Living (1914 = 100)

	Earnings Deflated by			*Cost of Living Indices*		
Year	*BLS CPI*	*Douglas*	*Rees*	*BLS CPI 1967 = 100*	*Douglas 1890–99 = 100*	*Rees 1914 = 100*
1890	0.63502	—	0.62596	27.0	—	91
1891	0.59622	0.73602	0.58132	27.0	101	92
1892	0.63150	0.77193	0.62248	27.0	102	91
1893	0.66325	0.82696	0.66104	27.0	100	90
1894	0.62648	0.77544	0.62923	26.0	97	86
1895	0.60200	0.71649	0.59524	25.0	97	84
1896	0.56009	0.65314	0.55380	25.0	99	84
1897	0.52580	0.60702	0.52616	25.0	100	83
1898	0.64772	0.74778	0.64816	25.0	100	83
1899	0.70488	0.79780	0.70535	25.0	102	83
1900	0.81156	0.88389	0.80244	25.0	106	84
1901	0.90300	0.96527	0.88235	25.0	108	85
1902	0.88659	0.95900	0.89049	26.0	111	86
1903	0.93490	1.00487	0.95296	27.0	116	88
1904	0.94195	1.02126	0.94937	27.0	115	89
1905	0.95254	1.03274	0.96003	27.0	115	89
1906	1.00545	1.05347	1.00211	27.0	119	90
1907	0.98076	0.97051	0.93590	27.0	126	94
1908	0.99134	1.02152	0.96657	27.0	121	92
1909	0.97723	1.00697	0.96328	27.0	121	91
1910	0.97295	0.98283	0.95270	28.0	128	95
1911	0.99676	0.97638	0.97602	28.0	132	95
1912	1.01494	1.02195	1.00809	29.0	133	97
1913	0.98461	0.98569	0.98133	29.7	137	99
1914	1.00000	1.00000	1.00000	30.1	139	100
1915	1.03714	1.07057	—	30.4	136	—
1916	1.08653	1.10115	—	32.7	149	—
1917	1.18819	1.17708	—	38.4	179	—
1918	1.25878	1.20258	—	45.1	218	—
1919	1.28169	1.24125	—	51.8	247	—
1920	1.48595	1.43957	—	60.0	286	—
1921	1.63139	1.64147	—	53.6	246	—
1922	1.71342	1.73451	—	50.2	229	—
1923	1.71494	1.72940	—	51.1	234	—
1924	1.50136	1.51699	—	51.2	234	—
1925	1.31178	1.32511	—	52.5	240	—
1926	1.29760	1.31778	—	53.0	241	—
1927	1.26760	—	—	52.0	—	—
1928	1.24777	—	—	51.3	—	—
1929	1.21620	—	—	51.3	—	—

Sources: For Greenslade's estimate of coal hourly earnings see Table 6-1. All deflated earnings are converted to 1914 = 100 for ease of comparison. BLS CPI is the BLS consumer price index for all goods in 1967 dollars, series E-135; Douglas's estimate of the cost of living is series E-185, 1890–99 = 100; and Rees's estimate of the cost of living is series E-186. All are from U.S. Bureau of the Census, *Historical Statistics of the United States, Colonial Times to 1970* (Washington, DC: U.S. Government Printing Office, 1975), p. 211. Correlations between the deflated earnings are 0.9908 between the CPI-deflated and Douglas-deflated earnings and 0.997 between the CPI-deflated and Rees-deflated earnings.

2. U.S. Bureau of the Census, *Sixteenth Census of the United States, Mineral Industries, 1939* (Washington, DC: U.S. Government Printing Office, 1944), p. 230.

3. The estimates of total output from the surveys by the Geological Survey and the Census are within 1 percent of each other, as are their estimates of total coal revenue.

4. Greenslade improved on earlier estimates by Paul Douglas by using information not available to Douglas in 1930. Douglass based his calculations for the 1909 benchmark year on the gross wages that were reported, although information in other census years were for wages net of the cost to the miner of supplies. The Census of 1939 later translated the 1909 figure into net wages paid. For the 1920s, Greenslade used alternative interpolations that could make full use of information throughout the decade, whereas Douglas was forced to stop in 1926. Rush V. Greenslade, "The Economic Effects of Collective Bargaining in Bituminous Coal Mining," Ph.D. dissertation, University of Chicago, 1952, p. 38 fn. 3, 42; Paul Douglas, *Real Wages in the United States, 1890–1926* (Boston, MA: Houghton Mifflin Company, 1930), pp. 343–58.

5. The anthracite strike of 1902 also created a similar problem for anthracite employment estimates. Bituminous coal also experienced a strike in 1902 but not of major proportions.

6. Douglas, *Real Wages*, pp. 344–45, quoting F.G. Tryon.

7. Greenslade, "Bituminous Coal," pp. 30, 34. In 1902 superintendents, foreman, managers, surveyers, and others accounted for 2.64 percent of all mine employees. U.S. Bureau of the Census, *Special Reports, Mines and Quarries, 1902* (Washington, DC: U.S. Government Printing Office, 1905), p. 709.

8. Greenslade, "Bituminous Coal," p. 35

9. The percentage figures are based on the ratio of December employment to average employment for the year as reported in the *Fifteenth Census of the United States, Mines and Quarries, 1929, General Report and Reports for States and for Industries* (Washington, DC: U.S. Government Printing Office, 1933), p. 284 and U.S. Bureau of the Census, *Special Reports, Mines and Quarries, 1902*, pp. 709–10.

10. Albert Rees offers alternative estimates of annual earnings in manufacturing, but they were designed primarily to calculate hourly earnings. His estimates were generally about 1 percent less than Douglas's. See Stanley Lebergott, *Manpower in Economic Growth: the American Record Since 1800* (New York: McGraw-Hill Book Company, 1964), p. 484, note 2.

11. The Bureau of the Census reported the total wages paid production workers and total production workers separately for male and female adult workers in 1899 and 1904, but not for later years. In both years the ratio of annual earnings for adult males to annual earnings for all adult workers in manufacturing was slightly less than 1.10. The figure is relatively low because females accounted for only about 20 percent of manufacturing workers, although the ratio of female to male annual earnings in manufacturing was 0.559 in 1904 and 0.568 in 1899. I calculated the ratio of all workers' earnings to male earnings in manufacturing for 1909, 1919, and 1929 using the following formula

$$W_t/W_m = (1 - p) + p\, W_f/W_m,$$

where W_t, W_m, and W_f are the average annual earnings for all workers, male workers, and female workers and p is the percent of the manufacturing workforce that is female. The percent female was 21 percent in 1929, 20.1 percent in 1919, and 20.6 percent in 1909 U.S. Bureau of the Census, *Fifteenth Census of the United States, Manufactures: 1929, Volume I, General Report* (Washington, DC: U.S. Government Printing Office, 1933), p. 42. Using the 0.559 ratio of female to male earnings in 1904 for W_f/W_m and taking the inverse of W_t/W_m, the ratio of male average annual earnings to average annual earnings for all workers was

1.102 in 1929, 1.097 in 1919, and 1.0996 in 1909. Given the constancy of this ratio over time it seemed reasonable to multiply the average for all earnings by 1.10 to get the measure for male earnings.

The 1.10 scalar may be an upper bound. The female-male ratio of weekly earnings in manufacturing from the National Industrial Conference Board ranged from 0.568 to 0.62 between 1914 and 1929; the female-male ratio for hourly earnings was 0.67 to 0.59 over the same period. These ratios of male to female earnings would have led to scalars less than 1.10. Ada Beney, *Wages, Hours, and Employment in the United States 1914–1936*, National Industrial Conference Board Studies Number 229 (New York: National Industrial Conference Board, 1936).

The annual earnings estimates for coal mining and manufacturing also included the earnings of children sixteen and under. This hinders the manufacturing-mining comparisons only slightly. Children composed 2.9 percent of manufacturing employment in 1904, 2 percent of coal employment in 1902. U.S. Bureau of the Census, *Census of Manufactures, 1905, Part I* (Washington, DC: U.S. Government Printing Office, 1907), pp. xxxv, lxxi–lxxiii; U.S. Bureau of the Census, *Special Reports: Mines and Quarries, 1902*, pp. 709–13. Both percentages declined over the next twenty years.

12. Douglas, *Real Wages*, p. 186. Annual earnings are twelve times monthly wages without board.

13. Manufacturing estimates for 1890 to 1914 are from Albert Rees, *Real Wages in Manufacturing, 1890–1914*, National Bureau of Economic Research Number 70 (Princeton, NJ: Princeton University Press, 1961), pp. 4, 23; after 1914 from Albert Rees, "New Measures of Wage-Earner Compensation in Manufacturing, 1914–57," National Bureau of Economic Research Occasional Paper 75, 1960, p. 3. Rees argues that his estimates of hourly earnings are more comprehensive than Paul Douglas's estimates in *Real Wages*. Douglas's data give too high a weight to union earnings. Although the payroll industries data are superior to those for union industries, Douglas used information for "selected occupations" peculiar to the industry. Therefore most unskilled workers and some semiskilled are excluded from his sample, an important consideration because most coal miners were unskilled or semiskilled.

14. Rees, *Real Wages*, pp. 28.

15. Greenslade, "Bituminous Coal," p. 61.

16. After 1922 the U.S. Bureau of Mines took over the task of preparing and publishing *Mineral Resources of the United States*, the series that contains most of the coal mining data.

17. The inquiry was phrased: "Total number of full days mine (tipple) was in operation during the year. Parts of days should be reduced to equivalent in full days." Quoted by Greenslade, "Bituminous Coal Mining," pp. 34–35

18. Waldo Fisher and Anne Bezanson, *Wage Rates and Working Time in the Bituminous Coal Industry, 1912–22* (Philadelphia: University of Pennsylvania Press, 1932), pp. 130–31.

19. The situation differed for tonnage workers and daymen. Tonnage workers in the 1920s worked between 7.2 and 7.5 hours per day in their workplaces after subtracting a half-hour for lunch. However, tonnage workers also spent roughly forty minutes a day in the mine travelling to and from their workplaces, raising the hours per day to 7.9 to 8.2. Daymen tended to work longer than the standard shift raising the average hours per day to the level in the text. U.S. Bureau of Labor Statistics, "Hours and Earnings in Bituminous Coal Mining, 1929," *Bulletin No. 516* (May 1930): 2–4; Greenslade, "Bituminous Coal Mining," pp. 37, 102.

APPENDIX B

Sources of Data for Panel of Twenty-three Coal States from 1901 to 1930

Throughout the book there are discussions of regressions based on the panel data set for twenty-three coal states from 1901 to 1930. The coal states include Alabama, Arkansas, Colorado, Illinois, Indiana, Iowa, Kansas, Kentucky, Maryland, Michigan, Missouri, Montana, New Mexico, Ohio, Oklahoma, Pennsylvania, Tennessee, Texas, Utah, Virginia, Washington, West Virginia, and Wyoming.

Accident Rates

Accident rates were calculated by dividing the measure of fatalities by a measure of hours worked. There were three measures of fatalities proposed in the text: underground deaths, underground deaths minus accidents killing five or more workers, and roof falls. The data for accidents killing five or more workers came from U.S. Bureau of Mines (BuMines), *Bulletin* 355, "Coal-Mine Accidents in the United States, 1930," by W. W. Adams, L. E. Geyer, and L. Chenoweth (Washington, DC: U.S. Government Printing Office, 1932), pp. 94–100. Data on the remaining fatalities come from the following sources: for 1930, BuMines *Bulletin* 355, pp. 8–9; for 1925–1929, U.S. Bureau of Mines, *Bulletin* 341, "Coal-Mine Fatalities in the United States, 1929," by W. W. Adams (Washington, DC: U.S. Government Printing Office, 1931), pp. 68–72; for 1922–1924, U.S. Bureau of Mines, *Bulletin* 283, "Coal-Mine Fatalities in the United States, 1926," W. W. Adams (Washington, DC: U.S. Government Printing Office, 1927), pp. 58–62; for 1919–1921, U.S. Bureau of Mines, *Bulletin* 241, "Coal-Mine Fatalities in the United States, 1923," by W. W. Adams (Washington, DC: U.S. Government Printing Office, 1924), pp. 31–36; for 1914–1918, U.S. Bureau of Mines, *Bulletin* 196, "Coal-Mine Fatalities in the United States, 1919," by Albert H. Fay (Washington, DC: U.S. Government Printing Office, 1920), pp. 42–47; for 1901–1913, U.S. Bureau of Mines, *Bulletin* 115 , "Coal-Mine Fatalities in the United States, 1870–1914," by Albert H. Fay (Washington, DC: U.S. Government Printing Office, 1916), pp. 142–355.

Underground hours worked are calculated as the product of total average underground workers and days worked and average hours worked per day. Days worked is defined as the average number of days the mines were open in each state in the following sources: for 1921–1930, BuMines *Bulletin* 355, p. 82; for 1913–1922, BuMines *Bulletin* 241, p. 52; for 1901–

1914, BuMines *Bulletin* 115, pp. 142–355. The Bureau of Mines did not report the average number of days the mines were open in 1909. I interpolated values for 1909 by calculating the ratio of net tonnage to total days worked (the product of average days worked and total employment) for 1908 and 1910 and then averaging them. I then used the average ratio to get an estimate of days worked for 1909. This technique gave odd estimates for Montana and North Dakota; so, missing values were left for those states. Average hours worked per day is calculated by using a weighted average of hours worked. The weights are the number of workers working that particular number of hours per day as a percentage of workers for whom hours per day were reported. The sources for these data include the following: for 1930, U.S. Bureau of Mines, *Mineral Resources of the United States, 1930, Part II—Nonmetals* (Washington, DC: U.S. Government Printing Office, 1932), (henceforth, to be referred to as BuMines Nonmetals, 1930), p. 654; for 1922–1929, BuMines *Bulletin* 341, pp.76–79; for 1919–22, BuMines *Bulletin* 241, pp. 44–46; for 1914–18, BuMines *Bulletin* 196, pp. 48–51; for 1903–30, BuMines *Bulletin* 115, pp 142–355.

The Bureau of Mines reported the number of underground workers directly for the years 1913 to 1930 in the following sources: for 1921–30, BuMines *Bulletin* 355, p. 82; for 1913–20, BuMines *Bulletin* 241, p. 53. The number of underground workers for 1901 to 1912 were interpolated using the total number of workers and benchmarks for the ratio of underground to total workers from 1902, 1909, and 1913. Ratios of underground workers to total workers were calculated for 1902 from Bureau of the Census, *Special Report: Mines and Quarries, 1902* (Washington, DC: U.S. Government Printing Office, 1905) pp. 709–11 using the total average number of wage earners underground and above ground; for 1909 from Bureau of the Census, *Thirteenth Census of the United States, Volume XI, Mines and Quarries, 1909*, pp. 232–33; and for 1913 from BuMines *Bulletin* 115, pp. 142–355. The ratios for intervening years were determined by a straight-line interpolation between 1902 and 1909 and then between 1909 and 1913. The interpolated ratios were then multiplied by the average total number of coal workers, also found in BuMines *Bulletin* 115.

Coal Prices, Technological Variables, Strikes, Union Strength, and Mine Size

Coal prices are defined as the average coal price received at the mine per ton. They were calculated by the Bureau of Mines as the total revenue at the mine divided by total coal production. The sources include the following: for 1925–30, BuMines, *Nonmetals*, 1930, p. 648); for 1915–24, BuMines *Bulletin* 275, p. 55; and for 1901–14, BuMines *Bulletin* 115, pp. 142–355. The coal prices were turned into real coal prices by deflating by the Consumer Price Index for the United States (1967 = 100), series E135 in U.S. Bureau of the Census, *Historical Statistics of the United States, Colonial Times to 1970* (Washington, DC: U.S. Government Printing Office, 1975), p. 211.

The percentage of tonnage mined with the machine cutter is reported directly in the document for 1901 to 1911. For 1911 and later, percent machine mined is the percent machine mined as a percentage of the total percentage of mines for which the technological information was reported. The sources for this information include for 1930, BuMines, *Nonmetals*, 1930, p. 661; for 1922–29, BuMines *Bulletin* 341, pp. 73–75; for 1919–21, BuMines *Bulletin* 241, pp. 37–38; for 1914–18, BuMines *Bulletin* 196, pp. 37–41; for 1901–14, BuMines *Bulletin* 115, pp. 142–355.

Potential strike variables include the ratio of men on strike to the average number of men employed and days idle on strike per employee. Information on the average number of men employed is discussed in the section on accident rates. Information on total days idle on strike and the number of men idle during strikes comes from the following sources: for the years

1923–30, BuMines, *Nonmetals* for the following years 1930 (p.659), 1929 (p. 748), 1928 (p. 480), 1927 (p. 372), 1926 (p. 483), 1925 (p. 439); for 1919–22, U.S. Geological Survey, *Mineral Resources of the United States, 1922, Part II—Nonmetals* (Washington, DC: U.S. Government Printing Office, 1925), p. 517 (henceforth referred to as U.S. Geo. Survey, *Nonmetals*); U.S. Geo. Survey, *Nonmetals*, 1921, p. 505; U.S. Geo. Survey, *Nonmetals*, 1918, p. 723; for 1914–18, BuMines *Bulletin* 196, pp. 51–52; and for 1901–13, BuMines *Bulletin* 115, pp. 142–355. To calculate days idle on strike per employee in the rest of the United States for state i, I subtracted state i's information for days idle (and employment) from the U.S. total and then calculated the ratio.

The relative strength of labor unions is based on data from the U.S. Coal Commission, *Report, Part III* (Washington, DC: U.S. Government Printing Office, 1925), p. 1052. The measure reported there is the ratio of paid up membership in the United Mine Workers of America as of November 30 to the average number of employees in each area as reported by the U. S. Geological Survey. The coverage of the variable is incomplete. It covers only the years 1902, 1905, 1908, 1912, 1915, 1918, 1921, and May 1923. Data is inserted for the remaining years prior to 1923 using straight-line interpolations between each pair of years for which data is reported. Several states were also combined in the reporting process, so the same value was inserted for each of the combined states. The combined states were: Arkansas, Oklahoma, and Texas; Colorado and New Mexico; Kentucky, Tennessee, and Virginia; Maryland and West Virginia; and Wyoming and Utah. There are missing data for the following states: North Dakota is not listed at all; Montana is not listed for 1902, 1905, and 1908; Washington for 1902; and Wyoming and Utah for 1902. The Coal Commission calculated the ratio for May 1923 using the number of employees for 1921. I readjusted the ratio so that the 1923 measure in the data base is the ratio based on the number of employees for 1923.

The mine size variable is the percentage of coal produced by mines producing less than 100,000 tons of coal per year. These figures are for commercial mines only and do not include wagon mines (small mines that deliver coal by wagon to the railroads). Most wagon mines were not regulated by state agencies. Mine size data was not available prior to 1909 and for the years 1915, 1916, and 1918. The remaining data come from the following sources: for 1922–30, BuMines, *Nonmetals* for the following years (pages in parentheses) 1930 (641–42), 1929 (713–14), 1928 (464–65), 1927 (396–97), 1926 (491–92), 1925 (461–64), 1923 (595–96); for 1909–14, 1917, and 1919–22, U.S. Geo. Survey, *Nonmetals* for the years 1922 (531–34), 1921 (520–23), 1917 (947–48), 1914 (610–13), 1912 (39–42), 1910 (36–39).

Wage Rates

The measure of real wages (listed in Table B-1) is the average hourly rate paid to daymen in each state deflated by the Consumer Price Index for the United States (1967 = 100), series E135 in U.S. Bureau of the Census, *Historical Statistics*. The wage rate data comes from two sources, Waldo Fisher and Anne Bezanson, *Wage Rates and Working Time in the Bituminous Coal Industry 1912–1922* (Philadelphia: University of Pennsylvania Press, 1932) pp. 248–53 and 338–43 and U.S. Bureau of Labor Statistics, "Hours and Earnings in Bituminous Coal Mining, 1929" *Bulletin No. 516,* (Washington, DC: U.S. Government Printing Office, 1930, pp. 31–39. The Bezanson and Fisher study is based on data collected by the U.S. Coal Commission from fifty-two coal districts located in twenty-three states at six month intervals beginning January 1, 1912 and ending January 1 1923. The Coal Commission collected data on pick mining piece rates, machine mining piece rates, and daily wages for various occupations inside the mine. Bezanson and Fisher then undertook the task of aggregating the data to the national level for piece rate workers and for day workers. The wage series used here for individual states are those for all inside day workers. Using the data for inside day workers allowed coverage of all twenty-three states in the sample. Furthermore, it reduced problems with comparing wage rates across states. As described in Chapter 5, piece rates were often adjusted to offset differences in the natural conditions of the mine and sometimes did not reflect all of the payments made to the miner because the miner might get paid extra for "deadwork." The daily pay to those who were paid on a time basis in most cases tended to move in the same directions as the average hourly earnings of workers paid by the piece; therefore, the day wages seem to be a reasonable approximation of the direction in the pay of piece rate workers. Piece rate workers and daymen were hired in the same labor market. Correlations of daymen's hourly wages and hourly earnings for piece rate workers were 0.902 for cross-state data from 1922 and 0.895 for pooled data for 1922 and 1924. The correlations are based on evidence from U.S. Bureau of Labor Statistics, "Hours and Earnings in Bituminous Coal Mining, 1929," *Bulletin No. 516*, (Washington, DC: U.S. Government Printing Office, 1930), pp. 27–35.

Bezanson and Fisher reported index values for the wages at the district level and at the national level but not aggregated to the state level (the level of aggregation for the remaining variables in the panel). For states containing several districts, I aggregated the values from the districts to provide a state wage. The first step was to calculate the average wage index for each year for each district, which was the average of the wages for December 31 the previous year, June 30 of the current year, and December 31 of the current year. These indexes were found on pp. 248–53 in Bezanson and Fisher. The indexes were then multiplied by the base wage rate for December 31, 1920. The average wage for the state was then calculated as a weighted average of the district wages with the weights determined by the district's share of bituminous coal produced that year (see pp. 338–43). This was done for all wages from 1912 to 1922. The wage for 1923 is based on the index from January 1 of that year.

Although the analysis of wages in the text was limited to the data for 1912 to 1923 above, the wage series can be extended to 1924, 1926, and 1929 using BLS data for the following states: Alabama, Colorado, Illinois, Indiana, Kentucky, Ohio, Pennsylvania, and West Virginia. For each state and year (1922, 1924, 1926, and 1929) the average wage for daymen is created as the weighted average of the wages across ten underground dayman occupations: brakeman, bratticeman and timberman, cager, driver, laborer, motorman, pumpman, trackman, trapper, and other. The weights were based on the number of workers in each occupation as a share of workers in all dayman occupations underground in that state and year. The two-wage series can then be spliced together using the ratio of the 1922 BLS wage (based on surveys taken between December 1921 and January 1922) to the December 1921 wage calculated from the data provided by Bezanson and Fisher.

Workers' Compensation Legislation

The Worker's Compensation law variable was compiled primarily from the volumes in the Bureau of Labor Statistics' Workmen's Insurance and Compensation Series. The law was assumed to go into effect at the beginning of the year after passage. The BLS volumes in the Workmen's Compensation Series were not published every year, so I treated them as benchmark volumes. If there was no change in the status of the compensation law in the benchmark volumes, the variable was given the same value for the years between the benchmarks. If there was a difference in the law in the benchmark volumes, I examined the BLS's annual descriptions of changes in labor law in particular volumes devoted to labor legislation in a particular year or in volumes of the *Monthly Labor Review* until I found the change in the law. The following *Bulletins* of the Bureau of Labor Statistics in the Workmen's Insurance and Compensation Series (date in parentheses) were used as benchmarks for the compilation: 92 (1911), 126 (December 1913), 189 (October 1915), 243 (September 1918), 272 (January 1921), 301 (April 1922), 332 (June 1923), 379 (January 1925), 423 (July 1926), and 496 (January 1929). The final benchmark volume was Bureau of Labor Statistics, "Handbook of Labor Statistics, 1931," *Bulletin No. 541* (Washington, DC: U.S. Government Printing Office, 1931), pp. 891–909.

The Employer Liability Law variable was constructed using information from Lindley D. Clark, "The Legal Liability of Employers for Injuries to Their Employees in the United States," *U.S. Department of Labor Bulletin No. 74*, Vol. 16 (Washington, DC: U.S. Government Printing Office, 1908). Additional dating of changes in the employer liability and workers' compensation laws came from examination of the annual or biennial state law volumes (for example, *Laws of Indiana*) and the compilations of statutes (for example, *Burn's Annotated Indiana Statutes*).

State Mining Legislation and Enforcement

The information on inspectors, inspectors' salaries, and the state laws were compiled from a variety of sources. The initial sources used as benchmarks included the following: U.S. Commissioner of Labor, "Labor Laws of the United States 1907," *22nd Annual Report of the Commissioner of Labor* (Washington, DC: U.S. Government Printing Office, 1908); U.S. Bureau of Labor Statistics, "Labor Laws of the United States with Decisions of the Courts Relating Thereto, April 10, 1914," *Bulletin No. 148* (Washington, DC: U.S. Government Printing Office, 1914); and U.S. Bureau of Labor Statistics, "Labor Laws of the United States with Decisions of the Courts Relating Thereto, May 1925," *Bulletin No. 370* (Washington, DC: U.S. Government Printing Office, 1925). From there the intervening years were filled in by examining the annual or biannual state statute volumes and the law compilations for various years from all of the states in the study. As with workers' compensation legislation, if there was a change in the law in a particular year, the change is not reflected in the data until the following year. Prior to statehood, Oklahoma (1907) and New Mexico (1912) came under the jurisdiction of U.S. territorial mining law.

Quantifying the laws was relatively straightforward once the definition of the law was established. There were relatively few problems with the laws concerning dusting the mines, requirements for fire bosses, provision of timbers by the operator, insulation of electric wires, riding on cars, use of permissible explosives, tests for inspectors, inspectors' ability to close the mines without a court order, police power, number of foremen's visits, licensing of foreman, licensing of miners by a state board, and licensing of miners by the foreman.

Compiling the number of inspectors and their salaries and therefore the budget for inspectors' salaries described in the text was considerably more complex. Typically, the state mining law established the number of inspection districts, the number of inspectors, their annual salaries , and the role of the chief of the mine department, which varied across states. Changes in salaries and the number of inspectors were usually legislated as amendments to the mining law. In many of the states the appropriations legislation also contains information on the budget for salaries of the mine inspectors. In most states both sources agree. Where possible, appropriations information is used as the basis for the salary budgets. Since the accident data is based on the calendar year and the states had a variety of fiscal years, the salary budgets are adjusted to the calendar year using appropriate weights.

The following states contained complete appropriations information: Alabama, Arkansas, Missouri, New Mexico, Virginia, West Virginia, and Wyoming. The Missouri appropriations are adjusted to reflect the fact that only part of the resources appropriated were devoted to coal mining inspections. These adjustments are based on the explicit allocations described in the mining statutes. In Virginia the state mining statutes actually provided for a mine inspector in 1912, but the appropriations legislation shows that the actual funding establishing the inspector's position did not occur until 1914.

In several states the appropriations were made in the mining legislation itself or no appropriations were listed. In those states the information is based purely on the statutes. New legislation on salaries or numbers of inspectors was treated as if it went into effect in the beginning of the fiscal year after the date of the legislation. For example, legislation approved in Illinois on June 5, 1911, was treated as going into effect at the start of the following fiscal year, beginning July, 1, 1911, and ending June 30, 1912. An exception was made for legislation that passed within a month after the beginning of the fiscal year. In all these cases it is clear that the change was designed to take place immediately. A law in Tennessee that passed on April 15, 1907, was treated as going into effect at the beginning of the fiscal year starting March 19, 1907, and ending March 18, 1908. Only statute information was used for each of the following states: Illinois, Indiana, Kentucky, and Michigan. In Indiana the appropriations and the statute information are dissimilar; data on disbursements are consistent with the statute information and are therefore used as the basis for inspectors' salary budgets.

In several states appropriations data were available for only part of the period; therefore, a mixture of statute and appropriations data was used. In those cases the rules above for the date the statute went into effect are followed. The mixture was used in the following states (with the period for which appropriations were used): Colorado (appropriations through March 31, 1913), Iowa (appropriations after July 1, 1919), Kansas (appropriations throughout except mine inspectors's salaries up to June 30, 1907; expense payments and salaries were not separated in the appropriations, but a daily salary was stated in the statutes; inspectors were treated as working 365 days a year), Maryland (appropriations to September 30, 1922), Montana (appropriations for State Coal Mine Inspector through February 28, 1916), Ohio (appropriations except for 1919, when a statute change took precedent over the appropriations legislation), Oklahoma (appropriations through June 30, 1929), Tennessee (appropriations after March 19, 1917), Texas (appropriations after August 31, 1909), Utah (appropriations through 1916 but missing values thereafter because mine inspection came under the Industrial Commission, which provided no detailed information after that date), and Washington (appropriations through March 31, 1919). In Pennsylvania the appropriations for mine inspectors were confusing because the mining department inspected both anthracite and bituminous mines. Statute information was used for the inspectors' salaries, while information on the number of bituminous districts and inspectors comes from the *Report of the Department of Mines of Pennsylvania, Part II—Bituminous, 1929–1930*, p. 53. The years listed on that page were treated as ending May 31 of the year listed, which was the end of Pennsylvania's fiscal year.

Several other factors deserve note. Both Indiana and Illinois state law allowed for appointments of county inspectors beyond the district inspectors. I found no appropriations for these inspectors in the state acts and no mention of them in the annual reports of the bureaus of mines in these states, so I left the county inspectors out of the calculations. In Kansas the number of inspectors was not listed directly in the state mining law. Instead they were included in laws for a mine safety association and then under the aegis of the commissioner of labor and industry. In later years the assistant commissioner of labor and industry was the *ex officio* chief inspector of mines. After 1917 the Montana industrial board oversaw mine inspection; as far as could be told Montana had only one inspector of coal mines at a constant salary from that time forward. Determining salaries in some cases was also complex. In some states travel expenses were mentioned as part of the mining law. However, the coverage was so scattered that I was unable to obtain a consistent series for such expenses and left them out.

In determining the number of inspectors, the role of the chief inspector also became an

TABLE B-1. Average Hourly Wage Rates by State for Inside Daymen (in 1967$)

State	1912	1913	1914	1915	1916	1917	1918	1919	1920	1921	1922
Alabama	0.65	0.66	0.66	0.65	0.66	0.66	0.88	0.86	0.86	0.90	0.73
Arkansas	1.18	1.17	1.15	1.14	1.08	1.21	1.36	1.23	1.29	1.72	1.83
Colorado	1.03	1.21	1.26	1.24	1.17	1.29	1.42	1.28	1.34	1.63	1.44
Illinois	1.16	1.15	1.14	1.13	1.09	1.20	1.35	1.21	1.28	1.70	1.82
Indiana	1.19	1.18	1.16	1.15	1.11	1.22	1.36	1.23	1.29	1.72	1.84
Iowa	0.92	0.91	0.90	0.89	0.85	0.94	1.06	0.96	1.01	1.35	1.44
Kansas	1.20	1.19	1.18	1.16	1.09	1.23	1.38	1.24	1.30	1.73	1.85
Kentucky	0.85	0.83	0.81	0.80	0.99	0.90	1.08	0.98	1.12	1.34	1.32
Maryland	0.81	0.79	0.78	0.78	0.76	1.12	1.33	1.20	1.27	1.71	1.82
Michigan	1.19	1.18	1.16	1.15	1.11	1.22	1.37	1.25	1.32	1.76	1.88
Missouri	1.20	1.19	1.17	1.16	1.09	1.23	1.38	1.24	1.31	1.74	1.86
Montana	1.52	1.50	1.48	1.46	1.38	1.45	1.56	1.40	1.44	1.88	2.01
New Mexico	1.32	1.29	1.29	1.32	1.23	1.30	1.44	1.30	1.43	1.71	1.43
Ohio	1.11	1.10	1.08	1.07	1.04	1.15	1.30	1.17	1.23	1.65	1.76
Oklahoma	1.16	1.14	1.13	1.12	1.05	1.198	1.33	1.20	1.26	1.67	1.75
Pennsylvania	1.03	1.01	1.00	0.99	0.98	1.15	1.34	1.21	1.27	1.59	1.62
Tennessee	0.66	0.64	0.63	0.63	0.59	0.70	0.91	0.84	0.97	1.22	1.01
Texas	1.20	1.19	1.17	1.16	1.09	1.22	1.37	1.23	1.30	1.73	1.73
Utah	1.38	1.34	1.33	1.31	1.23	1.33	1.50	1.36	1.41	1.84	1.96
Virginia	0.68	0.69	0.69	0.69	0.67	0.76	0.99	0.96	1.12	1.39	1.13
Washington	1.42	1.39	1.37	1.35	1.28	1.35	1.49	1.34	1.36	1.73	1.64
West Virginia	0.74	0.74	0.75	0.74	0.74	0.92	1.11	1.02	1.17	1.53	1.39
Wyoming	1.45	1.43	1.41	1.40	1.31	1.36	1.49	1.35	1.39	1.83	1.97
United States	1.02	1.00	0.99	0.98	0.97	1.09	1.26	1.14	1.22	1.57	1.56

Source: See text of wage rate section of Appendix B. The deflator does not adjust for differences in the cost of living across states.

issue. I constructed an alternative budget for inspectors' salaries across states in which chief inspectors whose job descriptions did not include direct inspections of mines were excluded from the budget. However, the correlation between the alternative budget and the budget in the text was above 0.9, so I did not pursue this line of inquiry further.

Another problem in calculating the budget for salaries of inspectors arose in determining the role of the chief inspector and deputy chief inspector of the Department of Mines in Pennsylvania, where they oversaw both bituminous and anthracite mine inspections. In this case I multiplied their combined salaries by the number of bituminous districts as a percentage of the number of all mining districts in Pennsylvania and then added this figure to the budget. A similar situation arose in Missouri, where the chief of the Department of Mines oversaw two coal mine inspectors and four inspectors of other mines. I allocated one-third of his salary to the coal mining inspection budget.

In all the states except Oklahoma prior to 1929 and Tennessee the mining laws specifically established the number of coal mine inspectors. In these two states the mining laws were more general. To establish what share of the inspection budget should be allocated to coal mining in these states, I examined the number of coal mines as a percentage of all mines reported in the United States Mining Censuses of 1902, 1909, 1919, and 1929. This examination showed that the coal mine share of all mines in Tennessee was 76 percent in 1902, 73 percent in 1909, 82 percent in 1919, and 87 percent in 1929. On this basis I assumed that 80 percent of the Tennessee mine inspection budget was spent inspecting coal mines between 1901 and 1930. For Oklahoma the percentages were 65 percent in 1909, 52 percent in 1919, and 55 percent in 1929, and I assumed that 60 percent of the Oklahoma mine inspection budget was expended on inspecting coal mines between 1907 and July 1, 1929.

APPENDIX C

Estimating the Relationship Between Wages and Accident Rates

Chapter 7 discusses a complex relationship between wage rates and accident rates and the impact of unions on safety and wages. Exogenous changes in wage rates altered the accident prevention decisions by employers and workers, differences in the accident proneness of workers affected the employers' demand for labor, and differences in the safety of the mines influenced coal workers' labor supply decisions. The empirical estimates of the wage-accident and the union-accident relationships presented in the text come from the following empirical model. An accident-rate equation (1) is included in a system of simultaneous equations along with labor-demand (2) and labor-supply (3) equations. The endogenous variables in the system are the real wage, total underground hours of work, and the accident rate.

The equations take the following linear forms:

(1) $ACCRATE = a_1 + a_2WAGE + a_3PRICE + a_4DAYS + a_5UNION + a_6MACHCUT + a_7SIZEU100 + a_8LWORCOMP + a_9LELIAB + a_{10}LAWS + a_{11}BUMINES + a_{12}INSBUDGET + a_{13}STATES + e_1$

(2) $WAGE = b_1 + b_2UNDHOURS + b_3ACCRATE + b_4PRICE + b_5PMACHCUT + e_2$

(3) $WAGE = c_1 + c_2UNDHOURS + c_3ACCRATE + c_4UNION + c_5STRIKE + e_3$

where *ACCRATE* is the number of underground fatalities per 10 million hours worked underground.[1] *UNDHOURS* is millions of hours worked by miners underground.[2] *WAGE* is the average daily wage rate for inside day workers[3] deflated by the U.S. Consumer Price Index.[4] *PRICE* is the average value per ton of coal at the mine deflated by the U.S. Consumer Price Index. *DAYS* is the average number of days the mines were open each year. *UNION* is paid-up membership in the United Mine Workers as a percentage of total average employment. *MACHCUT* is the percentage of coal mined by cutting machines. *SIZEU100* is the percentage of coal produced by mines that produced less than 100,000 tons per year. *LWORCOMP* is a dummy variable for a workers' compensation law. *LELIAB* is a dummy variable for laws limiting employers' defenses under negligence liability. *LAWS* is a vector of dummy variables for state mine safety laws.[5] *INSBUDGET* is the state budget for mine inspectors' salaries deflated by the CPI and normalized by total tonnage of coal in thousands produced that year. *STATES* is a vector of state dummies representing structural differences (often geological) in state accident rates. *STRIKE* is the days on strike divided by the number of workers employed. *BUMINES* represents the presence of the U.S. Bureau of Mines.[6]

Scholars who believe miners were stuck at subsistence incomes suggest that miners gambled their lives more when wages fell, implying that the coefficient of *WAGE* (a_2) in the accident rate equation (1) should be negative. Alternatively, if miners were at income levels that allowed them to maximize permanent income, the sign of the WAGE coefficient is ambiguous for risk-averse miners, positive if miners are risk-neutral (see Appendix D). In a model of profit maximization, a change in wages leads to an uncertain effect on the employers' efforts at accident prevention. Thus the *WAGE* coefficient (a_2) in the accident prevention equation is likely to have an ambiguous sign.

The coefficient (c_3) of *ACCRATE* in the labor supply equation (3) shows the extent to which miners sought higher wages when supplying labor to a more dangerous mine. The sign of the coefficient (b_3) of *ACCRATE* in the labor-demand equation (2) is uncertain because higher accident rates affect demand differently depending on the cause of the higher rates. To the extent that the higher accident rate in each state reflects a less risk-averse mining population, the demand for workers will increase and b_3 will be positive.[7] A higher accident rate may also reflect a more inexperienced, accident-prone population, that is a work force of lower quality. Demand for such a group will be lower and b_3 will be negative. Finally, the accident rate may reflect more unsafe geological conditions and therefore lower quality natural resources. Less labor is demanded in such regions because operators will combine more labor with resources of higher quality.

Both labor historians and economists expect that unions improved the welfare of their members in either of two ways. If unions effectively raised wages given the accident rate through their control of the labor supply, the *UNION* coefficient (c_4) in the labor-supply equation is positive. This coefficient reflects the structural impact on labor supply discussed in Chapter 7. The United Mine Workers may also have improved safety by providing such services as grievance procedures that allowed workers to negotiate for workplace public goods without fear of being fired. If so, the *UNION* coefficient (a_5) in the accident-rate equation should be negative. Collective action by miners was not limited purely to membership in the UMW, as nonunion miners sometimes struck. To the extent miners used strikes to raise wages, the coefficient of *STRIKE* (c_6) in the labor supply equation is positive.

Several cyclical and technical factors influence the accident rate. Coal demand fluctuated throughout the early 1900s, causing fluctuations in the coal *PRICE* and in the number of *DAYS* the mines were open. The signs of the *PRICE* and *DAYS* coefficients (a_3 and a_4) are unclear, a priori. Theoretically, increases in coal prices cause operators to promote reductions in accident rates, but price increases bring marginal mines into the market, causing accident rates to rise. A reduction in *DAYS* or opportunities to work has ambiguous effects on accident prevention by miners, while leading to more deterioration of the mine and thus more safety hazards.[8]

The set of technical variables includes the percentage of coal mined by cutting machines (*MACHCUT*), a mine size variable (*SIZEU100*), and a vector of state dummies (*STATES*). Contemporaries debated the impact on accidents of the diffusion of the cutting machine, which was the major change in mining technology during the early 1900s. Some argued that its introduction raised accident rates by increasing the employment of untrained workers, the risk of being caught in machine blades, and the incidence of electrocutions. The U.S. Bureau of Mines argued that the resulting decline in "shooting off the solid"—blasting of coal without making an undercut—more than offset such risks.[9] Similarly, observers disagree on the impact of mine size on accident rates. Contemporaries suggested that the smaller mines that moved in and out of production had higher accident rates. Alternatively, Drury noted that in Britain larger mines had higher accident rates.[10] The *STATES* dummies represent geological differences in the accident rates across states,[11] as the natural safety of the mines varied with respect to such factors as the composition of the roof, amount of methane gas present, and dustiness of the coal.[12]

The remaining factors are standard labor demand and supply relationships. *WAGE* and *UNDHOURS* should be negatively related in the labor-demand equation and positively related in the labor-supply equation. The coefficient of *PRICE* in the labor-demand equation should be positive. The introduction of cutting machines enhanced the productivity of miners, so *MACHCUT* is included in the labor-demand equation as a proxy for increased labor productivity. Its coefficient should be positive.

The simultaneous equations are estimated with two-stage weighted least squares on a pooled data set including the years 1912–14, 1917, 1919–23 for a sample of the twenty-three coal mining states listed in Table 7-4 in Chapter 7.[13] The equations were weighted by the square root of underground hours to avoid problems with heteroskedasticity caused by the fact that both wages and accident rates are means from state distributions of varying sizes.[14] Table C-1 reports the estimates of coefficients and t-statistics for the three-equation model. The discussion of wage effects in the chapter is based on these coefficients and t-statistics. Following a common procedure for discussing regression results in economics, I base the discussion on the results of t-tests. In this analysis with a sample size of 198, when the absolute value of the t-statistic exceeds 1.645, we can reject the hypothesis that the coefficient is zero at the 90 percent significance level. I feel comfortable in describing the magnitudes of effects implied by the coefficients that pass this test. If the absolute value of the t-statistic is less than 1.645, I am not confident that the coefficient is not zero.[15]

Coefficients describing the relationships between fatal accident rates and the various state safety laws and workers' compensation laws are reported both in Table C-1 and Table 7-5 in Chapter 7. Differences in the coefficients and t-tests reported in the two tables arise for two possible reasons. First, the results in Chapter 7 come from estimating a reduced-form accident equation based on the structural equations in this appendix. The results in Table C-1 examine the impact of the laws holding wages constant in the context of a simultaneous equations system. The reduced-form accident equation in Chapter 7 shows the total impact of the mine safety and workers' compensation laws on accident rates including all the feedback effects caused by changes in wages in the labor market.

Second, the panel data set used for estimation in Chapter 7 is larger because the reduced form allows us to omit the wage variable, which was unavailable for most years. The reduced-form should also include the union and mine size variables, but they were omitted because they also had large numbers of missing values. The larger data set allows us to examine the laws over a twenty-eight-year period which encompasses much more variation than the nine years of evidence in the simultaneous equations model in this appendix. One issue arises from the omission of the union and mine size variables from the reduced-form equation. Are differences in results caused by bias in the coefficients resulting from the omission of the union and mine size variables or are differences in the results caused by the increased size of the sample? The differences are caused by use of more data. When both union and mine size are included in the reduced-form regressions the sample is 264 observations. I ran the regressions for the sample of 264 both with union and mine size and without union and mine size and the coefficients and t-statistics of the remaining variables were changed very little. Thus, the coefficients are not biased by the omission of union and mine size.

The reduced-form accident-rate equation estimated in Chapter 7 is derived by solving the three-equation system in this appendix for ACCRATE as a function of all exogenous variables.

TABLE C-1. Weighted Two-Stage Least Squares Estimates from Pooled Annual Data for Twenty-Three Coal Mining States for the Years: 1912–14, 1917, 1919–23 (N = 198)

	Accident-Rate Equation		
Left-Hand Variable:	*SMALLACC*	*TOTALACC*	*ROOFACC*
Constant	39.64	−76.78	44.10*
	(1.69)	(−0.62)	(1.90)
PRICE	0.44	−1.93	0.53
	(0.58)	(−0.63)	(0.62)
WAGE	−3.98	44.67	−21.76
	(−0.21)	(0.55)	(−1.07)
MACHCUT	0.04	−0.48	0.05
	(0.48)	(−1.52)	(0.61)
UNION	−0.14	10.13	−4.59
	(−0.02)	(0.37)	(−0.79)
DAYS	−0.05	0.04	−0.07
	(−0.97)	(0.21)	(−1.37)
LDUST	—	−0.22	—
		(−0.22)	
LFIREBOSS	—	−0.93	—
		(−0.04)	
LTIMBER	−11.60*	94.87	−8.10
	(−1.85)	(3.73)	(−1.40)
LELEC	−3.27	60.67	—
	(−0.80)	(3.31)	
LNORIDE	5.36	−86.76*	—
	(1.11)	(−4.20)	
LSAFEXPL	6.37	−76.79	—
	(0.50)	(−1.40)	
LINSTEST	4.53	8.17	—
	(1.04)	(0.47)	
LCLOSE	−4.17	2.61	—
	(−1.21)	(0.21)	
LPOLICE	0.04	−29.35	—
	(0.01)	(−1.15)	
FVISIT	−0.61	2.34	2.61
	(−0.10)	(0.06)	(0.56)
FORELIC	0.37	21.50	−2.03
	(0.37)	(1.19)	(−0.53)
SBLICMIN	−6.22	−67.69	13.42
	(−0.46)	(−1.38)	(0.90)
FLICMIN	−0.13	21.96	8.67
	(−0.15)	(0.61)	(1.02)
INSBUDGET	−1.21	−3.30	0.62
	(−0.99)	(−0.70)	(0.51)
TIME	0.08	−2.03	1.11
	(0.08)	(−0.49)	(1.13)
LWORCOMP	0.26	8.06	−1.93
	(0.16)	(0.84)	(−0.84)
SIZEU100	−0.02	0.04	−0.11
	(−0.21)	(0.09)	(−1.08)

(*continued*)

TABLE C-1. *(Continued)*

	Labor Demand Equation *Left-Hand Variable: WAGE* *ADSUHOUR*	 *AUDUHOUR*	 *ARFUHOUR*
Constant	0.34*	0.29*	0.40*
	(2.80)	(2.43)	(3.22)
UNDHOUR	−0.00003	0.00006	−0.0001
	(−0.14)	(0.32)	(−0.64)
Accident Rate	−0.004	0.0002	−0.01*
	(−0.97)	(0.09)	(−1.89)
PRICE	0.13	0.13*	0.13*
	(7.65)	(7.57)	(7.53)
MACHCUT	0.005*	0.005*	0.005*
	(5.04)	(4.97)	(5.32)
F-statistic	845.78	841.99	845.48

	Labor Supply Equation *Left-Hand Variable: RWAGE* *ADSUHOUR*	 *AUDUHOUR*	 *ARFUHOUR*
Constant	0.64*	0.82*	0.76*
	(5.68)	(9.73)	(6.57)
Accident Rate	0.015*	0.006*	0.02*
	(3.50)	(2.69)	(2.28)
UNDHOUR	0.0005*	0.0004*	0.0004*
	(2.29)	(1.69)	(1.74)
PUNION	0.44*	0.40*	0.43*
	(5.37)	(4.92)	(4.86)
STRIKE	0.11	0.14*	0.11
	(1.38)	(1.70)	(1.25)
F-statistic	730.29	700.82	713.16

Source: These results were originally reported in Price V. Fishback, "Workplace Safety During the Progressive Era: Fatal Accidents in Bituminous Coal Mining, 1912–1923," *Explorations in Economic History* 23 (1986): 269–98, reprinted with the permission of Academic Press, Inc. Copyright © 1986 by Acadmic Press, Inc. All rights of reproduction in any form reserved. The coefficients of the state dummies can be fond there.

Notes: The accident rates used here are underground fatalities per 10 million hours worked underground. The accident rates reported in Chapter 7 are per million hours worked underground. *SMALLACC* refers to the number of deaths in accidents killing four or less, *TOTALACC* refers to the number of deaths from all types of accidents. *ROOFACC* refers to the number of deaths from roof falls.

All F-statistics for the equation as a whole are significant at the 1 percent level. R^2 are not reported because they are not good measures of goodness of fit in weighted least squares models. See R. Pindyck and D. Rubinfeld, *Econometric Models and Economic Forecasts* (New York: McGraw-Hill, 1981), p. 146.

*The hypothesis test rejects the null hypothesis that the coefficient is zero at the 90 percent significance level.

$$ACCRATE = d_1 + d_2PRICE + d_3DAYS + d_4UNION + d_5MACHCUT + d_6SIZEU100 + d_7LWORCOMP + d_8LELIAB + d_9LAWS + d_{10}BUMINES + d_{11}INSBUDGET + d_{12}STATES + d_{13}STRIKE + e_4$$

where

$$M = a_2b_2/(c_2 - b_2)$$
$$N = (1 - a_2b_3 - M)$$
$$d_1 = [a_1 + a_2b_1 + M\,(b_1 - c_1)]/N$$
$$d_2 = [a_3 + (a_2b_4 + b_4\,M)]/N$$
$$d_3 = a_4/N$$
$$d_4 = [a_5 - c_4\,M]/N$$
$$d_5 = [a_6 + a_2b_5 + b_5]/N$$
$$d_6 = a_7/N$$
$$d_7 = a_8/N$$
$$d_8 = a_9/N$$
$$d_9 = a_{10}/N$$
$$d_{10} = a_{11}/N$$
$$d_{11} = a_{12}/N$$
$$d_{12} = a_{13}/N$$
$$d_{13} = -c_5M/N$$
$$e_4 = [e_1 + a_2e_2 + M\,(e_2 - e_3)]/N$$

Each coefficient (d) in equation 4 is a function of the variable's direct impact on the accident rate (the a's) and the feedback effects on the accident rate caused by changes in the wage in the labor market (the b's and c's). The feedback effects are present in all coefficients in the form of the *M* and *N* functions. A priori, the signs of the reduced form coefficients are uncertain because the signs of *M* and *N* are uncertain. The uncertainty arises because a_2 (the coefficient of *WAGE* in the accident rate equation) has an uncertain sign. In Table C-1 we cannot reject the null hypothesis that a_2 was equal to zero. When a_2 equals zero, *M* equals zero, and *N* equals 1. The reduced-form coefficients in Table 7-5 of Chapter 7 are therefore theoretically similar to the structural coefficients in the accident-rate equation. Therefore, differences in the estimated impact of the laws on accident rates in Chapter 7 and in this appendix probably stem from the larger sample available in Chapter 7.

NOTES

Much of the work in this appendix appeared in Price V. Fishback, "Workplace Safety During the Progressive Era: Fatal Accidents in Bituminous Coal Mining, 1912–1923," *Explorations in Economic History* 23 (1986): 269–98. It is reprinted with the permission of Academic Press, Inc.

1. In seeking measures of exposure to risk, fatalities could be normalized in several other ways, by coal tonnage, by the number of men, and by the number of man-days. Fatalities per ton of coal is a relatively inaccurate measure of exposure to risk. Technological change could cause output per man-hour to rise without necessarily altering workers' exposure to risk; therefore, fatalities per ton increasingly would underestimate the true exposure to risk as the technology diffuses. Normalizing by the number of workers or by the number of days worked is less appealing than the hours worked measure because the number of days worked per year and hours worked per year varied across states.

2. Total underground hours is calculated as the product of the average number of underground employees per year, the number of days the mines were open, and the average number of hours worked per day. This measure overstates the number of underground hours worked, and therefore causes fatalities per man-hour to underestimate the true exposure to risk. Most of the miners were paid by the piece and often chose to work fewer days and hours per day than the amount of time the mine was open (See Chapter 6). The Bureau of Mines did not consider the overestimation a serious problem because they felt it was constant across states. Albert Fay, "Coal-Mine Fatalities in the United States, 1870–1914," *U.S. Bureau of Mines Bulletin No. 115*, (Washington, DC: U.S. Government Printing Office, 1916), p. 63.

3. The average hourly wage of daymen is a reasonable proxy for hourly wages for most workers. For more discussion of the issue, see the section on wage rates in Appendix B.

4. The CPI is not an unreasonable proxy for changes over time in the cost of living in the mining towns. Although food costs in company towns were sometimes higher than in independent towns, rent, fuel, water, and medical service were cheaper. For more discussion of the issue, see Chapter 8 and the notes to the discussion of real earnings in Chapter 6.

5. The safety laws, inspection budgets, employer liability laws and workers' compensation laws are discussed in Chapter 7. The state laws were passed at various times during the year and the machinery for administering the laws was often not available immediately upon passage. LWORCOMP and the vector of LAWS variables therefore are valued at zero for years prior to and including the year of passage of the law. They are valued at one for years after passage. The one exception to this rule is the employer liability law (ELIAB), which was replaced by workers' compensation and thus given a zero value when the workers' compensation law had a value of one.

6. In the reduced-form regressions in Chapter 7, the Bureau of Mines variables is a zero-one dummy variable reflecting the period when the Bureau of Mines went into operation. In the structural equations in this appendix, the Bureau of Mines variable takes a different form because the Bureau of Mines was put into place in 1911 and thus was in operation for the entire period in the sample. Lacking coercive power, the Bureau gathered and disseminated an increasing stock of safety information over time. The variable therefore appears as a time trend in the regressions in this appendix, and may represent other influences related to time, for example, improved accident records for immigrant miners as they lived in the United states longer. Price V. Fishback, "Discrimination on Nonwage Margins: Safety in the West Virginia Coal Industry, 1906–1925," *Economic Inquiry* 23 (1985): 651–69.

7. Richard Thaler and Sherwin Rosen, "The Value of Saving a Life: Evidence from the Labor Market," in N. E. Terlecky (Ed.), *Household Production and Consumption*, Studies in Income and Wealth Vol. 40, National Bureau of Economic Research (New York: Columbia University Press, 1975), pp. 281–82).

8. For a theoretical discussion of this issue, see Appendix D.

9. U.S. Bureau of Mines, *Bulletin* 115, "Coal-Mine Fatalities in the United States, 1870–1914," by Albert Fay (Washington, DC: U.S. Government Printing Office, 1916), pp. 111–15)

10. Doris Drury, *The Accident Records in Coal Mines of the United States* (Bloomington: Indiana University Department of Economics: 1964), p. 156.

11. An alternative way to control for geological differences across states is to include a lagged value for the accident rate in the equation. The qualitative results from weighted least squares estimates with a lagged accident rate rather than state dummies in the equation differed little from those reported. These alternative estimates are biased to the extent that the lagged accident rate is correlated with the other independent variables in the equation. Due to missing values for some years, however, estimation techniques that correct this problem cause the loss of most of the data in the sample.

12. In the results of this appendix the base case for the dummies combines Alabama, Missouri, and Ohio. Within the sample Ohio's dummy is a linear combination of the dummy for the law requiring foreman to ensure the training of miners and the dummy for Montana; Missouri's dummy is a linear combination of the dummy for the law requiring state boards to license miners and the dummies for Indiana and Illinois. Additional tests with other state dummies combined as the base case show that the coefficients for Missouri and Ohio were not statistically different from the Alabama coefficient.

13. Lack of data on wages limited the period of study to 1912 to 1923. The years 1915, 1916, and 1918 were lost because of missing data when mine size variables are included in the regressions.

14. Each fatal accident can be considered as an hour in which a fatal accident occurred. The fatal accident rate then is the mean number of hours in which a fatal accident occurred. Since the total hours worked varied greatly across states, we faced problems with heteroskedasticity similar to the problems discussed for the regression analysis in Table 6-8 in Chapter 6. Here the weight is the square root of total hours worked, since we might expect the variance of the error term in the regression to be inversely related to the total hours worked. The problem with heteroskedasticity was confirmed with a Glejser test on the OLS residuals. See J. Johnston, *Econometric Methods*, 2nd. edition (New York: McGraw-Hill, 1972), p. 220. Another possible technique for estimating the accident-rate equation would be the use of a logit or a probit model. Typically such techniques are used when the dependent variable is a truncated portion of the underlying distribution, or to ensure that the predictions from the regression model are all within the range suggested by theory. M. Intrilligator, *Econometric Models, Techniques, and Applications* (Englewood Cliffs, NJ: Prentice-Hall, 1978), p. 174. Neither of these problems arise here.

15. Although many economists use tests of statistical significance, Don McCloskey has expressed reservations about their use. Donald McCloskey, "The Rhetoric of Economics," *Journal of Economic Literature* 21 (June 1987): 493–99.

APPENDIX D

A Theoretical Model of Accident Prevention by Miners and Employers

Chapter 7 discusses the response of miners and employers to exogenous changes in the wage rate and Appendix C discusses an empirical three-equation model with an accident prevention equation. From the three-equation model we also derived the reduced-form accident-rate equation discussed in Chapter 7. This appendix describes how the accident prevention equation is derived from economic theory.

To determine the empirical impact of economic factors on accident rates, an accident-rate equation that incorporates the decisions made by miners and operators is specified.

$$p = p(s, A, B_1, \ldots, B_n, Z_1, \ldots, Z_m) \qquad \text{(D-1)}$$

where

p is the fatal accident rate per man-hour worked.
s is the percent of time in the mine that the miner devotes to ensuring safety.
A is the capital devoted to safety by operators.
B_1 to B_n are a series of governmental safety requirements.
Z_1 to Z_m are technological and geological factors affecting mine safety.

Increases in s or A lower the fatal accident rate per man-hour but at a diminishing rate; therefore, p_s and p_a (the derivative of p with respect to s and A, respectively) are negative and p_{ss} and p_{aa} (the second derivatives of p with respect to s and a) are positive.

We cannot measure directly the amount of resources devoted to safety by both miners and operators. By assuming that the miner maximizes the expected utility of his family's wealth and that owners maximize profits, we can derive their safety efforts as functions of wages, workmen's compensation, coal prices, and various other exogenous factors. Combining the comparative statics for these choice functions with the fact that changes in safety effort are inversely related with accident rates, hypotheses are developed about the impact of these factors on accident rates.

The Representative Miner

Assume a risk-averse miner maximizes the expected utility of the present value of his family's streams of income under two states of the world: He is killed in a work accident with probability g or he lives an infinite and productive life with probability $1 - g$. For ease of exposition, make the following assumptions: All accidents in the analysis are fatal accidents. If the miner survives the year, he lives an infinite life in which he earns the fruits of his labor, paid at the beginning of each year. If he is killed, his infinite-lived family will receive a workers' compensation perpetuity at the beginning of each year. The miner also has a full bequest motive. These assumptions can be relaxed to allow for disabling accidents and more complex income streams, but experiments with such changes suggest that the directions of change will remain the same. Mathematically, the worker will maximize the expected utility of his family's wealth,

$$E(s) = [1 - g(s,T,A)]\ U(X_n) + g(s,T,A)\ U(X_a) \qquad \text{(D-2)}$$

where

E is the expected utility of the family's wealth.
s is the percent of time underground devoted by the miner to workplace safety and is the choice variable in the equation.
$g(s,T,A)$ is the probability of being killed during a year of work.
T is the maximum total time the miner can spend in the mine.
A is the amount of capital devoted to safety by the mine operator.
U is the utility of money income. Risk aversion implies that U_x, the first derivative of U with respect to income, is positive and that U_{xx}, the second derivative of U, is negative.
X_n is the present value of the stream of family income when the miner is not killed.
X_a is the present value of the stream of family income when the miner is killed in a work accident.

The following equations provide more details on the relevant income streams faced by the miners.

$$X_n = W\ Q(L) + F/r \qquad \text{(D-3a)}$$

$$L = (1 - s)\ T \qquad \text{(D-3b)}$$

$$W = w\ m(A) \qquad \text{(D-3c)}$$

$$X_a = C + C/r \qquad \text{(D-3d)}$$

where

W is the miner's piece-rate wage.
$m(A)$ reflects the fact that in a competitive labor market the piece-rate rises (falls) to compensate for decreases (increases) in the safety capital provided by operators. This implies that m_a is negative. Assuming diminishing compensation, m_{aa} is positive.
w is a parameter representing exogenous changes in the wage.
Q is the output from labor effort applied to mining with a positive marginal product, $Q_l > 0$, and diminishing returns, $Q_{ll} < 0$.

L is labor effort applied to direct production of coal.
F is the expected annual future income of the miner.
r is the miner's discount rate.
C is the annual workmen's compensation payment.

After substituting equations D-3a through D-3d into equation D-2, the miner will optimize

$$E(s) = [1 - g(s,T,A)]\ U(w\ m(A)\ Q((1 - s)T) + F/r) + g(s,T,A)\ U(C + C/r) \quad \text{(D-4)}$$

Note that $g(s,T,A)$ in equations D-2 and D-4 differs from the accident rate in equation D-1 that will be examined empirically. Since $g(S,T,A)$ is the probability of being killed over the course of the year, it is a function of p. The function can be described by a binomial distribution where the probability of being killed in any hour will be p. If the miner works T hours, the probability of having an accident will be 1 minus the probability of not having an accident or,

$$g(s,A,T) = 1 - \binom{T}{0} (1 - p(s,A))^T (p(s,A))^0 \quad \text{(D-5)}$$

$$= 1 - [1 - p(s,A)]^T$$

From this formulation and the assumptions that increases in A and S reduce p, the following implications are derived: The annual accident rate falls with increases in A and or s (a_s and a_a are negative), although the signs of the second derivatives (a_{ss} and a_{aa}) are uncertain when there are diminishing returns to reducing the hourly accident rate (p_{ss} and p_{aa} are positive). The annual accident rate rises at a diminishing rate with increases in the total time spent in the mine (a_t is positive with a_{tt} negative). The cross partials of T and A with s (a_{ta} and a_{ts}) are negative; and cross partials of A and s (a_{sa}) are negative when the safety efforts of operators and miners are complementary or independent in reducing hourly accident rates (p_{sa} is negative or zero).

The first order condition for a maximum,

$$-g_s\ [U(X_n) - U(X_a)] = (1 - g)\ W\ T\ Q_l\ U_x(X_n) \quad \text{(D-6)}$$

implies that the worker equates the expected increase in the marginal utility of wealth from lowering accident rates with the increase in the expected marginal utility of wealth this year from increasing output. Based on the assumptions above and the first and second order conditions for a maximum, it can easily be shown that the worker will devote more effort to safety when his future income stream (F) increases and/or workmen's compensation payments (C) decrease. The impacts of wages (w), the miner's discount rate (r), the maximum time the mine is open for work (T), and safety effort by the operator (A) on the miner's safety effort are uncertain.

These results show the complexities of the miner's response to wage cuts. Graebner and Seltzer predict that when wages were cut miners reduced their safety efforts in order to maintain their standard of living.[1] However, the results above suggest that a wage cut will have an uncertain effect on a maximizing, risk-averse miner's safety efforts. The ambiguity of the miner's response lies in his risk aversion. It can easily be shown that a risk neutral miner's response to a reduction in wage rates is to increase safety effort, as long as the present value of future income (F/r) exceeds the present value of the stream of compensation payments ($C + C/r$), which in every state was true by law.[2] Intuitively, the opportunity cost of safety effort was lowered when the wages were cut, causing a risk-neutral miner to actually reduce his safety effort most during periods of high wages. Graebner and Seltzer may get a different result because they focus on current rather than permanent income. They seem to suggest that the miner's income was so low and sources of savings or loans so scarce that he could not maximize permanent income by waiting to increase his productive efforts during periods of high wages. Application of a permanent income model seems more reasonable because miners were able to accumulate savings during upturns, while running down those savings and sometimes going into debt during downturns.

Two additional results are worth mention. We get the standard moral hazard result that miners reduce safety effort when compensation payments increase. However, the miner's reaction to increases in the operator's safety efforts is found to be ambiguous in contrast to Viscusi's earlier theoretical result that miners reduce their safety effort in such cases.[3]

The Operator

The mine operator is assumed to maximize a profit function of the following mathematical form:

$$F(A,N,K) = [P - w\,m(A)]\,Q[N\,(1 - s),K] - R\,K - R\,A - C\,b(A) \qquad \text{(D-7)}$$

where

A, s, w, $m(A)$, Q, and C have the same interpretations as in the previous section.
F is total profits.
P is the market price of coal.
N is the total amount of piece rate labor hired, equal to the product of the number of workers hired and T in the previous section.
K is mining capital.
R is the rate of payment to both safety and mining capital.
$b(A)$ represents the company's share of compensation payments, which changes inversely with the amount of safety capital provided by the firm (b_a is negative).

Additional assumptions include positive and diminishing marginal products for both labor and capital ($Q_N > 0$, $Q_K > 0$; $Q_{NN} < 0$, $Q_{KK} < 0$). Increases in capital cause the marginal product of labor to increase (Q_{lk} is positive). The last assumption seems to be borne out empirically in the labor demand equation, where increases in the percentage of coal mined by cutting machines caused miners' wages to rise.

The first order conditions for the maximum are

$$(P - w\,m(A))\,Q_l = 0 \qquad \text{(D-8a)}$$

$$(P - w\,m(A))\,Q_k = R \qquad \text{(D-8b)}$$

$$-w\,m_a\,Q - C\,b_a = R \qquad \text{(D-8c)}$$

They imply that the operator will seek to hire labor until the marginal product of labor is zero because empirically coal prices exceeded piece rate wages. The operator will seek to equate the marginal product of capital with the ratio of the cost of capital to the difference per unit between prices and wages. Finally, the firm will seek to equate the marginal cost of safety resources with the benefits gained in terms of lower wages and lower insurance payments.

From the conditions of a maximum and the assumptions above, several implications follow. The firm devotes more capital to safety when the price of coal (P) rises and when workers' compensation payments (C) rise. In a situation similar to that for miners, when there is a change in the piece rate wage (w) or in the safety effort by miners (s), the change in safety capital provided by the operators is ambiguous. Further, the operator's response to increases in the rate paid to safety or other capital (R) is indeterminant.

Combining the Results

To examine the impact of the exogenous factors above on the hourly accident rate, substitute the choice functions derived from the first order conditions (equations D-6 and D-8a to D-8c) into equation D-1.

$$p = p[s(T,w,F,r,C,A),\ A(P,w,R,C,s),\ B_1, \ldots ,B_n,\ Z_1, \ldots ,Z_m] \qquad \text{(D-9)}$$

Then differentiate equation D-9 with respect to the parameter. For example, differentiating with respect to w gives us:

$$p_w = p_s\, s_w + p_a\, a_w + p_s\, s_a\, a_w + p_a\, a_s\, s_w \qquad \text{(D-10)}$$

The last two terms in equation D-10 represent the feedback effects that changes in the operator's safety resources have on safety decisions made by miners and vice versa. These are assumed to be of small enough size that they do not offset the direction of change represented by the first two terms of equation D-10 for several reasons. As noted earlier, the responsibility for various safety tasks was in most cases clearly defined. Where there was overlap, one party accepted most of the responsibility. For example, although the foreman helped the miner inspect his roof, most of the safety effort was expended by the miner, who was typically responsible for this task. Further, there are few empirical cases that have been found where the feedback effects offset the major effects. Finally, the signs of these feedback effects are ambiguous for both workers and employers in the theoretical model, suggesting offsetting effects that would keep these terms close to zero.

With the assumptions above, we get the following implications, *ceteris paribus*. Changes in piece-rate wages (w) have uncertain effects, because their impact on safety effort is uncertain for both miners and operators. When expected future annual income (F) increases, miners increase safety effort, and accident rates fall. As coal prices rise, accident rates should fall, as operators increase their safety efforts. When compensation payments per accident (C) rise, the impact is uncertain as miners reduce their safety effort, while employers increase theirs. When the time the mine is open (T) changes, the impact on accident rates is uncertain because the miner's response is uncertain. Finally, increases in the price of capital (R) and the miner's discount rate (r) have uncertain impact because the change in safety effort by operators and miners, respectively, is uncertain.

NOTES

1. Curtis Seltzer, *Fire in the Hole: Miners and Managers in the American Coal Industry* (Lexington: University of Kentucky Press, 1985), pp. 10, 112; William Graebner, *Coal-Mining Safety in the Progressive Period* (Lexington: University of Kentucky Press, 1976), p. 10.

2. The risk-neutral miner also increases his safety effort when the discount rate falls. All other implications for the risk-neutral miner are similar to those for the risk-averse miner.

3. W. Kip Viscusi, "The Impact of Occupational Safety and Health Regulation," *The Bell Journal of Economics* 10 (1979): 117–40.

APPENDIX E

Measuring Segregation in Job Hierarchies

Tables 10-4 and 10-5 in Chapter 10 define the various coal jobs in terms of whether they were open to blacks and southern Europeans. The bases for these definitions come from procedures testing whether the distribution of ethnic groups in jobs can be considered random or not. A complete lack of segregation would imply that the percentages of blacks in each job perfectly matches their percentage in the work force. But that is an extremely hard standard to meet, particularly when there are small numbers of workers in some jobs. Given the laws of probability, even if an employer totally ignored race and ethnicity in his hiring practices, it is highly unlikely that we would see a perfect matchup of percentages in all jobs. Therefore, the standard for the absence of job segregation used here is a test to see whether blacks and native whites are randomly distributed across the jobs, just as if a manager picked black and white balls out of an urn to determine who would be placed in each job.

A chi-square test for contingency tables with two categories, job and ethnic group, is used to test for randomness in particular job categories.[1] A nonrandom distribution suggests that differences in experience or discrimination affected the distribution of ethnic groups among the major job categories. We use four ethnic groups: blacks, southern European immigrants, native whites, and northern European immigrants. The latter two groups are generally not considered victims of discrimination.[2]

The tests of randomness are performed at two levels. The first explores segregation for each job across all ethnic categories. Segregation in, say, a motorman's job is defined in terms of a chi-square test for a contingency table with four ethnic groups and two jobs, motorman and a composite of all other jobs. If the null hypothesis of randomness for this two-by-four table is rejected at a significance level of 5 percent by a chi-square test with 3 degrees for freedom, the motorman's job can be said to have been closed to some group or groups. If it is not rejected, the motorman job can be defined as open for all groups.[3]

To define open and closed jobs for blacks (or southern Europeans), the second level of measures compares blacks with northern Europeans and whites, the nonvictims of discrimination. For blacks, a contingency table is created with two ethnic groups: blacks and the combined grouping of native white and northern European workers. Continuing with the motorman example, the table also includes two jobs, the motorman and the composite of all other jobs. In this case we are assuming that decisions are made to fill the jobs with blacks and native whites first, then southern Europeans are used to fill the remaining slots. A job is considered an open job for blacks if the chi-square test does not reject a null hypothesis of randomness at the 95 percent level. If the test rejects the null hypothesis, the job is a black job, when the percentage black of the grouping of blacks, native whites, and northern Europeans in the job exceeds that percentage in the overall work force. It is nonblack when the reverse is true. A similar process was used for southern Europeans. Note that the definitions refer to comparisons of blacks (southern Europeans) with native whites and northern Europeans; therefore the same job can be both a black and southern European job at the same time in cases where both are overrepresented relative to native whites and northern Europeans.

The information for 1906 to 1925 is derived from data on individuals killed from 1906 to 1925 and workers seriously injured from 1906 to 1915 in West Virginia. When a miner was killed or seriously injured, the mine management was expected to fill out a report on the accident and send it to the West Virginia Department of Mines. Much of the information was then published in the department's Annual Report. I recorded the victim number, nationality, mining experience, age, occupation, marital status, type of accident, and whether the accident was inside or outside the mine. To reduce problems with geographical segregation, only

TABLE E-1. Distribution of Ethnic Groups in the West Virginia Job Hierarchy, 1906–10

		Percentages of Group in Job				*Segregation Statistics*		
Job	*Sample Size*	*American White*	*Northern European*	*Black*	*Southern European*	*General*[a]	*Black*[b]	*Southern European*
Machine Runner	78	59.0	6.4	18.0	16.7	14.71**	3.80*	12.87**
Miner	2016	33.1	4.3	21.4	41.3	164.66**	12.81**	142.03**
Loader	152	30.9	4.0	9.2	55.9	41.40**	4.44**	22.09**
Driver	462	49.8	1.5	35.1	13.6	114.82**	13.13**	61.84**
Motorman	58	86.2	3.5	5.2	5.2	49.83**	19.03**	31.07**
Trackman	67	62.7	1.5	7.5	28.4	15.24**	11.07**	3.48*
Bratticeman and Timberman	15	66.7	6.7	6.7	20.0	c	c	c
Brakeman	110	76.4	0.9	17.3	5.5	62.66**	10.34**	48.80**
Pumpman	9	77.8	0.0	0.0	22.2	c	c	c
Laborer	351	30.8	2.0	29.3	37.9	25.54**	22.36**	14.27**
Machine Helper	65	53.9	0.0	24.6	21.5	7.63*	0.05	3.85**
Slateman	76	25.0	7.9	22.4	44.7	12.40**	1.16	5.81**
Tippleman	32	56.3	3.1	18.8	21.9	3.08	0.88	2.52
Boss	74	79.7	9.5	4.1	6.8	60.77**	25.94**	36.87**
Other	331	58.3	2.7	19.3	19.6			
Total	3896	41.5	3.6	22.0	33.0	629.50**		

Source: Aggregated from information on workers killed and injured in West Virginia. West Virginia Department of Mines, Annual Report, for the years between 1906 and 1925. The sample is from the counties listed in note 4. Differences between these tables and those appearing in Fishback (1983, pp. 281–85) are due to the deletion of several minor counties that had fewer than a hundred black workers from the accident sample.

[a]The general segregation statistic is the chi-square statistic for a contingency table with the four ethnic groups and two jobs, the job in the row, and a composite of all other jobs. The grand statistic, listed in the row for the total, is the chi-square with all jobs and the four ethnic groups.

[b]Chi-square statistic for a contingency table with two jobs, the job in the row and a composite of all other jobs, and two ethnic groups, black (southern European) and a combination of native whites and northern Europeans.

[c]Not reported for jobs with less than twenty-five workers sampled.

*Test statistic exceeds the rejection value for 10 percent significance.

**Not an open job because the segregation statistic rejects the null hypothesis that the percentages are the same at the 95 percent level.

TABLE E-2. Distribution of Ethnic Groups in the West Virginia Job Hierarchy, 1911–15

		Percentages of Group in Job				*Segregation Statistics*		
Job	*Sample Size*	*American White*	*Northern European*	*Black*	*Southern European*	*General*[a]	*Black*[b]	*Southern European*
Machine Runner	216	60.2	2.8	13.9	23.2	35.93**	11.93**	29.75**
Miner	2450	29.7	2.5	18.5	49.4	294.87**	38.28**	289.66**
Loader	446	30.9	3.4	10.8	54.9	67.36**	3.80**	40.13**
Driver	512	40.2	0.6	34.0	25.2	102.50**	48.58**	10.00**
Motorman	153	76.5	3.3	5.9	14.4	85.52**	34.84**	58.07**
Trackman	119	55.5	1.7	16.0	26.9	10.99**	2.86*	8.59**
Bratticeman and Timberman	50	50.0	10.0	8.0	32.0	15.07**	5.47**	2.53
Brakeman	400	54.8	2.5	27.3	15.5	93.39**	0.87	79.14**
Pumpman	23	82.6	4.4	4.4	8.7	17.79**	6.41**	12.40**
Laborer	279	43.7	2.9	18.6	34.8	1.33	0.22	1.30
Machine Helper	105	44.8	1.9	14.3	39.0	1.63	1.36	0.03
Slateman	129	23.3	4.7	23.3	48.8	17.91**	7.57**	11.93**
Tippleman	71	57.8	2.8	12.7	26.8	8.70**	4.08**	6.29**
Boss	112	78.6	7.1	4.5	9.8	84.61**	31.13**	57.63**
Other	437	63.2	2.5	16.5	17.9			
Total	5502	40.9	2.6	18.7	37.7	946.21**		

For sources and notes see Table E-1.

TABLE E-3. Distribution of Ethnic Groups in the West Virginia Job Hierarchy, 1916–20

		Percentages of Group in Job				*Segregation Statistics*		
Job	*Sample Size*	*American White*	*Northern European*	*Black*	*Southern European*	*General*[a]	*Black*[b]	*Southern European*
Machine Runner	61	47.5	4.9	16.4	31.1	4.36	0.58	0.02
Miner	583	35.7	1.5	21.1	41.7	86.67**	12.09**	87.09**
Loader	153	36.0	0.0	16.3	47.7	31.25**	0.18	26.42**
Driver	63	39.7	0.0	36.5	23.8	10.71**	8.63**	0.02
Motorman	83	69.9	1.2	19.3	9.6	19.51**	2.33	18.27**
Trackman	49	65.3	2.0	12.2	20.4	5.89	3.69**	3.28**
Bratticeman and Timberman	21	66.7	9.5	4.8	19.1	c	c	c
Brakeman	162	61.7	0.0	29.6	8.6	41.96**	0.93	31.49**
Pumpman	8	50.0	0.0	25.0	25.0	c	c	c
Laborer	56	48.2	3.6	25.0	23.2	2.25	0.26	0.55
Machine Helper	38	73.7	7.9	18.4	8.1	10.84**	2.17	11.29**
Slateman	35	31.4	2.9	31.4	34.3	4.80	3.99**	1.98
Tippleman	19	79.0	0.0	21.1	0.0	c	c	c
Boss	45	77.8	4.4	8.9	8.9	19.49**	7.70**	12.93**
Other	168	66.1	3.6	15.5	14.9			
Total	1544	48.7	1.8	20.7	28.8	290.90**		

For sources and notes, see Table E-1.

TABLE E-4. Distribution of Ethnic Groups in the West Virginia Job Hierarchy, 1921–25

Job	Sample Size	*Percentages of Group in Job* American White	Northern European	Black	Southern European	*Segregation Statistics* General[a]	Black[b]	Southern European
Machine Runner	77	59.7	0.0	18.2	22.1	1.98	0.20	0.15
Miner	522	44.6	2.3	24.0	29.1	30.91**	16.57**	21.54**
Loader	433	39.0	1.2	17.6	42.3	113.54**	3.34*	110.19**
Driver	62	56.5	0.0	35.5	8.1	15.61**	5.03**	5.51**
Motorman	111	80.2	0.9	10.8	8.1	30.84**	11.37**	20.69*
Trackman	63	65.1	4.8	7.9	22.2	8.92**	6.52**	0.75
Bratticeman and Timberman	36	63.9	11.1	5.6	19.4	21.70**	5.52**	1.25
Brakeman	196	63.3	0.5	31.1	5.1	50.29**	5.33**	33.99**
Pumpman	12	50.0	8.3	25.0	16.7	*c*	*c*	*c*
Laborer	32	59.4	3.1	21.9	15.6	1.33	0.00	1.04
Machine Helper	59	71.2	0.0	15.3	13.6	7.21*	1.84	4.32**
Slateman	37	37.8	0.0	37.8	24.3	8.91**	8.68**	1.12
Tippleman	10	100.0	0.0	0.0	0.0	*c*	*c*	*c*
Boss	65	86.2	9.2	0.0	4.6	55.41**	22.58**	19.85**
Other	188	73.4	0.5	14.4	11.7			
Total	1903	55.0	1.8	19.8	23.4	388.32**		

For sources and notes, see Table E-1.

TABLE E-5. Distribution of Ethnic Groups in the West Virginia Job Hierarchy, 1932

Job	Sample Size	*Percentages of Group in Job* American White	Black	Immigrant[c]	*Segregation Statistics* General[a]	Black[b]	Immigrant[c]
Machine Runner	226	76.1	15.9	8.0	63.0**	56.60**	17.18**
Laoder	3415	38.9	41.3	18.3	514.12**	308.0**	313.6**
Motorman	300	66.3	28.3	5.3	36.65**	16.05**	26.8**
Trackman	322	55.0	33.9	11.2	3.46	1.25	3.15*
Brakeman	304	55.6	42.1	2.3	33.88**	0.81	33.50**
Tippleman	323	90.7	7.4	1.9	221.8**	159.8**	73.70**
Other	272	82.4	15.8	1.8			
Total	5162	50.6	35.5	13.8			

Source: James T. Laing, "The Negro Miner in West Virginia," Ph.D. dissertation, Ohio State University, 1933, p. 195.

[a]The segregation statistic for each job is the chi-square statistic for a contingency table with three ethnic groups and two jobs, the job in the row and a composite of all other jobs.

[b]Chi-square statistic for a contingency table with two jobs, the job in the row and a composite of all other jobs, and two ethnic groups, black (foreign-born) and native whites.

[c]Includes both southern Europeans and northern Europeans because Laing did not report them separately.

*Test statistic exceeds the rejection value for a 10 percent level of significance.

**Not an open job because the segregation statistic rejects the null hypothesis that the percentages are the same at the 95 percent level.

workers from counties in West Virginia that employed more than one hundred black workers in a particular year were selected for that year.[4]

Immigrant workers were divided into northern European and southern European workers in the way used by McGouldrick and Tannen. Northern Europeans included Canadians, Danish, Dutch, English, Finnish, French, German, Norwegian, Scotch, Swedish, and Welsh. All other nationalities are under the catchall category of southern European.[5]

To be included in the sample a worker had to be killed or seriously injured. Unsafe occupation, individuals with less experience, and groups discriminated against through placement in more dangerous jobs are likely to be overrepresented. The sample bias toward unsafe jobs has its biggest effects on inside versus outside jobs. Thus, when I talk about the division between inside and outside jobs, I use the direct evidence reported by the West Virginia Department of Mines. The bias towards overrepresentation of less-experienced workers is not a severe problem for comparisons of black and white workers because they had similar experience. However, southern Europeans, who had less experience on average, probably are overrepresented in the first three time periods. The segregation measure limits the sample bias by comparing ethnic employment in a particular job to ethnic employment in the remaining jobs in the sample, not the entire mining population. Using this technique is unbiased under the assumption that the danger in each job is affected by less experience and discrimination in the same manner as it is in the remaining jobs.

Tables E-1 through E-5 show the percentages of each ethnic group in each job and the chi-square test statistics for the general contingency table with all ethnic groups and the separate contingency tables for blacks and for southern Europeans.

NOTES

Most of the material in this appendix first appeared in Price Fishback, "Segregation in Job Hierarchies: West Virginia Coal Mining, 1906–1932," *Journal of Economic History* 44 (September 1984): 763. It is reprinted here with the permission of The Economic History Association and Cambridge University Press.

1. The contingency tables can also be described in the context of a multinomial distribution. See Robert Hogg and Elliot Tanis, *Probability and Statistical Inference* (New York: MacMillan, 1977), pp. 352–57.

2. See Paul McGouldrick and Michael Tannen, "Did American Manufacturers Discriminate Against Immigrants Before 1914?" *Journal of Economic History* 37 (September 1977): 723–46; Oscar Handlin, *The Uprooted* (Boston: Little, Brown, 1952); Oscar Handlin, *Race and Nationality in American Life* (Boston: Little, Brown, 1948); Michael Novak, *The Rise of the Unmeltable Ethnic* (New York: MacMillan, 1971).

3. The statistic measured here is not a perfect description of the job assignment process. For each job it assumes that the employer makes the choice between that job and all other jobs first and then assigns workers to the other jobs later. Since this assumption is used for the assignment process for each job, we miss some of the interdependence of job assignments. A similar caveat is relevant to the separate comparisons of blacks and southern Europeans with native whites and northern Europeans. A chi-square that captures all the interdependencies is one for a contingency table with all four ethnic groups and all fifteen major jobs, but it provides information only on segregation across the entire hierarchy and not for individual jobs.

4. The counties included were McDowell, Fayete, Raleigh, Mercer, Kanawha, Harrison, Mingo, Logan, and Marion for the years 1906–25; Putnam in 1906–09, 1912–16; Preston in

1906; Wyoming in 1916–25, Ohio in 1920, 1922–25; Brooke in 1920–25; Barbour in 1916, 1918–25; Greenbrier in 1922, 1924, 1925; Monongalia in 1920–25 and Clay in 1922–24. I made exceptions to the hundred-black-minimum rule for Harrison in 1910, 1911, 1913, and 1914, and Marion in 1910 because they exceeded the minimums in all other years. The selection of counties accounted for 97 percent of the black miners, 85 percent of the native whites, and 83 percent of the immigrants in the state.

5. For more details, see Price V. Fishback, "Employment Conditions of Blacks in the Bituminous Coal Industry, 1900–1930," Ph.D. dissertation, University of Washington, 1983, p. 232.

APPENDIX F

An Empirical Test of the Influence of Coal Companies on Equalizing Black and White Schools in West Virginia

The section on segregated schools in Chapter 10 describes the results of econometric tests of the influence of the coal companies on the equality of segregated schools in West Virginia. The tests are incorporated in an empirical model of the racial division of school spending. The school board's decisions on allocations of funds between black and white schools were affected by the demands of their voting constituents and of special interest groups. White and black voters generally lined up on opposite ends of the spectrum. Given the constraint on expenditures, whites stood to gain at the expense of blacks as the black/white ratio of school expenditures declined. Since blacks rarely composed more than 10 percent of the population, white constituents were the predominant voters on the racial split of funds. The empirical model thus focuses primarily on their decision with additional variables to capture the impact of special interests. Blacks could organize as a special interest group and act as swing voters in the election. Coal companies also wielded ample influence in local governments.

To capture the influences of white voters and the special interests of blacks and coal companies, the empirical equation described in Table F-1 was estimated with the black/white ratio of expenditures per child on teachers' salaries as the dependent variable. Because data on other expenditures were not reported separately for blacks and whites, the expenditure data are confined to expenditures on teachers' salaries—65 percent of the expenditure on schooling by school boards in 1910.

The regression equation is estimated using ordinary least squares on cross sections of West Virginia counties and independent municipal districts in 1910 and West Virginia counties in 1920 that spent money on black education. The log-log format allows the coefficients to be interpreted as elasticities and prevents the dependent variable from being bounded below by zero. Table F-1 contains the regression results and means of the logs of the variables for 1910 and 1920. See Table F-1 for more details on the sources and the construction of variables.

The results show clearly the countervailing pressures applied to school boards by their white constituents and the coal companies. In both 1910 and 1920 the coefficient of the percentage of black schoolchildren is negative and statistically significant. The coefficients show that white constituents pressured the school board to redistribute funds from black to

TABLE F-1. Regression Results for West Virginia Schools (Dependent Variable = Black/White Ratio of Expenditures per Pupil on Teachers' Salaries)

Variable	1910 Mean	1910 Regression Coefficients	1920 Mean	1920 Regression Coefficients
Mean of Dependent Variable	0.003 (0.5)		0.17 (0.4)	
CONSTANT		−6.82 (0.81)		−15.1* (2.24)
Percent Black of School Children	0.85 (1.7)	−0.15* (3.70)	0.96 (1.15)	−0.13* (2.39)
Ratio of Coal Miners to Adult Male Population	0.52 (2.65)	0.061* (1.84)	1.47 (2.60)	0.045* (1.84)
Wealth per Child	1.30 (0.48)	−0.35 (2.04)	1.39 (0.36)	−0.10 (0.54)
Literacy Rate	4.51 (0.05)	1.54 (0.82)	4.52 (0.04)	3.43* (2.29)
Number of Children per Square Mile	2.9 (1.6)	0.14* (2.81)	2.64 (0.81)	0.02 (0.24)
R^2		0.39		0.27
N		44		42

Sources: This table first appeared in Price V. Fishback, "Can Competition Among Employers Reduce Governmental Discrimination? Coal Companies and Segregated Schools in West Virginia in the Early 1900s" *Journal of Law and Economics* 32 (October 1989): 321, 325. It is reprinted with the permission of the University of Chicago. © 1989 by the University of Chicago. All rights reserved. Black/white ratio of expenditures per pupil on teachers' salaries: Ratio of disbursements of teachers' fund to white teachers (State Superintendent of Free Schools in West Virginia, *Biennial Reports* for the Two Years Ending June 30, 1910, p. 135 and for 1920, pp. 166–67, referred to as WVA10 and WVA20, respectively) divided by the number of white children enumerated ages six to sixteen (WVA10, pp. 160–61; WVA20, pp. 123–24) to disbursements of teachers' fund to black teachers (WVA10, p. 135; WVA20, pp. 168–69) divided by the number of black children enumerated ages six to sixteen (WVA10, pp. 162–63; WVA20, pp. 125–26). The disbursement measure is payments to black teachers, not teachers at black schools. In some districts with few black students, where it was costly to obtain black teachers, there may have been cases where whites taught black pupils. In these areas the expenditures on black schooling may be underestimated.

Percent Black of School Children: Number of black children enumerated ages six to sixteen as a percentage of the total number of children enumerated ages six to sixteen.

Ratio of Coal Miners to the Adul Male Population: Number of coal and coke workers in the county (West Virginia Department of Mines, Annual Reports for the Years Ending June 30, 1910, pp. 106–07 and ending June 30, 1920, pp. 259–60) as a percentage of the male population twenty-one and over. U.S. Bureau of the Census, *Thirteenth Census of the United States, Population, 1910,* vol. 4 (1914) (CEN10), pp. 1032–41; U.S. Bureau of the Census, *Fourteenth Census of the United States, Population, 1920* vol. 4 (1923) (CEN20) pp. 1105–09.

Wealth per Child: Value of real and personal property (WVA10 at pp. 188–89; WVA20 at pp. 188–242) divided by the number of children enumerated ages six to sixteen. The assessments of property values in West Virginia were consistently underestimated. When compared with census data for 1920, the underestimation rated from 62 percent in Barbour County to 21 percent in Preston County, West Virginia. See National Industrial Conference Board, *The Tax Problem in West Virginia* (1925), pp. 101–05.

Literacy Rate for Adult White Males: Percent literate of white males of voting age (CEN10 at pp. 1032–43) in 1910 and white males and females of voting age in 1920 (CEN20 at pp. 1105–09).

Number of Children per Square Mile: Number of children enumerated ages six to sixteen divided by the number of square miles in the county (CEN10 at pp. 1032–41; CEN20 at pp. 1105–09). All municipal independent districts in 1910 were assumed to have square mileage of four miles.

Notes: The absolute value of Students' t-statistics are in parentheses under the coefficients. Standard deviations for the variables are listed under the means in parentheses. All variables are in natural logs.

*The coefficient is significantly different from zero at the 90 percent level.

white schools as the black percentage of the school population rose. This pressure from white constituents more than offset any increase in pressure that black constituents applied as they became a larger share of the population.

In contrast, the coal companies worked to counteract white appropriation of black school funds, represented by the coefficient of the ratio of coal miners to the adult male population. In both 1910 and 1920 the mining coefficients are positive and statistically significant. The mining coefficient is slightly smaller in 1920 than in 1910, possibly due to differences in the tightness of coal labor markets. The coal boom was in full swing in 1910, but 1920 was in the midst of a period of slackening coal demand and labor strife following World War I.[1]

The coal companies' did not fully offset white appropriation of funds. In absolute values, the MINING elasticities were roughly 60 to 70 percent smaller than the PERBLACK elasticities. To give the elasticities more meaning, consider a situation where a county described by the sample mean experienced a one standard deviation increase in MINING that also led to a one standard deviation increase in the percent black in 1910. Given the increase in percent black, whites would have appropriated enough school funds that after taking anti-logs, the black-white ratio of school expenditures per child would have fallen from around 1 to 0.78. However, assuming the increase in the black population was primarily miners, the coal companies would have counteracted this decline somewhat, pushing the ratio back up to 0.87. The estimates of the impact of the coal companies may understate the efforts of the coal companies to the extent that they operated outside the school system. Extra spending outside the school system may have caused the school board to reduce spending inside the system.

The coefficients of the remaining variables generally did not have unexpected signs, although in each case they are statistically significant in one year but not in the other. The wealth per child variable reflects the tax base per child for school funds and is also positively correlated with income. A larger tax base allows greater local spending on both black and white education, but the impact on the black-white ratio is uncertain. Whites have an incentive to use the larger tax base to raise white but not black spending, although wealthier whites might discriminate less. The wealth coefficients are negative, suggesting that increases in wealth were appropriated more for white than for black education, offsetting any nondiscriminatory attitudes of wealthier whites.

The white literacy variable is included to examine differences in the taste for discrimination by white voters. Greater white literacy might have reduced ignorance-based discrimination. The positive coefficients on white literacy are consistent with lesser discrimination by more literate white constituents. Finally, the child population density captures several effects associated with more urban areas. Schooling may have been more highly valued in urban areas, leading to higher expenditures for both black and white schools. The positive coefficient of population density is consistent with Pritchett's findings for some southern states in 1910 that urban areas had more equal schooling than rural areas.[2]

NOTES

Part of this appendix first appeared in Price V. Fishback, "Can Competition Among Employers Reduce Governmental Discrimination? Coal Companies and Segregated Schools in West Virginia in the Early 1900s" *Journal of Law and Economics* 32 (October 1989): 311–28 and are reprinted with permission of the University of Chicago.

1. Following World War I, the labor market in West Virginia had loosened such that 15 percent more men were employed to produce the same amount of coal in 1920 that was

produced in 1918. The number of days worked fell from 238 in 1918 to 198 in 1920. Real wages fell approximately 8 percent in 1919 before returning to their 1918 level in 1920. This was also a period of tremendous labor strife. In 1919 50 percent of West Virginia miners had struck such that days idle on strike accounted for approximately 6 percent of the man-days worked that year. In 1920 only 12 percent struck, but each for a longer period so that strike days accounted for 2.5 percent of the man-days worked that year. In 1910 only 2 percent of the men struck for a period accounting for 0.08 percent of the man-days worked. The data sources are U.S. Bureau of Mines and U.S. Geological Survey publications described in Appendix B.

2. Jonathon Pritchett, "The Racial Division of Education Expenditures in the South, 1910," Ph.D. dissertation, University of Chicago, 1986, pp. 165–78.

APPENDIX G

Piece Rate Regressions for West Virginia Counties

Chapter 5 and Chapter 10 contain regressions that examine the relationships between piece rates, how tough it was to mine coal, and the location of blacks and immigrant workers. The regressions treat piece rate wages as a function of the price of coal at the mine, the effect of mine conditions on the workers' productivity, the percentage of workers who were black, the percentage of workers who were southern European immigrants, and a random error term, which includes unmeasured factors not mentioned above.

The West Virginia Department of Mines reported information by county on each of the variables listed above. The basic equation is estimated for pick mining rates and for loading rates. The measure of the pick mining piece rates used is the average run-of-mine rate per long ton, in other words, the rate for 2240 pounds of coal before it was run over the screens.[1] The West Virginia mining reports do not specify how the county averages were obtained. Since the statewide average reported is a simple average of the county information, the county averages are also probably simple averages of the wages at the mines. Pick mining became less important as the cutting machine technology spread and the job of loader, also known as machine miner, became the primary occupation in the coal industry. The Department of Mines also reported the piece rates paid to these workers, defined as run-of-mine rates per long ton of coal paid to machine miners.[2] Regressions are estimated with both pick rates and machine mining rates as the dependent variable.

In general, the selling price of coal should be positively related to the piece rate paid in the county. It should reflect the demand conditions for the final product, which in turn help determine the demand for labor in coal mining. The measure used is the average selling price of a long ton of coal for each county as reported by the West Virginia Department of Mines. As with the wage rates, this average is probably an unweighted arithmetic average of the prices at the mines in the county.

To measure the effect of mine conditions on the productivity of miners, a measure of output per man day was developed. For pick miners, the pick-mined tonnage of coal per pick miner per day is used; for the loader, or machine miner, the measure is the amount of machine-mined coal per machine miner (loaders plus machine cutters) per day. These figures are rough estimates obtained by dividing the coal tonnage, pick-mined or machine-mined, by the number of pick miners or machine miners, respectively. These tonnage-per-man measures are then divided by the average days worked by the mines in the counties.[3] The analytical framework implies that piece rates rise when the conditions in the mine worsen. The only problem with this measure is that it may capture differences in the productivity of the miners themselves as well as differences in the natural conditions of the mines in the county. At this level of aggregation the average productivity of the miners probably did not differ much between counties. If it did, the better miners probably were concentrated in the counties offering better employment packages. With zero information costs, it is uncertain how this would bias the coefficient, because the better employment package might be in counties with high wages and worse conditions or in counties with low wages and better conditions. In this case, the variance in the coefficient would increase, but the coefficient would not be biased. With positive information costs, the wages would not have adjusted fully to differences in mine conditions; they would not rise as much for worse conditions nor would they fall as much for better conditions; therefore, employment packages would be better in counties with better conditions and lower wages, and the better miners would be concentrated in these counties. In this case the estimate of the coefficient for the mine conditions proxy would be less negative than the true coefficient.

An additional variable is added to the machine mining rate equation to adjust for differences in the machine miner's tasks in the various mines. In some mines the machine miner drilled holes, blasted the coal, loaded it and did his own timbering of the roof and bailing of water. In these mines the only difference between the loader and the pick miner was that the pick miner made the cut at the base of the wall. In other mines the loader might specialize in only loading coal, as other workers, such as shotfirers and timbermen, performed the other tasks. The loader's piece rate would be lower in these mines. The Department of Mines did not report the number of timbermen, shotfirers, and other workers in each occupation; it lumped them into a group labelled inside laborers. If the loader specialized, the number of inside laborers per loader in the mines should have increased. This figure is included in the regression and should be negatively related to the machine mining piece rate.[4]

The estimate used for the percent black for both the pick mining rate and the machine mining rate is the percentage of workers of known nationality inside the mine who were black. For southern Europeans a similar estimate is used; the division of immigrants into southern European and northern Europeans followed that used in Appendix E. The percent of inside workers is a reasonable proxy for the concentration of blacks and immigrants in these jobs, because both loader and pick mining jobs were open to all ethnic groups.[5]

Linear regressions for several years are estimated using weighted least squares. The number of workers in each county varied dramatically, creating problems with heteroskedasticity. (See the notes of Chapter 6 for further discussion of heteroskedasticity). The variance of the error terms is probably inversely correlated with the number of workers in the county. The pick mining regression is weighted by the square root of the number of pick miners. Several years are selected to test the robustness of the results under a variety of market conditions, including 1907, 1910, 1914, 1915, 1918, and 1923. Piece rates in 1907–10 were close to the average rates for the early 1900s. The average pick rate in the state reached a minor peak in 1907, was slightly lower in 1910, and reached another minor peak in 1914. The wage dipped to a minor trough in 1915. The years 1918 and 1923 were chosen to represent the run-up in wages during World War I and the period afterward, when the wage had leveled off at the high peak. A future consideration is to check the wages in later periods, when coal demand has declined and black employment had become more concentrated in southern West Virginia again.

The coefficients reported in Tables G-1 and G-2 for the output per man-hour variable are the bases for the elasticities reported in Table 5-1. As discussed in Chapter 5, nearly all the coefficients are negative as expected, and roughly half of them were statistically significant. In most cases the coal price had the expected effect on piece rates. The coefficient was usually positive, although statistically significant in only five of the twelve regressions.

Blacks were apparently concentrated in counties with low pick rates, but not in counties

TABLE G-1. West Virginia Pick Mining Piece Rate Regressions, 1907–23 (Dependent Variable = Pick-Mining Piece Rate, per 2240 lb. ton)

Variable	*1907*	*1910*	*1914*	*1915*	*1918*	*1923*
Weight	0.61*	0.66*	0.24*	0.72*	0.82*	0.81*
	(5.70)	(5.50)	(3.10)	(3.61)	(3.92)	(14.35)
Coal Price	0.07	0.09	0.34*	−0.04	−0.01	0.06*
	(0.80)	(0.84)	(5.04)	(0.21)	(0.12)	(3.37)
Pick Mining Output per Pick Miner per Day	−27.6*	−33.6*	−3.02	−31.7*	−3.40	−1.96
	(2.81)	(4.55)	(0.61)	(2.35)	(0.41)	(0.59)
Percent Black	−0.24*	−0.40*	−0.58*	−0.06	−0.10	−0.18*
	(2.87)	(6.34)	(7.75)	(0.18)	(0.66)	(2.10)
Percent Southern European	−0.09*	−0.16*	−0.08	−0.12	−0.02	0.03
	(1.72)	(3.19)	(1.56)	(0.96)	(0.17)	(0.72)
Number of Observations	30	25	29	23	34	34

Source: West Virginia Department of Mines, *Report,* 1907, 1910, 1914, 1915, 1918, 1923. See also notes to Appendix. G.

Notes: The weight is the square root of the number of pick miners. Students' t-statistics are in parentheses.

Coal counties with missing values which were left out of regression: 1907, Gilmer, Lewis. 1910, Lewis, Clay, Lincoln, Logan, Brooke, Hancock, Marshall, Ohio. 1914, Gilmer, Putnam, Wayne, Lincoln. 1915, Gilmer, Greenbrier, Lincoln, Mason, Putnam, Wayne, Lewis, Logan, Boone, Upshur. 1918, Wetzel, Webster. 1923, Summers.

*Statistically significant at the 90 percent level in a two-tailed t-test.

with low machine rates. The sign of the coefficient of the black variable is negative in all six of the pick mining rate regressions. In four of the years the coefficient was negative and significant. The lack of significance in the other two equations may be a statistical artifact, but it is interesting to note the years in which the coefficient is not significant in these regressions. Black employment in the southern counties, except McDowell County, declined during 1915, just prior to the surge in coal demand. It increased rapidly during World War I as piece rates and coal prices increased to their peak in 1918. These changes would appear to be consistent with expanding opportunities for blacks during World War I. According to the regressions, by 1923 they were once again concentrated in low wage regions, despite geographical expansion of employment within West Virginia. A heartening fact for blacks was that they were not concentrated in counties where machine mining rates were low. Although the coefficients of the black variable are negative in five of the six machine mining rate regressions, only the one for 1918 is significant at the 90 percent level. If this result is not a statistical artifact, the blacks' relative wage status was continually improving as the new machine cutting technology spread within the fields. Blacks were not cut off from entering these machine mines. The correlation between the percent black and the ratio of pick miners to machine miners in southern West Virginia mines is only about 0.28 for 1910 and 0.25 for 1913.[6] Southern Europeans do not appear to have been located in low piece rate counties in West Virginia. The coefficents of the southern European variable are negative in five of the six regressions, but in only two is the coefficent significantly negative. In the machine mining rate regressions, the coefficents are positive in four of the regressions, and one of them is significant at the 90 percent level.

TABLE G-2. West Virginia Loader Piece Rate Regressions, 1907–23 (Dependent Variable = Loader Piece Rate, per 2240 lb. ton)

Variable	*1907*	*1910*	*1914*	*1915*	*1918*	*1923*
Weight	0.15	0.40*	0.25*	0.38*	0.31*	0.84*
	(1.07)	(2.56)	(2.81)	(4.04)	(2.70)	(8.84)
Coal Price	0.25*	−0.05	0.15*	0.07	0.07*	−0.05
	(2.23)	(0.36)	(2.05)	(0.80)	(1.77)	(1.61)
Machine Mining Output per Loader and Machine Cutter per Day	−20.7*	−7.68	−11.13*	−4.51	2.23	−8.03*
	(2.57)	(1.10)	(2.63)	(0.91)	(0.48)	(1.75)
Percent Black	−0.15	0.006	−0.08*	−0.18	−0.26*	0.20
	(0.93)	(0.08)	(1.18)	(0.91)	(2.83)	(1.46)
Percent Southern European	0.07	−0.05*	0.05	−0.01	0.10*	0.07
	(1.30)	(0.76)	(1.20)	(0.22)	(1.88)	(1.45)
Laborers per Loader	−0.005	0.005	−0.02	−0.04	0.02	0.025
	(0.46)	(0.68)	(1.28)	(0.98)	(1.35)	(0.96)
Number of Observations	21	24	26	22	28	31

Source: West Virginia Department of Mines, *Report*, 1907, 1910, 1914, 1915, 1918, 1923. See also notes to Appendix G.

Notes: The weight is the square root of the number of loaders. Students' t-statistics are in parentheses.

Coal counties with missing values which were left out of each regression: 1907, Hancock, Ohio, Gilmer, Lewis, Upshur, Mineral, Randolph, Braxton, Putnam, Greenbrier, Wayne. 1910, Brooke, Hancock, Braxton, Putnam, Greenbrier, Wayne, Logan, Clay, Lewis. 1914, Greenbrier, Lewis, Putnam, Wayne, Wyoming, Gilmer, Lincoln. 1915, Greenbrier, Lewis, Putnam, Wayne, Wyoming, Lincoln, Logan, Boone, Mason, Tucker, Upshur. 1918, Braxton, Greenbrier, Lewis, Putnam, Summers, Wayne, Webster, Wetzel. 1923, Lincoln, Summers, Webster.

*Statistically significant at the 90 percent level in a two-tailed t-test.

NOTES

1. Several different rates were given for McDowell and Fayette Counties for three years: 1907, 1910, and 1914. I chose the rates that represented the largest percentage of types of coal produced in the area. For McDowell County, the Pocahontas No. 3 and No. 4 wage was used; for Fayette, the Kanawha River Series. After 1914 a single rate was reported for each county.

2. The pick mining rates and the average coal price appear in the table titled "Wages Paid and Selling Price of Coal and Coke," and the loading rates in the table "Summary of Wages Paid Machine Miners, Runners, and Helpers" in the West Virginia Department of Mines, *Report*, 1907, 1910, 1914, 1915, 1918, and 1923.

3. The total tonnage figures are from the table entitled "A Comparative Statement of the Pick and Machine Mined Coal, by Counties." The number of pick miners, machine miners, and average days worked are from the table "Detail of Men Employed at the Mines and Ovens" in the West Virginia Department of Mines, *Report*.

4. There is one problem with this measure. The number of inside laborers should also increase as the size of the mine expands. In the pure machine mine this should create few problems, but in a mine with a large group of pick miners, the number of inside laborers may

rise even when the loader does all the tasks. This variable will understate the task performed by the loader in these mines and therefore where pick mining is prevalent. Therefore, it will overstate the actual number of specialized workers performing tasks like shotfiring and timbering in the rooms.

5. The information on the number of workers of different ethnicities is from tables titled "Nationalities of Mine Employees" in the West Virginia Department of Mines, *Report*, various years.

6. The correlation is from information on 353 mines in 1910 and 443 mines in 1913 in southern West Virginia counties. For each mine the West Virginia Department of Mines reported the ethnic breakdown and the number of pick miners and machine miners, but wage and price information was not reported by mine.

Index